Microsoft Wo
on the IBM PC
Release 2.0

Timothy J. O'Leary
Brian K. Williams
Linda I. O'Leary

Print = printer setup
pana 11 P1180
120 dpi

Syscon
system info

Mitchell **McGraw-Hill**
55 Penny Lane
Watsonville, CA 95076

Microsoft Works in the IBM PC
Release 2.0

1 2 3 4 5 6 7 8 9 0 KGP KGP 9 0 9 8 7 6 5 4 3 2 1

ISBN 0-07-048807-x

CONTENTS

Exploring Works 2.0

CONTENTS
Exploring Works 2.0

INTRODUCTION TO THE WORKS 2.0 LABS

The labs that follow each require about one hour to complete.

The labs are designed to provide you with practical skills in using the Microsoft Works 2.0 software program. Works is an integrated software program. It contains the following four tools:

- Word Processor
- Spreadsheet and Charting
- Database and Reporting
- Electronic Communications

The labs describe not only the most important commands and concepts, but also explain why and under what circumstances you will use them. That is, by presenting an ongoing case study—The Sports Club, which is based on input from actual health-club managers—we show how Works is used in a real business setting. The labs demonstrate the use of the word processing, spreadsheet and charting, and database tools. The electronic communications tool is not covered because of the hardware requirements needed to use this tool.

Organization of the Labs

The Labs Are Organized in the Following Categories: Overview, Objectives, Case Study, Lab Activities, Key Terms, Matching and Practice Exercises, and Functional Summary of Selected Commands.

Overview The overview, which appears in the first of the succession of labs, describes (1) what the program can do for you, (2) what the program is, (3) the generic terms that this and all similar programs use (e.g., all word processing programs, regardless of brand name), and (4) the case study to be presented in the labs covered by the program.

Objectives The objectives list the concepts and commands to be learned in that particular lab.

Case Study The case study introduces the specific case covered by the particular lab—the general problems that the software activities will help you solve.

Lab Activities The lab activities consist of detailed, step-by-step directions for you to follow in order to solve the problems of the case. Display screens show how a command or procedure is supposed to look. Labs should be followed in sequence, because each succeeding lab builds on the ones preceding it. In addition, screen displays and directions become less specific. This feature allows you to think about what you have learned, avoids simple rote learning, and reinforces earlier concepts and commands, helping you to gain confidence.

Key Terms Terms that appeared in **boldfaced (dark) type** throughout the lab are also listed at the end of each lab.

Matching and Practice Problems Each lab concludes with a matching exercise and with several practice problems. The practice problems, which require use of a microcomputer, are designed to reinforce concepts and commands presented in the lab.

Functional Summary of Selected Commands Each section of labs also concludes with a quick-reference source for selected commands for that particular tool. The commands are categorized by the type of function performed.

The only lab that does not follow this organizational pattern is Lab 1, "Exploring Works 2.0." This lab is designed as an overview to the three tools covered in the labs: word processing, spreadsheet and charting, and database. Its main function is to teach students how to use the menus and access the different tools.

How the Case Study Explains Software

The Sports Club Ongoing Case Study Shows How to Solve Real-World Business Problems Using the Word Processor, Spreadsheet, and Database Tools.

The ongoing case study of the Sports Club, a health and athletic club offering many activities (swimming, tennis, weight room, sauna, and so on), was written with the help of experience contributed by actual health-club managers. In our scenario, the club has recently had great growth in membership and is trying to update its facility and management procedures, using the newly purchased software program Works 2.0 with their microcomputer system.

The reader follows Sports Club employees as they perform their jobs with this software, as follows:

Section I: An Introduction to Works—Lab 1 This section first describes what the Works program is and the three tools covered in the labs. It then shows you how to use the program to access the tools and how to use the menu and Help system.

Section II: Word Processing—Labs 2–4 The word processing program is explained by showing how a letter welcoming new club members is edited, formatted, saved, and printed.

Section III: Spreadsheets—Labs 5–8 Use of the spreadsheet tool is shown by depicting how the operating budget for the Courtside Cafe is created and modified. A proposal to expand services that will produce a 20 percent profit margin in one year is analyzed. Growth in club membership over five years is charted.

Section IV: Database—Labs 9–11 Creating, modifying, updating, and making a report of a database of employee information are demonstrated.

Section V: Integrating Works—Lab 12 The final lab demonstrates how the three tools can be used together. Specifically, the student learns how to combine a word processing document with a spreadsheet and chart.

Directions and Commands

Commands and Directions Are Expressed Through Certain Standard Conventions.

We have followed certain conventions in the labs for indicating keys, key combinations, commands, command sequences, and other directions.

Keys Computer keys are expressed in abbreviated form, as follows:

Computer Keys	Display in Text
Alt (Alternate)	ALT
← or Bksp (Backspace)	Bksp
Caps Lock (Capital Lock)	CAPS LOCK
Ctrl (Control)	CTRL
Cursor Movement	
↑ (Up)	↑
↓ (Down)	↓
← (Left)	←
→ (Right)	→
Del (Delete)	DEL
End	END
ESC (Escape)	ESC
↵ (Enter/Return)	↵
Function Keys	
F1 through F10	F1 through F10
Home	HOME
Ins (Insert)	INS
Num Lock (Number Lock)	NUM LOCK
Pg Dn (Page Down)	PGDN
Pg Up (Page Up)	PGUP
Prt Sc (Print Screen)	PrtScr
Scroll Lock	SCROLL LOCK
⇧ (Shift)	SHIFT
⇆ or Tab	TAB

Key Combinations Many programs require that you use a combination of keys for a particular command (for example, the pair of keys CTRL and F4). You should press them in the order in which they appear, from left to right, holding down the first key while pressing the second. In the labs, commands that are used in this manner are separated by a hyphen—for example: CTRL - F4.

Directions The principal directions in the labs are "Press," "Move to," "Type," and "Select." These directions appear on a separate line beginning at the left margin, as follows:

- *Press:* This means press or strike a key. Usually a command key will follow the direction (such as DEL for "Delete"). For example:

  Press: DEL

- *Move to:* This means you should move your cursor or cell pointer to the location indicated. For example, the direction to move to line 4, position 12, would appear as:

  Move to: Ln 4 Pos 12

- *Type:* This means you should type or key in certain letters or numbers, just as you would on a typewriter keyboard. Whatever is to be typed will appear in **boldface (dark) type.** For example:

  Type: **January**

- *Select:* Many programs use a sequence of selections to complete a command. In the beginning, we will introduce these commands separately. Later, as you become more familiar with the software, we will combine the commands on a single line. Each command will be separated by a ">". The command sequences will follow the word *Select.* If the first letter of a command appears in **boldface**, you can select that command by typing the letter. Other parts of the command sequence that are to be typed will also appear in **boldface.** For example, the command to open a file will appear as:

  Select: **F**ile>**O**pen Existing File>**MEMBERS.WKS**>⏎

  This means you should type the letter "F" to select File, type the letter "O" to select Open Existing File, select "MEMBERS.WKS" from a list of files or type in the filename, and then press ⏎ to execute the command.

General System Requirements To complete the labs you must have the Microsoft Works 2.0 software program for IBM PCs and compatibles. Works requires the following system specifications:

- A minimum of 512K memory
- MS or PC-DOS versions 2.0 or higher
- Two 360K disk drives or one 720K disk drive or a hard disk drive
- CGA, EGA, VGA MCGA, Tandy 1000 Video Graphics, or Hercules graphics adapter card for charting
- A printer

A Microsoft mouse or compatible mouse is optional.

User data diskette The files needed to perform the labs and to complete the practice exercises are included on a separate diskette that is supplied by your instructor.

Hardware/Software Assumptions The directions and figures in the book assume the use of an IBM or IBM-compatible computer system with two disk drives. If you have a computer system with one disk drive, a hard disk drive, or a system that is networked, your instructor will provide you with alternative directions.

Installation

Works Must Be "Installed" in Order to Run on Certain Equipment. Consult Your Instructor.

Most software has to be installed or "custom-tailored" to run with specific computers and printers. Works must be installed on your computer using the program called Setup. The documentation accompanying the software gives details. If you find that, for some reason, your software will not print out correctly and won't run on your microcomputer, ask your instructor for assistance.

LAB

1 Exploring Works 2.0

CASE STUDY

Ernie Powell, the manager of the Sports Club, has just purchased the Microsoft Works computer program. Works is an **integrated program,** consisting of a collection of four software tools: a **word processor,** a **spreadsheet,** a **database,** and a **communications** program. Each tool can be used independently, or information can be easily exchanged among tools. The word processor is used to write, edit, and present text. The spreadsheet is used to enter, calculate, present, and chart numerical data. The database is used to store, access, and organize lists of information. The communications tool lets you send and receive information from one computer to another. Because Works is an integrated program, you can share information between tools. For example, you can easily incorporate data from a spreadsheet file into a word processing file.

This lab will introduce you to the word processing, spreadsheet, and database tools. The Sports Club plans to use the Works word processing tool to produce letters, memos, and a newsletter. The spreadsheet tool will be used to produce financial and budget reports. The database will be used to maintain member and employee records. You will explore the different areas of Works and take a quick look at several files the club uses in each of these areas. The purpose of this lab is to learn how to move around and select commands from the menu and to briefly explore the three tools. The communications tool will not be demonstrated, as it requires that your computer be connected with another computer through a modem or cable.

OBJECTIVES

In this lab you will learn how to:

1. Load the Works program.
2. Use the menu system.
3. Use the keyboard.
4. Use the mouse.
5. Open a file.
6. Close a file.
7. Exit the program.

Loading Works Version 2.0

Boot the system by turning on the computer and loading DOS. If necessary, respond to the DOS date and time prompts.

Note: The instructions in these labs assume you are using a floppy disk system. If you are using a hard disk system or a network system, consult your instructor for instructions on loading DOS and Works.

The A> should appear on your display screen. Remove the DOS diskette and place the backup Works program diskette in drive A and your data diskette in drive B.

To load the Works Version 2.0 program, at the DOS prompt,

Type: **works**
Press: ⏎

After a few moments, your display screen should be similar to Figure 1-1. This is the Works **opening screen.** It is displayed every time you load the program.

FIGURE 1-1

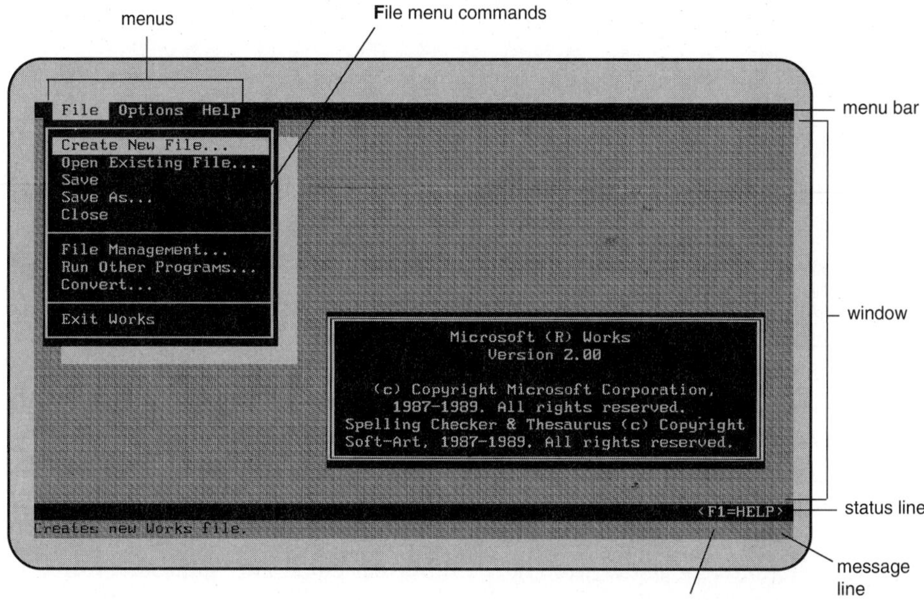

Note: If your computer is connected to a mouse device, a highlighted rectangle or arrow will appear on your screen. You will learn how to use the mouse to move around the screen and select commands shortly.

Exploring the Works Screen

The Works screen consists of many parts that are the same in each tool. The top line of the screen is the **menu bar.** It lists the names of three menus that can be opened: File, Options, and Help. The opening screen has fewer menu choices than the tools screens; otherwise, they operate in the same way. The box below the File menu displays the nine command names associated with the open File menu.

Directly below the menu bar is the **window.** In the tools screens the window displays each open file, and is where you enter text and data. The window in each tool consists of many common parts. As you use each tool in this lab, the parts of the window will be explained.

At the bottom of the screen are two lines of information: the **status line** and the **message line.** The status line advises you of various key and program conditions. The information provided varies with the tool you are using. However, in all tools, the status line will display the Help reminder <F1=HELP>. The message line displays program prompts, descriptions, or instructions that are mainly provided to help you use the menus. The different areas of the screen will be described in detail as you are using the different tools.

Moving Through the Menus

To issue commands, you select the appropriate command from a **menu.** Since Works is an integrated program, all the tools use a similar menu structure. This means that once you learn how to select and execute commands using one tool, the same procedure will be used in the other tools.

Generally, when you first load Works, you will want either to create a new file or use an existing file. That is why the File menu is already opened. The first command, Create New File, is highlighted with an inverse video box, called the **highlight bar** (see Figure 1-1). A brief description of what this command does is displayed in the message line.

Press: (↓)

The second command, Open Existing File, is highlighted and the message line displays a brief description of this command.

Notice that the next three commands are "grayed out" or displayed in **inverse video.** This is because they are not available for selection at this time.

Press: (↓)

The message line tells you that you cannot save a file because there are no files opened. Therefore, the Save command is inactive. Read the message line as you continue to move the highlight bar to each of the commands as follows:

Press: (↓) (7 times)

You have moved through each of the command choices and are back on the first command, Create New File.

Using the (→) and (←) keys moves the menu highlight bar to each menu title in the menu bar. To move to the right one menu selection on the menu bar,

Press: (→)

The Options menu is opened. It lists four commands that allow you to set screen colors, the number of lines for your screen display, country settings, units of measure, and phone-dialing settings.

Press: (→)

The Help menu is displayed. Every tool in Works has a Help menu. It provides on-screen information about commands and procedures appropriate to the tool you are using. Since the opening screen is displayed, the Help commands provide introductory information about using the Works program. The first command, Using Help, provides information on how to use Works' Help.

Selecting Commands

So far you have learned how to move around the menus and highlight commands. However, you have not yet selected or executed a command. You select a command by highlighting the option and pressing ↵ or by typing the underlined or **mnemonic letter** (the highlighted letter) associated with the command.

If you move the highlight to the command first, you can verify that it is the command you want to use by checking the message line before you press ↵ to select it. If you type the mnemonic or underlined letter, the command is executed immediately.

If you accidentally find yourself in a command that you did not intend to select, press (ESC). This action will cancel the command and deactivate the menu bar.

In this case, since the highlight bar is already on the command you want to use, to select it,

Press: ↵

Following the instructions on the screen, insert the "Spell and Help" disk in drive A and press ↵.

Note: If you are using a hard disk or networked system, Works will access the Help program directly from the hard disk. Therefore, you will not be instructed to change disks.

Your screen should be similar to Figure 1-2.

FIGURE 1-2

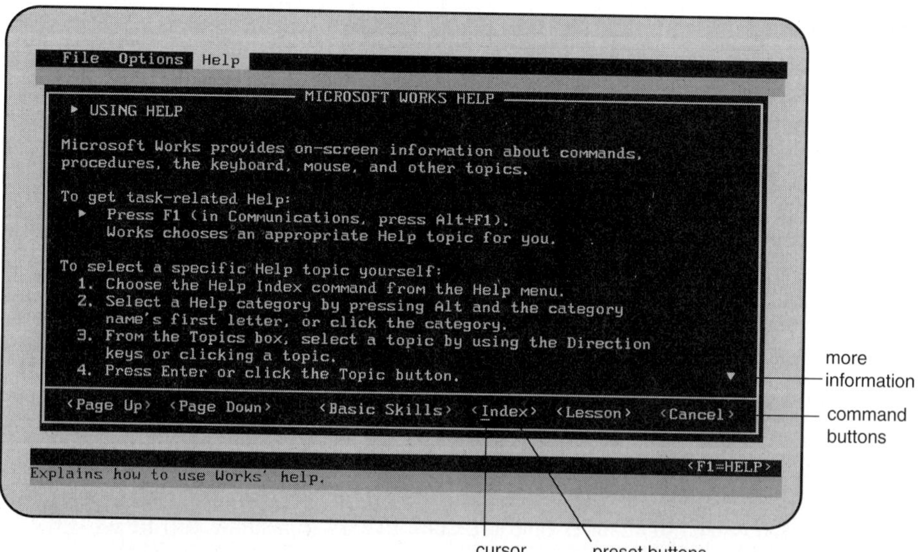

The information displayed in the window tells you how to use Help. The lower-right corner of the window displays an arrow ▼. This tells you that there is more information available about this topic on the next Help window.

At the bottom of the Help window, Works displays six **command buttons.** The command buttons in Help let you move to different parts of the Help program. Notice that the brackets surrounding the <Index> button are highlighted and the **cursor** (the flashing underscore) is positioned under the "I" of "Index." This tells you that the Index button is the **preset** button and can be selected by pressing ↵. The preset button is the **default** setting that is automatically selected by Works. The default settings are generally the settings most commonly selected. Works has many preset or default settings, as you will see as you use the program. Works specifies preset settings to save you the time it would take to make the selection. All you need to do is press ↵ to accept the default setting. To select the other buttons in Help, press the bold or underlined letter. If there is no bold or underlined letter, as with the <PageUp>, <PageDown>, and <Cancel> buttons, press the keyboard key associated with the button. To use the <PageUp> and <PageDown> buttons, press PGUP and PGDN, respectively. To select the <Cancel> button, press ESC. Alternatively, you could move the cursor to the button of your choice using TAB or the → or ← keys and press ↵. This method, however, is much slower.

To move from one Help window to the next,

Press: PGDN

Again, after reading the information in this Help window, for more information,

Press: PGDN

Your screen should be similar to Figure 1-3.

FIGURE 1-3

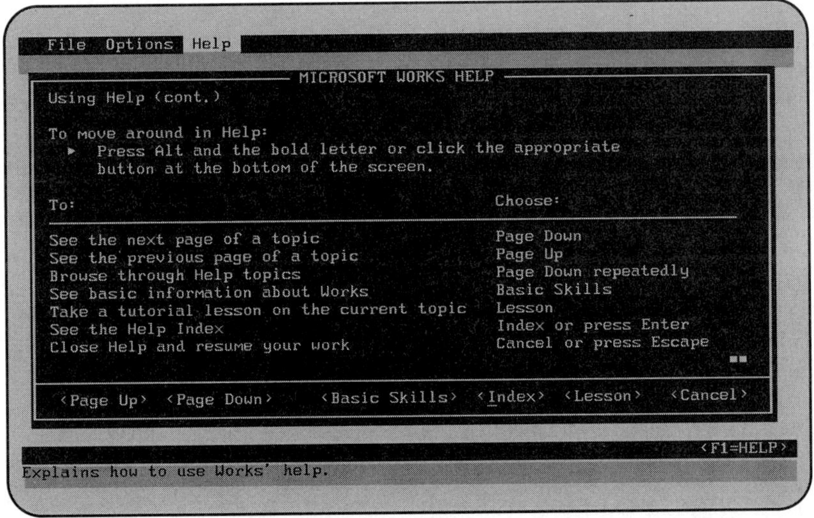

This is the last window of help information about using Help. You can tell that the topic ends on this window because there are two rectangles (■■) displayed in place of the arrow in the lower-right corner of the window.

You will be learning more about using Help for information throughout the series of labs.

To leave Help, you press ESC to choose the <Cancel> button.

Press: ESC

Following the instructions on the screen, remove the Spell and Help disk from drive A, insert the working copy of the program disk, and press (↵).

Note: If you are using a hard disk or networked system, you will not be instructed to change disks.

Note: From this point forward, the lab instructions will not direct you to insert and remove the Spell and Help disk whenever you activate Help. If you are using a floppy disk system, follow the instructions displayed on the screen.

Your screen should be similar to Figure 1-4.

FIGURE 1-4

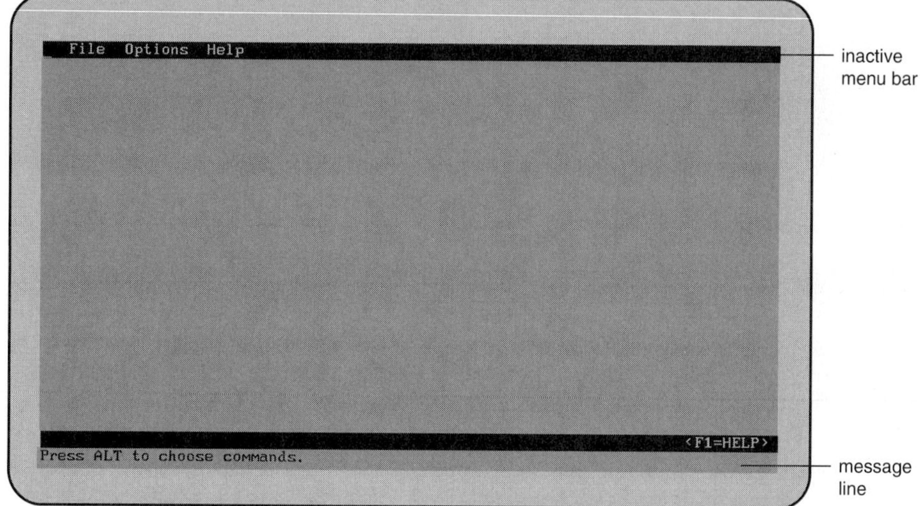

Opening and Closing Menus

You are returned to the opening screen menu. However, the copyright message is no longer displayed, the Help menu is no longer open, and the menu bar is not active. If you have a mouse, the only thing you will see in the work area is the **mouse pointer** (either a rectangle or arrow).

You can tell that the menu bar is not active because the first letter in each menu name is not highlighted and there is no highlight box over a menu title. Also, the message line directs you to press (ALT) to choose commands. This is how the menu bar will appear when you open a Works tool. To reactivate the menu bar,

Press: (ALT)

Your screen should be similar to Figure 1-5.

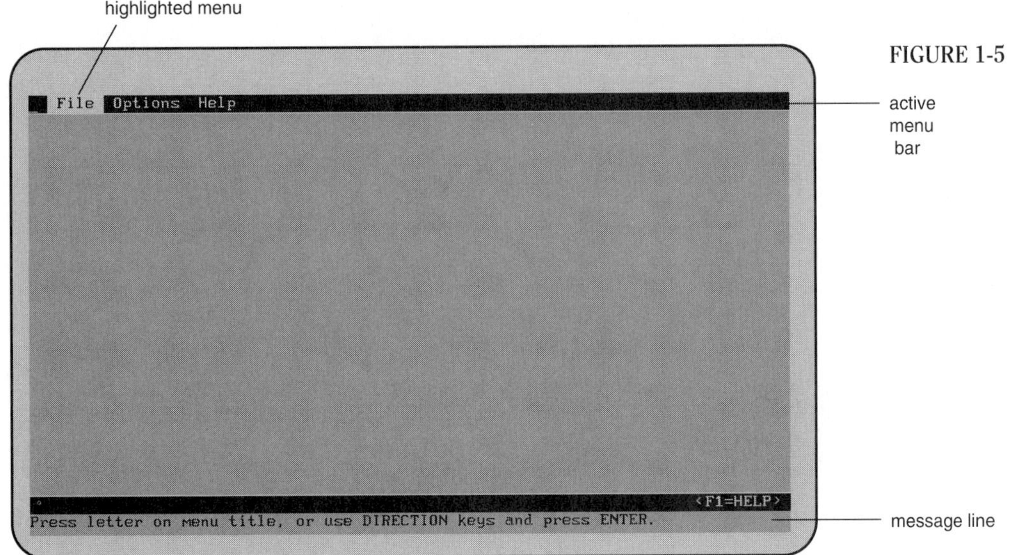

FIGURE 1-5

Now the menu bar displays one letter bold or underlined in each menu title and shows a highlight box. The message line tells you how to open a menu.

To open a menu, you can type the bold or underlined letter of the menu title or use the direction keys to move the highlight to the menu title and press (↵).

To open the Help menu again,

Type: **H**

The Help menu is open, and the titles in the menu bar no longer display a bold or underlined letter. The Help commands in the list now contain the bold or underlined letter.

Choosing a command from a menu is much like opening a menu: press the bold or underlined letter of the command. Once a menu is opened, you cannot select another menu by typing the letter of the menu title. Instead, use the (→) or (←) keys to move to the menu of your choice.

To close a menu without deactivating the menu bar,

Press: (ALT)

To open the Help menu again,

Press: (↵)

To close the Help menu and deactivate the menu bar at the same time,

Press: (ESC)

Using the Mouse

If you have a mouse attached to your computer, follow the instructions below. If you do not have a mouse, skip to the next section, "Opening a File."

The mouse controls a pointer on your screen, which appears as a solid rectangle or an arrow. On the top of the mouse are two or three buttons that are used to make selections. You move the pointer on the screen by moving the mouse over the desktop in the direction you want the pointer to move.

There are four mouse actions you use to select commands or enter instructions. They are:

Point	To move the mouse until the pointer rests on what you want to point to on the screen.
Click	To press and release the mouse button without moving the mouse.
Double-click	To press the mouse button quickly twice without moving the mouse.
Drag	To press and hold down the mouse button while moving the mouse pointer to a new location on the screen.

Move the mouse in all directions (up, down, left, and right) and note the movement of the pointer on the screen.

Pick up the mouse and move it to a different location on your desktop. The pointer will not move on the screen. This is because the pointer movement is controlled by the rubber-coated ball on the bottom of the mouse. This ball must move within its socket for the pointer to move on the screen. The ball's movement is translated into signals that tell the computer how to move the on-screen pointer.

To open a menu, position the pointer anywhere on the menu title (this includes one blank space to each side of the title) and click the left mouse button. You do not need to activate the menu bar by pressing (ALT) as you do when you use the keyboard keys to open a menu. Using the mouse both activates the menu bar and opens the menu the pointer is on. To open the File menu,

Point: File (The pointer can be positioned anywhere on the word *File* on the menu bar.)

Click: Left button

Your screen should be similar to Figure 1-6.

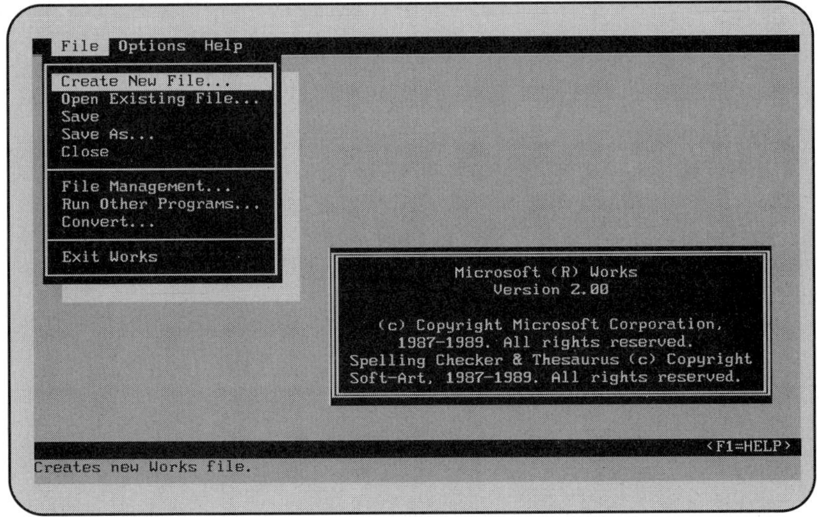

FIGURE 1-6

The pull-down File menu is displayed. This is the same as if you had pressed (ALT) to activate the menu and pressed (↵) to open the File menu.

Note: If the pointer is not on File or is on an incorrect menu title when you click the left button, either nothing will happen or the wrong menu will open. To correct this, position the pointer over File and click the left button again.

Point: Options
Press: Left button

Point: Help
Press: Left button

The Help menu should be open. You can move quickly from one menu to another by dragging the mouse from one menu title to another. As soon as you release the button, the menu you are positioned on is opened.

Drag the pointer slowly to the left and then back to the right over the menu titles. Do not release the left button until the pointer is positioned over Help again.

When you release the button, the highlight is displayed over the first command in the pull-down menu. Dragging the mouse along the menu bar has the same effect as using the (→) and (←) keys to move from one menu to another when a menu is opened.

Note: If you release the left button when the pointer is not on a menu option, the menu bar is deactivated. If this happens, click on the Help menu and try again.

You select a command by moving the pointer to the command name (anywhere on the line within the box) and clicking the left button. This has the same effect as typing the mnemonic letter of the command; it selects the command immediately. You can also drag the pointer within the open menu. This moves the highlight to each command, and the message line displays information about the command. This lets you verify that the highlighted command is the command you want to use, just as if you were moving the highlight using the arrow keys. However, as soon as you release the left button, the option is selected. Be careful when dragging the menus that you have the pointer on the correct command before you release the left button. If you decide you do not want to select a command, move the pointer anywhere outside the menu box and release the left button. This is the same as pressing (ESC); it deactivates the menu.

Try this by dragging the pointer to each of the commands in the Help menu and reading the message in the message line. Move the pointer outside the menu area and release the left button.

Developing the skill for moving the mouse and correctly positioning the pointer takes some time. If you accidentally find yourself in a command that you did not intend to select, press (ESC). This action will cancel the commands and deactivate the menu bar.

To select the Help menu command, which will provide information on using the mouse,

Point: Help
Click: Left button
Point: Mouse
Click: Left button

Your screen should look similar to Figure 1-7.

FIGURE 1-7

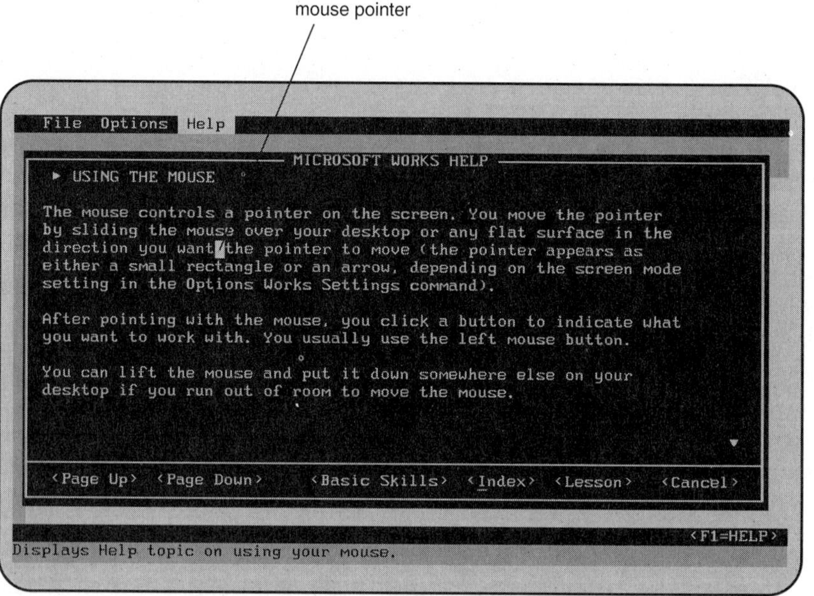

The first window of information about using the mouse is displayed. Now you can press the PGDN key to view the next screen of information, or you can point to the <Page Down> command button and click the left mouse button to select it.

Point: <Page Down>
Click: Left button

This is the last window of help information on this topic. To exit Help,

Point: <Cancel>
Press: Left button

This has the same effect as pressing ESC. Sometimes it is faster to use the key equivalent than it is to use the mouse to perform a task. You can always use a combination of the two methods.

The opening screen is displayed again.

Opening a File

You are now ready to open a file that has already been created for you and should be on your data disk. To do this, you need to open the File menu and select the Open Existing File command.

Note: Instructions in this lab will appear as "Select:" followed by the menu title, the command, or both. The appropriate letter will be **boldfaced.** To select a command, either type the bold letter or move the highlight to the menu or command and press ↵. If you have a mouse, click on the menu title both to activate the menu bar and select the menu. Then click on the appropriate command.

To open the File menu,

Press: ALT
Select: **F**ile

The highlight should be over the first command, Create New File. Notice the three dots or **ellipsis** following this command. This tells you that before Works can execute this command, the program will request further information. (If there are no dots following the command, it is executed as soon as it is selected.)

The command you will use, Open Existing File, will require additional information when it is selected.

Select: **O**pen Existing File

Your screen should look similar to Figure 1-8.

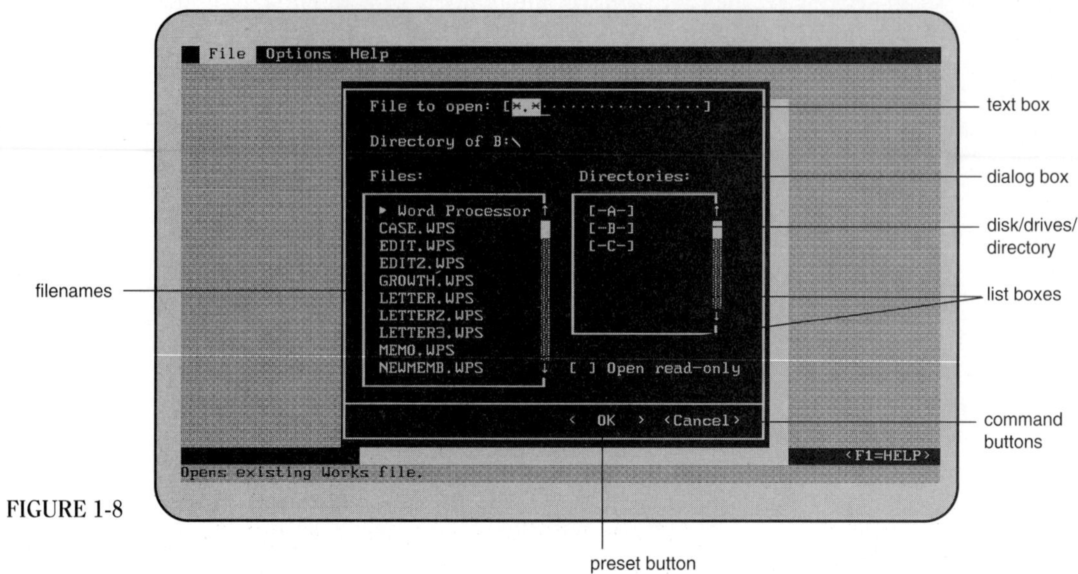

FIGURE 1-8

Whenever Works needs more information, a **dialog box** is displayed on the screen. This is how Works communicates with you to obtain the information it needs to complete a command. You will fill out the information in this box to specify how you want the command carried out.

The first line displays "File to open: [*.*.........]." This is called a **text box** because you enter the new information on the line by typing the appropriate text or information. Whenever you see text or numbers between square brackets, you can type instructions. Works wants to know the name of the file you want to use. The blinking cursor shows that Works is ready to accept information on this line. Whenever a dialog box appears, the cursor is in the top-most or left-most box.

The second line tells you the drive Works is using to access files. Works assumes the drive that was used to load the program is the drive you want to use to retrieve and save files to (most likely A: for a two-disk-drive system and C: for a hard disk system).

The two boxes, Files and Directories, contain a list of options that allow you to change the settings in the dialog box. They are called **list boxes.** The Files box displays the names of the files on the disk in the current drive. The Directories box displays the drives that can be accessed. List boxes are used when the options may vary or when the list of options is long. The Files box options will vary with the files on your disk and the Directories box options will vary with the computer system you are using.

Before you can select the filename you want to open, you need to change the directory to the drive containing your data disk (most likely B: for a two-disk-drive system and A: for a hard disk system).

The cursor is in the File to open: text box. To move from one box to another, hold down the (ALT) key and press the bold or underlined letter of the option you want to use. To open the D**i**rectories box,

Press: (ALT) - I

The cursor moves to the first line in the box to show it is ready for you to select information from this box. Now, just like with a pull-down menu, you use the ↑

and ↓ keys to move to the item you want to select. In addition, END will move the cursor to the last item in the box and HOME will move it to the first item.

Press: END

The cursor and highlight should be on the last option in the list. (Your screen may display different drives than those in Figure 1-8, depending upon your computer system.) The File to open: text box should display the selected drive.

Press: HOME

The highlight is back on the first list option.

Note: If the first option is "..", this means the current directory is a subdirectory. Selecting this option would take you to the next higher directory.

Mouse Note: You can move the cursor into the box and select the option at the same time by using the mouse. To do this, move the pointer to the option you want to select and click the left button.

If you are using a two-disk-drive system, the drive containing your data files should be drive B. If you are using a hard disk or network system, you will select the drive containing your data disk.

Move the highlight box to the appropriate drive for your system.

Next, you need to tell Works to carry out the command or to cancel it. Every dialog box contains at least two command buttons, generally, <OK> and <Cancel>. <OK> tells the program to carry out the instructions in the dialog box and <Cancel> cancels the command. The command button <OK> is the preset button and can be selected by pressing ↵ or by clicking on it using the mouse.

To complete the command by selecting OK,

Press: 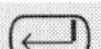

Mouse Note: You can double-click (press the left mouse button twice quickly) to both select an item and select OK at the same time in any dialog box.

The text box should show your new drive selection. Works will use this drive to open and save files until you change it again or exit Works. The Files list box should display the names of the files on your newly selected drive. This is now the current drive. If you selected the wrong directory, select the correct directory from the Directories list box and select OK.

You do not need to change every item in a dialog box if the displayed settings are correct. For example, if the directory is correct for your system, you would not need to change the setting.

Next, you need to enter the name of the file you want to open in the text box. You can type the filename in the text box or you can select it from the Files box. Using the Files box to select the filename is often easier and more accurate. If you are not sure of the name of the file, you can see all the filenames and select the name from the list. In addition, selecting the filename from the list avoids typing errors.

Before selecting the filename, you will use Help for information about opening a file. Since you are in the middle of a command, you cannot select Help from the menu. The status line displays the Help reminder button. You can however, press (F1) at any time to receive help information. Whenever you are using a dialog box, (F1) is your link to the Help system.

Mouse Note: You can click the button <F1=HELP> to access Help.

Press: (F1)

Your display screen should be similar to Figure 1-9.

FIGURE 1-9

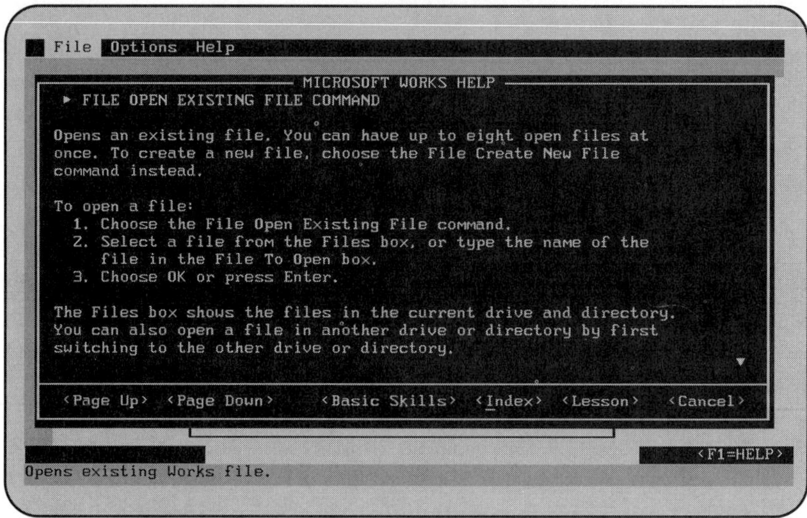

The Works Help system is **context-sensitive**. This means that whenever a command is in use, Works will display the Help topic about the command that is being used. This window tells you how the File>Open Existing File command works.

Read the four windows of information about this command.

To leave Help,

Press: (ESC)

You are returned to the same place you were before using Help and are ready to select the name of the file to open. To move the cursor to the Files box, you could press (ALT) - F or you can press (TAB). It is easier to press (TAB) to move within a dialog box; however, (TAB) will not work in all cases. If you cannot use (TAB) to move the cursor, then you must use the appropriate (ALT) - letter combination.

Press: (TAB)

The filenames are displayed in the Files box according to the type of tool used to create the file (Word Processor, Database, Spreadsheet, Other). The word processing files are listed first. Since there is limited space in the Files box, to see the names of the other files that do not have enough space to be displayed, you can press (PGDN) to see the next group of filenames,

Press: (↓)

The second group of filenames is displayed in the box. The spreadsheet group of files begins in the middle of the box. To quickly move to the last filename,

Press: (END)

The database filenames are displayed and the highlight is over the last filename in the list box. To return quickly to the first filename,

Press: (HOME)

The highlight should be on the first filename in the list.

The ↑ and ↓ keys are used to move the highlight in the direction of the arrow from one filename in the list to the next.

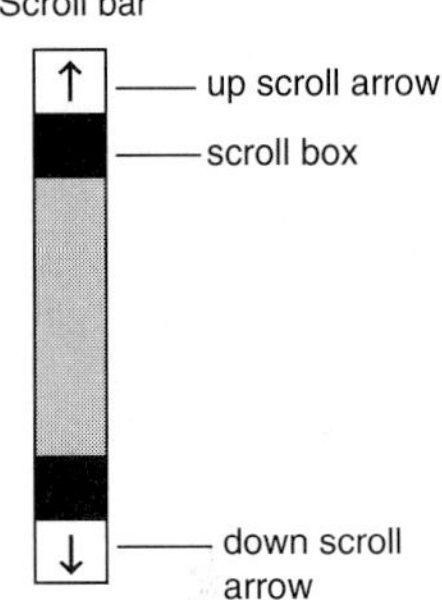

Press: ↓ (two times)

The third filename should be highlighted.

If you hold down the ↑ or ↓ keys or the (PGUP) or (PGDN) keys you can quickly move through the list of filenames. This is called **scrolling**.

Try this by holding down the ↓ key until the highlight is positioned over the last filename in the list.

As you moved the highlight through the list of filenames, new filenames scrolled into view at the bottom of the list box as others scrolled out of view at the top of the list box.

To return quickly to the first filename in the list box,

Press: (HOME)

Mouse Note: Notice on the right side of both of the list boxes that there is a bar with an up arrow at the top and a down arrow at the bottom. This is called the **scroll bar.** The arrows are called **scroll arrows.** If you place the pointer on the arrow and click, the list of items in the box will advance in the direction of the arrow. Try this by moving to the down scroll arrow and clicking the left button several times. Then move to the up scroll arrow and click on it until you are back to the first filename on the list.

To select the word processing file GROWTH.WPS on your data disk, using the arrow keys, move the highlight box to GROWTH.WPS.

The filename should be highlighted and displayed in the File to open: text box.

Mouse Note: To select the file, move the pointer to the filename and click the left button. You do not need to press (ALT) - F first.

To complete and execute the command by selecting OK,

Press: (↵)

Mouse Note: You can also double-click on the filename to select it and select OK at the same time.

After a few moments, your display screen should be similar to Figure 1-10.

FIGURE 1-10

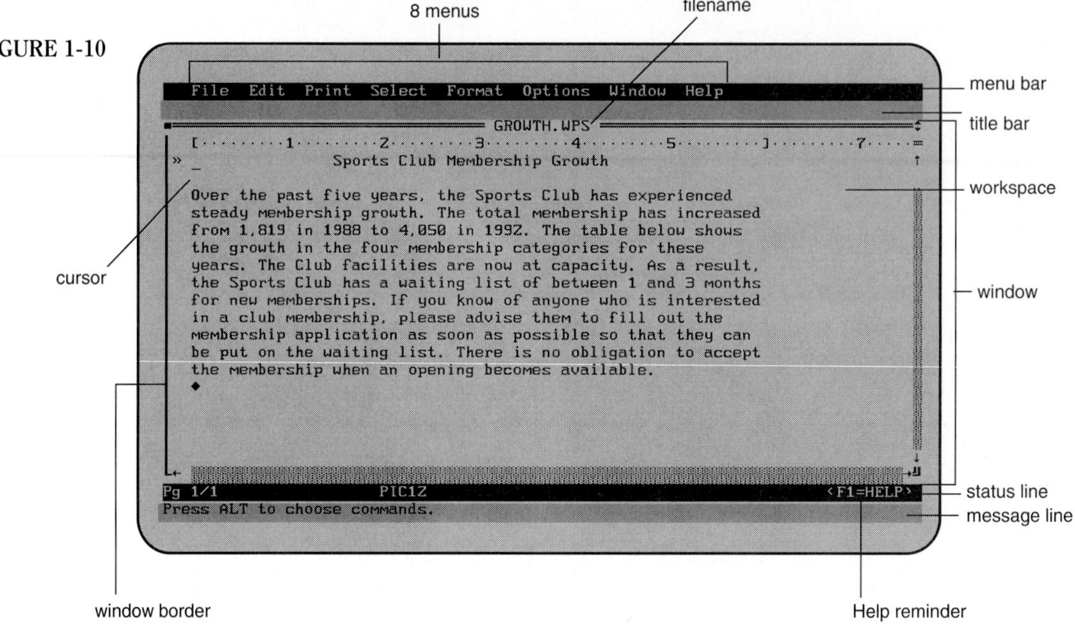

The File>Open Existing File command loads a copy of the file from the diskette into memory. The original file remains on the diskette. This file contains an article about the Sports Club membership growth.

Exploring the Word Processing Tool

The Works word processor can help you create and edit a text document such as a letter, memo, or a report. It allows you to easily design your printed document using different styles to create the appearance you want. Some of these features include boldfacing text, underlining, centering, changing margins, and selecting different **fonts,** or typestyles, and sizes. You will be learning about these features and more in the word processing labs.

The word processing screen looks similar to the opening screen in many ways. The menu bar is displayed at the top of the screen. However, it now lists eight menus that can be opened. The bottom two lines are still the status line and the message line. The status line contains information specific to the word processor as well as the Help reminder. You will learn about the specific information in the status line when you use the labs on word processing. The message line tells you what action to take—in this case, how to activate the menu bar.

The word processor window displays the name of the open file, in this case GROWTH.WPS, in the first line of the window. This is the **title bar.** The contents of the file, in this case the text for the article, are displayed in the **workspace.** This is the area of the screen where you enter text. The **window border** separates the window from the screen. All the tools have a title bar, workspace, and a window border. The other features in the word processor window will be explained in the word processing labs.

The cursor shows your location in the workspace. The arrow keys are used to move the cursor around the workspace.

Press: ↓ (4 times)

The cursor has moved down four lines.

Press: (→) (5 times)

Your screen should be similar to Figure 1-11.

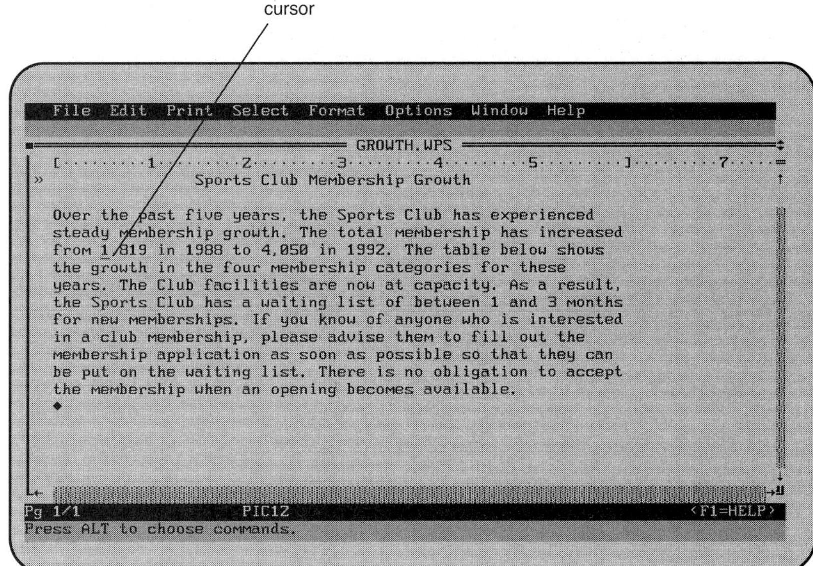

FIGURE 1-11

The cursor has moved to the right five spaces and should be under the number "1" in 1,819.

You will learn about more about moving around the word processing workspace in Lab 2.

To open the File menu,

Press: (ALT)
Select: **F**ile

The same commands are available for selection as in the opening screen. The cursor is no longer displayed in the workspace because you cannot use the workspace while the menu is active.

Press: (→)

The Edit menu is opened. It lists commands that are used to makes changes to your text.

To browse through the other word processing menus,

Press: (→) (6 times)

The Help menu should be open. The same six Help commands are listed.

Press: (→)

The File menu should be open.

To close this file before opening another file,

Select: Close

You will learn how to use the word processing tool in Labs 2–4.

Exploring the Spreadsheet Tool

The opening screen menu is displayed again. Next, to look at the spreadsheet tool, you will open the spreadsheet file MEMBERS.WKS. To do this,

Select: Open Existing File

The dialog box should display the correct directory and filenames. To move to the Files list box,

Press: (TAB) or (ALT)-F

Using the (↓), move the highlight down through the list of word processor filenames. When the spreadsheet category of filenames comes into view in the Files box, highlight the file MEMBERS.WKS.

To open this file,

Press: (↵)

Your screen should be similar to Figure 1-12.

FIGURE 1-12

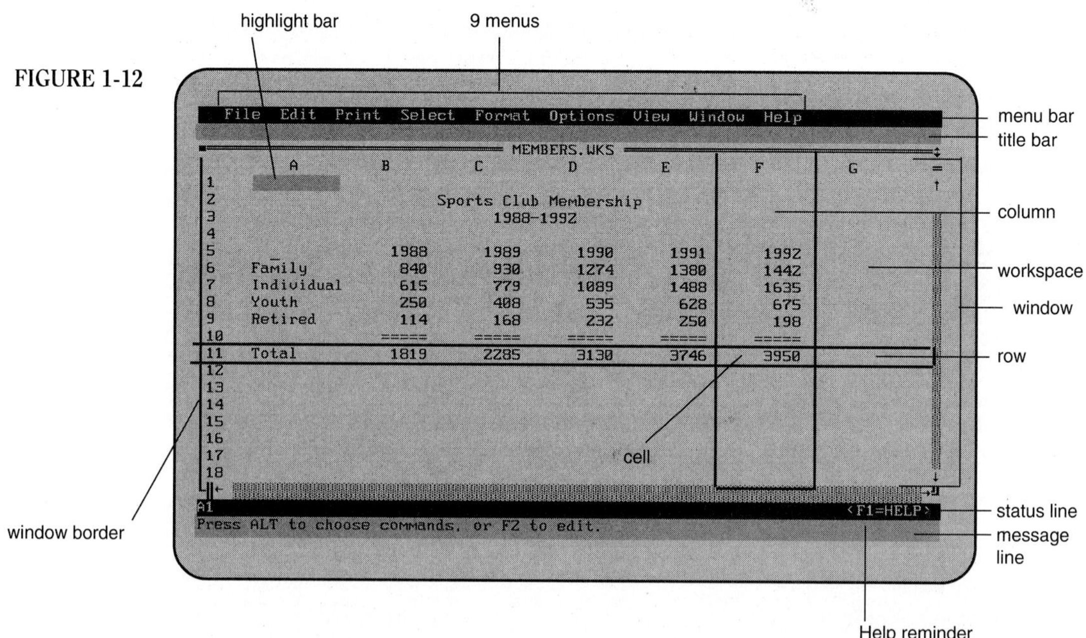

The spreadsheet is similar to an accountant's ledger. It is used to prepare, analyze and present budgets, cost estimates, and other types of financial or statistical information.

The screen is again similar to the word processing and opening screens. Nine menus are available in the menu bar. Eight are the same as in the word processing screen. The status line contains new information specific to the spreadsheet as well as the Help reminder. The message line displays information on command usage.

The window displays the filename of the open file in the title bar. The contents of the open file are displayed in the workspace. Unlike the word processor window, the spreadsheet workspace is bordered by letters across the top of the workspace and numbers along the left side. The numbers identify the **rows** in a spreadsheet and the letters identify the **columns.** The intersection of a row and column creates a **cell.** Data is entered into a **cell**. The cursor is now a highlighted bar that shows you which cell you are currently located in. To move the highlight,

Press: ↓ (5 times)

The highlight should be over the cell containing the entry "Family."

Press: →

Your screen should be similar to Figure 1-13.

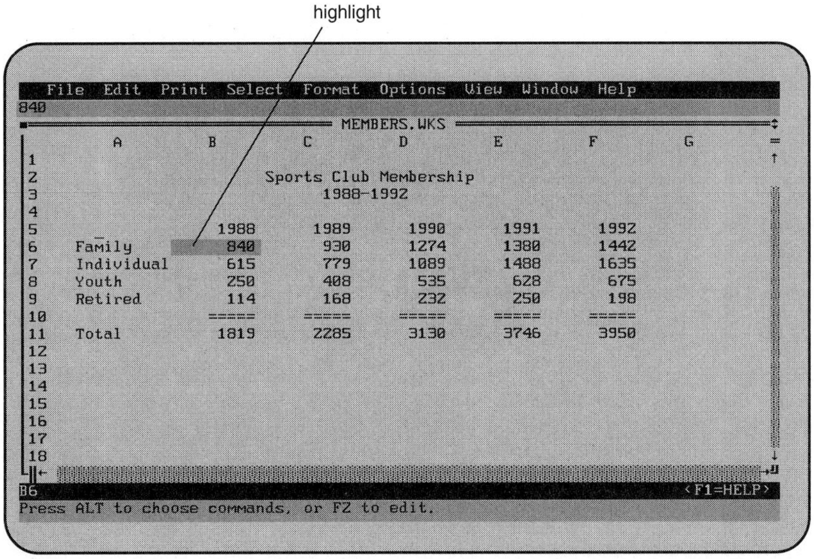

FIGURE 1-13

highlight

File Edit Print Select Format Options View Window Help
840
MEMBERS.WKS

	A	B	C	D	E	F	G
1							
2			Sports Club Membership				
3			1988–1992				
4							
5		1988	1989	1990	1991	1992	
6	Family	840	930	1274	1380	1442	
7	Individual	615	779	1089	1488	1635	
8	Youth	250	408	535	628	675	
9	Retired	114	168	232	250	198	
10		=====	=====	=====	=====	=====	
11	Total	1819	2285	3130	3746	3950	
12							
13							
14							
15							
16							
17							
18							

B6 <F1=HELP>
Press ALT to choose commands, or F2 to edit.

The highlight should have moved to the right one cell and should be highlighting the number 840.

You will learn how to move around, enter data, and use the spreadsheet tool in Labs 5–8.

To open the File menu,

Press: ALT
Select: File

The File commands are again the same as in the word processing and opening screen menu.

Press: (→)

Many of these commands are the same as in the word processing Edit menu; however, some are different. You will find as you explore and use the menus that many commands will be the same from tool to tool. Others will be different and specific to the tool you are using.

Press: (→) (5 times)

The View menu should be open. This menu lets you create and view charts using Works.

To view a bar chart of the data in this spreadsheet (it has been already been created for you), move the highlight to the menu option 1 Growth.

Press: (↵)

If you are using a floppy disk system, the program will direct you to insert the Accessories Disk in drive A and press (↵). Follow these directions.

Your screen should be similar to Figure 1-14.

FIGURE 1-14

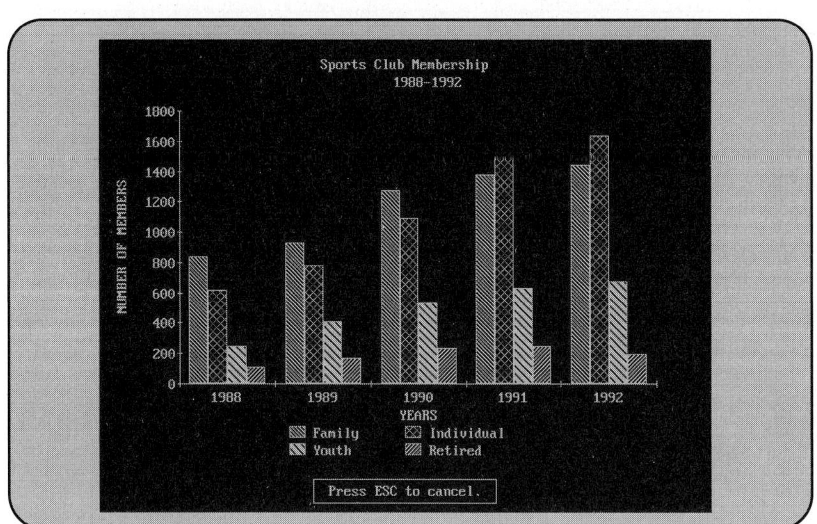

A bar chart of the data is displayed on your screen. You will learn how to chart spreadsheet data in Lab 8.

To return to the spreadsheet,

Press: (ESC)

Notice that the menu bar displays eight menus and the status line displays CHART. Whenever you create and view a chart, Works changes from the normal Spreadsheet view to Chart view. The commands in Chart view are used to create and modify charts. To return to Spreadsheet view and menu,

Press: F10

If you are using a floppy disk system, you will be instructed to insert the working copy of the program disk in drive A and press ↵. Follow these directions.

To close the spreadsheet file,

Press: ALT
Select: **F**ile
Select: **C**lose

Exploring the Database Tool

The last tool you will look at is the database tool. A database is like a filing system. It helps you keep track of and organize records that contain common information. The Sports Club has several database files. One contains information about each member. Another contains information about each employee. The club frequently uses the information in the database files to create mailing labels and reports.

To take a look at the employee database file,

Select: **Op**en Existing File

Using ↓, move the highlight through the list of filenames in the word processor and spreadsheet sections. When the database section of filenames is displayed, highlight the file named EMPLOY.WDB.

To open this file,

Press: ↵

Your screen should be similar to Figure 1-15.

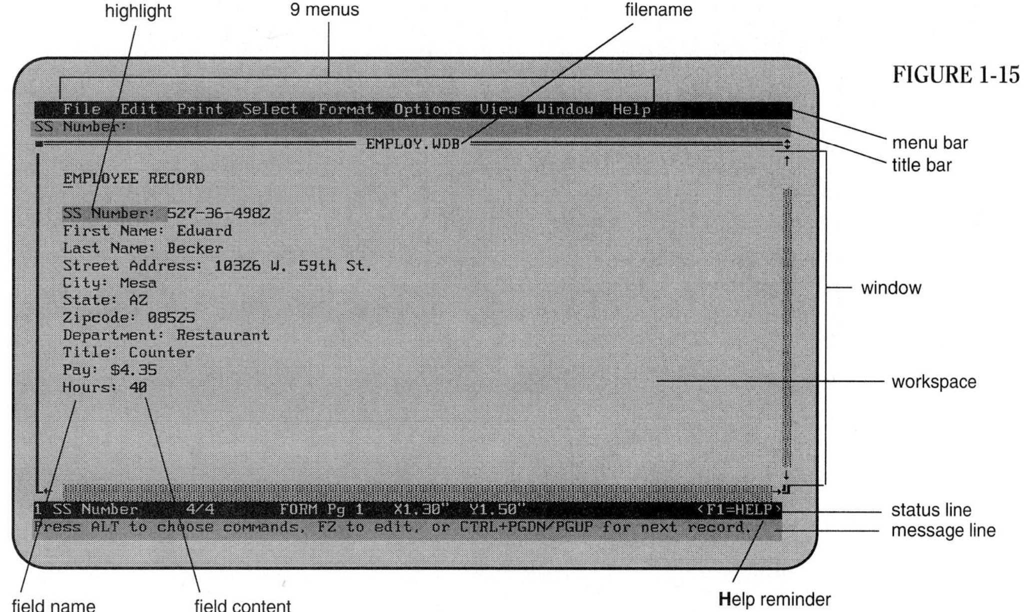

FIGURE 1-15

The database file on employees includes information such as the employee's name, address, pay, and hours worked.

The screen is again similar to the other tools you have looked at. Nine menus are available in the menu bar. They are the same as in the spreadsheet tool. The status line contains new information specific to the database tool as well as the Help reminder. The message line displays information on command usage and database creation. The database window displays the filename of the open file in the title bar. The contents of the open file are displayed in the workspace. The database tool stores and displays the information in the file differently than the other tools. Currently, the workspace displays the information for one club employee, Edward Becker. This is called a **record.** A record consists of **fields** of information. Each field is made up of a **field name** and **field contents.** The field name describes the information displayed in the field contents.

Like the spreadsheet tool, the cursor is a highlight bar that identifies your location in the workspace. It is over the field name "SS Number:."

Press: →

The cursor is over "527-36-4982." This is the field contents of the social security number field.

Pess: CTRL - PGDN

A second record of information is displayed. It contains the same type of information as the first record, except for a different employee.

Your screen should be similar to Figure 1-16.

FIGURE 1-16

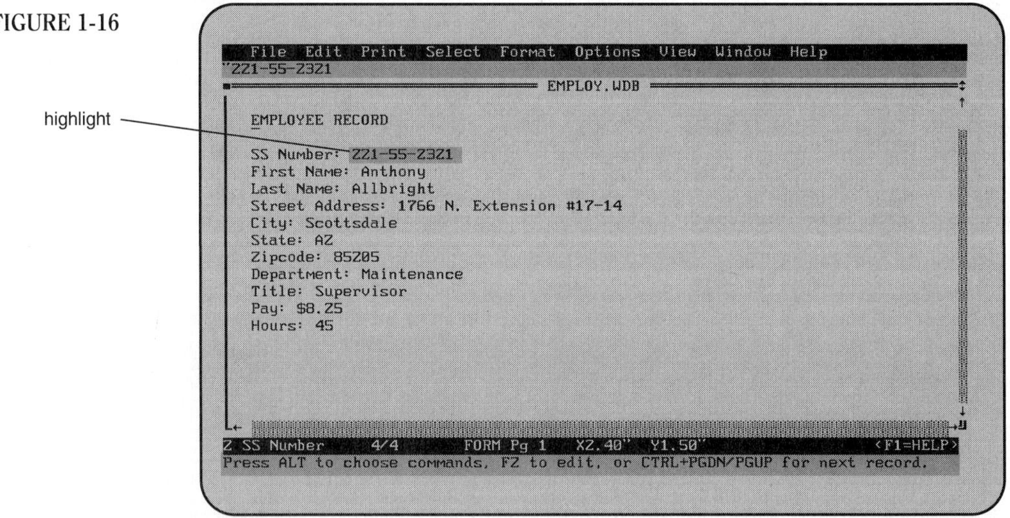

You will learn how to create a database, enter data, and use the database tool in Labs 9–11.

To open the File menu,

Press: ALT
Select: File

The File commands are again the same as in the spreadsheet, word processing, and opening screen menu.

Press: →

Many of these commands are the same as in the word processing and spreadsheet Edit menu; however, some are different.

Press: (→) (8 times)

The File menu should be open again. To close this file,

Select: Close

You will learn more about each of these tools throughout the series of labs. In the last lab (12), you will learn how you can integrate the tools.

The opening menu should be displayed. To exit the program,

Select: Exit Works

The DOS prompt should be displayed on your screen again.

Key Terms

integrated program	cursor	scrolling
word processor	preset	scroll bar
spreadsheet	default	scroll arrows
database	mouse pointer	fonts
communications	point	title bar
opening screen	click	workspace
menu bar	double-click	window border
window	drag	row
status line	boldface	column
message line	ellipsis	cell
menu	dialog box	record
highlight bar	text box	field
inverse video	list box	field name
mnemonic letter	context-sensitive	field contents
command buttons		

Matching

1. menu bar	4	**a.** activates menu
2. cursor	7	**b.** opens File menu
3. (ESC)	1	**c.** lists available menus
4. (ALT)	3	**d.** cancel
5. mnemonic letter	10	**e.** accept command
6. (F1)	2	**f.** shows location
7. (ALT) - F	8	**g.** displays chart
8. View>1	9	**h.** moves pointer on screen
9. mouse	5	**i.** bold letter in menu/command
10. OK	6	**j.** activates Help

Practice Exercises

1. Identify the parts of the screen.

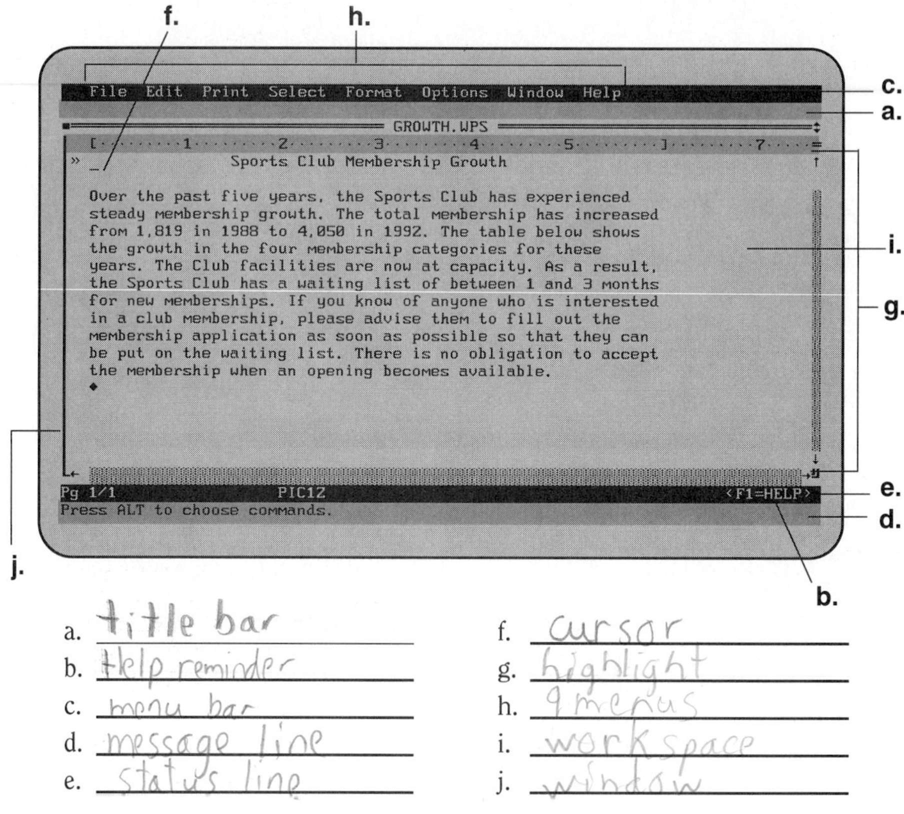

a. title bar
b. Help reminder
c. menu bar
d. message line
e. status line
f. cursor
g. highlight
h. 9 menus
i. workspace
j. window

2.
- Open the file GROWTH.WPS.
- Move the cursor to the 4 in the third line of text. What were the keystrokes you used to move to this position? 4 down →22
- Activate the menu.
- Open the Edit menu. How many commands are there in this menu? 10
- Move the highlight to the Move command.
- Use Help for information about this command. From the information provided by Help, complete this statement: When you move in the word processor, Works does this: inserts text at cursor.
- Close the file.

3.
- Open the file MEMBERS.WKS.
- Move the highlight to the cell containing the entry 779. What were the keystrokes you used to move to this cell? 6 down two →
- Activate the menu.
- Open the Edit menu. How many commands are there in this menu?
- Move the highlight to the Delete Row/Column command.
- Use Help for information about this command. From the information provided by Help, answer this question: What are the two step instructions under "To Delete:"?

1. select what you want to delete.
2. choose edit delete command.

- Close the file.

4.
- Open the file EMPLOY.WDB.
- Move the highlight to the field containing the entry 08525. What were the keystrokes you used to move to this field? 6 down
- Activate the menu.
- Open the Edit menu. How many commands are there in this menu?
- Move the highlight to the Move Record command.
- Use Help for information about this command. Complete this statement from information provided in Help: When you are in Database Form view, Works does this: moves fields, labels, or entire records.
- Close the file.

Command Summary

Keystroke vs. Mouse

Function	Keystroke	Mouse
Selecting Commands:		
Activate menu bar	(ALT)	
Open a menu	Type bold letter or highlight name and press (↵)	Click the menu name
Select a command name	Type bold letter or highlight command and press (↵)	Click the command
Close a menu	Press (ESC)	Click outside menu
Selecting Options:		
Text box	(TAB) to box, type information	Click on box, type information
List box	(TAB) to box, highlight option or press (ALT) plus bold letter	Click on option
Command button	(TAB) to button, press (↵) or press (ALT) plus bold letter	Click on button

Command	Shortcut	Action	Page
File>**O**pen Existing File...		Opens file	17
File>**C**lose		Closes file	24
File>E**x**it Works		Exits the Works program	29
	(F1)	Displays task related Help information	20
Help>**U**sing Help		Displays information on using Help	10
Help>**M**ouse		Displays help topic on using your mouse	16

CONTENTS
WORD PROCESSING

OVERVIEW
WORD PROCESSING

The most popular applications software used on a microcomputer today is a word processor. To put your thoughts in writing, from the simplest note to the most complex book, is a time-consuming process. Even more time-consuming is the task of editing and retyping the document to make it perfect. There was a time when perfection in written communication was difficult, if not impossible, to achieve. With the introduction of word processing, errors should be nearly nonexistent—not because they are not made, but because they are easy to correct. Word processors let you throw away correction fluid, scissors, paste, and erasers. Now, with a few keystrokes, you can easily correct errors, move paragraphs, and reprint your document.

Definition of Word Processing

Word processing programs help you create any type of written communication via a keyboard. A word processor can be used to manipulate text data to produce a letter, a report, a memo, or any other type of correspondence. Text data is any letter, number, or symbol that you can type on a keyboard. The grouping of text data to form words, sentences, paragraphs, and pages of text results in the creation of a document. Through a word processor you can create, modify, store, retrieve, and print part or all of a document.

Advantages of Using a Word Processor

The speed of entering text data into the computer depends on the skill of the user. If you cannot type quickly, a word processor will not improve your typing speed. However, a word processor will make it easier to correct and change your document. Consequently, your completed document will take less time to create.

Where a word processor excels is in its ability to change, modify, or edit a document. Editing involves correcting spelling, grammar, and sentence-structure errors. With a word processor, the text is stored on the diskette. As errors are found, they are electronically deleted and corrected. Once the document is the way you want it to appear, it is printed on paper. Good-bye, correction fluid!

In addition to editing a document, you can easily revise or update it by inserting or deleting text. For example, a document that lists prices can easily be updated to reflect new prices. A document that details procedures can be revised by deleting old procedures and inserting new ones. This is especially helpful when a document is used repeatedly. Rather than recreating the whole document, only the parts that change need to be revised.

Revision also includes the rearrangement of pieces or blocks of text. For example, while writing a report, you may decide to change the location of a single word or several paragraphs or pages of text. You can do it easily by using Block and Move commands. Blocks of text can also be copied from one area of the document to another. This is a real advantage when the text includes many recurring phrases or words.

Combining text in another file with your document is another advantage of word processors. An example of this is a group term paper. Each person is responsible for writing a section of the paper. Before printing the document, the text for all sections, which is stored in different files, is combined to create the complete paper. The opposite is also true. Text that may not be appropriate in your document can easily be put in another file for later use.

Many word processors include special programs to further help you produce a perfect document. A spell checker will check the spelling in a document by comparing each word to a dictionary of words. If an error is found, the program will suggest the correct spelling. A syntax checker electronically checks grammar, phrasing, capitalization, and other types of syntax errors in a document. A thesaurus will display different words, each with a meaning similar to the word you entered.

After changes are made and the document appears ready to be printed, the word processor also makes it easy to change the document's design or appearance. For example, a word processor lets you set the line spacing of a document. You can decide how large you want the right, left, top, and bottom margins. The number of lines printed on each page can be specified. In addition, you can quickly specify whether the pages will or will not be numbered and where (top or bottom, centered or not) the page number will appear. Further, a word processor will let you enter headers and footers on each page or on specified pages.

If, after reading the printed copy, you find other errors or want to revise or reformat the document, it is easy to do. Simply reload the document file, make your changes, and reprint the text! Now that saves time!

Word Processing Terminology

The following list of generic terms and definitions are associated with most word processing programs.

Block: Any group of characters, words, lines, paragraphs, or pages of text.

Boldface: Produces dark or heavy print.

Center: To center a line of text evenly between the margins.

Character string: Any combination of letters, numbers, symbols, and spaces.

Delete: To erase a character, word, paragraph, or block of text from the document.

Flush right: To align text on the right-hand margin.

Format: To define how the printed document will appear; includes settings for underline, boldface, print size, margin settings, line spacing, etc.

Insert mode: New text is entered into a document between existing text.

Justified: The text has even left and right margins, produced by inserting extra spaces between words on each line.

Merge: Combine text in one document with text in another.

Overstrike: Causes the printer to print one character over another to make the type darker.

Search: Scans the document for all matching character strings.

Search and replace: Scans the document for all matching character strings and replaces them with others.

Template: A document, like a form letter, that contains blank spaces for automatic insertion of information that varies from one document to another.

Typeover mode: New text is entered in a document by typing over the existing text on the line.

Unjustified: The text has an even left margin and an uneven, or ragged, right margin.

Word wrap: Automatic adjustment of the number of characters or words on a line while entering text; eliminates pressing the ⏎ key at the end of each line.

Case Study for Labs 2–4

Karen Barnes is the membership assistant for the Sports Club. The club just purchased the Works 2.0 software program. Her first assignment using this program is to create a letter welcoming new members to the club using the word processing tool.

In Lab 2, the rough draft of the letter entered by Karen is corrected. During this process, the basic cursor-movement keys and editing features are demonstrated.

Lab 3 continues with modifying the welcome letter. You learn how to create and save a new file, open and use multiple files, and copy and move text within and between files. In addition, you learn how to improve the appearance of the document by adjusting the margins and tabs. Finally, the search and replace feature is covered and the document is previewed and printed.

In Lab 4, you follow Karen as she uses Works to create an announcement for the club's bulletin board and prepares an article to be used in the club's newsletter. You will learn how to center, boldface, and underline text to add visual interest. In addition, you will learn how to create tabular columns, align paragraphs, create headers and footers, and use windows to view multiple documents on the screen at the same time. Finally, you will spell-check and print the documents.

LAB

2 Word Processing: Editing a Document

CASE STUDY

Karen Barnes, the Membership Assistant for the Sports Club, has been asked to create a letter welcoming new members to the club. The letter should briefly explain the services offered by the club. Karen has written a rough draft of the welcome letter using Works 2.0. However, the letter contains many errors. You will follow Karen as she uses Works 2.0 to correct and modify the letter.

OBJECTIVES

In this lab you will learn how to:

1. Move around a word processing document.
2. Delete characters, words and lines of text.
3. Insert and replace text.
4. Select text.
5. Insert and delete blank lines.
6. Display hidden codes.
7. Undo mistakes.
8. Print a document.

Exploring the Word Processor Screen

Load the Works program. If you need help, refer back to the instructions in Lab 1.

Karen created the first draft of the welcome letter yesterday using the word processor and saved it on the diskette in a file named LETTER.

Note: In this lab and all subsequent labs, when the direction to "Select:" a command appears, you will need to activate the menu bar by pressing (ALT) before you can select the menu and commands. The instruction to press (ALT) will not appear.

To open this file,

Select: **O**pen Existing File

Specify the appropriate drive for your system.

Select: **LETTER.WPS**
Press: (↵)

Reminder: To cancel an incorrect menu selection, press (ESC) to terminate the command or (ALT) to close a menu without deactivating the menu bar.

Your display screen should be similar to Figure 2-1.

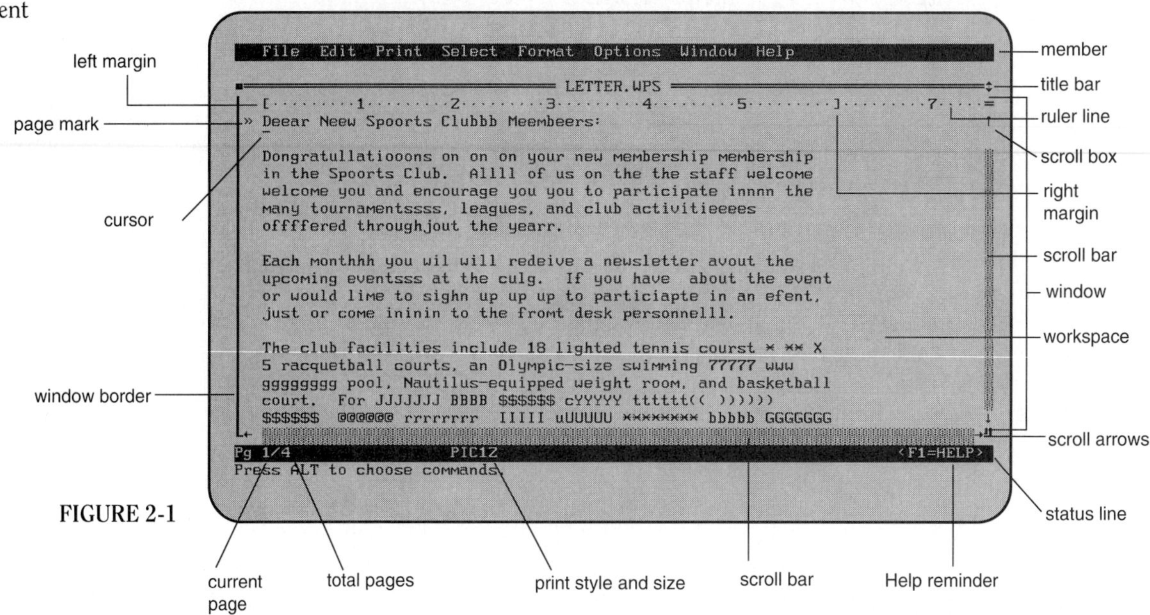

FIGURE 2-1

At the top of the screen, the **menu bar** displays the eight menus available in the word processor tool. The **title bar** displays the name of the file you are viewing.

The borders of the **window** create a frame around the **workspace**. This separates the window from the screen and is where your work is displayed. The first three paragraphs of the rough draft of the welcome letter are displayed in the workspace. As you can see, it contains many errors, which you will correct in this lab.

Just below the title bar in the window is the **ruler line.** It shows where tabs and indents are set. The zero mark of the ruler is at the left margin. The brackets on both ends of the ruler line are the left and right indents or margins. They show you where your text begins and ends and create the margins on both sides of the paper when the document is printed. The dots show each space or column on the line. The ruler line settings are preset or **default settings**. Works comes with many default settings. These settings are generally those that are the most commonly used. For example, the default left margin setting is 1.3" from the left edge of the paper.

The symbol >> on the first line of the workspace is called a **page mark.** It identifies the beginning of a page. The blinking underline is the **cursor.** As you type, text appears to the left of the cursor. It marks your location in the file.

In addition to the **Help reminder**, the **status line** displays several pieces of information specific to the word processor. The status line helps you keep track of where you are and what you are doing. It currently tells you several pieces of information about the current location of the cursor:

Pg 1/4 This first number tells you the number of the **page** on which the cursor is located. It is currently on page 1. The second number tells you the number of pages in the file. In this file there are four pages.

PIC12 This tells you the **font** or print style (Pica) and size (12) of the print Works will use to print out your document. It will vary with your printer. For example, your printer may use Courier, in which case COU would be displayed instead of PIC.

The status line will also display other information, such as key conditions, command prompts, and descriptions that are mainly designed to help you use the menus.

The **message line** provides suggestions and brief descriptions of the commands.

Mouse Note: The Word Processor Screen for Mouse Users

Even if you do not have a mouse, the symbols for mouse users will appear on your screen. These symbols are located in the right, left, and bottom borders of the window surrounding the workspace. At the right and bottom of the window are **scroll bars** that allow you to use the mouse to move quickly through long files. The box inside the scroll bar is called the **scroll box.** It indicates approximately what part of the file is currently displayed in the window. For example, when the scroll box is in the middle of the scroll bar, you are looking at the middle of the file. The **scroll arrows** in the scroll bar let you move up, down, left, or right in the file by line, character, row, or column. Many of the other symbols let you control the size of the window. You will be learning how to use many of these symbols later in this lab.

Moving the Cursor

The cursor is moved around the screen by using the directional (arrow) keys and key combinations or by using the mouse. The directional keys, located on the numeric keypad or on the separate cursor key area, move the cursor one character space to the right or left or one line up or down.

Note: Be careful to use only the keys specified as you are following the directions in this section. If you do, the instructions and figures in the text should be the same as what you see on your screen. Also, make sure the (NUM LOCK) (number lock) key is not on when you use the numeric keypad area. If it is on, NL will be displayed in the status line. When (NUM LOCK) is on, numbers are entered rather than the cursor moving through the text. If NL appears in the status line, press (NUM LOCK) to turn it off.

Press: (→) (6 times)

Your display screen should be similar to Figure 2-2.

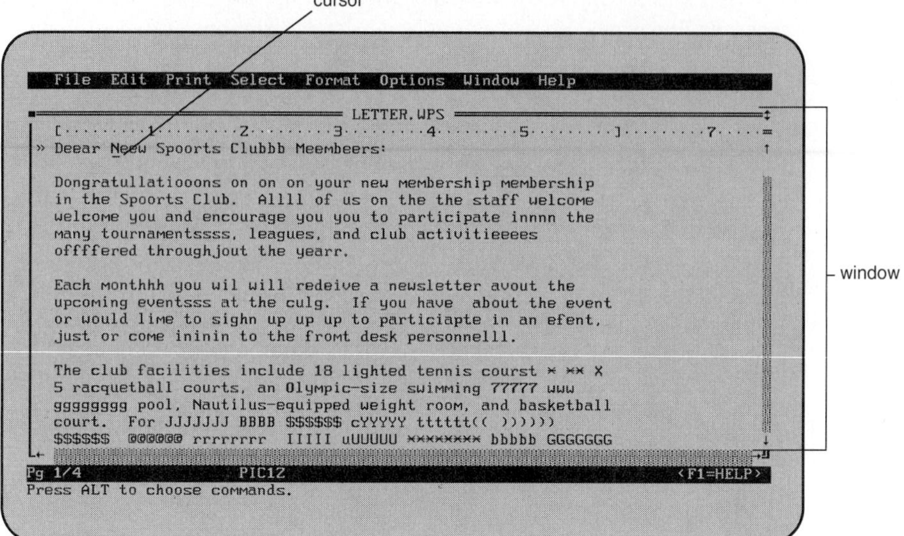

FIGURE 2-2

The cursor moved six character spaces or columns to the right along the line. It should be positioned under the "N" in "Neew," the seventh column on the line.

Press: ↓

The cursor moved down one line. Since this is a blank line, the cursor moved back to the left margin on the line.

Press: ↓

The cursor moved down to the next line and back to the seventh column. This is the same relative position in the line the cursor was located on when it was last positioned on a line containing text. The cursor will attempt to maintain its position in a line of text as you move up or down through the document.

By holding down either ← or →, the cursor will move quickly character by character along the line.

To see how this works, hold down → and move the cursor to the right along the line until it is under the "p" in the first "membership."

If you moved too far to the right along the line of text, use the ← to move back to the correct position.

This saves multiple presses of the arrow key. Many of Works' cursor movement keys can be held down to execute multiple moves.

Press: ↑ (2 times)

The cursor moved up two lines. It should be positioned at the end of the first line.

Using the arrow keys,

Move to: X at end of first line of third paragraph

The default right margin setting is 1.2 inches from the right side of the paper. To see what happens when the cursor reaches the right margin,

Press: (→) (2 times)

The cursor automatically moved to the beginning of the next line. Unlike a typewriter, you did not need to press (↵) to move from the end of one line to the beginning of the next. It is done automatically for you.

The cursor can also move word by word in either direction on a line using (CTRL) in combination with (→) or (←). (CTRL) is held down while pressing the arrow key.

Press: (CTRL) - (→) (5 times)

The cursor skipped to the beginning of each word and moved five words to the right along the line. It should be positioned on the "O" in the word "Olympic."

To move back to the first word in this line,

Press: (CTRL) - (←) (5 times)

The cursor should be positioned on the "5," the first character in the line. If the cursor is positioned in the middle of a word, (CTRL) - (→) will move the cursor to the beginning of the next word. However, (CTRL) - (←) will move the cursor to the beginning of the word it is on, rather than to the beginning of the preceding word.

The cursor can be moved quickly to the end of a line of text by pressing (END). To move to the end of this line,

Press: (END)

Similarily, you can move to the beginning of a line of text by pressing (HOME). To move back to the beginning of the line,

Press: (HOME)

The cursor should be back on the "5."

The letter is longer than what is currently displayed in the workspace of the window. To move to the bottom line of the workspace,

Press: (↓) 3 times

The cursor should be on the first "$."

The workspace can display only 18 lines of text at a time. If the cursor is positioned on either the top or bottom line of the workspace, using (↑) or (↓) will bring more lines of the document into view. As you move line by line up or down through the document, the lines at the top or bottom of the workspace move out of view to allow more text to be displayed. This is called **scrolling.**

To scroll the rest of the letter into view in the window,

Press: (↓) (20 times)

The cursor should be at the beginning of the word "Sports."

Your display screen should be similar to Figure 2-3.

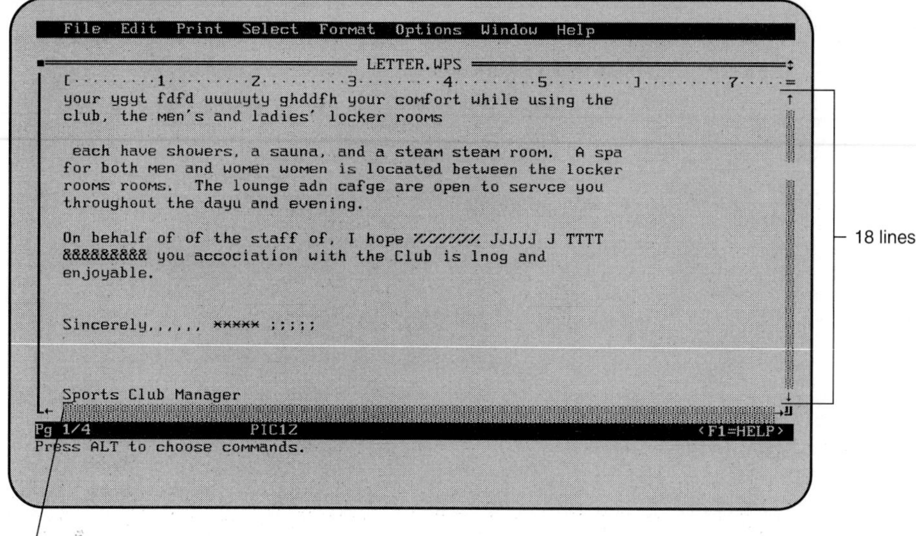

FIGURE 2-3

Each time you pressed (↓), a new line of text was brought into view at the bottom of the workspace. At the same time, a line of text scrolled out of view at the top of the workspace.

The workspace still displays only 18 lines of the letter. You can move the cursor quickly to the top line of the workspace by pressing (CTRL) - (PGUP).

Note: Key combinations that require you to hold down one key while pressing another will be separated with a hyphen throughout the rest of the text.

To move to the top line of the workspace,

Press: (CTRL) - (PGUP)

The cursor should be on the "y" in "your."

(CTRL) - (PGDN) will move the cursor to the last line of the workspace.

Press: (CTRL) - (PGDN)

The cursor should be positioned back at the beginning of "Sports" on the last line of the workspace.

The window is positioned over 18 lines of text on page 1 of the document (see Figure 2-3).

The cursor can also be quickly moved from one window of text to another using the (PGUP) and (PGDN) keys.

To move back to the top of the previous window,

Press: (PGUP)

The cursor should have moved up 18 lines and should be positioned on the "i" in the word "in."

To move down one full window,

Press: (PGDN)

The cursor should be on the "y" of the word "your" on the first line of the next window.

Works differentiates between a window and a page. A window can display only 18 lines of text in the workspace at one time. A page refers to the physical printed page. Works uses the default page length settings of 54 single-spaced lines of text. This is the standard number of lines that can be printed on an 8.5" x 11" piece of paper with 1" top and bottom margins.

To move to the top of page 2,

Press: (PGDN) (2 times)

The cursor should be positioned on the first line of page 2. The status line show that you are on Pg 2/4. The **page mark** (>>) symbol shows you where page 2 begins. Works inserts an automatic page break to tell the printer where to end one page and begin printing a new one. The automatic page break is entered whenever you have typed enough text to fill a page.

Press: (↑)

Your display screen should be similar to Figure 2-4.

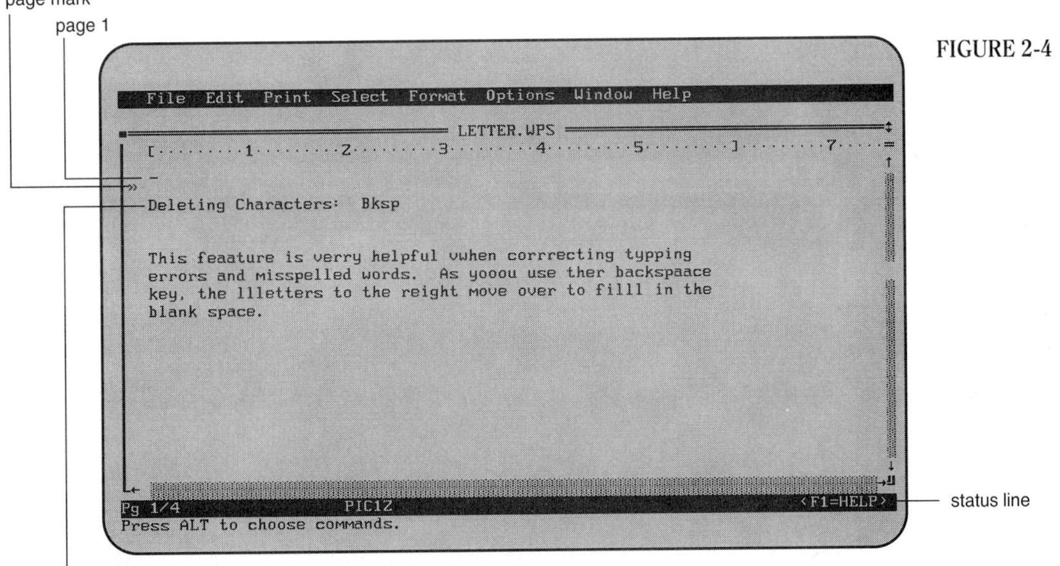

FIGURE 2-4

The status line shows that you are on Pg 1/4. The cursor is positioned on the last line of page 1.

To move through several pages of the document at once, you could press (PGDN) or (PGUP) over and over to move window by window through the file. However, using the Select>Go To command. When you use the Go To command, you can jump from one location in the file to another without scrolling text you do not want to see.

To move to page 3 of this document,

Select: Select
Select: Go To

Your screen display should be similar to Figure 2-5.

FIGURE 2-5

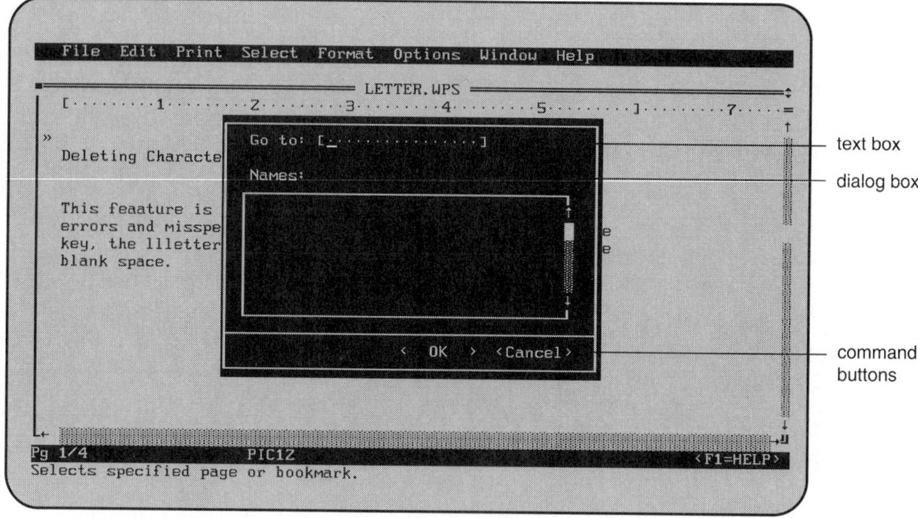

A **dialog box** is displayed. The cursor is positioned in the Go to: **text box**. You need to enter the page number you want to move to.

Type: 3

To complete the command by selecting OK,

Press: ⏎

Your display screen should be similar to Figure 2-6.

FIGURE 2-6

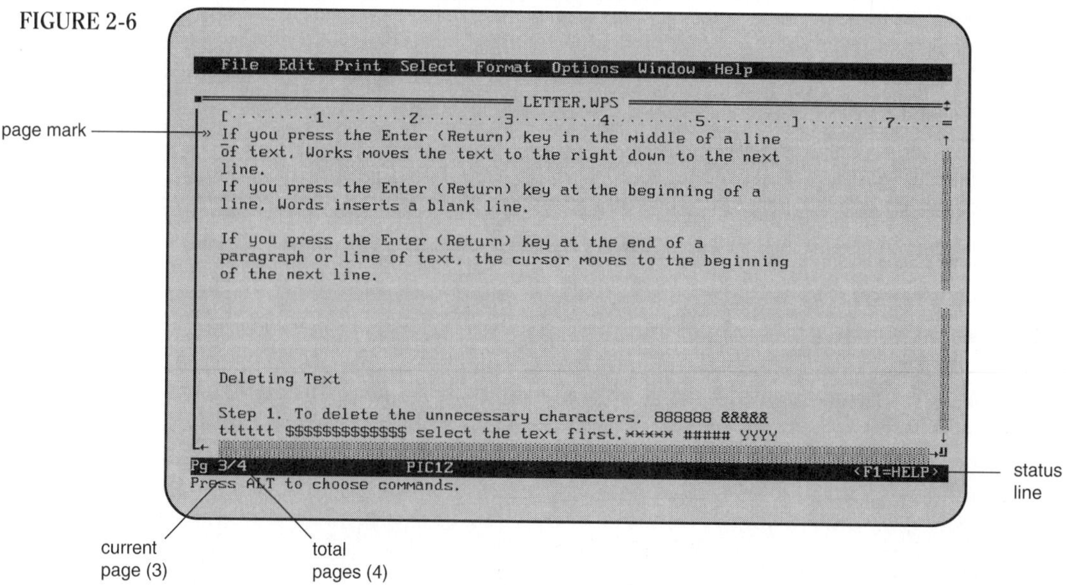

The cursor is positioned on the first line of page 3. The Go To command is very useful for moving around in a large file.

Works has several **shortcut keys** for frequently used commands. A shortcut key generally consists of a function key or other key combination that initiates a command without using the menu. The shortcut key to the Go To command is (F5). To see how this works,

Press: (F5)

The Go To dialog box is displayed. To move back to page 2,

Type: 2
Press: (↵)

The cursor is positioned on the first line of page 2. Shortcut keys will be introduced as they are used throughout the labs. They are available for commands that are used frequently.

The biggest jump the cursor can make is to move to the beginning or end of a document. To move to the end of this document,

Press: (CTRL) - (END)

Your display screen should be similar to Figure 2-7.

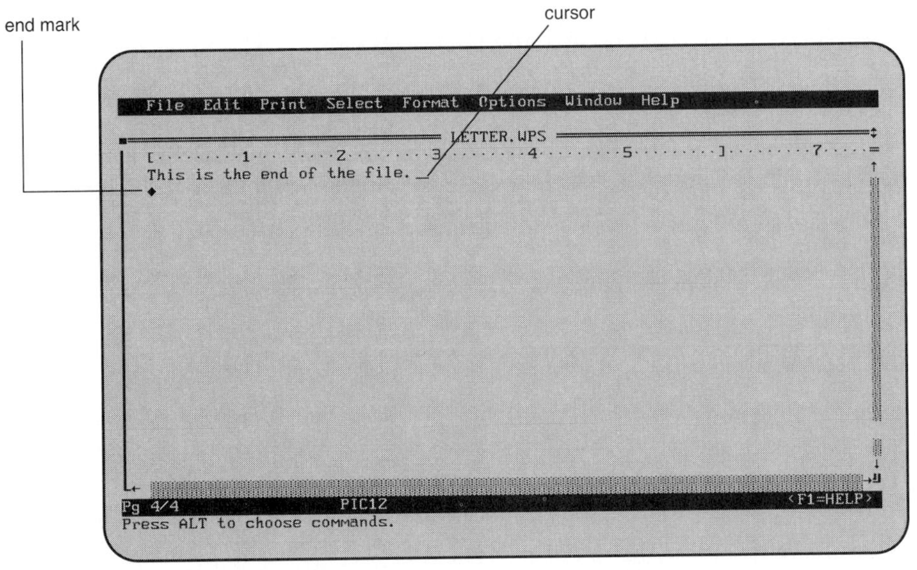

FIGURE 2-7

The cursor should be positioned on the last line in the file.

The diamond symbol is called the **end mark**. It identifies the end of a file. It cannot be deleted or erased.

Press: (↓)

The computer beeps and the program will not let you move the cursor to the line containing the end mark.

To move quickly back to the first line of text in the document,

Press: CTRL - HOME

The cursor should be positioned on the first line of page 1 of this document.

To review, the following cursor movement features have been covered:

Key	Action
→	One character to right
←	One character to left
↑	One line up
↓	One line down
CTRL - →	One word to right
CTRL - ←	One word to left
HOME	Left edge of line
END	Right edge of line
Select>Go To>[page number]↵	Top of page number specified
F5 [page number]↵	Top of page number specified
PGUP	Up a window
PGDN	Down a window
CTRL - HOME	Top of document
CTRL - END	Bottom of document

Using the Mouse to Move the Cursor

Note: If you do not have a mouse, skip to the next section, "Editing a Document."

If you have a mouse, you can use it to move the cursor to a specific location in a document. To do this, position the mouse pointer at the location in the text where you want to move the cursor, then click the left button.

Point: "y" of "your" (first line of first paragraph)

Notice that the cursor has not moved.

Click: Left button

The cursor is now positioned under the "y."

Practice using the mouse to move the cursor by moving it to the following locations on the workspace:

Move to: "E" in "Each" (first line of second paragraph)

Move to: "b" in "basketball" (third line of third paragraph)

Your screen should be similar to Figure 2-8.

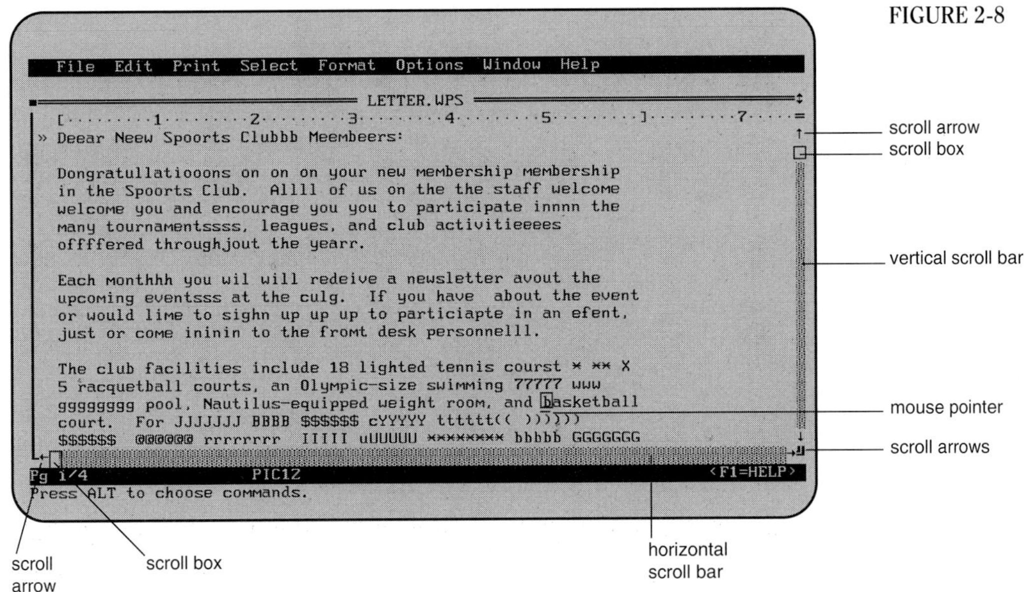

FIGURE 2-8

Three symbols are used to scroll the text in the window with the mouse; the scroll bar, the scroll arrows, and the scroll box.

To scroll the text line by line, position the mouse pointer on the arrow located on the ends of the scroll bar and click the left button. Each time you click the button, the text scrolls in the direction of the arrow. The arrows on the right scroll bar scroll the document vertically line by line. The arrows on the bottom scroll bar scroll the window horizontally.

Move the mouse pointer to the down arrow on the right scroll bar.

Click: Left button (20 times)

The text scrolled line by line in the workspace. As you scroll the text, the scroll box moves in the scroll bar, showing you the approximate vertical location in the document.

Next, position the mouse pointer on the right-facing arrow on the bottom scroll bar.

Click: Left button (10 times)

The text scrolls horizontally in the window. Again, notice that the scroll box has moved along the bottom scroll bar to show your approximate horizontal location in the document.

To return the document to its original position, move the mouse pointer to the left-facing arrow on the bottom scroll bar and click the left button until the text is properly positioned in the window.

To scroll the window one full window at a time, position the mouse pointer in the scroll bar and click the left button. If you position the mouse pointer below the scroll box, the text will move downward window by window. If you position the mouse pointer above the scroll box, it will scroll upward.

Try this by positioning the mouse pointer anywhere below the scroll box on the right scroll bar and click the left button several times. If the scroll box lines up with the mouse pointer location on the scroll bar, as you continue to click the button, the window will repeatedly jump up and down one window.

Next, move the window upward by positioning the mouse pointer on the right scroll bar anywhere above the scroll box and clicking the left button several times.

To scroll the document by large amounts, you can drag the scroll box on the scroll bar. To do this, position the mouse pointer on the scroll box. Hold down the left button while dragging the mouse pointer downward on the scroll bar. Release the left button when the space box is near the bottom of the scroll bar.

Your screen should be over text near the end of the file. When you scroll the document using the mouse, the cursor remains in its original location. Therefore the status line does not reflect the change in the page number. To move the cursor to the page you are viewing, click on a character in the window. The status line will then reflect the page you are viewing. Click on any character in the workspace. The page number in the status line should reflect the location of the cursor in the file.

Scroll the document upward by dragging the mouse on the scroll box until it is at the top of the scroll bar.

Click: the "D" in "Deear"

The status line should show that you are back on Pg 1/4.

The same procedure is followed using the scroll box in the bottom scroll bar to scroll the text horizontally on the window.

These features are used in all Works tools to scroll the document.

To review, the following mouse movement features have been covered.

Button	Action
Clicking Left button	Positions cursor
Dragging on scroll box	Scrolls document
Clicking in scroll bar	Scrolls window by window
Clicking on scroll arrows	Scrolls by line, character

Editing a Document

Now that you have learned how to move the cursor around the document, you are ready to learn how to **edit**, or revise and correct errors in a document.

The next part of this lab contains a series of exercises. Each exercise will show you a Works editing feature and allow you to practice using it. As you read the text in the book, you will be directed to use the editing feature to correct the exercise on your display screen. When you have completed the exercise, a figure in the book will show you how your display screen should appear. After completing each exercise, press (PGDN) the number of times directed to go to the next exercise.

To begin the exercise,

Press: (PGDN) (3 times)

Deleting Characters

Your display screen should be similar to Figure 2-9.

FIGURE 2-9

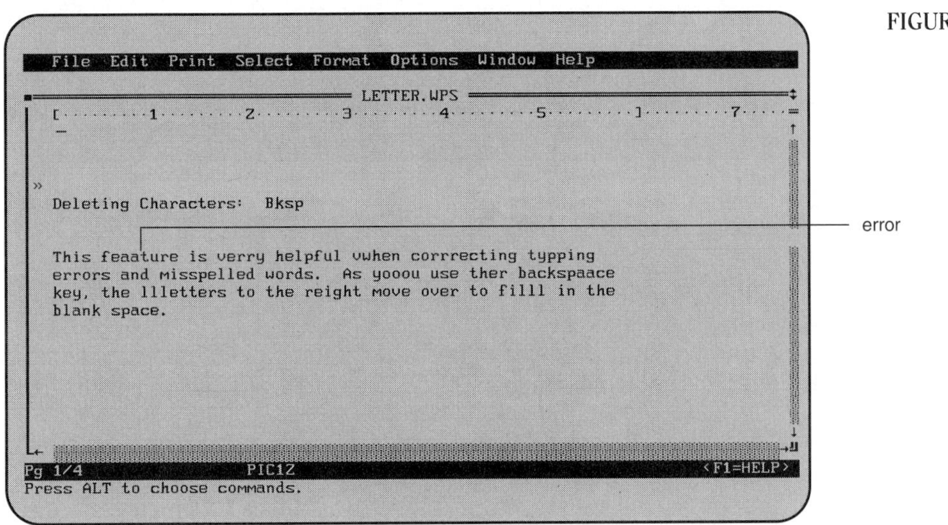

The first exercise, "Deleting Characters: Bksp," should be on your display screen.

The (Bksp) (backspace) key will **delete** or erase a character to the left of the cursor. This key may be labeled with a left-facing arrow, the word "Backspace" or "Bksp," or a combination of the two. It is located above the (↵) key.

The paragraph in the exercise on the display screen contains several errors that you will correct using the (Bksp) key. The first error on the screen is in the second word, "feaature." The word should be "feature." The extra "a" needs to be deleted.

To position the cursor to the right of the first "a,"

Move to: second "a" in "feaature"

Note: You can use the arrow keys or the mouse to move the cursor.

As a character is deleted, the text to the right will move over to fill in the space left by the deleted character. Watch your screen carefully as you

Press: (Bksp)

The character to the left of the cursor, in this case the "a," is deleted. The text to the right then moves over one space to fill in the space left by the character that was deleted.

There is now an extra space at the end of this line. Works constantly examines the number of characters on a line to see whether the word beginning on the next line ("errors") can be moved up to fill in the space without exceeding the margin setting. This process of filling in the spaces is called **reformatting**. Watch your screen carefully as you correct the next two errors. To delete the extra "r" in "verry,"

Move to: second "r"in "verry"

Press: (Bksp)

To delete the "v" before the word "when,"

Move to: **"w" in "when"**
Press: Bksp

Your display screen should be similar to Figure 2-10.

FIGURE 2-10

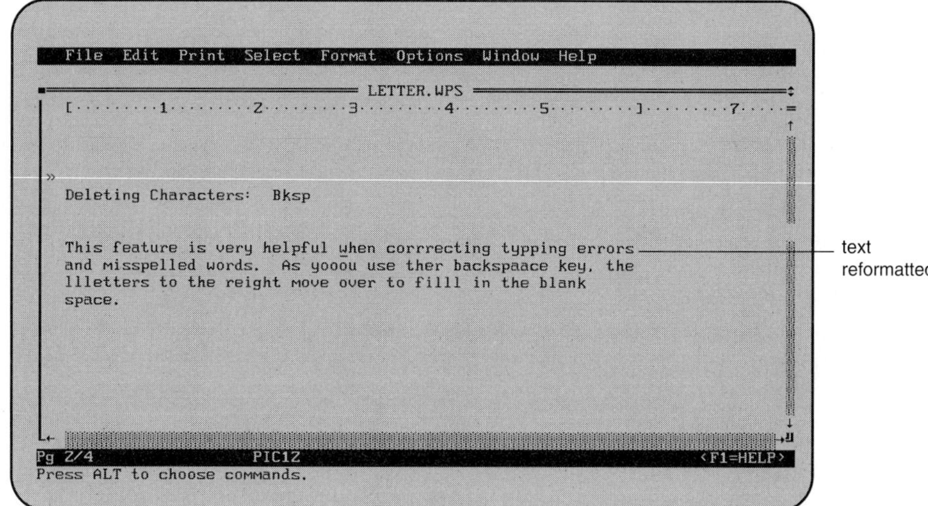

The word "errors" from the beginning of the line below moved up to the end of the current line. The deletion of the extra characters created enough space for the whole word to move up a line. The lines below this line are also automatically reformatted.

Continue this exercise by using Bksp to correct the text on the display. As you edit and move through the text, Works will constantly re-examine the margin space and adjust the text as needed.

When you are finished, your display screen should be similar to Figure 2-11.

FIGURE 2-11

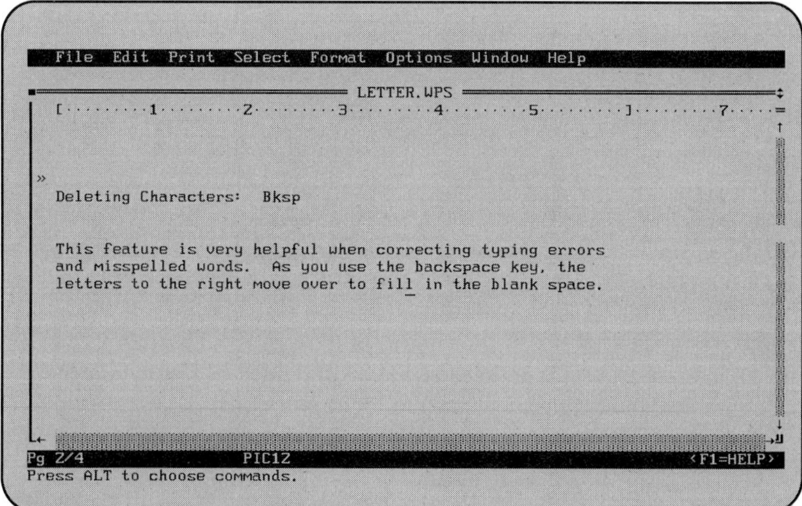

As you can see, each time you press (Bksp), the cursor "backs up" through the text, deleting the character to the left of the cursor. The text is reformatted as needed.

Deleting Characters

To move to the next exercise,

Press: (PGDN)

The second exercise, "Deleting Characters: Del" should be on your screen.

A second way to delete a character is with (DEL). On most keyboards, the (DEL) (delete) key is at the right side of the keyboard beneath the numeric keypad. This key will delete the character the cursor is positioned under.

The first error is in the second word in the first line of the exercise, "uyou."

Move to: first "u" in "uyou"

To delete the "u,"

Press: (DEL)

The "u" was removed, and the text to the right moved over to fill in the blank space. The paragraph was reformatted.

Complete the exercise by using (DEL) to correct the text on the screen. When you are done, your display screen should be similar to Figure 2-12.

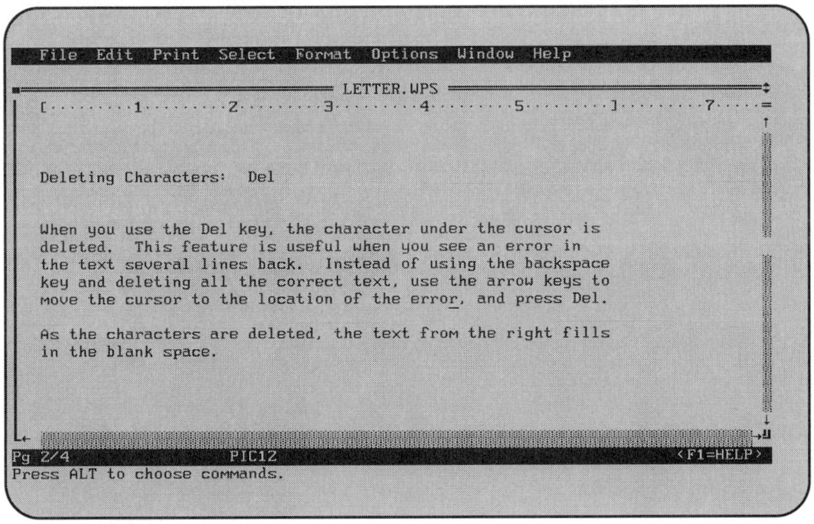

FIGURE 2-12

```
File  Edit  Print  Select  Format  Options  Window  Help
                              LETTER.WPS
 [·········1·········2·········3·········4·········5·········]·········7·····

 Deleting Characters:  Del

 When you use the Del key, the character under the cursor is
 deleted.  This feature is useful when you see an error in
 the text several lines back.  Instead of using the backspace
 key and deleting all the correct text, use the arrow keys to
 move the cursor to the location of the error, and press Del.

 As the characters are deleted, the text from the right fills
 in the blank space.

Pg 2/4          PIC12                                        <F1=HELP>
Press ALT to choose commands.
```

Inserting Characters

Press: (PGDN)

The third exercise, "Inserting Characters," should be on your screen.

Often you may want to add or insert characters or text in the middle of words you have already typed. When you insert text, the new characters are entered by moving the existing text to the right.

The first sentence on the screen should read: "You can insert or add text in the middle of words you have already typed." The missing words are "insert," "add text," "middle," and "text." These words can be entered without retyping the entire line of text.

To enter the word "insert" following the word "can" in the first sentence,

Move to:	the "o" in "or"
Type:	**insert**
Press:	Space bar

The word "insert" has been entered into the sentence by moving everything to the right to make space as each letter is typed.

Next, to enter the words "add text" following the word "or,"

Move to:	the "i" in "in"
Type:	**add text**
Press:	Space bar

The line is now almost completely full. Watch your screen carefully as you insert the next missing word, "middle."

Move to:	the "o" in "of"
Type:	**m**

Your display screen should be similar to Figure 2-13.

FIGURE 2-13

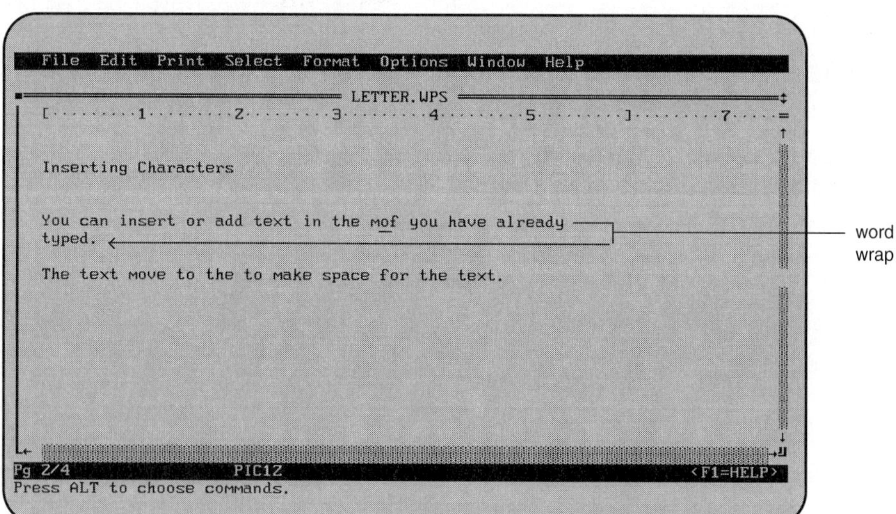

Notice that the word "typed" automatically moved to the next line to make space for the text you are entering. When there is not enough space at the end of the line, Works moves it to the next line for you. This is called **word wrap.** Word wrap automatically ends your lines for you. The program determines when to move text to the next line or back to a previous line (after a deletion). You do not need to press a carriage return as you would if you were using a typewriter to move to the next line.

Continue entering the word as follows:

Type: **iddle**
Press: Space bar

Finally, enter the word "text" following the word "of." Notice that the word "already" wrapped to the next line.

In a similar manner, correct the second sentence on the screen to read: "The **old** text moves to the **right** to make space for the **new** text."

Inserting and Deleting Blank Lines

Press: (PGDN)

The fourth exercise, "Inserting and Deleting Blank Lines," should be on your screen.

The (↵) key is used to insert a blank line into text or to mark the end of a paragraph. A special character called a **paragraph mark** is entered at the location in the text whenever you press (↵). You cannot see this mark because it is hidden. You will learn how to display these special symbols shortly.

If (↵) is pressed in the middle of a line of text, all text to the right of the cursor moves to the beginning of the next line. For example,

Move to: "m" of "middle" in the first line of this exercise
Press: (↵)

A paragraph mark is entered at the end of the first line, and the text from the cursor to the right moves down to the beginning of the next line.

If (↵) is pressed at the beginning of a line, a blank line is inserted into the document. To see how this works,

Move to: "I" of "If" on the fourth line of this exercise
Press: (↵)

A blank line is inserted into the text, forcing the line the cursor is on to move down one line.

If (↵) is pressed at the end of a paragraph or line of text, the cursor moves to the beginning of the next line.

Move to: end of last line in the exercise
Press: (↵)

The cursor moves to the beginning of the next line.

To delete a blank line, remove the paragraph mark by placing the cursor at the beginning of the blank line and press (DEL). To try this,

Move to: beginning of the blank line between second and third paragraphs
Press: (DEL)

Your display screen should be similar to Figure 2-14.

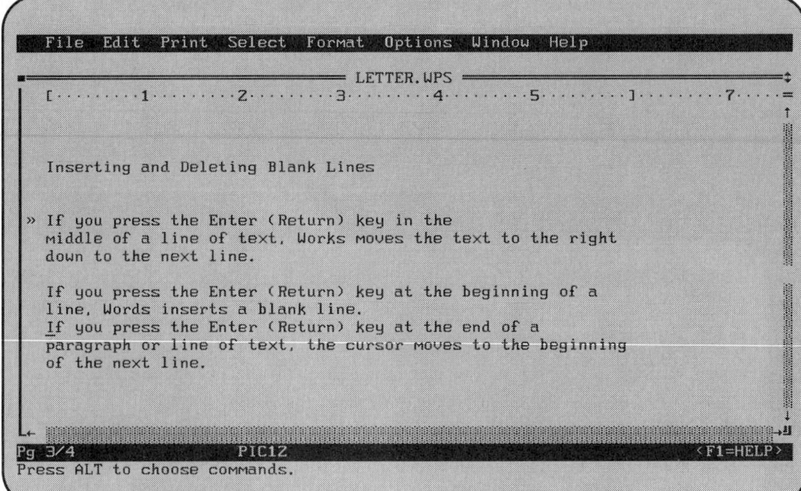

FIGURE 2-14

The blank line is deleted and the text below moves up one line.

Displaying Hidden Symbols

As mentioned, every time you press ⏎, Works inserts a paragraph mark into the file. There are other **hidden symbols** entered by the program also. For example, each time you press the Space bar, Works enters a dot as the space symbol. Works does not display these symbols because they clutter the screen. However, there are times when you need to delete a hidden symbol and have to find out where it is located. To display the symbols, the Show All Characters command in the Options menu is used.

Select: Options

The Options menu contains commands that let you set screen colors, number of lines, units of measure, and other screen and program settings. The menu is divided into four boxes or categories of commands. The command to display the hidden symbols is in the second category of commands. This category affects the action and display of the screen. For example, the Show Ruler command displays the ruler at the top of the workspace. The ruler is displayed by default. The diamond to the left of the command tells you it is active.

Select: Show All Characters

Your display screen should be similar to Figure 2-15.

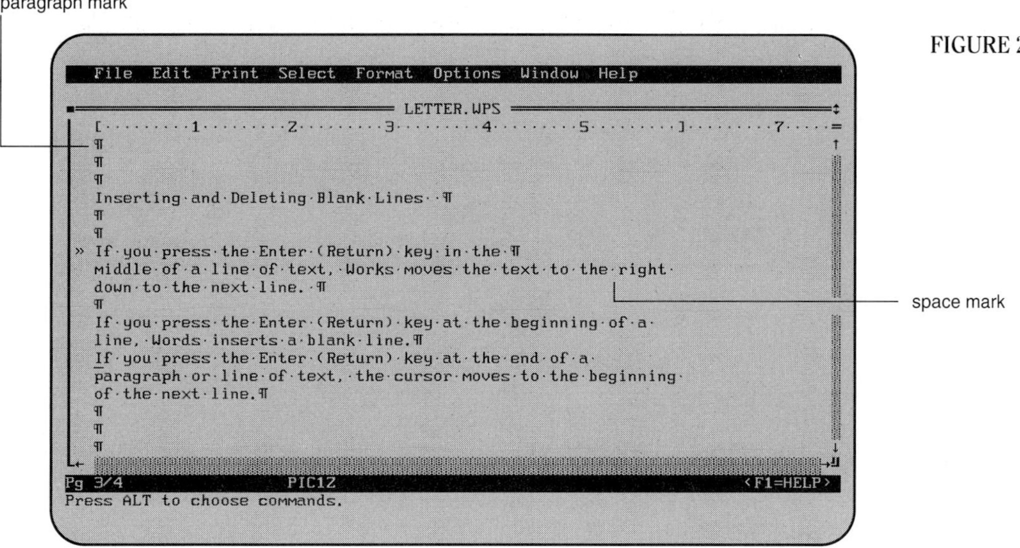

FIGURE 2-15

The ¶ symbol is displayed wherever (↵) was pressed. Between each word, a **space mark** (.) shows where the space bar was pressed. You can use Works with or without the symbols displayed. It does not affect how the program operates.

Move to: "I" of "If" in the last paragraph if you are not already there.

To reenter the blank line,

Press: (↵)

A paragraph mark is inserted, and the text moves down one line to make space for the blank line.

To delete a paragraph mark or any hidden symbol, you can position the cursor on the symbol and press (DEL), or you can position the cursor to the right of the symbol and press (Bksp).

Move to: "m" of "middle"

The paragraph mark you want to delete is at the end of the previous line or to the left of the cursor. To remove it,

Press: (Bksp)

To reenter the paragraph mark,

Press: (↵)

This time, to delete it using (DEL),

Press: (←)

The cursor should be positioned on the paragraph mark.

Press: (DEL)

You will find that displaying the hidden symbols is helpful in many editing situations. For normal entry of text, you will probably not want the symbols displayed. To hide them again, the command is selected again. To do this,

Select: Options

Notice the diamond symbol to the left of the "Show All" character command. This tells you that the command is active.

Select: Show All Characters

The screen returns to normal display. Now that you know how to turn this feature on and off, you can use it whenever you want when entering and editing text. You will be directed to use it periodically to display other symbols as the actions that enter them are performed.

Deleting Text

Press: (PGDN)

You can delete text by using (Bksp) or (DEL) repeatedly; however, this is very slow. Instead, Works has a feature called **selecting,** which lets you specify a block of text you want to change (in this case, delete). A block of text can be any group of characters, words, phrases, sentences, paragraphs, or the entire file. Once the text is selected, you can choose from many different commands to change it, such as moving, copying, or deleting it. When you select text, the cursor changes to a highlight bar. The highlight bar covers the text you have selected.

Text can be selected using several different methods. One way is to use (SHIFT) plus the directional arrow keys or key combinations. To demonstrate this method first to select text, move the cursor to the beginning of the text you want to select.

Move to: "S" of "Step 1"
Press: (SHIFT) - (→) (4 times)

Note: Hold down (SHIFT) while pressing (→) four times. If you forget to hold down (SHIFT), any selected text is cleared.

The highlight covers one character at a time. The word "Step" should be highlighted.

To highlight text a little faster, the key combination (SHIFT) - (CTRL) - (→) will extend the highlight word by word. To do this, hold down (SHIFT) and (CTRL) while pressing the (→).

Press: (SHIFT) - (CTRL) - (→) (7 times)

Your display screen should be similar to Figure 2-16.

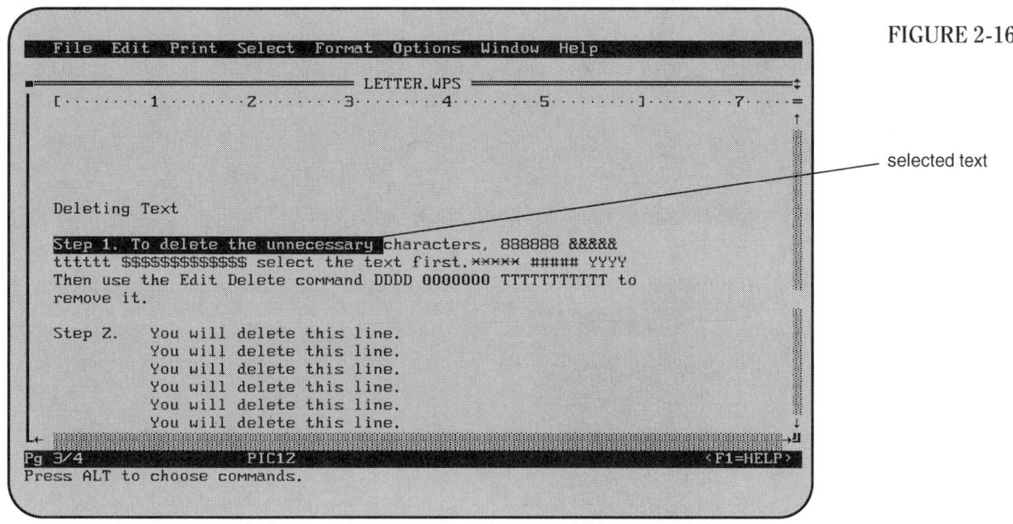

FIGURE 2-16

The first half of the sentence is highlighted. To highlight an entire line, use (SHIFT) - (END). To see how this works,

Press: (SHIFT) - (END)

The highlight extends to the end of the line of text.

To highlight the next three lines,

Press: (SHIFT) - (↓) (3 times)

You can use the other key combinations while holding down (SHIFT) to extend the highlight as follows:

To the beginning/end of file	(CTRL) - (HOME)/(CTRL) - (END)
To the next/previous window	(PGUP)/ (PGDN)
To the beginning/end of window	(CTRL) - (PGUP)/(CTRL) - (PGDN)

To shrink the selection character by character, word by word, and line by line,

Press: (SHIFT) - (←) (3 times)
Press: (SHIFT) - (CTRL) - (←) (5 times)
Press: (SHIFT) - (HOME)
Press: (SHIFT) - (↑) (2 times)

You should have removed all the highlighting from the screen.

Next, to select text and delete it,

Move to: the first "8" in the first line

Select the text to the last "$."

Once the text is selected, you can issue the command to be used on it. In this part of the exercise you want to delete the unnecessary text in the sentence. The Delete command in the Edit menu is used to remove selected text.

Select: Edit

Your display screen should be similar to Figure 2-17.

FIGURE 2-17

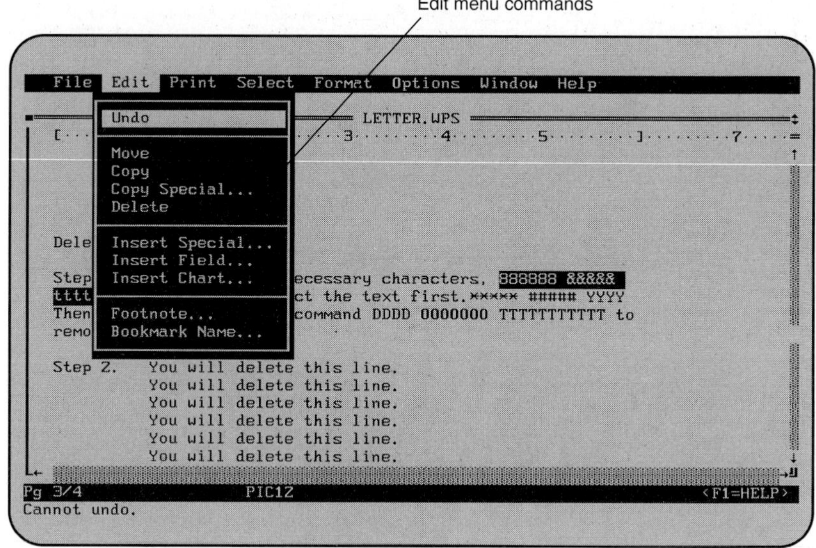

The Edit menu contains four boxes or categories of related commands. The second box contains commands that let you move, copy, or delete text.

Select: Delete

The highlighted text is removed, and the text is reformatted on the line.

In a similar manner, select and delete the unnecessary characters in the two sentences in step 1. In step 2, select and delete the six sentences.

When you are done, your screen should be similar to Figure 2-18.

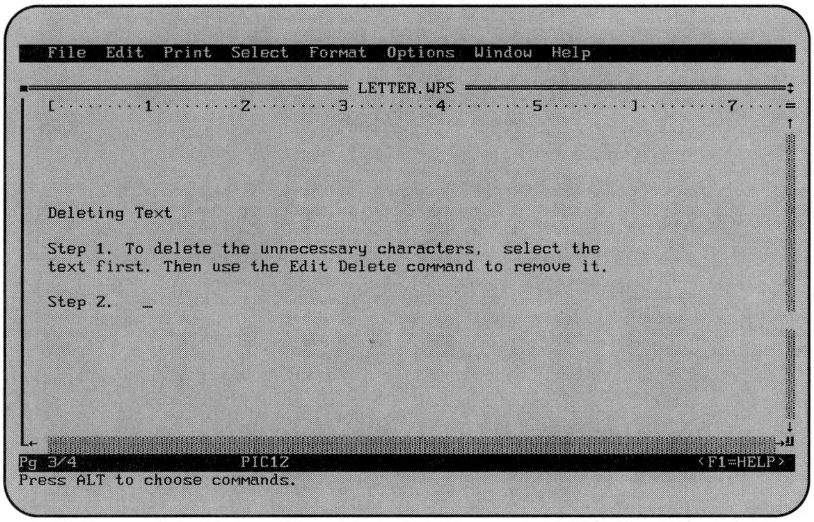

FIGURE 2-18

```
 File  Edit  Print  Select  Format  Options  Window  Help
                         LETTER.WPS
 [·········1·········2·········3·········4·········5·········]·········7·····=

 Deleting Text

 Step 1. To delete the unnecessary characters,  select the
 text first. Then use the Edit Delete command to remove it.

 Step 2.   _

Pg 3/4                PIC12                                      <F1=HELP>
Press ALT to choose commands.
```

This method of selecting text is useful for making small selections quickly. However, it is cumbersome because it often requires that you hold down several keys at the same time. The next exercise will demonstrate another way to select text.

Press: (PGDN)

Deleting Logical Blocks

Another method of selecting text is to use the Text command in the Select menu. The (F8) or Extend key is the shortcut for this command. To demonstrate this method,

Move to: "c" in the first "command."

The Text command in the Select menu (or (F8)) lets you specify the text you want to change.

Select: Select
Select: Text

or

Press: (F8)

The status line displays EXT (for "extend"). This is to remind you that you are in the process of extending the highlight to select text using the Select>Text command. Now you can use the directional keys or combinations (without holding down the (SHIFT) and (CTRL) keys) to select the text. This works just as if you were using the (SHIFT) - (CTRL) directional key method above and is useful for selecting parts of a word, sentence, or paragraph. However, if you want to select a logical block of text, such as an entire word, a full sentence, or an entire paragraph, you can press (F8) repeatedly to extend the selection in increments of a word, a sentence, a paragraph, and the entire file. To select a word,

Press: F8

The word the cursor is positioned on is highlighted. Notice also that one blank space after the word is included in the highlight. If the cursor is placed on a blank space immediately after a word, then using F8 highlights the word to the left of the cursor and the blank space the cursor is on.

To select a sentence,

Press: F8

To select a paragraph,

Press: F8

To select the entire file,

Press: F8

Your screen should be similar to Figure 2-19.

FIGURE 2-19

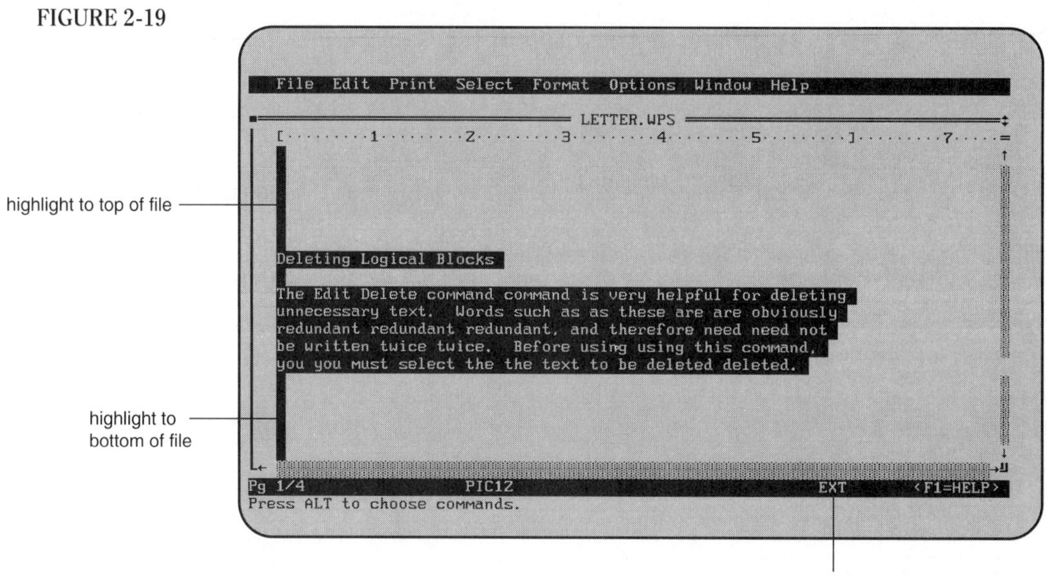

Although you cannot see the entire file, it is highlighted. The highlights along the left edge of the screen show you that the highlight extends up and down through the file.

Note: If at any point you decide you do not want to select text and want to cancel the command, press ESC. EXT will disappear from the status line. Then press any arrow key; the highlight will disappear and the cursor will reappear.

Since this is more text than you want selected, to shrink the selection made by pressing (F8) repeatedly, press (SHIFT) - (F8) as many times as needed. In this case, to shrink the highlight to cover the word "command" only,

Press: (SHIFT) - (F8) (3 times)

Now only the word "command" should be highlighted or selected.

Once the text is selected, you can issue the command to be used on it. In this exercise you want to delete the duplicate words in the sentence. The Edit>Delete command is used to remove selected text. Another shortcut is to use the (DEL) key instead of the Edit>Delete command to remove the word. This is much quicker. As you become familiar with the program, you will probably rely less on the menus to issue commands and more on the shortcut keys. This is because the shortcut keys accomplish the same procedure with fewer keystrokes.

Press: (DEL)

The highlighted word is removed, and the text is reformatted on the line.

Mouse Note: To select text using the mouse, point to the first character you want to select and then drag over the text you want to select. This is the same as using the directional keys. Try this by positioning the pointer on any character in the workspace and dragging the mouse in different directions. Then, to clear the selected text, click the left button. This has the same effect as pressing (ESC).

You can also select a logical block as follows:

One word	Position the pointer on the word and press the right button
One sentence	Position the pointer anywhere in the sentence and press both buttons at the same time
One line	Position the pointer in the left margin and press the left button
One paragraph	Position the pointer in the left margin and press the right button
An entire file	Position the pointer in the left margin and press both buttons

Try each of the above methods of selecting blocks of text using the mouse. When you are done, clear any selected text.

Delete the other duplicate words in the sentences. When you are done, your screen should be similar to Figure 2-20.

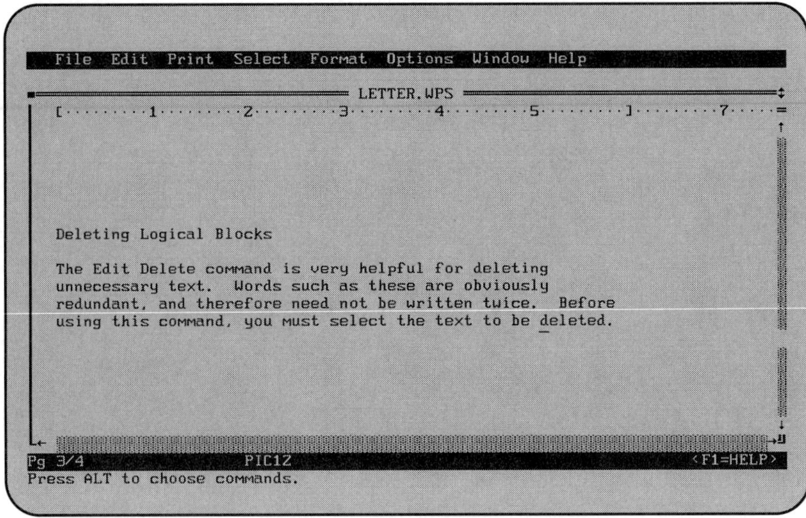

File Edit Print Select Format Options Window Help
LETTER.WPS
Deleting Logical Blocks
The Edit Delete command is very helpful for deleting
unnecessary text. Words such as these are obviously
redundant, and therefore need not be written twice. Before
using this command, you must select the text to be deleted.
Pg 3/4
PIC12
<F1=HELP>
Press ALT to choose commands.

FIGURE 2-20

Press: (PGDN)

Replacing Text

The usual method for replacing text is to select it, delete it, and then type in the new text. However, there is another method that lets you automatically delete selected text and replace it with the text you type. Many word processor programs call the feature **overtype.** The command to turn on this feature is Typing Replaces Selection in the Options menu.

Select: **O**ptions>**T**yping Replaces Selection

Note: For the remainder of the labs, command sequences will be shown following the word "Select:" with a > symbol separating the menu or commands. You can open the menu and select the commands using the keyboard or the mouse. If there is a shortcut key equivalent, it will be shown below the command, preceded with the »→ symbol.

Next, you need to select the text you want to replace when you type in the new text. To select the entire paragraph in this exercise,

Move to: anywhere within the paragraph
Press: (F8) (4 times)

The paragraph should be highlighted. Now, as soon as you begin typing, the selected block of text will be deleted and replaced with the text you are typing.

Type: With the Options>Typing Replaces Selection command on, new text you type, move, copy, or insert replaces any selected text.

Your screen should be similar to Figure 2-21.

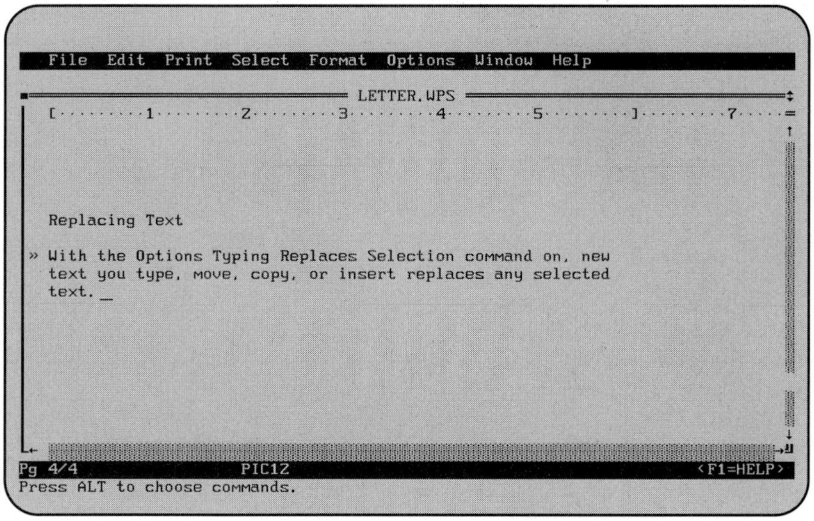

FIGURE 2-21

```
 File  Edit  Print  Select  Format  Options  Window  Help
                          LETTER.WPS
 [·········1·········2·········3·········4·········5·········]·········7·····

 Replacing Text

» With the Options Typing Replaces Selection command on, new
  text you type, move, copy, or insert replaces any selected
  text. _

Pg 4/4              PIC1Z                                    <F1=HELP>
Press ALT to choose commands.
```

Once this feature is on, whenever you select text and then begin typing, the selected text is deleted and the text you are typing replaces it. Be careful not to accidentally delete selected text. The next exercise will show you how to recover text you may have accidentally deleted.

To turn off this feature,

Select: Options

Notice the diamond mark beside the command name. This mark was entered when you turned this feature on by selecting the command. Whenever the diamond mark appears beside a command name on the menu, it tells you this feature is in effect.

Select: Typing Replaces Selection

The mark beside the command name is removed, and the feature is no longer active. Now, to replace text, you would need to delete the text you do not want and enter the new text by inserting it in the appropriate location.

Press: (PGDN)

Undoing Mistakes

It is easy to accidentally delete text that you did not intend to delete. Fortunately, the Undo command in the Edit menu lets you reverse your most recent editing action. You can undo many Works actions using this command; however, it must be used immediately after the action was performed.

To select the first sentence in this exercise and then delete it,

Move to: anywhere within the first sentence
Press: (F8) (3 times)
Press: (DEL)

To restore it,

Select: **E**dit>**U**ndo

The sentence is restored to its original location in the document.

Delete the second sentence in this exercise.

To restore the selected sentence, use the Edit Undo shortcut key (ALT) - (Bksp) as follows:

Press: (ALT) - (Bksp)

Another use of the Undo command is to delete any typing or deleting since the last command was carried out or since you last moved the cursor. To demonstrate this,

Move to: any blank line below this exercise
Type: The Undo feature can save you much time.

To undo this typing,

Select: **E**dit>**U**ndo
⋙ (ALT) - (Bksp)

The line of text is removed from the document.

Exiting a File

Now that you know how to move around a document and how to use several different types of editing keys, you will correct the welcome letter Karen created. A copy of this letter is in another file, named LETTER2. Before opening a new file, you will close the current file using the Close command in the File menu.

Select: **F**ile>**C**lose

Mouse Note: You can quickly close a file by clicking the close box (the black box in the left corner of the title bar). This has the same effect as selecting File>Close from the menu.

The prompt in the dialog box "Save changes to: LETTER.WPS?" is asking whether you want to save the changes you made to the active file, LETTER. When you create or edit a file, the changes you make are recorded in your computer's memory only. Not until you save the file with the changes you have made to it are your changes permanently stored on disk. In most cases, before you close a document that is on the screen, you will want to save the work you have done onto a diskette. In this way you would be able to open the file again and resume work on it if needed. If you close a file, exit a program, or turn off the computer before saving the file, your work will be lost.

The default response to the question in the dialog box is "Yes." To accept the default setting and save the document to the diskette, you can simply press (↵) and the changes you have made will be saved on the disk using the same filename. In this case, however, you do not want to save the edited version of the document. By responding No, the changes you made to the document file LETTER will not be saved. The original version of the file LETTER remains on the diskette unchanged. You can retrieve it again and repeat the exercises for practice. To indicate that you do not want to save the document as it appears on the screen,

Select: No

The opening screen and menu bar are displayed.

Select: **O**pen Existing File>LETTER2.WPS

The welcome letter is displayed on the screen. Using the commands presented in this lab, correct this letter. Use Figure 2-23 as a guide to how your letter should appear when you are done. Check that there is only one blank space between words (use the Display All Characters command).

Saving a File

This time, you will save the edited version of the file that is displayed on your screen. Another way to save a file is to use the File Save command.

Select: **F**ile>**S**ave

Works automatically saves the file using the same filename. The file remains open and displayed on the screen.

Printing a Document

Karen wants to print a hard copy of the welcome letter to give to the Membership Coordinator. If you have printer capability, you can print a copy of the document.

Note: Please consult your instructor for printing procedures that may differ from the directions below.

The Print command is in the Print menu.

Select: **P**rint>**P**rint

Your display screen should be similar to Figure 2-22.

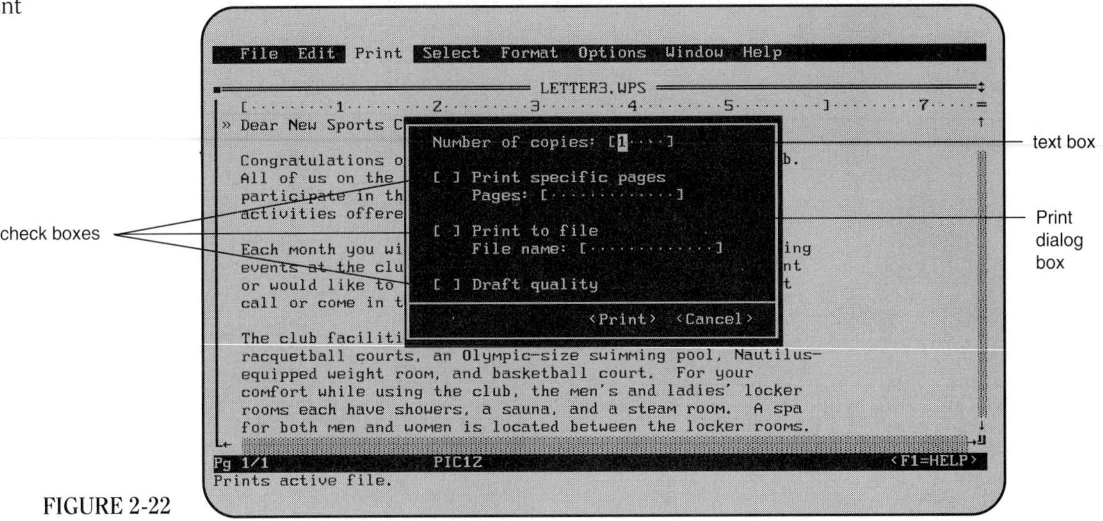

FIGURE 2-22

The print dialog box is displayed. The first three options in this box are common to all tools. The default setting of one copy is entered in the Number of copies text box. This setting is acceptable. The next three settings can be turned on or off only. They appear as **check boxes.** By default, Works prints the entire file. If you wanted to print a single page or specific pages, you would select the "Print specific pages" box and specify the pages in the text box below it. The second option lets you create a file that contains printing information. This lets you print the file from DOS or another application. The only setting you may want to select is Draft Quality (check with your instructor). This setting prints faster.

To select an item in a check box, move to the box using (TAB) or the arrow keys and press the Space bar. Alternatively, you can press (ALT) and the bold letter.

Note: In many of Works dialog boxes, you can simply type the bold letter to select an option. In many other cases, however, you need to hold down (ALT) while pressing the bold letter. The second method will work in all situations, whereas the first will not. Therefore, it is generally safer to use the (ALT)-bold letter combination to select options.

Select: Draft quality

An "X" appears in the box to let you know this option is on. To turn off a check box option, select the option again and the "X" will be removed. If your instructor does not want you to change to draft quality print, turn off this option.

Now you are ready to instruct Works to print the letter. If necessary, first turn the printer on and make sure it is on-line. Then adjust the paper so that the perforation is just above the printer scale. To complete the command by selecting the Print button,

Press: 

If you are using a floppy disk system, follow the directions on the screen to insert the Accessories disk in drive A and press ⏎.

Your printer should be printing out the document. The Print menu is cleared from the screen.

The printed copy of the welcome letter should be similar to Figure 2-23. It may not match exactly because Works will use the print and type size specified by your printer.

FIGURE 2-23

```
Dear New Sports Club Member:

Congratulations on your new membership in the Sports Club.
All of us on the staff welcome you and encourage you to
participate in the many tournaments, leagues, and club
activities offered throughout the year.

Each month you will receive a newsletter about the upcoming
events at the club.  If you have questions about the event
or would like to sign up to participate in an event, just
call or come in to the front desk personnel.

The club facilities include 18 lighted tennis courts, 5
racquetball courts, an Olympic-size swimming pool, Nautilus-
equipped weight room, and basketball court.  For your
comfort while using the club, the men's and ladies' locker
rooms each have showers, a sauna, and a steam room.  A spa
for both men and women is located between the locker rooms.
The lounge and cafe are open to serve you throughout the day
and evening.

On behalf of the staff of the Sports Club, I hope your
association with the Club is long and enjoyable.


Sincerely,



Sports Club Manager
```

Exiting Works

If you are using a floppy disk system, follow the instructions on the screen to insert the working copy of the program disk in drive A.

To exit Works,

Select: File>Exit

Since you just saved the changes you made to the document, Works exits back to DOS immediately. If you had not saved your changes, Works would display a dialog box asking you if you want to save the current document. This is a safeguard against accidentally exiting the program without saving the file.

Key Terms

menu bar
title bar
window
workspace
ruler line
default settings
page mark
cursor
Help reminder
status line
page
font
message line
scroll bar
scroll box
scroll arrow
scrolling
page mark
dialog box
text box
shortcut key
end mark
edit
delete
reformat
word wrap
paragraph mark
hidden symbols
space mark
selecting
overtype
check box

Matching

1.	(DEL)	5	**a.**	opens the menu
2.	(ESC)	2	**b.**	cancels a command
3.	(CTRL)-(PGDN)	9	**c.**	the Extend key
4.	status line	10	**d.**	moves cursor to next word
5.	(ALT)	7	**e.**	creates a paragraph mark
6.	check box	3	**f.**	moves cursor to bottom of screen
7.	(↵)	1	**g.**	deletes selected text
8.	(ALT)-(Bksp)	8	**h.**	reverses most recent editing action
9.	(F8)	6	**i.**	turns on or off an option in a dialog box
10.	(CTRL)-(→)	4	**j.**	displays your location in the file

Practice Exercises

1. Open the file EDIT. Follow the directions in the file to correct the sentences. When you have completed the exercise, print a copy of the file. Save the edited version of the file using the same filename.

2. Retrieve the file EDIT2. Follow the directions above the six paragraphs to correct the text in this file. Your corrected document should look like the text beginning on page 30 in the section "Advantages of Using a Word Processor" in the Overview to Word Processing. When you have completed the exercises, print a copy of the file. Save the edited file using the same filename.

3. Retrieve the file MEMO. This is a Works Version 2.0 document that is similar to the document you edited in Lab 1. It contains many errors. Edit the document using the commands you learned in this lab. Your edited document should look like:

```
Enter your name:   Student name
Enter the date:   current date

TO:  All Sports Club Employees

FROM:  Ernie Powell, Sports Club Manager

DATE:  December 1, 1992




The Sports Club will have the following holiday hours:

December 24, 1992 - 6:00 AM to 3:00 PM
December 25, 1992 - closed all day
December 31, 1992 - 6:00 AM to 3:00 PM
January   1, 1993 - closed all day
```

Print a copy of the edited document. Save the file using the same filename

4. Retrieve the file CASE. Correct the text in this file using the commands you learned in this lab. Your corrected document should look like the text on page 36 in the section "Case Study for Labs 2–4" in the Overview to Word Processing. Print the edited document. Save the corrected version of the file using the same filename.

Command Summary

Command Key	Shortcut	Action	Page
File>**O**pen Existing File		Makes selected file active	37
File>**S**ave		Saves active file to disk	65
File>**C**lose		Closes active file	64
File>**E**xit Works		Exits Works	67
Edit>**U**ndo	(ALT)-(Bksp)	Reverses most recent edit	64
Edit>**D**elete	(DEL)	Deletes selected text	51
Print>**P**rint		Prints active file	65
Select>T**e**xt	(F8)	Highlights text	59
Select>**G**o To	(F5)	Moves to location	43
Options>Show **A**ll Characters		Displays hidden symbols	54
Options>T**y**ping Replaces Selection		Replaces selected text	62

LAB

Creating and Formatting a Word Processing Document

3

OBJECTIVES

In this lab you will learn how to:

1. Create a new word processing document.
2. Save a new word processing document.
3. Move and copy text.
4. Open and use multiple files.
5. Align text flush with the right margin.
6. Set margins.
7. Use tabs.
8. Search and replace text.
9. Preview the document.

CASE STUDY

After editing the rough draft of the welcome letter, Karen showed it to the membership coordinator. The coordinator would like the letter to include information about monthly club fees and the new automatic fee payment program. We will follow Karen as she enters the new information into a file, combines it with the welcome letter, and adds some finishing touches to the letter.

Creating a File

Boot the system by turning on the computer and loading DOS. If necessary enter the current date when responding to the DOS date prompt. Load Works. If you are not sure of the procedure, refer to Lab 1, "Exploring Works 2.0."

Karen will enter the information about the monthly fees and automatic fee payment program into a new word processing document. To create a new file,

Select: Create **N**ew File>New **W**ord Processor

Your screen should be similar to Figure 3-1.

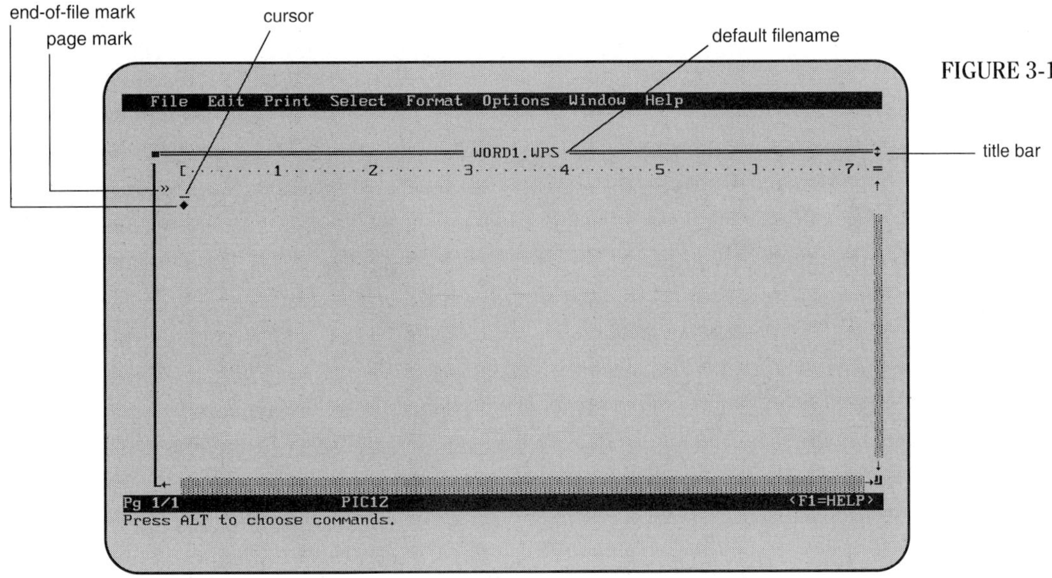

FIGURE 3-1

A word processing screen is displayed with an empty workspace. The cursor is on the first space of the first line of the workspace. The end-of-file mark is immediately below the cursor. A blank workspace is like a blank piece of paper you put into the typewriter. To create a new document, simply begin typing the text. When the cursor reaches the end of a line, remember, do not press ⏎. Works will automatically decide when to wrap text to the next line, based on the margin settings. The only time you need to press ⏎ is at the end of a paragraph, to insert blank lines, or to create a short line such as a title.

Notice the filename displayed in the title bar. This is the default filename Works assigns a new file. You will change this filename to a name that is more descriptive of the contents of the file when you save it.

As you type the text shown below, do not press ⏎ until you are directed to at the end of the paragraph. There should be two spaces following a period at the end of a sentence. If you make typing errors as you enter the text, use the editing features you learned in Lab 2 to correct your errors.

Type: **The Sports Club is offering a new program to all its members that will save you writing a check each month. Upon your authorization, the bank will send payment of your monthly charges directly to the club. You will receive a copy of your monthly statement to confirm the accuracy of your bill. If you are interested in the automatic fee payment program, please contact the accounting department to make the necessary arrangements.**

Press: 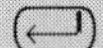

Your display screen should be similar to Figure 3-2.

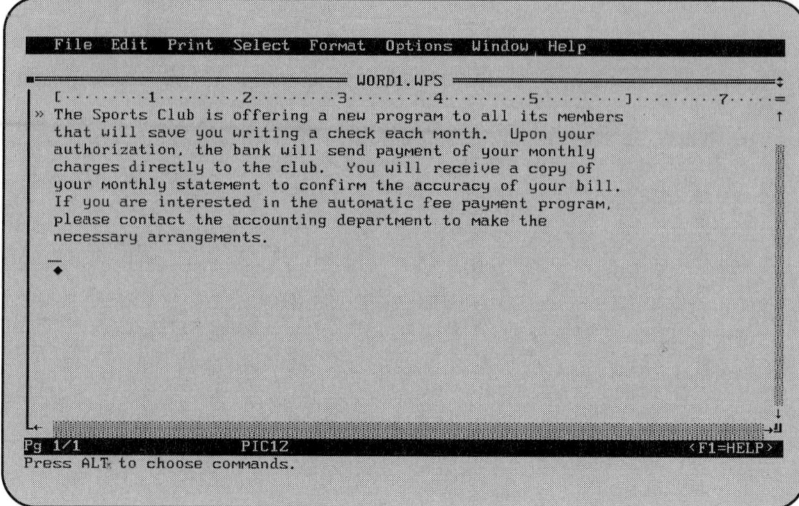

FIGURE 3-2

As you can see, the automatic word wrap feature makes entering text in a document much faster than typing. This is because a carriage return does not need to be pressed at the end of every line.

To insert a blank line,

Press: ↵

To enter the second paragraph,

Type: **The regular monthly membership fee is $45.00. Other expenses, such as league and lesson fees, pro-shop purchases, and charges at the Courtside Cafe can also be billed to your account. The charges will be itemized on your monthly statement and added to your regular monthly fee.**

To end the second paragraph,

Press: ↵

Your display screen should be similar to Figure 3-3.

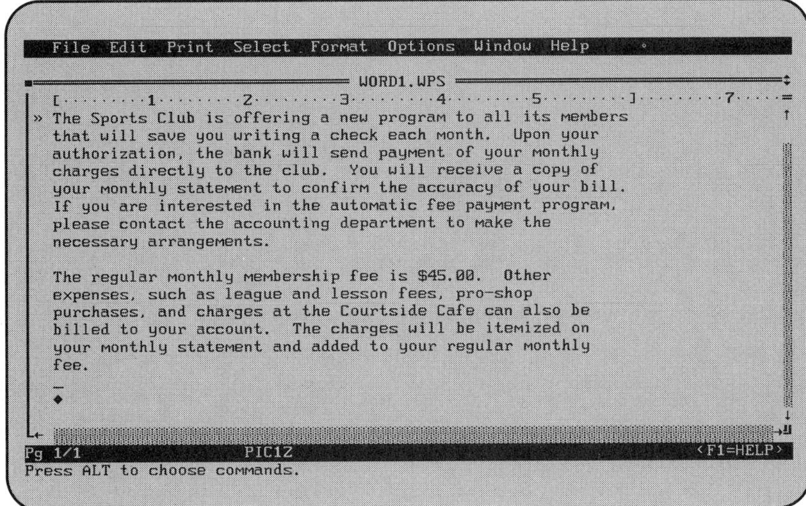

FIGURE 3-3

Check that you have entered the two paragraphs correctly. If you find any errors, correct them using the editing features you learned in Lab 2.

Saving a File

When you are entering text, it is stored in temporary memory (RAM) only. Not until you **save** the document to the diskette are you safe from losing your work due to power failure or other mishap. Saving your work frequently is a safety precaution that may save you a lot of time and aggravation.

The first time you save a new file, use the File>Save As command. This command lets you save a file using a new filename. The default filename, WORD1.WPS, is the filename Works automatically assigned the new file. You will replace this filename with a more descriptive filename.

Select: File>Save As

Your screen should be similar to Figure 3-4.

FIGURE 3-4

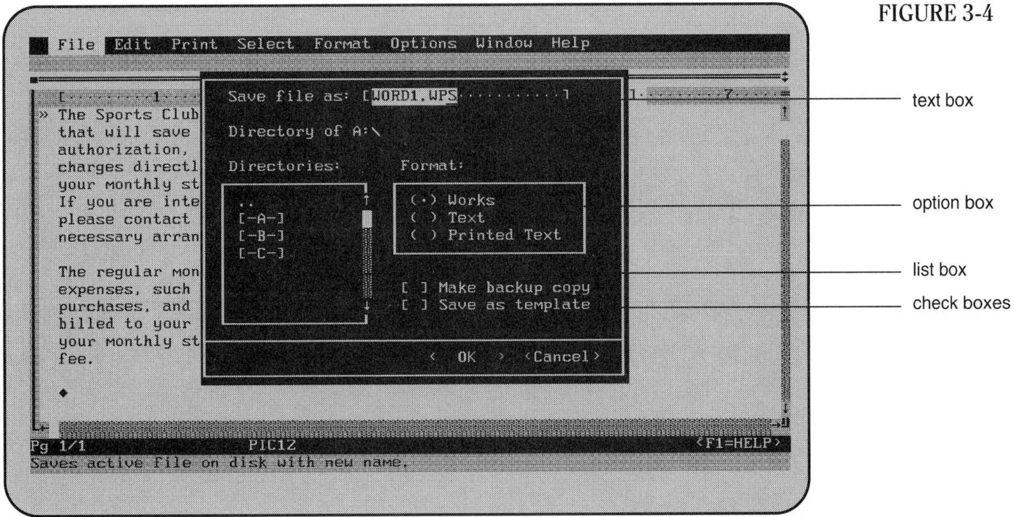

A dialog box is displayed. This is very similar to the dialog box that is displayed when you open an existing file. The cursor is positioned in the text box ready for you to enter the name of the file.

The **filename** consists of two parts. The first part of the filename is required and can be up to eight characters long. There can be no spaces within it. If you want to use two words in the name, separate them with a hyphen or an underscore. You will use the filename AUTO-PAY.

The second part of the filename is the **file extension**. It can be up to three characters long and is separated from the first part of the filename by a period. Works automatically assigns the extension .WPS to all files created using the word processor.

The filename can be entered in either upper- or lowercase letters. As soon as you begin typing, the existing filename will be erased.

First, you need to specify the drive where you want the file saved (most likely B: for a floppy disk system and A: for a hard disk system). Just as you specified the drive when opening a file, specify the appropriate drive for your system in the Directories list box.

Next, to enter the new filename, move to Save file as: text box.

You do not need to erase the default filename before entering the new filename. As soon as you type a character the default filename will disappear.

Type: **Auto-pay**

The default setting in the Format **option box** will save the file as a Works file. The mark beside the option (.) means that it is the selected option. An option box is similar to a check box, except that in an option box only one option can be selected at a time. You could also save the file in a format for use or printing by other products. You do not need to change this setting.

The last two check box options let you create a backup copy of the file each time it is saved or save it as a template file, which contains frequently used settings, text, and formats. You do not need to select either of these options. To complete the command,

Press: ↵

After a few moments, the document is saved on the diskette. The filename is displayed in the title line. You are returned to the exact location in the document you were at before saving the file. This allows you to continue working on the file.

Copying Text

Now Karen decides she needs to add the telephone number for the accounting department to the document. She will add it to the end of the first paragraph.

Move the cursor under the period at the end of the first paragraph.

Press: Space bar
Type: **(931-4285 ext. 33)**

After reading over the paragraphs, she is unsure about the location of the telephone number in the document. She thinks it might read better if the number followed the reference to the accounting department in the same sentence. To see how the number would look in a new location without deleting it from its current location, she can make a **copy** of the number. To do this, first you need to select the text and then use the Edit>Copy command.

Select the telephone number, including the opening and closing parentheses (press (F8) and then extend the highlight).

Karen wants to copy this block of text to another location in the document. The Edit>Copy command copies selected text to a new location. The shortcut key for this command is (SHIFT) - (F3).

Select: Edit>Copy
➽ (SHIFT) - (F3)

Reminder: The shortcut key equivalent will be displayed below the command. It will be preceded with the ➽ symbol.

The status line displays COPY to tell you this command is in effect. The message line tells you to select the new location and press (↵). The telephone number is still highlighted and in its original location. If you used the menu rather than the shortcut key to select this command, the menu is no longer displayed so that you can see the entire workspace.

Press: (↑)

As soon as you press a directional key, the cursor reappears so that you can move the cursor to specify the new location. You can now move it to the location where you want a copy of the selected text to be entered.

To specify the new location as immediately after the word "department" on the previous line,

Move to: blank space after "department"

You are now ready to copy the selected text. To do this, you can select Edit>Copy again, or press (SHIFT) - (F3), or press (↵).

Press: (↵)

Your display screen should be similar to Figure 3-5.

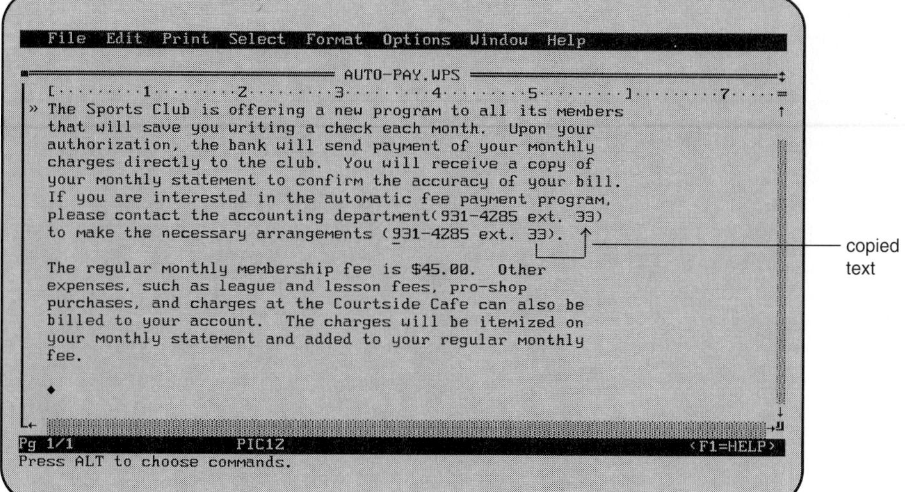

FIGURE 3-5

The telephone number is now in two locations in the document.

To insert a space before the opening parenthesis of the telephone number,

Press: Space bar

Karen decides she prefers the appearance of the telephone number in the new location. She wants to delete the original telephone number.

Select the original telephone number again and delete it. If necessary, delete the extra space before the period at the end of the paragraph.

The Copy command is very useful if you need to enter the same information repeatedly in a file. You can copy the same text again by simply moving to the new location and by pressing (SHIFT) - (F7).

Opening Multiple Files

Karen is satisfied with the revised document. Next, she will retrieve the file containing the welcome letter and add the new paragraphs to it.

A complete corrected copy of the welcome letter is saved for you in a file named LETTER3. Although you made changes to the AUTO-PAY file since last saving it, Works lets you continue working on a file without saving or closing it before opening another file. You can have up to eight files open at one time.

To open a second file,

Select: File>**O**pen Existing File>LETTER3.WPS>(↵)

Your screen should be similar to Figure 3-6.

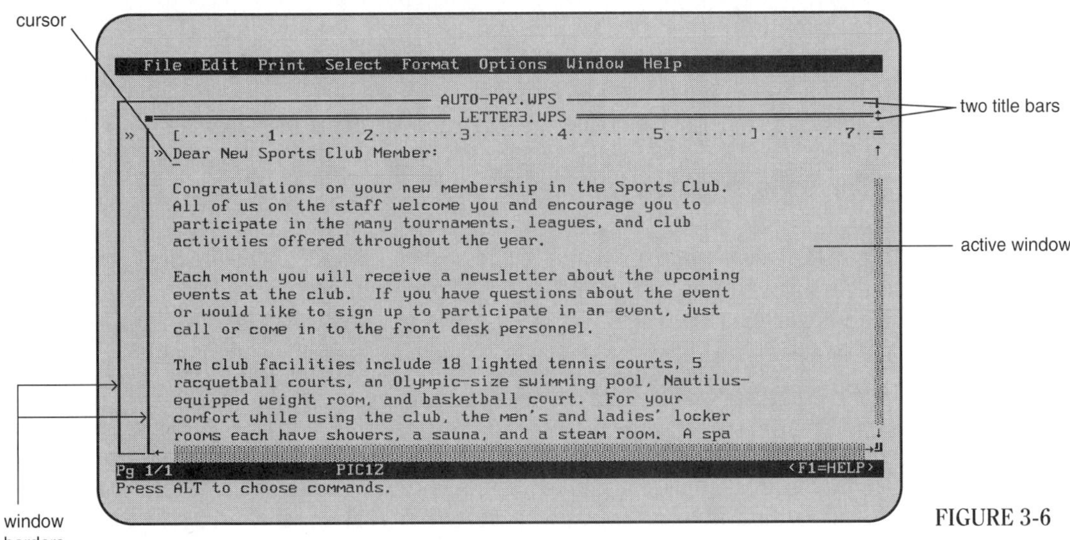

FIGURE 3-6

The welcome letter is displayed in the workspace. The AUTO-PAY file is obscured by the LETTER3 file, but it is still open. It is behind the LETTER3 file. Both files can now be used at the same time. Each file occupies a window.

The LETTER3 file is displayed in the **active window.** You can identify the active window by its different colors (if you have a color monitor), double top border lines in the title bar, and scroll bars. The active window, which always contains the cursor, is the window you can work in. The menu bar, status line, and message line always correspond to the active window. The AUTO-PAY file is in the window behind the LETTER3 window. The title bars and window borders for both windows are visible.

To switch the active window to the window containing the AUTO-PAY file,

Select: Window

Your screen should be similar to Figure 3-7.

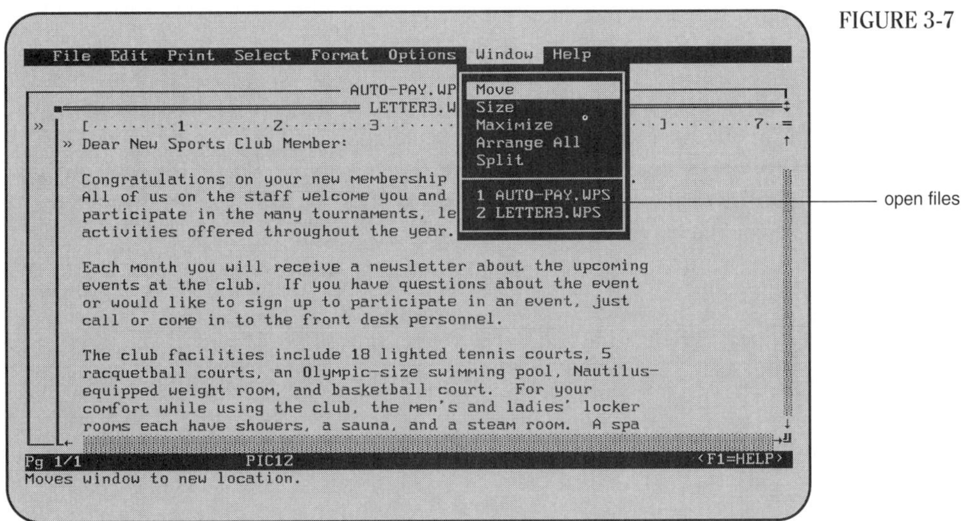

FIGURE 3-7

The top box of the Window menu contains commands that control the display of up to eight windows at a time on the screen. You will be learning how to use these features in the next lab.

The lower box displays the filenames of all open files. The two open files are numbered in the order they were opened. To make the AUTO-PAY file the active file, choose the numbered command that corresponds to the file you want to work on.

Select: **1** AUTO-PAY.WPS

The AUTO-PAY file is displayed in the active window. Since it is the first window, the title bar and window border for the second open window are not displayed. There are no other windows open behind this window. To switch back to the LETTER3 window,

Select: **W**indow>**2** LETTER3.WPS

Mouse Note: To switch to another window using the mouse, click on the window you want to work in. However, you cannot click the window you want to make active when it is the first open window because the other windows are not displayed. In that case you must use the menu.

Again, the double bar border is in the LETTER3 title bar and the AUTO-PAY window title bar is visible behind the active window.

As with many other commands, Works has a shortcut key to let you quickly move from one window to another. The shortcut key to switch to the previous window (lower number window) is (CTRL) - (F6).

Press: (CTRL) - (F6)

The AUTO-PAY window is active. The shortcut key to switch to the next window (higher number window) is (SHIFT) - (CTRL) - (F6).

Press: (SHIFT) - (CTRL) - (F6)

The LETTER3 window is again the active window.

Copying Text Between Files

Karen wants to copy the two paragraphs from the AUTO-PAY file into the LETTER3 file. You can copy text between open files just as you did when you copied the telephone number within the file. The only difference is that you switch from one open file to another during the process. The file you copy text from is the **source file** and the file you copy text to is the **destination file.**

Text from one open file can be copied easily into another open file by following these steps:

- Select the text to be copied from the source file.
- Select Edit>Copy or (SHIFT) - (F3).
- Switch to the destination file.
- Move the cursor to the location where you want the text entered.
- Select Edit>Copy ((SHIFT) - (F3)) or press (↵).

To copy the text from the source file (AUTO-PAY) to the destination file (LETTER3), begin by selecting the text to be copied from the source file. To make the source file the active window,

Press: (CTRL) - (F6)

To select the entire AUTO-PAY file, you could press (F8) five times. However, it is quicker to use the Select>All command.

Mouse Note: Remember, you can turn on Extend and highlight the text you want to select at the same time simply by dragging the mouse across the text.

Select: Select>**A**ll

The entire file is highlighted. Next, to activate the Copy command,

Select: **E**dit>**C**opy
(SHIFT) - (F3)

COPY appears in the status line to tell you this feature is on. Now you need to switch to the destination file to mark your location.

Press: (CTRL) - (F6)

Karen wants the copied text to be entered following the third paragraph of the letter. To move to this location,

Press: (PGDN)
Move to: Blank line above the last paragraph

To copy the text to this location,

Press: (↵)

Your display screen should be similar to Figure 3-8.

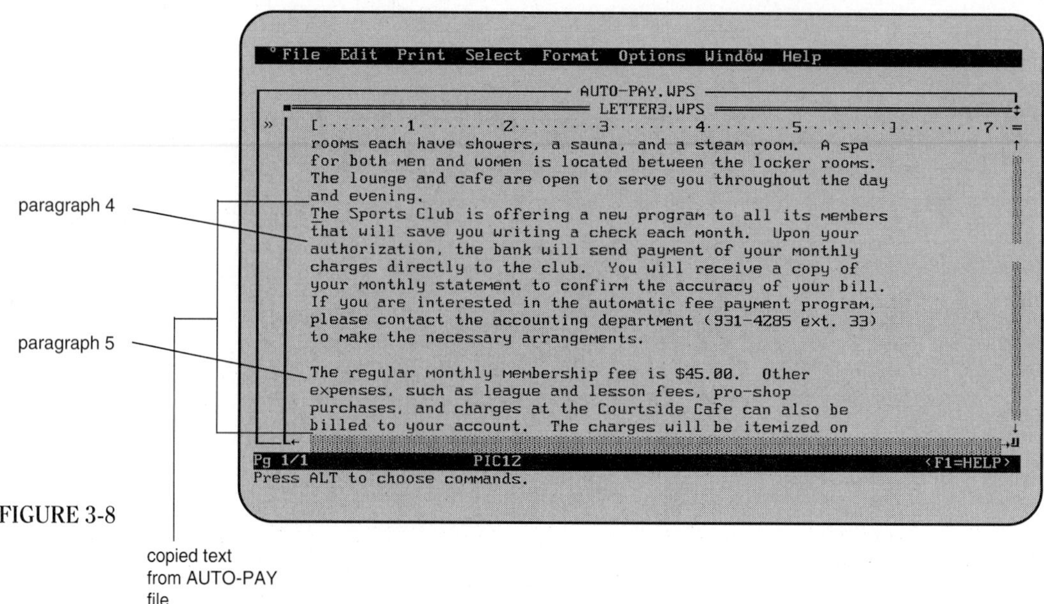

FIGURE 3-8

The two paragraphs from the AUTO-PAY file have been inserted into the welcome letter at the location of the cursor.

To separate paragraphs 3 and 4 with a blank line,

Press: 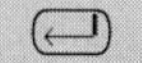

Moving Text

After looking over the welcome letter, Karen decides she would like to change the order of the paragraphs in the letter. She wants the paragraph about the monthly membership fees (paragraph 5) to precede the paragraph about the automatic fee payment program (paragraph 4).

She could use the Edit>Copy command to copy the paragraph to the new location and then delete the original paragraph. However, using the Edit>Move command is faster. It will make a copy of the original selected text, copy it to the specified location, and delete the original text automatically for you. The procedure is the same as copying text, except that you select Move instead of Copy from the Edit menu. The shortcut key for the move command is (F3).

Select the fifth paragraph (press (F8) four times). This is the paragraph beginning with "The regular monthly...".

Select: Edit>**M**ove

⋙ (F3)

"MOVE" appears in the status line and the message line tells you to select the new location and press (Enter). The selected paragraph is still highlighted. As soon as you move the cursor to the new location, the highlight will disappear to allow you to specify the new location.

Move to: blank line above the paragraph beginning "The Sports Club..." (paragraph 4)
Press: ⏎

Your display screen should be similar to Figure 3-9.

FIGURE 3-9

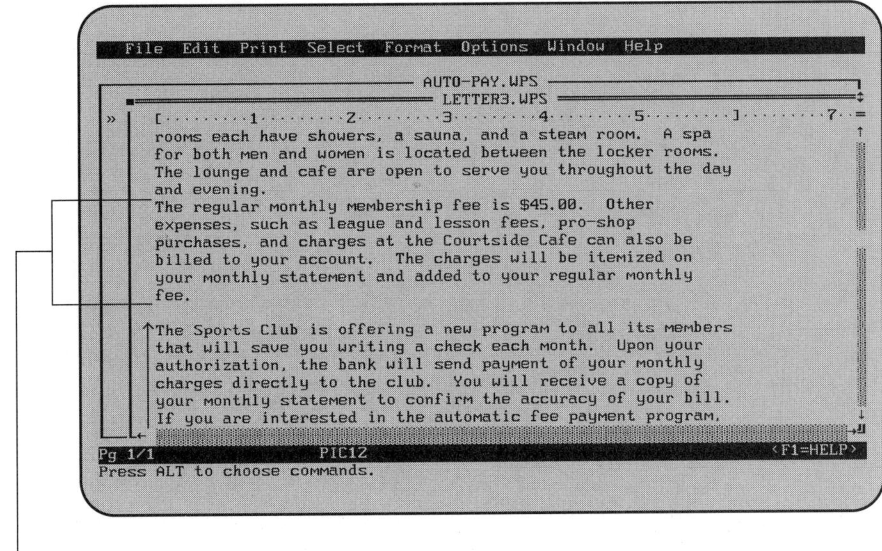

The selected paragraph moved from its original location to the new location marked by the cursor. That was a lot quicker than retyping the whole paragraph!

To correct the spacing between paragraphs, insert a blank line between the paragraphs at the cursor location (3 and 4) and delete the extra blank line between the last two paragraphs in the letter (5 and 6).

After looking over the letter for a while, Karen decides she wants to make the following changes:

- Increase the margin width.
- Indent the first line of each paragraph.
- Replace the word "club" with "Sports Club."

You will follow Karen as she makes these changes to the welcome letter.

Saving the Document with a New Filename

There have been many changes made to the LETTER3 file since you opened it. It is always a good idea to save your changes to disk periodically. Then, if there is a power failure or other mishap, you will not lose the time and effort you have put into your changes.

You will save the edited version of the welcome letter that is displayed on the screen in a new filenamed WELCOME. This will allow the original file, LETTER3, to remain unchanged on the diskette in case you would like to repeat the lab for practice.

To save the document and enter a new filename, use the File>Save As command as follows:

Select: File>Save **As**

To enter the new filename in the Save file as: text line,

Type: **welcome**

You do not need to select the directory again; the setting you specified when you first opened the file remains the selected directory until you change it or exit Works.

Press: (↵)

The revised letter has been saved on the disk as WELCOME. The original file, LETTER3, remains unchanged on your disk and is no longer an open file. The new filename is displayed in the title bar.

Setting Margins

The **margins** are the blank areas between the edges of the paper and the printed text. The size of the printed area can be controlled by increasing or decreasing the margin setting. The larger the margins, the smaller the printed area.

Works automatically uses a standard page size of 8 1/2 inches by 11 inches and sets standard margins. The top and bottom margins are preset at 1 inch. The right margin is preset at 1.2 inches, and the left margin width is 1.3 inches. Karen would like to increase the right and left margins to 1.5 inches.

The margins determine the line length and consequently the number of characters that can be entered on a line. The default line length is 6 inches (60 characters at 10 characters per inch). On the ruler line, the 0 marks the left margin and the 6 the right margin. The square brackets ([ ]) are currently positioned on the left and right margin settings. The brackets represent left and right indents. Indents are used to change the distance between text and margins for selected paragraphs. By default, indents are set at the left and right margins.

To change the left and right margin settings of a document, use the Page Setups & Margins command on the Print menu.

Select: Print>Page Setup & **M**argins

Your display screen should be similar to Figure 3-10.

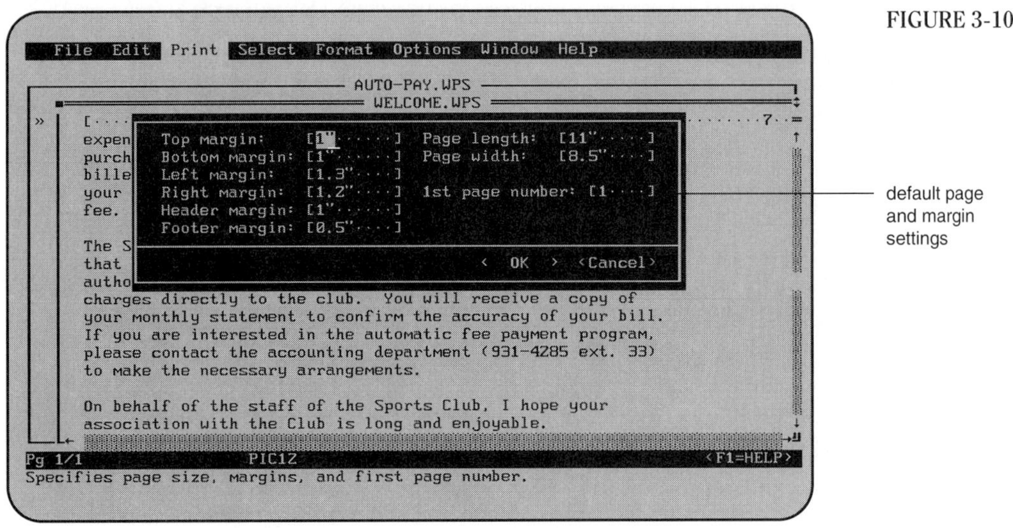

FIGURE 3-10

The current margin settings and page size are displayed in the dialog box. To change the left margin,

Select: Left Margin

In the text box,

Type: **1.5**

It is not necessary to enter the inches symbol.

To change the right margin,

Select: **R**ight margin
Type: **1.5**

To complete the command,

Press: ⏎

To move to the top of the document,

Press: (CTRL) - (HOME)

Your display screen should be similar to Figure 3-11.

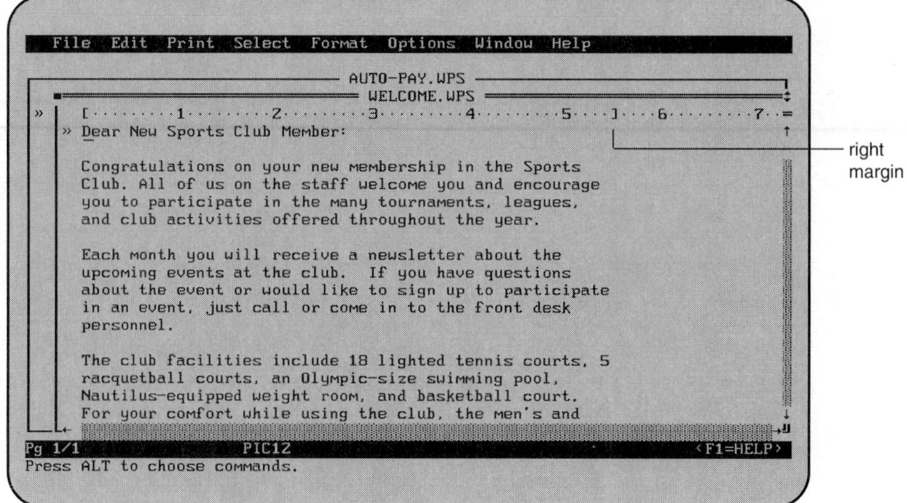

FIGURE 3-11

The letter has been reformatted to fit within the new margin settings. The left margin still begins at the 0 marker on the ruler line. The right margin setting is now at position 55. This tells you there are 55 characters per line (at 10 characters per inch). The indent markers will always correspond to your margin settings unless you change the indent setting for selected lines or paragraphs.

Using Tabs

Next, Karen wants to enter the current date on the first line of the letter. To enter a blank line as the first line of the file,

Press: (↵)
Press: (↑)

She does not want the date to begin at the left margin. The (TAB) key lets you easily indent text on a line. Each time you press (TAB), the cursor moves over a preset number of spaces along the line. Each position the tab moves the cursor to is called a **tab stop.** Works has set the default tab stops at every .5 inch. As with other default settings, the tab stops can also be changed. You will learn how to do this in the next lab. The default tab stops are not displayed on the ruler line. The tab settings apply to the entire document, unlike indent settings, which apply only to the selected lines or paragraphs.

Whenever you want to enter text on a blank line, if you do not want to begin at the left margin, you need to press the Space bar or (TAB) to move to the right along the line. Then you can enter text. To move the cursor to position 35 to enter the date,

Press: (TAB) (7 times)

Your display screen should be similar to Figure 3-12.

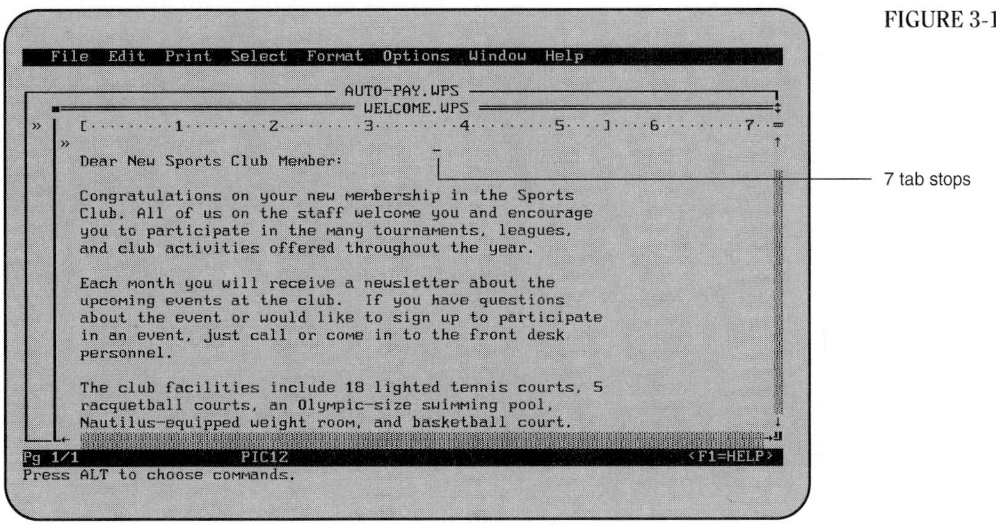

FIGURE 3-12

Using (TAB) to move along a line is much faster than pressing the Space bar. Now you can enter the current date. You will enter the date as the month, day, and year (e.g., May 10, 1992).

Type: Today's date

To separate the date from the salutation by four blank lines,

Press: (↵) (4 times)

Next, Karen wants to indent the first line of each paragraph and the closing. To indent text that is already typed, position the cursor under the first letter of the text you want to move and then press (TAB) until the text is in the correct position.

Move to: "C" in "Congratulations" of the first line of the first paragraph
Press: (TAB)

The first line of the paragraph is indented five spaces and the paragraph is reformatted. Each time you press (TAB), a hidden symbol is entered in the document. To view the hidden symbols,

Select: **O**ptions>Show All Characters

Your display screen should be similar to Figure 3-13.

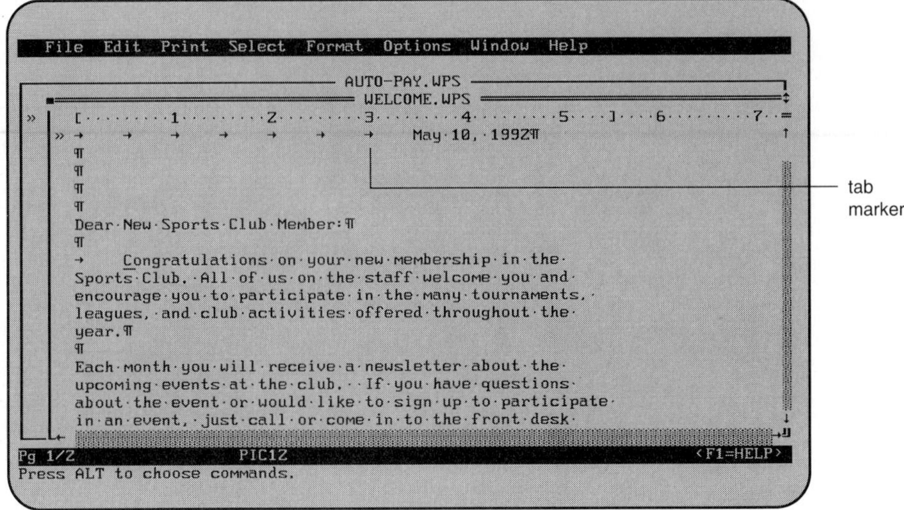

FIGURE 3-13

Each place you pressed (TAB) is marked with a tab mark (→) symbol.

In a similar manner, indent the first line of the next five paragraphs. Notice as you enter a tab that each paragraph is automatically reformatted.

To indent the closing lines,

Move to: "S" in "Sincerely"
Press: (TAB) (7 times)
Move to: "S" of "Sports"
Press: (TAB) (7 times)

Notice that the cursor is on the first line of page 2 (the status line displays Pg 2/), and a page break marker (>>) is displayed. The last line of the letter is on the first line of page 2. Since this is not acceptable, Karen decides to reset the right and left margins back to the default settings. This would allow more text to be printed on each line and would make the letter shorter.

To return the margin settings back to the default settings,

Select: Print>Page Setup & **M**argins>Le**f**t margin>**1.3**>**R**ight margin>**1.2**>(↵)

The letter is reformatted to the new margin settings. The right margin mark on the ruler line is back at position 60. As you can see, because the margin widths were decreased, more text can be displayed on a line. The status line tells you the cursor is on Pg 1/1, and a page break mark is no longer displayed because the file is only one page long.

Press: (CTRL)-(HOME)

To turn off the all characters display,

Select: Options>Show All Characters

Searching and Replacing Text

Karen wants to find all occurrences of the word "club" in the letter and change it to "Sports Club." The Select menu contains two commands that will search a file to the locate the first occurrence of any combination of letters, characters, or numbers you specify.

Select: Select

The **Search** command will move the cursor forward from its current location in the file to the location of the first occurrence of the character sequence you are searching for. The **Replace** command will also locate the matching character sequence. In addition it will replace it with another character sequence you have specified. Since you want to locate and replace a character sequence,

Select: Replace

Your screen should be similar to Figure 3-14.

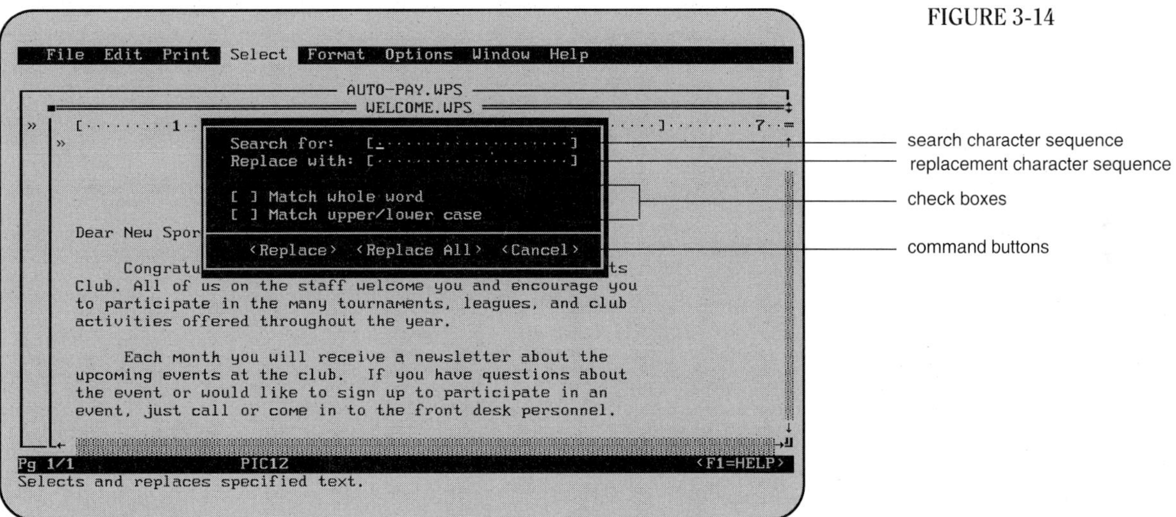

FIGURE 3-14

The Replace dialog box is displayed. In the Search for: text box, enter the word or phrase you want to locate.

Type: **club**

To move to the Replace with: text box and enter the replacement character sequence,

Press: (TAB)
Type: **Sports Club**

The replacement sequence must be entered exactly as you want it to appear in your document.

If you want Works to search for a word as an entire word and not as a part of a longer word, you need to select the Match whole word check box. If you do not select this box, Works will search for the character sequence anywhere within a word. For example, it would locate "clubhouse" because the character sequence "club" is part of the word.

Reminder: To select a check box, hold down the (ALT) key and press the bold letter.

Select: Match whole word

The next check box, Match upper/lower case, tells Works to match the capitalization of the replaced text. You do not want Works to use the same capitalization as in the text. Therefore, you do not need to select this option.

The two command buttons, Replace and Replace All, let you specify how you want the Replace command carried out. If you select Replace, Works locates the first match and asks you if you want to replace it. You then have the option of accepting or rejecting each replacement. If you select Replace All, Works automatically replaces all instances. It is much safer to select Replace. Sometimes Works will locate character sequences you did not anticipate and will automatically replace it with the replacement text string. If this happens, use the Undo>Replace All command immediately.

To select Replace,

Press: (↵)

Your screen should be similar to Figure 3-15.

FIGURE 3-15

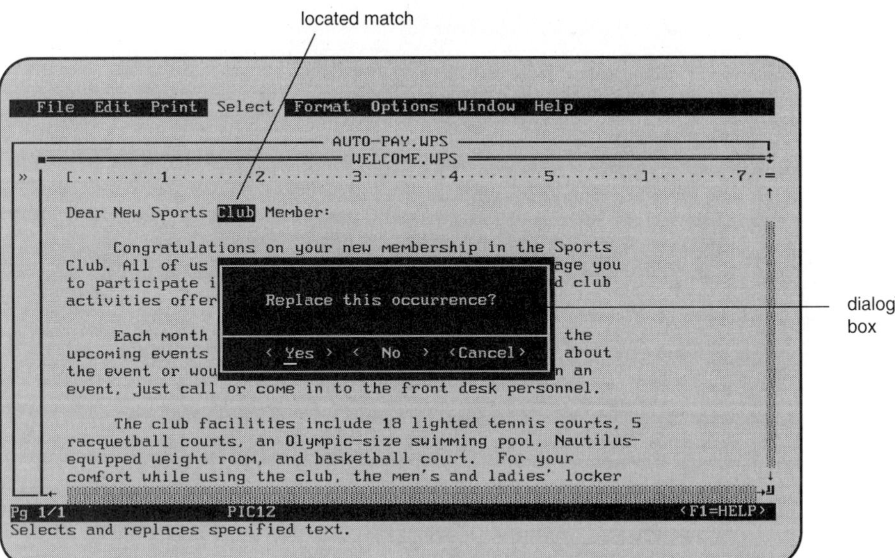

Immediately, the cursor moves to the first word matching the search sequence "club" and highlights the match. Notice that the cursor is positioned on "Club." Works will locate all matching text, regardless of capitalization; it does not distinguish between upper- and lowercase letters when searching the text for matching sequences.

The prompt "Replace this occurrence?" is displayed in the dialog box. The first occurrence is acceptable as it is (you do not want to replace it because it already has the word "Sports" in front of it).

Select: No

The cursor skips to the next occurrence of the word "club" and waits for your response. Again, it is already correct.

Select: No

The cursor moves to the third occurrence of the word "club." This time you want to replace it with "Sports Club."

Select: Yes

The word "club" is replaced with the word "Sports Club." The cursor moves to the next match.

Respond to the remaining prompts to replace "club" with "Sports Club" whenever the word "Sports" does not appear before the word "club." When no more matches are located, the message "No more matches" is displayed. To end the search,

Press: ↵

It was difficult to see how the text was replaced because it scrolled off the screen so quickly. To move to the top of the file,

Press: CTRL - HOME

Scroll through the file to look at how the word "club" was replaced with "Sports Club." When you are done, return to the top of the file.

Previewing the Document

To see how the printed letter will look before printing the file, you can use the Preview command in the Print menu.

Select: Print>Preview

The Print dialog box is displayed. This allows you to specify print settings to be followed after previewing the file. Select the Draft quality option if instructed to by your teacher.

Note: If you are using a floppy disk system, follow the directions displayed on your screen to insert the Accessories disk and the Working Copy disk at the appropriate times.

To complete the command by selecting "Preview," the default button,

Press: 

The Preview command displays a page of the document at a time as it will appear when printed. The instruction box to the left tells you how to move to the next page. Since this is the only page of the document, you will not need to press (PGDN).

To print the letter (make sure your printer is set up correctly),

Press: Print

Your printed letter should be similar to Figure 3-16.

FIGURE 3-16

May 10, 1992

Dear New Sports Club Member:

Congratulations on your new membership in the Sports Club. All of us on the staff welcome you and encourage you to participate in the many tournaments, leagues, and Sports Club activities offered throughout the year.

Each month you will receive a newsletter about the upcoming events at the Sports Club. If you have questions about the event or would like to sign up to participate in an event, just call or come in to the front desk personnel.

The Sports Club facilities include 18 lighted tennis courts, 5 racquetball courts, an Olympic-size swimming pool, Nautilus-equipped weight room, and basketball court. For your comfort while using the Sports Club, the men's and ladies' locker rooms each have showers, a sauna, and a steam room. A spa for both men and women is located between the locker rooms. The lounge and cafe are open to serve you throughout the day and evening.

The regular monthly membership fee is $45.00. Other expenses, such as league and lesson fees, pro-shop purchases, and charges at the Courtside Cafe can also be billed to your account. The charges will be itemized on your monthly statement and added to your regular monthly fee.

The Sports Club is offering a new program to all its members that will save you writing a check each month. Upon your authorization, the bank will send payment of your monthly charges directly to the Sports Club. You will receive a copy of your monthly statement to confirm the accuracy of your bill. If you are interested in the automatic fee payment program, please contact the accounting department (931-4285 ext. 33) to make the necessary arrangements.

On behalf of the staff of the Sports Club, I hope your association with the Sports Club is long and enjoyable.

Sincerely,

Sports Club Manager

Closing Two Files

To close the current file,

Select: File>**C**lose

Mouse Note: Remember, you can click on the close box.

Works asks you if you want to save your changes. To confirm that you do,

Select: **Y**es

The AUTO-PAY file is displayed. To close this file,

Select: File>**C**lose>**Y**es

Exit Works.

Key Terms

save	copy	margins
filename	active window	tab stop
file extension	source file	search
option box	destination file	replace

Matching

1. word wrap	2	**a.**	repeats a copy
2. File close	7	**b.**	automatic adjustment of words on a line
3. →	4	**c.**	shortcut key for Copy command
4. CTRL - F6	5	**d.**	a word processing file extension
5. .WPS	8	**e.**	moves the cursor a set number of spaces
6. F3	10	**f.**	switches to next window
7. margin	6	**g.**	hidden symbol for TAB
8. TAB	3	**h.**	shortcut key for Move command
9. SHIFT - F3	1	**i.**	border of white space around the printed document
10. SHIFT - CTRL - F6	4	**j.**	switches to previous window

Practice Exercises

1. This problem will give you practice in creating, combining, and rearranging text.

- Enter the first paragraph from the Overview to Word Processing (page 30) into a Works document.
- Save the file as OVER-WP.
- Open the file DEF-WP. Copy the text in the file DEF-WP into the file OVER-WP. The copied text should be entered at the end of the text in OVER-WP. Leave a blank line above the heading "Definition of Word Processing."
- Rearrange the paragraphs in the text so they are in numerical order. Correct the spacing between sentences if necessary.
- Rearrange the order of sentence 4. It should read "The grouping of text to form words, sentences, paragraphs, and pages of text results in the creation of a document."
- Enter your name and the current date on the first line of the document. Separate your name from the text with two blank lines.
- Print the document.
- Save this new document as DEF-REV.

2. You are the public relations assistant at the local zoo, and you are working on a news release about the various fund-raising activities at the zoo.

- Enter the three paragraphs below. Save the file as EVENTS. Print the file.

  The zoo Wine Tasting Event is sponsored by the zoo Wine Tasting Society. The second annual event was a 1978 Cabernet Sauvignon tasting party. It raised $3,600 to top off the Roadrunner Exhibit campaign.

  The Aid-To-Zoo National Horse Show is the major fund-raising activity of the Friends of the zoo Auxiliary. This event has raised funds for numerous exhibits throughout the zoo, including the Nocturnal Exhibit, Elephant Exhibit, Galapagos Exhibit, and the Graphic Signage and Deer Exhibit in the Children's zoo. Proceeds from the 1992 Horse Show exceeded $100,000 and were directed toward the Educational Graphics Exhibit.

  The Black-Tie Ball, an annual event held under the stars at the zoo, is sponsored by the men's Wildest Club in Town. Proceeds from the 1992 Black-Tie Ball amounted to $24,000 and are earmarked for architectural drawings for a proposed Bear Exhibit. Past proceeds have gone toward such projects as the Animal Nursery in the Children's zoo.
- Open the file ZOOFARI (on your data diskette).
- Copy the text in the file ZOOFARI into EVENTS. The text should be entered below the second paragraph, and there should be a blank line between paragraphs.

- Change the order of the paragraphs so that the first paragraph is about the Horse Show event, the second paragraph is about the Black-Tie Ball event, the third paragraph is about the Wine Tasting event, and the last paragraph is about the Zoo-Fari. Again, there should be a blank line between paragraphs.
- Find and replace all occurrences of the word "zoo" with "Zoo."
- Enter your name on the first line and the current date on the second line. Leave one blank line below the date.
- Print the completed document. Save the file as EVENTS.
- Exit Works.

3. You are the managing director of the local zoo. Every quarter you need to update the zoo Advisory Board about the current status of the zoo.

- Enter the memo below using 1-inch margin settings.

TO: Advisory Board

FROM: [Your Name], Managing Director

DATE: [Enter current date]

One year after creating a Marketing Department, we are seeing excellent results. We are not budgeting for advertising, and our public relations, promotions, and publications are rapidly improving. With this boost in our profile, we believe that a 912,500 attendance figure is within reach and we hope to cross the 1,000,000 mark soon.

The animal inventory has increased this quarter, making our collection to this date 292 specimens from 1,280 species. Our collection is well cared for and its health is excellent. Our breeding success is above normal and our animals enjoy an excellent quality of life, a reflection of our feeding and veterinary programs.

The other major project this quarter has been the updating of the Zoo Master Plan. The architectural firm and the Society Board have produced a well thought out plan to guide us through the next decade. We hope to begin the renovation of the Arizona exhibit using these guidelines in the next quarter.

The major construction project for this quarter continues to be the new Children's Zoo. We expect completion of the project in the next quarter. It has been the largest construction project since our opening twenty-five years ago. Every department at the Zoo has helped in its

```
planning and construction. We are looking forward
to its opening scheduled for next quarter.
    This quarter has been very productive and
exciting as we near the completion of the
Children's Zoo project.
```

- Rearrange the paragraphs so that the paragraph about the construction of the Children's Zoo is paragraph 2, the Zoo Master Plan is paragraph 3, and the animal inventory is paragraph 4.
- Delete the second sentence in the second paragraph.
- The animal inventory figures in the fourth paragraph are switched. They should be "1,280 specimens from 292 species." Use the Edit>Move command to correct this.
- Print the memo. Save the file as STATUS.

4. In this problem you will create and format a document.

- Set margins to left= 2" and right= 1.5".

Enter the letter below:

```
Current Date


Ms. Peg Mitchell
Admissions Department
Arizona State University
Tempe, AZ  85257

Dear Ms. Mitchell:

Thank you for taking the time to speak with me
yesterday about the possibility of employment in
your department.

I feel my professional background in personnel
services and my educational background in higher
education would meet many of your requirements.

I am enclosing a complete resume and hope that if
a position becomes available in the near future,
you will consider my credentials.

Sincerely,


(enter your name)
```

- Indent the date six tab stops.
- Indent each paragraph in the letter one tab stop.
- Indent the closing six tab stops.
- Change the margins to left= 1", right=1.5".
- Preview the letter.
- Print the letter.
- Save the letter using the filename JOB.

Command Summary

Command	Shortcut	Action	Page
File>Save **A**s		Saves file with new name	73
Edit>**C**opy	(SHIFT) - (F3)	Copies selected text	75
Edit>**M**ove	(F3)	Moves selected text	80
Print>Page Setup & **M**argins		Sets page and margins	82
Print>Pre**v**iew		Displays text as it will appear when printed	89
Select>**A**ll	(F8) (5 times)	Selects entire file	79
Select>**R**eplace		Finds and replaces text	87
Window>**#**	(CTRL) - (F6)	Switches to previous window	77
Window>**#**	(SHIFT) - (CTRL) - (F6)	Switches to next window	78

LAB

Refining Documents

4

OBJECTIVES

In this lab you will learn how to:

1. Center, bold, and underline text.
2. Create tabular columns.
3. Justify text.
4. Set line spacing.
5. Create headers and footers.
6. Arrange, move, and size windows.
7. Spell check the document.

CASE STUDY

Karen needs to create an announcement for the Club bulletin board about new member orientation meetings. She needs to make the announcement attractive and plans to use many of the Works format settings to create an interesting design and to emphasize important information in the announcement. As a second project, she will use Works' Window feature to help create an article for the monthly newsletter. You will follow Karen as she works on these two projects.

Centering Text

Karen needs to add several finishing touches to the announcement to be posted on the club's bulletin board about new member orientation meetings. She has already started the announcement and saved it in a file named NEWMEMB.

To open this file,

Select: **F**ile>**O**pen existing file

Set the directory appropriately for your computer system.

Select: NEWMEMB.WPS

The announcement about a new member orientation meeting is displayed on the screen. Scroll through the text and read the announcement. When you are done, return to the top of the file.

Karen needs to enter the headline "NEW MEMBER ORIENTATION MEETING" above the announcement. She will enter it as two lines. To enter it in all capital letters,

Press: CAPS LOCK

Your display screen should be similar to Figure 4-1.

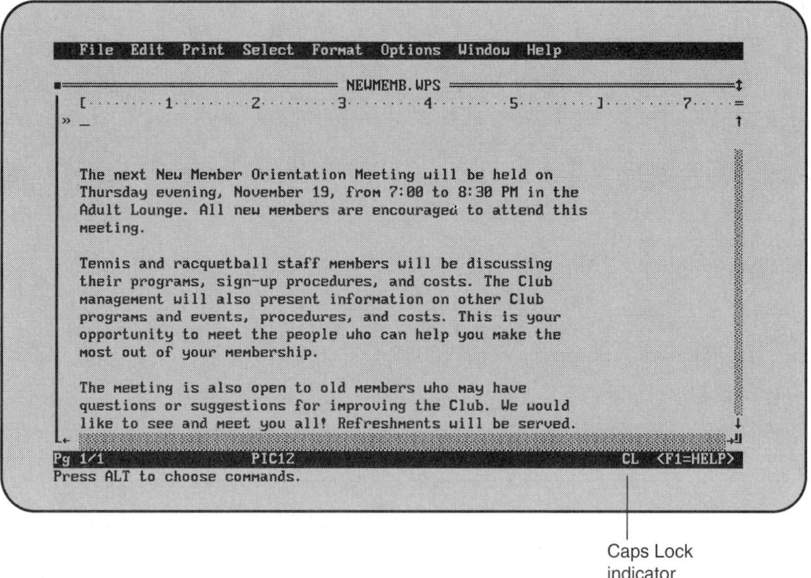

FIGURE 4-1

Notice in the status line that "CL" is displayed. This is how Works tells you that the (CAPS LOCK) key is on. The (CAPS LOCK) key affects only alphabet keys. Other characters will require that you use the (SHIFT) key.

To enter the first line of the heading on the first line of the document,

Type: **NEW MEMBER**

Next, she wants to **center** the heading on the line between the left and right margins. Works has a set of commands that let you control the display of paragraphs of text. Works defines a paragraph as text of any length ending with a paragraph mark. These commands are located in the Format menu. When working with paragraph format commands, the cursor should first be positioned within the paragraph to be affected.

The cursor should be positioned anywhere on the heading line.

Select: Format

The Format menu contains commands that control the appearance of the printed text. The commands in the first box on this menu let you control the display of any number of characters of text. They are the text format commands. Before using these commands, the text must be selected. The commands in the second box affect paragraphs (text ending with a paragraph mark) of text only. They are paragraph format commands. When you use these commands, the cursor must be positioned anywhere within the paragraph. The command to center text is a paragraph format command.

Select: Center

The first heading line is centered between the margins on the line. To move to the next line and enter the second heading line,

Press: (↓)
Type: **ORIENTATION MEETING**

The shortcut key for the Center command is (CTRL) - C.

With the cursor positioned on the second heading line, center it using the shortcut key.

To turn off all capital letters,

Press: (CAPS LOCK)

Your screen should be similar to Figure 4-2.

FIGURE 4-2

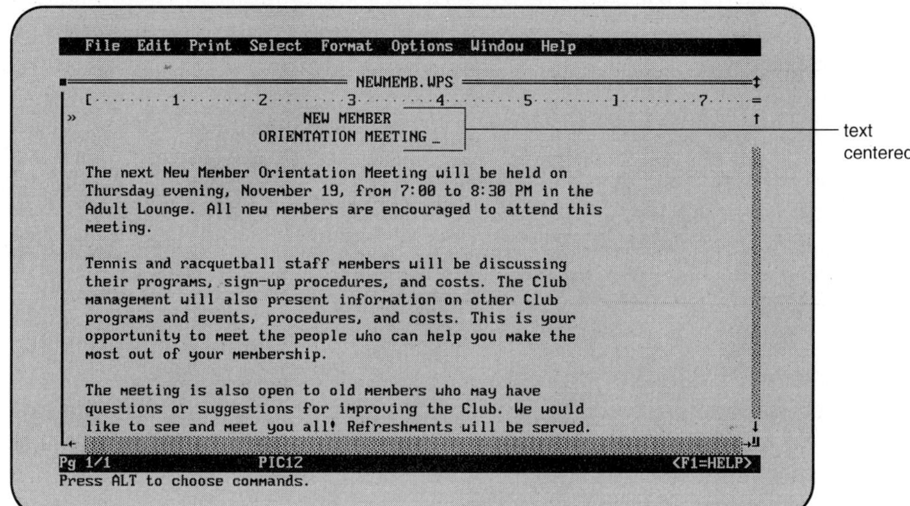

Both heading lines are centered between the margins.

Bolding Text

Karen also wants the heading to be printed in **bold** characters. Bold text is printed darker than normal text. On the screen, it is displayed brighter than surrounding text or in color if you have a color monitor. The command to produce bold text is Format/Bold or (CTRL) - B. It is a text format command, and it requires that you select the text to be formatted first.

Select the text "NEW MEMBER ORIENTATION MEETING" (press (F8); then extend the highlight).

To format the selected text to be printed bold,

Select: Forma**t**>**B**old
⋙ (CTRL) - B

To clear the highlight,

Press: 

The formatted text is displayed brighter on your screen or in color if you have a color monitor, to show the area that is to be printed in bold text.

Karen would like the first line of the heading to begin and end with a series of three asterisks (***). To add this to the heading,

Move to: N of New
Type: ***
Press: Space bar

Move to: The space after the R of MEMBER
Press: Space bar
Type: ***

The line of text adjusts to remain centered between the margins as the additional characters are inserted. The inserted text is also bold. You can delete and add text to a centered paragraph and Works will automatically adjust the text so that it remains centered.

Underlining Text

Karen wants to emphasize the date and time of the meeting by **underlining** it. The Format/Underline command is a text format command. Like the Bold format command, you must first select the text before using the Underline command.

To do this, select the text, November 19, from 7:00 to 8:30 PM in the first paragraph (press 8; then extend the highlight).

The Underline command shortcut key is CTRL - U. To underline the selected text,

Select: Format>**U**nderline
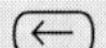 CTRL - U

To clear the highlight,

Press: ←

Your screen should be similar to Figure 4-3.

FIGURE 4-3

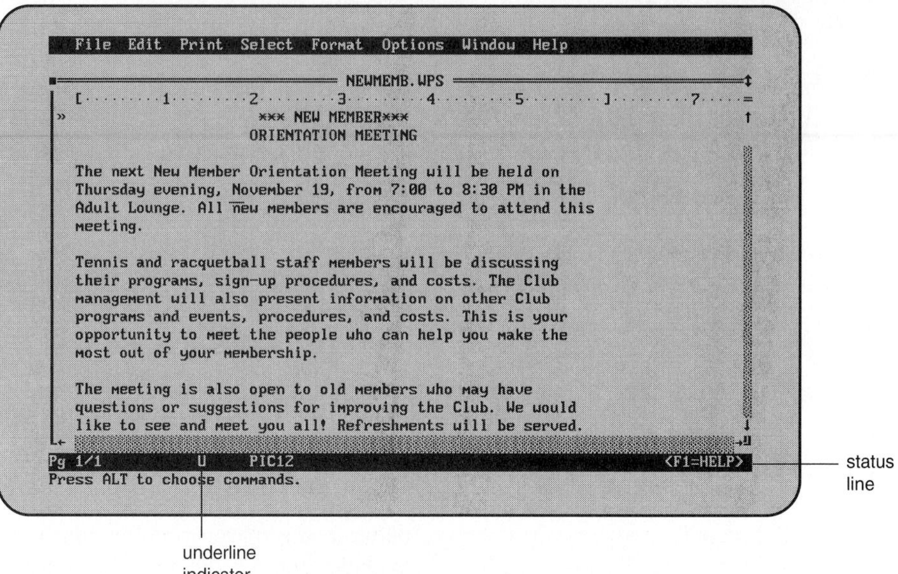

The underlined text is displayed in color or appears brighter on your screen if you have a monochrome monitor. On some monitors it will be underlined. The different colors help you tell which format has been applied to the text. With a monochrome monitor you cannot tell what format setting has been applied. For that reason, Works displays a U in the status line to tell you that the text the cursor is positioned on is underlined. In addition, Works displays a B for Bold and an I for Italicized when the text the cursor is positioned on is formatted in either of those styles.

Creating Tabular Columns

Karen wants to add information about future orientation meetings in a table at the bottom of the announcement. To move to this location,

Press: (PGDN)

The cursor should be positioned on the second blank line below the last line of the announcement. If it is not, move it there.

Type: **Other New Member Orientation Meetings:**
Press: (↵) (2 times)

Karen wants to set up three columns of text that will contain the following information:

DATE	LOCATION	TIME
Dec. 13	Courtside Cafe	7:00 PM
Jan. 15	Lounge	10:00 AM
Feb. 17	Lounge	8:00 PM

When you create columns, you could use the Space bar to move along the line and then enter the text at the desired location. However, it is much faster and more precise to use (TAB) to move the cursor to the position on the line where you want to enter the text. When you insert text at the same tab stop on many lines, you create a column of text. If you use the Space bar instead of (TAB), the columns may appear correct on the screen but may not print correctly. Using the (TAB) key assures that your columns will always be aligned correctly.

You could use the preset tab stops at every .5 inch to tab along the line, or you can set your own tab stops. To enter your own tab stops, figure the position on the page using the ruler at the top of the workspace. There are 10 spaces or characters per inch on the ruler line. Each inch from the left margin is marked on the ruler with the appropriate number. Karen wants to set tab stops at 1, 3, and 4.5 inches from the left margin.

Select: Forma**t**>**T**abs

Your screen should be similar to Figure 4-4.

FIGURE 4-4

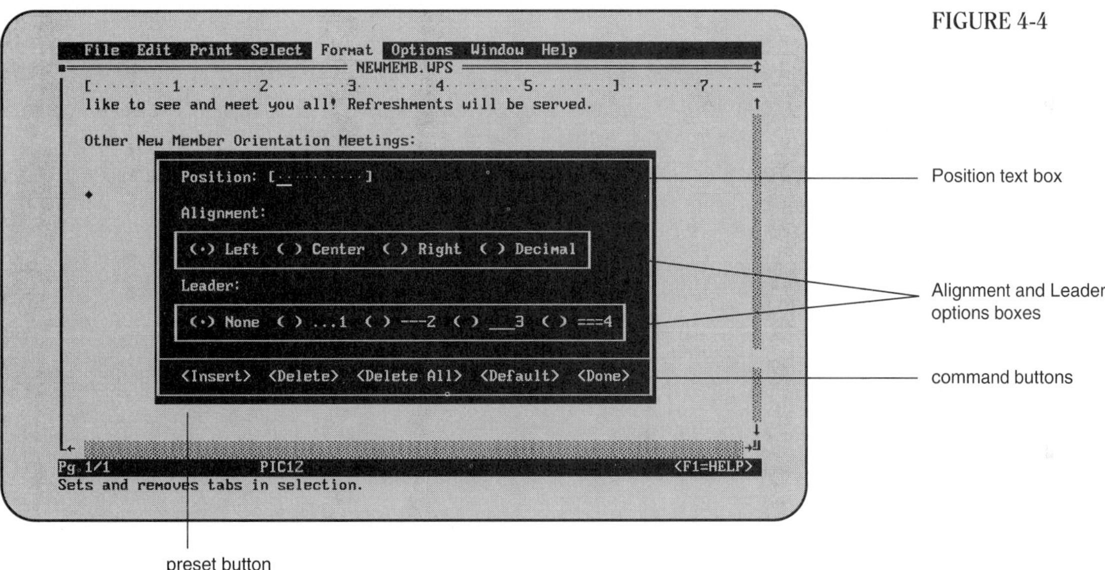

The Tabs dialog box is displayed. In the Position text box, you need to enter the position where you want the first tab stop. To enter one inch,

Type: 1

You do not need to enter the inches symbol (").

The Alignment options box lets you choose how you want the characters to be positioned or **aligned** with the tab stop. There are four tab alignment settings; Left, Center, Right, and Decimal. They have the following effects:

Left	Positions the left edge of each entry at the tab stop
Center	Centers each entry at the tab stop
Right	Positions the right edge of each entry at the tab stop
Decimal	Positions the decimal point of each entry at the tab stop

Left tab alignment is the preselected or default setting and is appropriate for this tab stop.

The Leader options box lets you specify if you want to fill the space between columns with **leader characters** and specify the style of leader characters such as dots. The default is none. Leader characters are used for listings such as tables of contents. For example, in a table of contents a title or heading is often separated from the page number by a series of leader characters (Section I..........12).

Both the default alignment and leader settings are appropriate, so you do not need to make selections from these boxes.

The Insert command button lets you confirm or set the tab as specified in the dialog box. Since it is the active (highlighted) button, to use it,

Press: ↵

The new tab stop is displayed on the ruler line as an L. This tells you it is a left-aligned tab stop.

Whenever a tab stop is set, the default settings to the left of the new setting are removed. The settings to the right of the new tab stop remain in effect at every .5 inch.

The dialog box continues to be displayed to let you set other tab stops. The cursor is in the Position box, waiting for you to enter another position value. The second tab stop will be at position 30 (3 inches). It will be a center-aligned tab. Another way to enter the position value is to use CTRL - → or ← to move the cursor on the ruler line to the position. As you move the cursor, the position value is displayed in the Position text box.

Press: CTRL - → (20 times)

Mouse Note: You can click on the position on the ruler line to specify the position of a tab stop. In addition, you can move a tab stop by dragging it to the new position.

The cursor should be over the 3" mark on the ruler line, and 3" should be displayed in the Position text box. To make this a center-aligned tab with no leader,

Select: Center (ALT - C)

To complete this tab stop by selecting the Insert button,

Press: ↵

A C is displayed on position 30 of the ruler line.

Finally, set the last tab stop at position 4.5". It should be left-aligned with no leader.

Your screen should be similar to Figure 4-5.

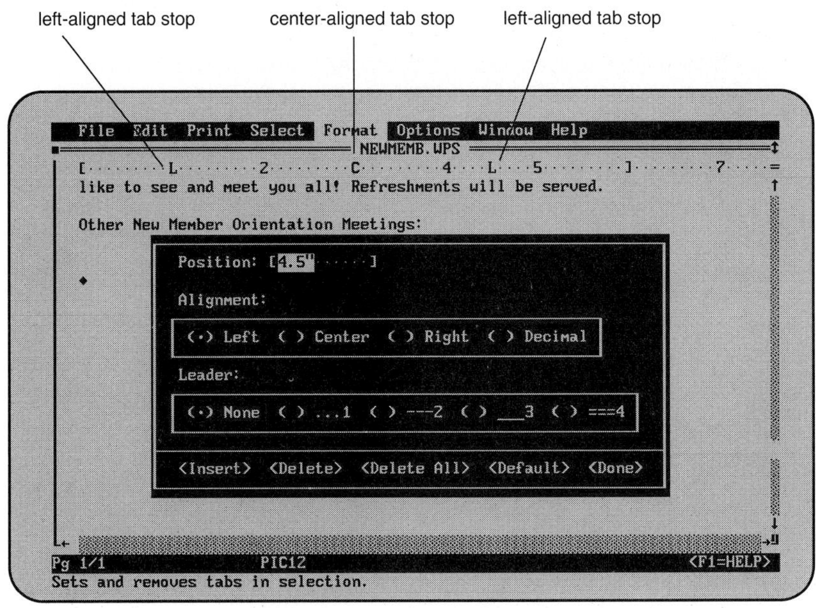

FIGURE 4-5

To close the dialog box and return to the document,

Select: Done (ALT - D)

You are now ready to enter the column headings.

Press: TAB
Press: CAPS LOCK
Type: **DATE**

The cursor moved over to the 1" position, and the text you entered is aligned with the left edge of the tab stop.

Press: TAB
Type: **LOCATION**

The cursor moved to position 30. This time, however, the text is centered on the tab stop.

Press: TAB
Type: **TIME**
(Do not press ↵)
Press: CAPS LOCK

Your screen should be similar to Figure 4-6.

FIGURE 4-6

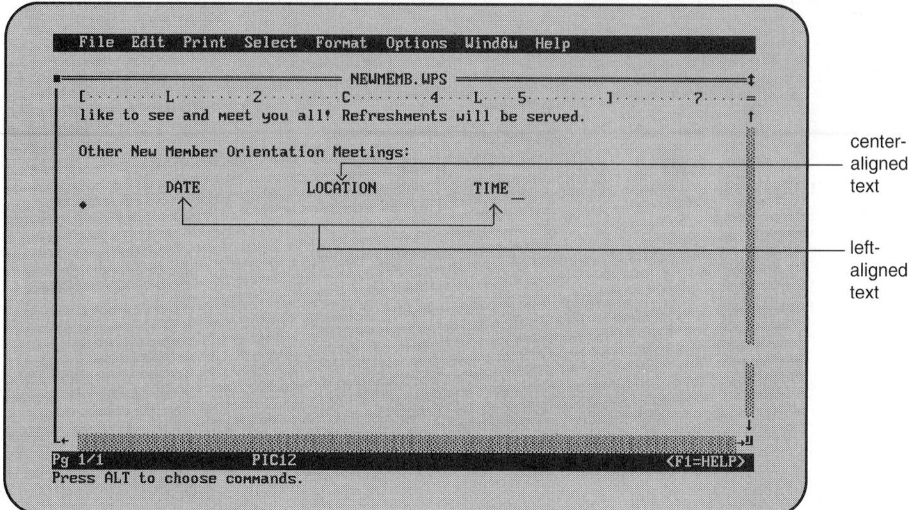

Normally, you would press ⏎ to move to the next line to begin entering the information in the table. However, if you press ⏎, Works inserts a paragraph mark and defines that first line as a paragraph. You would then need to redefine the tab settings for each line of the table. Instead, to move to the next line and enter a blank line without entering a paragraph mark,

Press: SHIFT - ⏎ (2 times)

The SHIFT - ⏎ combination allows you to format the table as a paragraph by inserting an **end-of-line mark** rather than a paragraph mark. To see this mark,

Select: **O**ptions>Show **A**ll characters

Your screen should be similar to Figure 4-7.

FIGURE 4-7

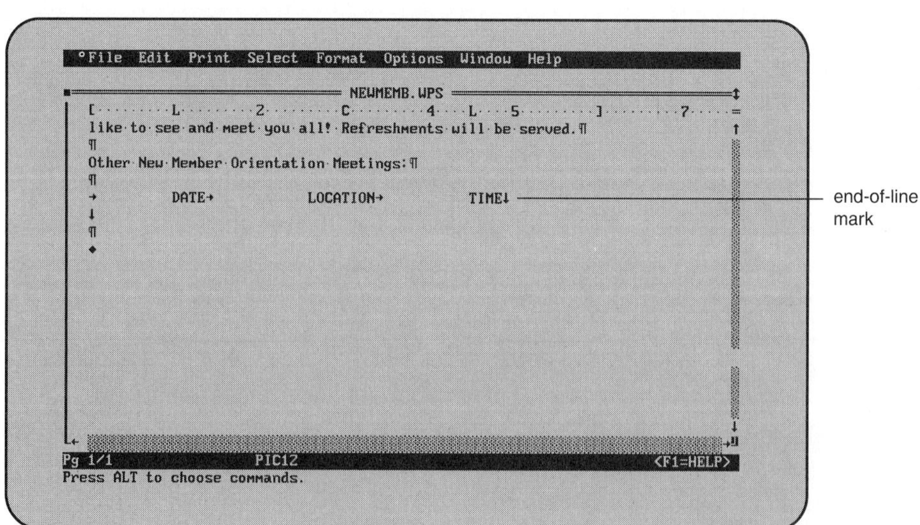

The end-of-line mark is the arrow (⓵) symbol. It has the same effect as pressing (↵): it lets you move to the next line, except that it does not end the paragraph.

To enter the first row of information for the table,

Press: (TAB)
Type: **Dec. 13**
Press: (TAB)
Type: **Courtside Cafe**
Press: (TAB)
Type: **7:00 PM**
Press: (SHIFT) - (↵)

In the same way, enter the following information as the second and third rows of the table.

Jan. 15	Lounge	10:00 AM
Feb. 17	Lounge	8:00 PM

To end the table and complete the paragraph,

Press: (↵)

Your screen should be similar to Figure 4-8.

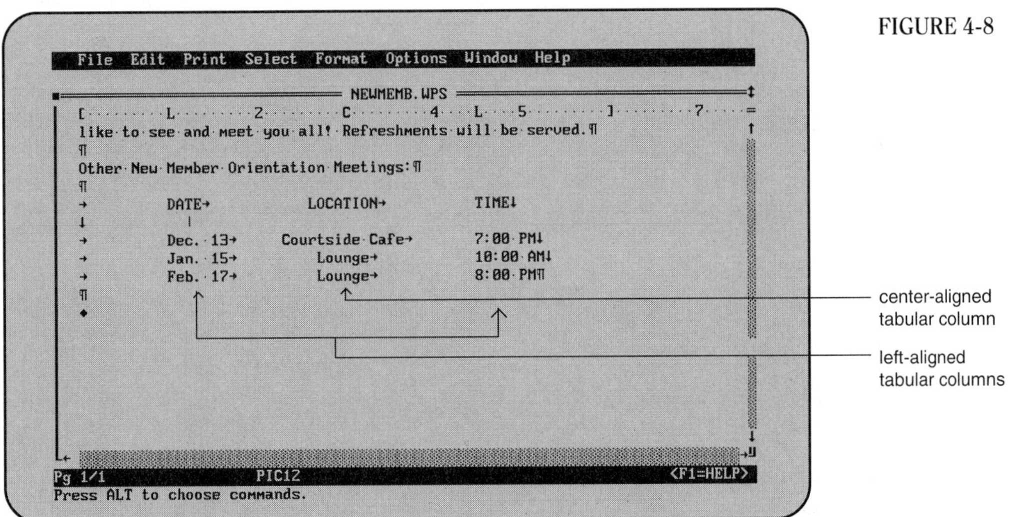

FIGURE 4-8

The middle column of text is centered at the tab. The first and last columns are left-aligned. Using the (TAB) key to move along a line lets you quickly and accurately format columns of information.

The tab settings you enter apply only to the paragraph. The rest of the document still uses the default tab stops. If you want the tab stops to apply to the entire document, use the Default command button. It will change the preset interval for all tab stops. If you need to clear tab stops you have entered, select the paragraph that contains the tab stops, select Format/Tabs, and then type the position of the tab you want to remove. The Delete command button will then remove it. To remove all tab stops not preset by Works, use the Delete All command button. When tab stops are removed, the default settings are restored and the text is repositioned at the preset tab stops.

To turn off the All Characters display,

Select: Options>Display All Characters
Press: CTRL - HOME

Aligning Paragraphs

On the screen the announcement has even left margins and uneven right, or **ragged-right,** margins. This is also how it will appear when the document is printed.

The Format menu contains four commands that control the alignment of a paragraph. They are Left, Center, Right, and Justified. Left alignment is the default setting. The alignment settings have the following effect:

Left	Aligns text against the left indent, leaving the right edge ragged
Center	Aligns text evenly between the left and right indents
Right	Aligns text against the right indent, leaving the left edge ragged
Justified	Aligns text evenly against the right and left indents

In this document, the margin and indent settings for all paragraphs are the same (the default). Therefore the paragraph will be aligned with the margin settings. Each paragraph can have its own alignment as well as indent settings. If a paragraph has indent settings that are different from the margin settings, the text will be aligned with the indent settings.

Karen wants the announcement to have text on both the right and left margins evenly aligned, or **justified.** To justify text, Works inserts extra spaces between some of the words on a line to force the line to end evenly with the right margin setting.

Works will change the paragraph alignment for the paragraph the cursor is in, or for selected paragraphs. If there is no selection, Works applies the new alignment to the paragraph as you type.

To change the alignment of the first paragraph, move the cursor anywhere within the first paragraph.

Select: Format

To change justification to have even left and right margins,

Select: Justified

Your screen should be similar to Figure 4-9.

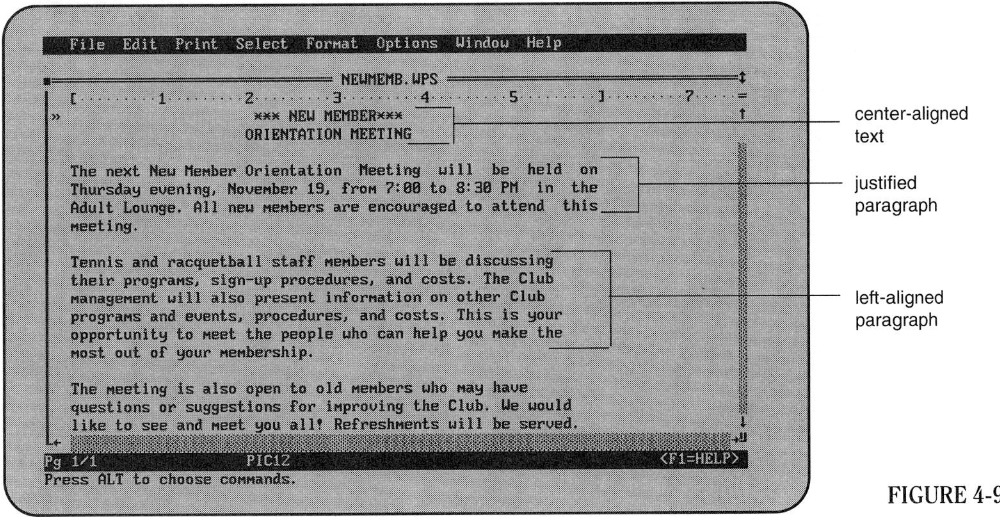

FIGURE 4-9

The text is realigned in the paragraph, and each full line ends even with the right margin.

Next, you need to justify the other paragraphs in the announcement. You could justify each paragraph individually, or select the text you want to justify first and then choose the Justify command. This is much quicker.

Select the next two paragraphs and justify them using the shortcut key CTRL - J.

To clear the highlight,

Press: ↑

The shortcut key for left alignment is CTRL - L, for center alignment is CTRL - C, and for right alignment is CTRL - R.

Setting Line Spacing

Karen decides the announcement would be easier to read if it were printed double spaced instead of single spaced. To change to double-spaced text, the Format/Double Space command is used. The shortcut key for this command is CTRL - 2. She wants the entire file to be double spaced. To select the entire file,

Select: Select>**A**ll
Select: Format>**D**ouble Space
⋙ CTRL - 2

To return to the top of the file,

Press: CTRL - HOME

Your screen should be similar to Figure 4-10.

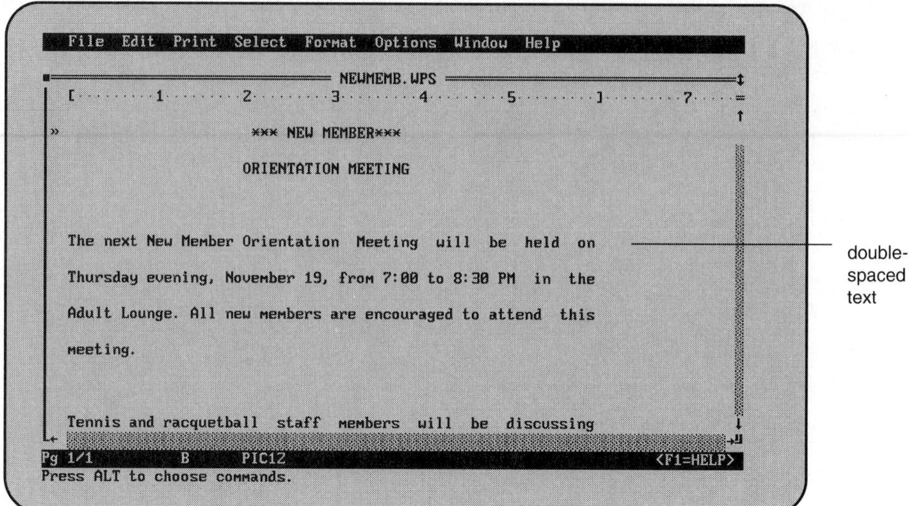

FIGURE 4-10

The text appears double spaced.

To make sure the announcement still fits on a single sheet of paper, move to the bottom of the document. The page marker is not displayed, and the status line shows that you are still on page 1 and there is only one page in the file.

Defining Multiple Text Formats

Karen is pleased with how the document appears. She wants to make one last change. She would like to underline and bold the column heads. You can do this quickly by selecting the text, then choosing one text format after another while the text is still highlighted.

Select the three column headings DATE, LOCATION, and TIME.

To apply the bold format setting,

Press: (CTRL) - B

The highlight is still over the selected text. To underline the selected text,

Press: (CTRL) - U

Both a B and a U appear in the status line to identify this text as being formatted using both format settings. Do not be concerned if you accidentally formatted incorrect words. You will learn shortly how to correct this.

To return to the top of the document,

Press: (CTRL) - (HOME)

Changing the Screen Mode

Note: You must have a computer with graphics capability to complete this section. If you do not, skip to the next section, "Clearing Format Settings."

Karen would like to see how the bold and underline formats will appear when printed. The Preview screen shows the layout of the page, but it does not show the different text formats. To see how the text formats will appear when printed, you need to change the screen mode to graphics.

Works can display information on your screen in two modes: text and graphics. The default is **text mode**. In this mode, the character styles (such as bold and underline) are displayed in color if you have a color monitor or in a brighter intensity if you have a monochrome monitor. You cannot tell how these character styles will appear when printed. In **graphics mode**, Works displays character styles on your screen similar to how they will appear when printed. To change modes,

Select: Options>Works Settings

Your screen should look similar to Figure 4-11.

FIGURE 4-11

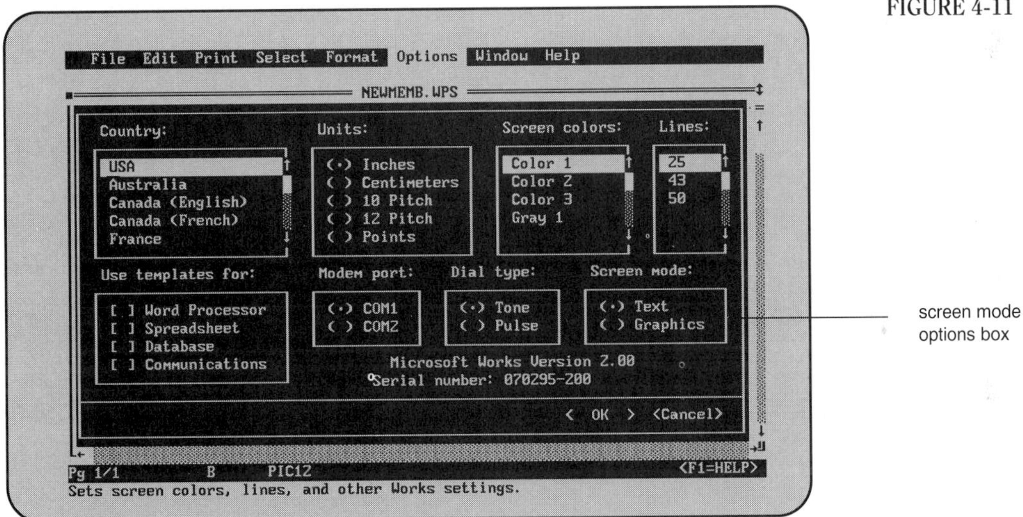

The options displayed on your screen may be different from those in Figure 4-11. This is because Works displays only those options that are appropriate for your computer system. The default settings are highlighted or selected.

This dialog box lets you customize the Works display and control certain preset options. When you make changes to the Works settings, they are remembered from session to session, so they need to be selected only once.

The Screen mode option box shows that the current screen mode of display is text. To change it to graphics,

Select: Graphics (ALT - G)

The graphics option is now selected. To complete the command,

Press: ↵

After a few moments, your screen should appear similar to Figure 4-12.

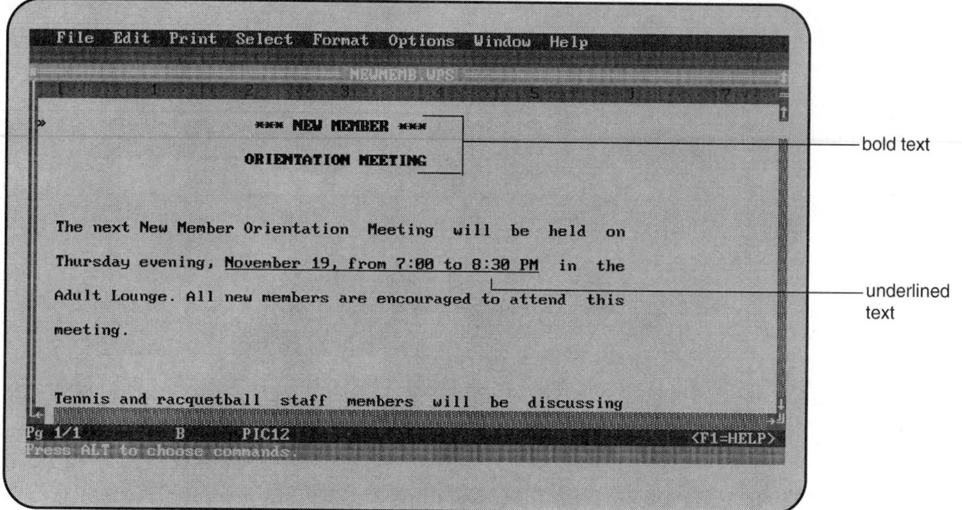

FIGURE 4-12

The underline and bold formats are displayed as they will appear when printed. If you have a mouse, the pointer is now an arrow.

Scroll through the document until you are at the end of the file.

Clearing Format Settings

Karen does not like how the underlining appears in the column heads. She wants to change it so that each head is individually underlined. To remove the bold and underline format from the column heads,

Select the three column heads DATE, LOCATION, and TIME.

Select: Format>**P**lain Text

The bold and underline formatting is removed. Plain text returns the selected text to normal display.

To clear the highlight,

Press: (←)

To bold and underline the Date column heading, select the DATE column head. Do not extend the highlight beyond the word.

To specify the formats,

Press: (CTRL) - B
Press: (CTRL) - U

The DATE column heading appears bold and underlined on the screen.

Note: If you were not able to complete the previous section on changing the screen mode, the text will not appear bold or underlined on your screen.

Select and format the other two column headings in the same way.

Note: If you were not able to complete the previous section on changing the screen mode, skip the end of this exercise and proceed to the next section, "Adding Headers and Footers."

To clear the highlight,

Press: 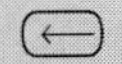

Your screen should be similar to Figure 4-13.

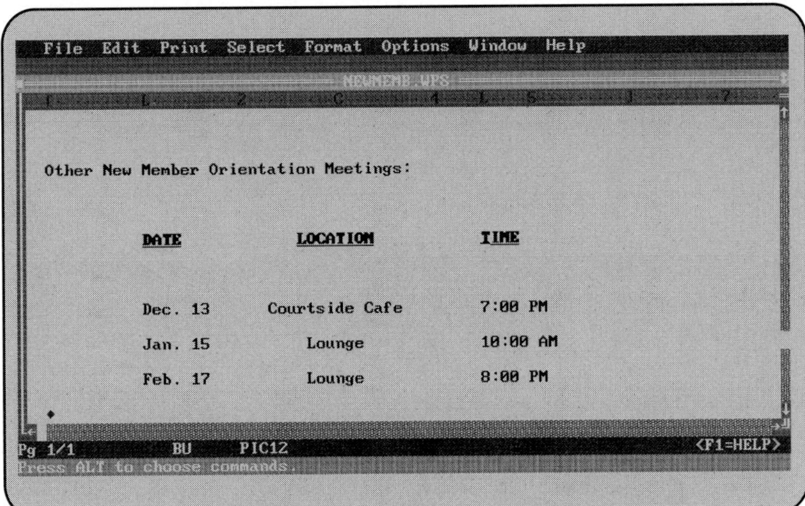

FIGURE 4-13

Karen likes how this formatting looks.

If you completed the previous section, Changing the Screen Mode, to turn off graphics mode display,

Select: Options>Works Settings>Text>(↵)

The screen returns to text mode display.

Generally, you will want to use text display mode when entering text. This is because the graphics display mode is slower when scrolling the screen. Graphics mode is convenient when you want to see how your character format settings will appear.

Adding Headers and Footers

The last thing Karen needs to add to the announcement is a header and a footer. A **header** is text that appears at the top of every page and a **footer** is text that appears at the bottom of every page. The command to enter headers and footers is in the Print menu.

Select: Print>Headers & Footers

Your screen should be similar to Figure 4-14.

FIGURE 4-14

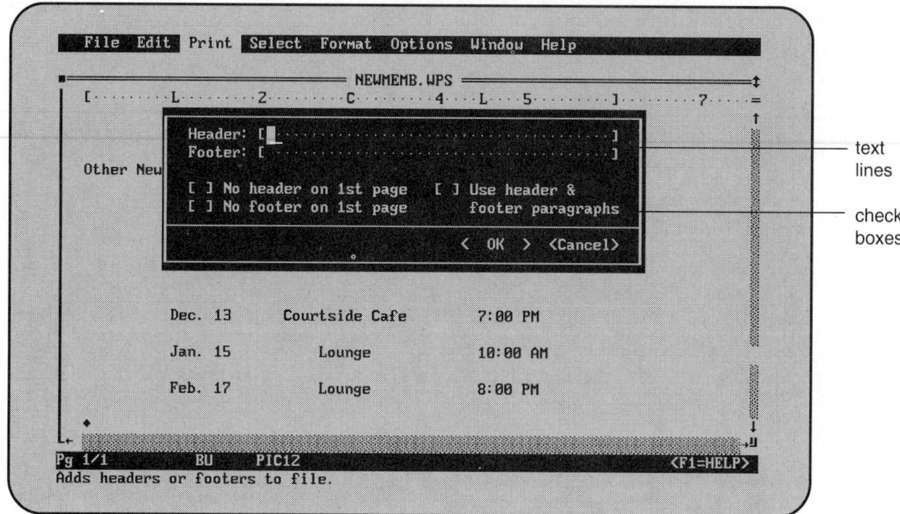

A dialog box appears with a text line for you to enter the header and footer text. The text line lets you enter a single line header or footer only.

The header you will enter is the name of the sports club. The footer will be the sports club slogan, followed by your name. They are single-line headers and footers. If you make a mistake entering the header or footer text, correct it using the keys you would use when entering normal text. In the header text line,

Type: **THE SPORTS CLUB**

To move to the footer text box,

Press: TAB

In the footer text line,

Type: **A Sports Club to meet all your exercise needs - Your Name**

Your screen should be similar to Figure 4-15.

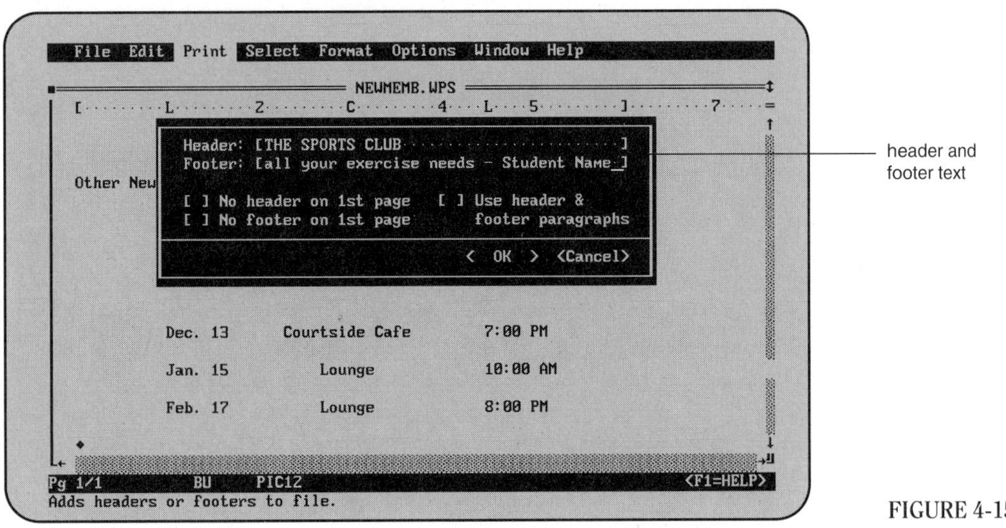

FIGURE 4-15

The check box options in the dialog box let you suppress headers and footers on the first page. The Use header and footer paragraphs check box is used to create multiple-line headers and footers.

To close the dialog box,

Press: ↵

The header and footer are not displayed on the screen. To see how they will appear, you can preview the page.

Note: If you are using a floppy disk system, follow the instructions to insert the Accessories disk and the Working Copy disk when using this command.

Select: Print>Preview

Before previewing the announcement, set the print quality to draft by selecting the "Draft quality" option.

To complete the command,

Press: ↵

The header and footer are displayed centered at the top and bottom of the page. Headers and footers are automatically centered and placed .5 inch from the top and bottom edge of the page.

You can now print the announcement. If necessary, turn on your printer and make sure it is ready to print.

Select: Print

Your printed document should be similar to Figure 4-16.

THE SPORTS CLUB

***** NEW MEMBER *****

ORIENTATION MEETING

The next New Member Orientation Meeting will be held on Thursday evening, <u>November 19, from 7:00 to 8:30 PM</u> in the Adult Lounge. All new members are encouraged to attend this meeting.

Tennis and racquetball staff members will be discussing their programs, sign-up procedures, and costs. The Club management will also present information on other Club programs and events, procedures, and costs. This is your opportunity to meet the people who can help you make the most out of your membership.

The meeting is also open to old members who may have questions or suggestions for improving the Club. We would like to see and meet you all! Refreshments will be served.

Other New Member Orientation Meetings:

DATE	LOCATION	TIME
Dec. 13	Courtside Cafe	7:00 PM
Jan. 15	Lounge	10:00 AM
Feb. 17	Lounge	8:00 PM

A Sports Club to meet all you exercise needs - Student Name

FIGURE 4-16

Save the revised announcement as ORIENMTG using the File/Save As command.

Using Windows

Karen shows the printout of the announcement to the manager. He is very pleased with how it looks. In fact, he is so pleased that he wants her to use the same information in an article for the club's monthly newsletter. He also wants her to write another article for the newsletter about the automatic fee payment program. He wants both articles in one file, and they should not exceed a single page.

The first thing Karen needs to do is change the spacing of the announcement back to single spacing. To do this,

Select: Select>**A**ll
Select: Format>**S**ingle Space
⋙→ (CTRL) - 1
Press: (CTRL) - (HOME)

Next, she needs to remove the header and footer lines. To delete this information,

Select: Print>**H**eaders & Footers

To remove the text in the header and footer lines, simply press (Bksp) or (DEL) with the cursor positioned in the text box.

Press: (DEL)

The header text should be deleted.
Delete the footer text in the same way. To complete the command,

Press: (↵)

Finally, she wants to separate the body of the article from the title with two blank lines. To do this, move to the first line of the first paragraph and insert a blank line.

Arranging Windows

Now Karen is ready to enter the information about the automatic fee payment program. To save time, she will copy the text about the program from the WELCOME file or from the AUTO-PAY file into the announcement. She is not sure which file she will copy it from, so she will open and look at both of them. Then she will copy the paragraph into the file to be used as an article.

Select: File>**O**pen Existing File>**WELCOME.WPS**>(↵)

The welcome letter is now displayed in the active window and the ORIENMTG file is hidden behind it.
To open the AUTO-PAY file,

Select: File>**O**pen Existing File>**AUTO-PAY**>(↵)

Your screen should be similar to Figure 4-17.

FIGURE 4-17

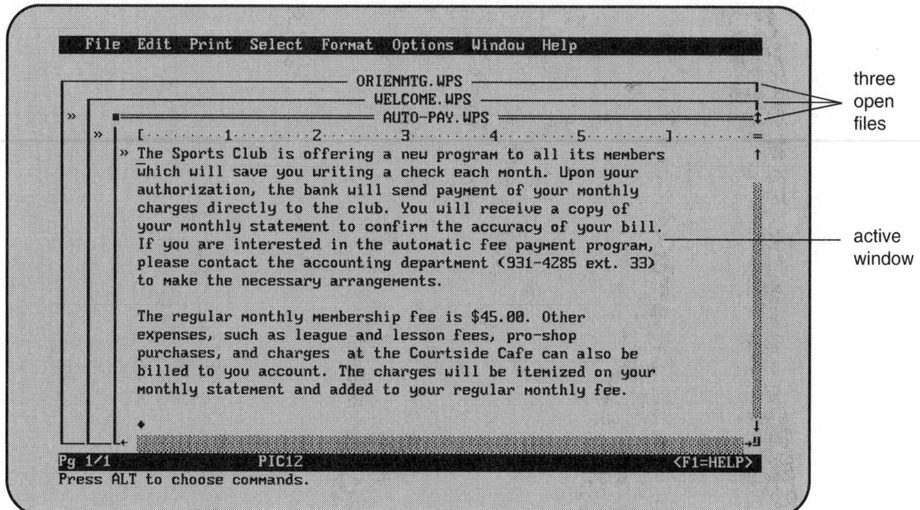

Now there are three open files, stacked one behind the other. The filenames are displayed in the title bars. The active window contains the cursor, the double top border, and the scroll bars. Although three files are open, only the text in the active file is visible in the workspace of the active window. With Works you can display up to eight windows at a time on the screen.

To move to the previous window,

Mouse Note: To switch between windows, click on the window you want to make active.

Press: (CTRL) - (SHIFT) - (F6)

The previous window containing the file WELCOME is now the active window. The active window is the window you can work in.

Press: (CTRL) - (SHIFT) - (F6)

The active window is now the first file that was opened, ORIENMTG. To move back through the windows,

Press: (CTRL) - (F6)

The WELCOME file is the active window.

Press: (CTRL) - (F6)

The AUTO-PAY file is the active window.

To arrange the windows so that they are all visible at the same time in the workspace,

Select: Window

Your screen should be similar to Figure 4-18.

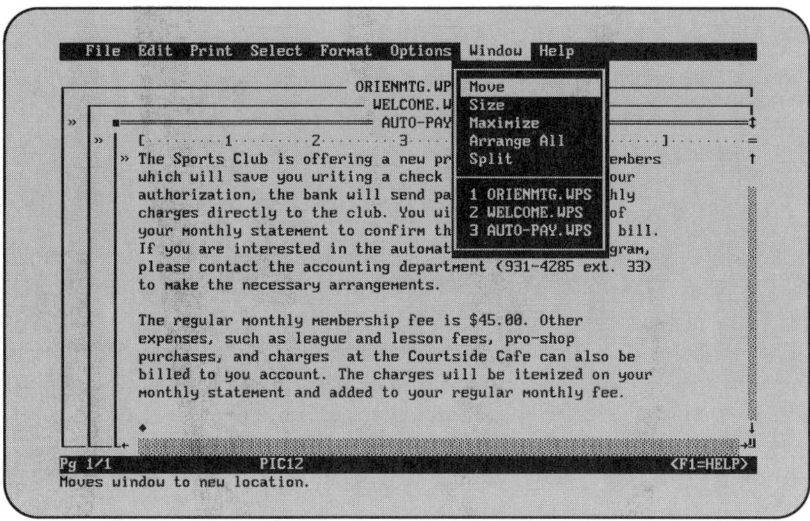

FIGURE 4-18

The five window options in the upper box let you control the display of multiple windows in the workspace. To make all the open windows visible on the screen at the same time,

Select: Arrange All

Your screen should be similar to Figure 4-19.

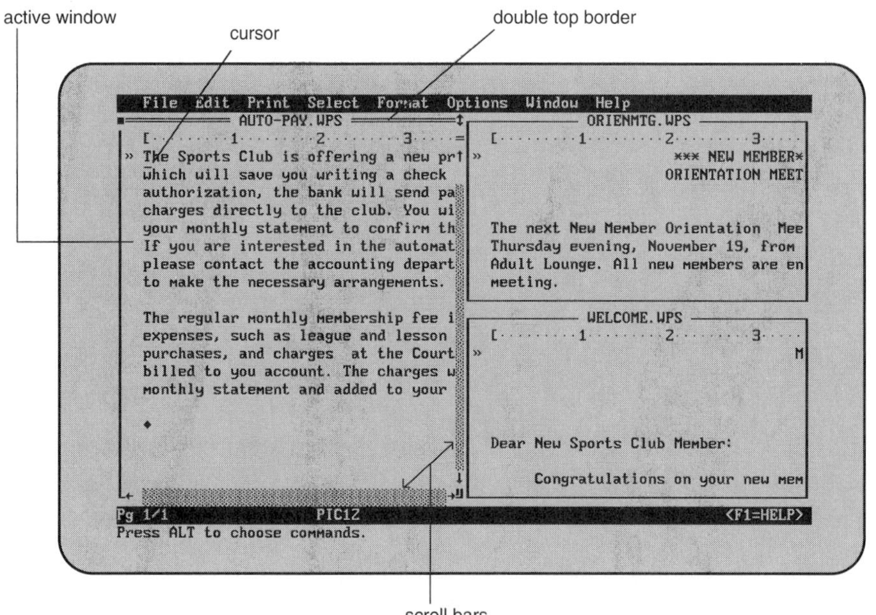

FIGURE 4-19

The three files are displayed in three windows in the workspace. Limited space on the screen controls how much of each file can be displayed. The AUTO-PAY window is the active window. It contains the double top border, scroll bars, and cursor. The menu bar, status line, and message line always correspond to the active window.

To make the ORIENMTG file the active window,

Press: CTRL - F6

Use the ↓ to move through the file until you are at the end of the file. This is the location where the text for the second article will be entered.

To switch to the WELCOME file,

Press: CTRL - F6

Scroll the document until the paragraph beginning "The Sports Club is offering..." is displayed as the first line in the window.

Karen could copy the paragraph about the automatic fee payment program from either the AUTO-PAY file or the WELCOME file into the ORIENMTG file. To enlarge the workspace of the active window to see more of the text,

Select: Window>Maximize

Mouse Note: You can click the maximize arrow (↕) in the upper-right corner of the window instead of using the menu to maximize the window area.

The current window occupies the entire screen. Karen decides to use the text from this file for the article because it reflects the change made earlier when she replaced "club" with "Sports Club."

The Window Maximize command acts as a toggle between the initial size of a window and its enlarged size. When this command is active, any window you make active is enlarged, too. To return the window to its previous size so you can view the other files,

Select: Window

Notice the diamond symbol next to the Maximize command. This tells you this feature is on. To deactivate this command,

Select: Maximize

The three files are displayed on the screen again.

Moving and Sizing Windows

Karen no longer needs the AUTO-PAY file opened. To make that file the active file,

Press: CTRL - F6

The AUTO-PAY file window should be the current window. To close the file,

Select: File>Close

Now there is empty space on the screen and the window containing the WELCOME file is the active window. To make use of the extra space, you can move and enlarge the two windows. To move them to the left edge of the screen,

Select: Window>Move

A highlighted box appears around the window. The arrow keys are used to move the window to the new location.

Press: (←) (10 times)

Your screen should be similar to Figure 4-20.

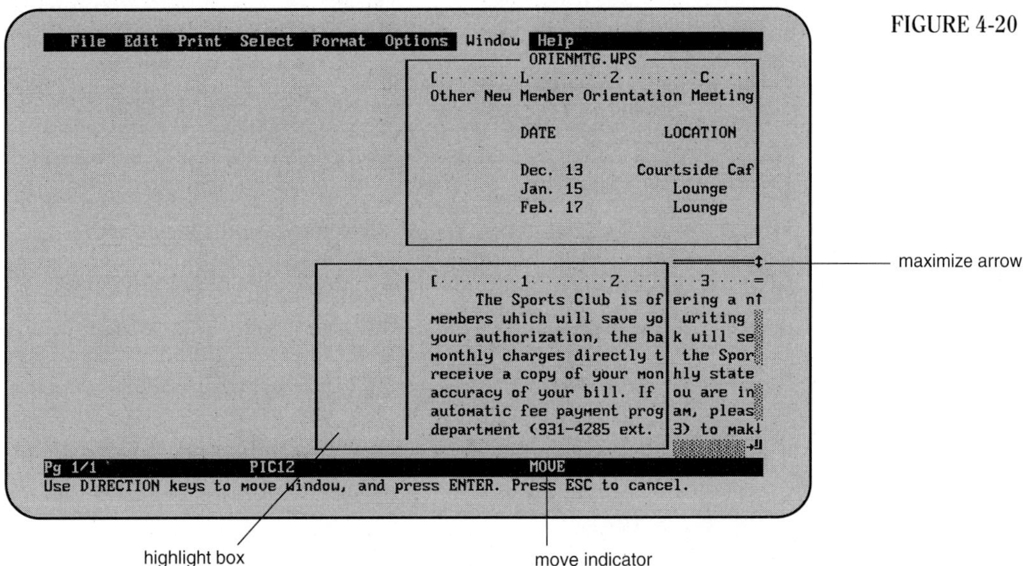

FIGURE 4-20

The window moves to the left 10 character spaces. A window can be moved in the direction of the arrow anywhere on the screen. You can even move it so that part of it is off the screen, as long as the upper-left corner is still visible on the screen.

Press: (↑) (5 times)

By pressing (←), continue to move the window until the left edge is on the left edge of the screen.

To return the window to the bottom half of the screen,

Press: (↓) (5 times)

The window should be in the lower-left corner of the workspace. To set the window at the marked location,

Press: (↵)

Your screen should be similar to Figure 4-21.

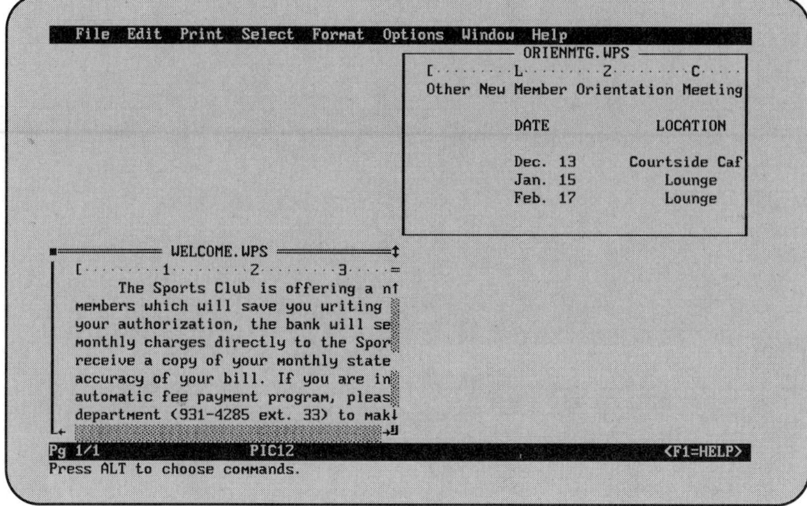

FIGURE 4-21

The text moves from the original window into the new window location.

Mouse Note: To move the window, you can position the pointer on the window's title bar or left border and drag it to the new location.

Make the ORIENMTG file current and move it to the left edge of the workspace above the lower window.

To increase the size of this window,

Select: **W**indow>**S**ize

The arrow keys will change the size of the window in the direction of the arrow.

Press: (→) until the window extends across the workspace
Press: (↵)

Mouse Note: To size a window, position the mouse pointer on the size box (the ⅃ in the lower-right corner of the window) you want to change; then drag the size box to change the window's size.

Your screen should be similar to Figure 4-22.

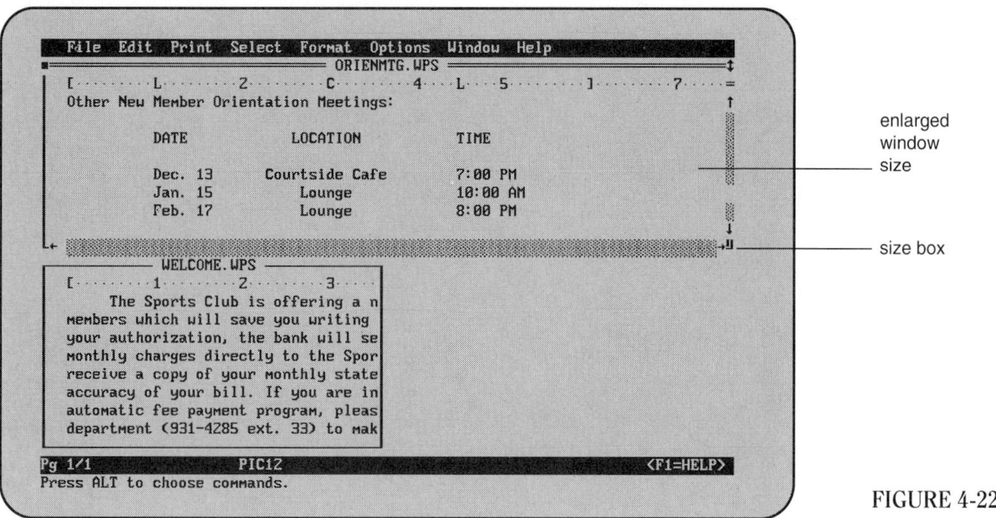

FIGURE 4-22

Make the lower window active and increase its size in the same way. Your screen should be similar to Figure 4-23.

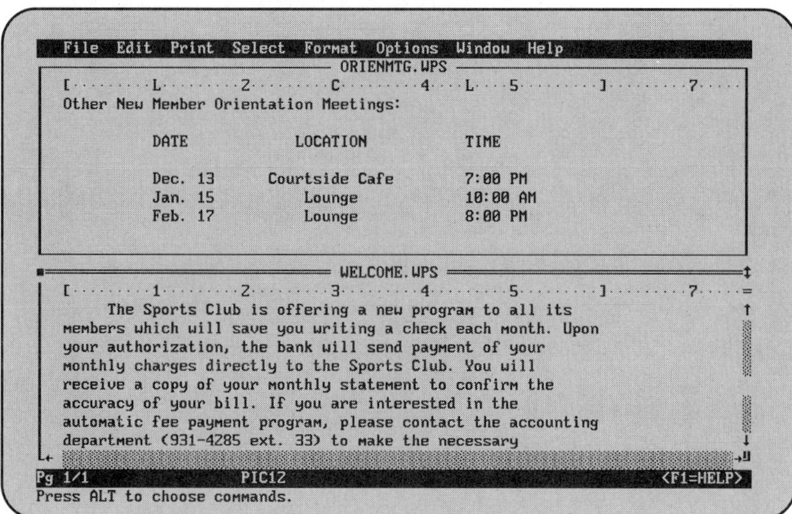

FIGURE 4-23

Now the full width of both documents is visible.

Now Karen is ready to copy the paragraph on the automatic fee payment program from the WELCOME file into the ORIENMTG file.

Position the cursor anywhere within the automatic fee payment paragraph.

To select it to be copied,

Press: F8 (4 times)

Next, to activate the Copy command,

Select: Edit>Copy
⋙ (SHIFT) - (F3)

To switch into the upper window,

Press: (CTRL) - (F6)

The cursor should be positioned at the end of the file. If it is not, move it there. To copy the paragraph into the file,

Press: (↵)

The paragraph is copied into the file in the upper window. Since Karen no longer needs to see the WELCOME file window, to maximize the current window,

Select: Window>Maximize

Your screen should be similar to Figure 4-24.

FIGURE 4-24

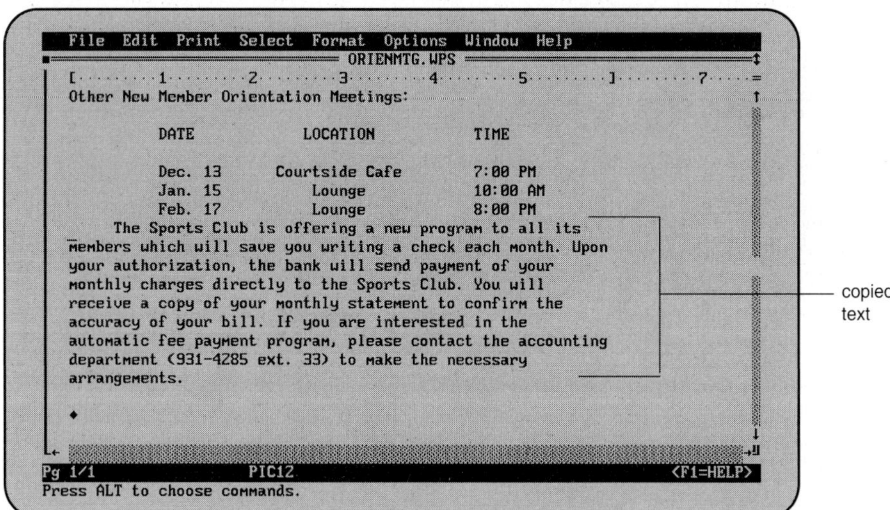

Next, Karen needs to add a title and change the format of the paragraph so that it is like the orientation meeting article.

To format the paragraph so that it is like the other, do the following:

Enter four blank lines to separate the two articles.

Delete the paragraph tab by positioning the cursor under the Tab mark and pressing (DEL).

Justify the paragraph.

Bold and underline the telephone number.

Next, she needs to enter a title.

Move to the blank line immediately above the paragraph about the automatic fee payment program. The title will be on two lines.

Type: ***** NEW PROGRAM *****
Press: (↵)
Type: **AUTOMATIC PAYMENT**
Press: (↵) (2 times)

Center and bold the title lines.

To clear the highlight,

Press: (←)

When you are done, your screen should be similar to Figure 4-25.

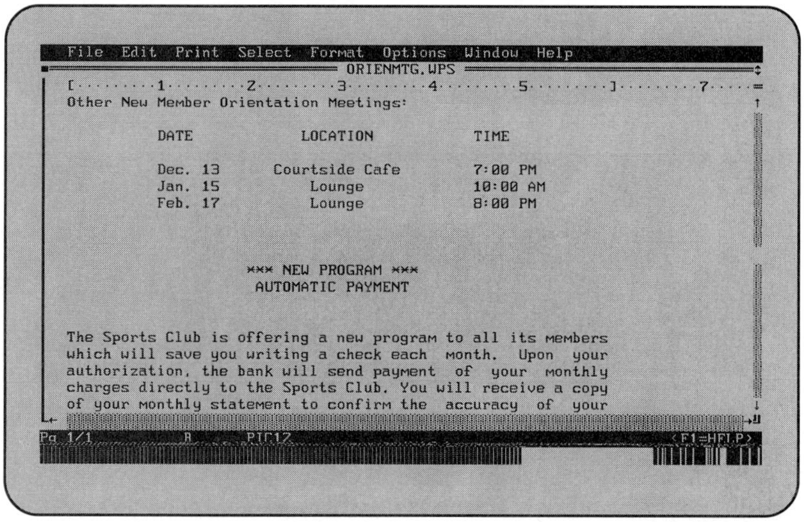

```
 File  Edit  Print  Select  Format  Options  Window  Help
                         ORIENMTG.WPS
 [·········1·········2·········3·········4·········5·········]·········7·····
 Other New Member Orientation Meetings:

              DATE              LOCATION              TIME

              Dec. 13         Courtside Cafe          7:00 PM
              Jan. 15            Lounge               10:00 AM
              Feb. 17            Lounge               8:00 PM


                        *** NEW PROGRAM ***
                         AUTOMATIC PAYMENT

 The Sports Club is offering a new program to all its members
 which will save you writing a check each  month.  Upon  your
 authorization, the bank will send payment  of  your  monthly
 charges directly to the Sports Club. You will receive a copy
 of your monthly statement to confirm the  accuracy  of  your
 Pg 1/1        B     PIC12                                   <F1=HELP>
```

FIGURE 4-25

Using the Spell Checker

Press: (CTRL) - (HOME)

Karen is pleased with how the announcement looks. However, before printing it out she wants to check its spelling. To help you do this quickly, Works has a built-in dictionary that checks for spelling errors. In addition, it will look for words that are incorrectly capitalized and hyphenated, and for duplicate words.

To enter several intentional errors in this document,

Change the spelling of "Orientation" in the title to "Orentation".

Change the spelling of "held" to "eld" (in the first line of the first paragraph).

Add the word "meeting" before "meeting" in the last line of the first paragraph.

Begin by positioning the cursor at the point in the document where you want to begin spell checking. To begin at the top of the document,

Press: CTRL - HOME

To begin spell checking,

Select: **O**ptions>Check **S**pelling

Note: If you are using a floppy disk system, insert and remove the Spell and Help disk when directed.

Your screen should be similar to Figure 4-26.

FIGURE 4-26

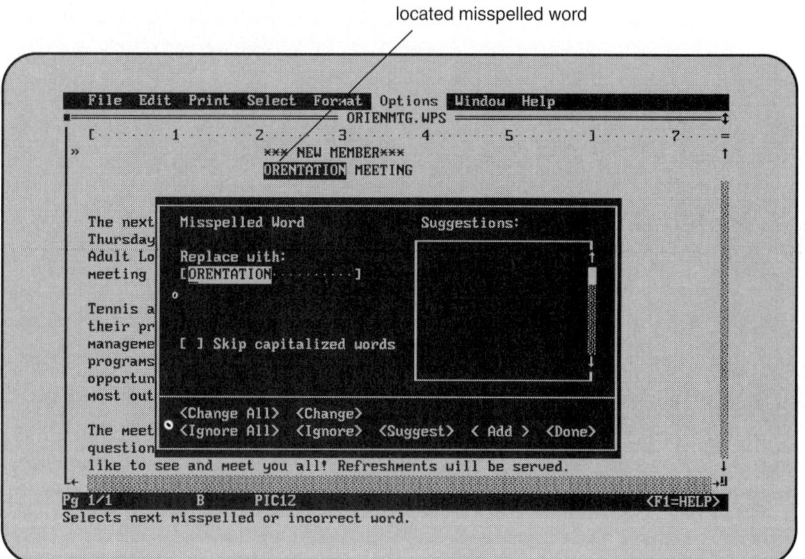

A dialog box is displayed. Works has located the first word it does not recognize. It displays the word in the Replace with: text box and highlights it in the text. You can type in the correct spelling yourself if you know how to spell the word, or you can ask Works to display a list of proposed spellings in the Suggestions box. To view a list of proposed spellings you use the Suggest button.

Select: Suggestions (ALT - S)

Your screen should be similar to Figure 4-27.

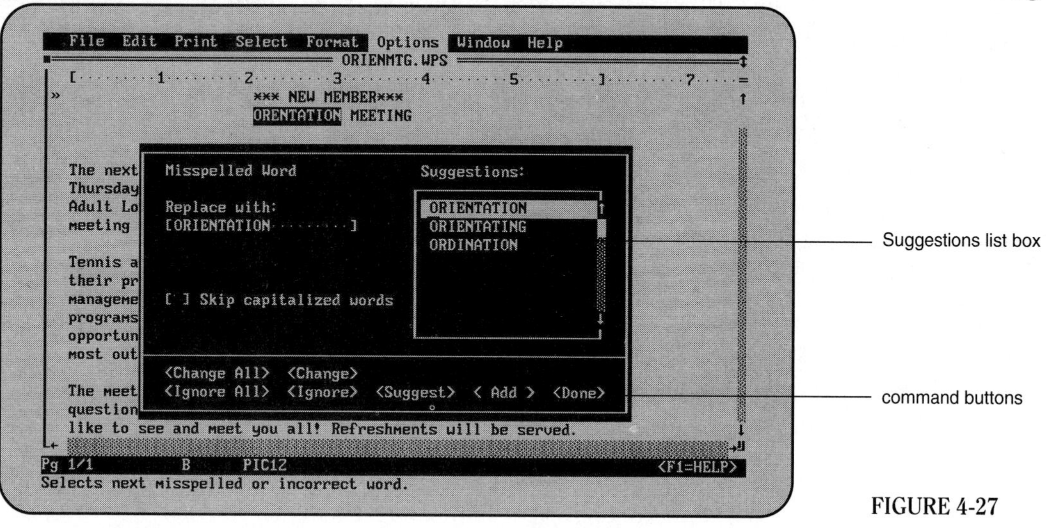

FIGURE 4-27

Three possible spellings are proposed and the cursor and highlight are displayed in the Suggestions box. The first choice is highlighted and the spelling of the word in the Replace with: box is the same as the highlighted suggestion.

Press: ↓

The second choice is highlighted and the spelling of the word in the Replace with: box is now the same as the highlighted suggestion.

The first choice is the correct one. Highlight it.

The buttons at the bottom of the dialog box instruct Works as to how you want to proceed. They have the following effects:

<Change All>	Changes all occurrences of this word
<Change>	Changes the spelling of the word
<Ignore All>	Skips all future occurrences of the word
<Ignore>	Leaves the located word unchanged
<Suggest>	Displays a list of possible correct spellings
<Add>	Adds the word to the dictionary
<Done>	Completes the command

Change is the preset button. To select it,

Press: ↵

The selected word replaces the incorrectly spelled word. The spell checker moves on to locate the next error, "eld." To see what suggestions Works has,

Select: Suggest (ALT - S)

None of the suggestions are appropriate. This time, you will need to change the spelling by typing in the correction in the Replace with: box. To move the cursor back to the Replace with box and type the correct spelling,

Select: **R**eplace with ((ALT) - R)
Type: **held**

To change the spelling by selecting the Change button,

Press: (↵)

Works moves to the next error, the duplicate word "meeting." The dialog box tells you this is a repeated word. Only three command buttons are available for selection. To make the correction by deleting one of the duplicate words, the change button is used. Since this is the preset button, to select it,

Press: (↵)

The next located word is "Courtside." Works located this word because it did not find a match for it in the dictionary. However, in this case it is correct. To leave the word as it is,

Select: **I**gnore ((ALT) - I)

Finally, no other errors are located. To leave the spell checker,

Press: (↵)

Return to the top of the document. Scroll through the text to verify that Works corrected the spellings as you specified.

Enter your name two lines below the last line of text in the file.

If you have printer capability, print a copy of the article. Your print out should be similar to Figure 4-28.

Save the current document as ARTICLE.

Close the file.

The second open document is displayed. Close this file.

Exit Works.

```
                    *** NEW MEMBER ***
                   ORIENTATION MEETING

The next New Member Orientation Meeting will be held on
Thursday evening, November 19, from 7:00 to 8:30 PM in the
Adult Lounge. All new members are encouraged to attend this
meeting.

Tennis and racquetball staff members will be discussing
their programs, sign-up procedures, and costs. The Club
management will also present information on other Club
programs and events, procedures, and costs. This is your
opportunity to meet the people who can help you make the
most out of your membership.

The meeting is also open to old members who may have
questions or suggestions for improving the Club. We would
like to see and meet you all! Refreshments will be served.

Other New Member Orientation Meetings:

         DATE            LOCATION            TIME

         Dec. 13       Courtside Cafe        7:00 PM
         Jan. 15           Lounge            10:00 AM
         Feb. 17           Lounge            8:00 PM


                    *** NEW PROGRAM ***
                   AUTOMATIC PAYMENT

The Sports Club is offering a new program to all its members
that will save you writing a check each month.  Upon your
authorization, the bank will send payment of your monthly
charges directly to the Sports Club.  You will receive a
copy of your monthly statement to confirm the accuracy of
your bill.  If you are interested in the automatic fee
payment program, please contact the accounting department
(931-4285 ext. 33) to make the necessary arrangements.

Student Name
```

FIGURE 4-28

Key Terms

center
bold
underline
align
leader characters
end-of-line mark
ragged right
justify
text mode
graphics mode
header
footer

Matching

1. CTRL - U	_____	**a.**	shortcut key for Bold command
2. Format>Justified	_____	**b.**	inserts end-of-line mark
3. .5"	_____	**c.**	shortcut key for Underline command
4. CTRL - J	_____	**d.**	preset tab setting
5. 8	_____	**e.**	number of files that can be opened at one time

6. Window>Maximize _____ f. shortcut key for Justify command

7. CTRL - C _____ g. toggles between initial size of window and enlarged size

8. CTRL - B _____ h. displays character styles as they will appear when printed

9. SHIFT - ↵ _____ i. aligns text evenly against right and left indents

10. graphics mode _____ j. shortcut key for Center command

Practice Exercises

1. To complete this problem, you must first have completed problem 1 in Lab 3. Open the file DEF-REV.

- Enter the title **OVERVIEW OF WORD PROCESSING** on the third line of the document. It should be in all capital letters, centered, and boldfaced.
- Enter one blank line below the heading.
- Underline the title DEFINITION OF WORD PROCESSING.
- Open the file TEXT-WP.
- Display both windows.
- Copy the entire contents of the file TEXT-WP into DEF-REV. It should be entered at the end of the file.
- Enlarge the window containing the file DEF-REV.
- Separate the heading "Advantages of Using a Word Processor" from the text above and below it with a blank line.
- Add the header "Word Processing Tool." Add the footer "Section II."
- Set the left and right margins at 1 inch.
- Spell check the document.
- Print the document.
- Save the new document as DEF-REV4. Close both files.

2. To complete this problem, you must first have completed problem 2 in Lab 3. Retrieve the file EVENTS. The text in this file will be used in the zoo bulletin board.

- Enter the heading shown below for the article, centered and in bold, as two lines. Leave a blank line below your name and date, and two blank lines below the heading.

  SPECIAL ZOO

  EVENTS

- The announcement needs an introductory paragraph. This has already been created and saved for you as EVENT1. Open this file and display it on the screen in a second window. Copy the entire contents of EVENT1 into EVENTS. It should be the first paragraph of the announcement (two lines below the heading).

- Maximize the window containing EVENTS.
- Boldface the name of each event in the first line of paragraphs 2 through 4.
- Justify all paragraphs of the announcement.
- Change the body of the announcement to double spacing.
- Spell check the announcement.
- Enter the current date on the second line of the document. Print the document.
- Save the announcement as EVENTS 2.

3. Enter the following article. Use tabular columns to create the table with left-aligned tab settings of .3, 2.0, 4.5, and 5.5. Set the left and right margins at 1 inch. Format the article as it appears below. (Source: *Money Magazine,* June 1990). Spell check the document. Save it as HOTTEST. Enter your name and the current date on the first line of the document. Print the document.

The Ten Hottest Jobs of the 90's

Experts forcast that workers starting out now will switch careers—that's careers, not jobs—an average of more than three times during their lives. To help newcommers to the workforce, the following table presents the hottest careers of the 1990's. To qualify for this list, these professions are growing fast, relatively lucrative, challenging, and prestigious.

Career	**Training**	**Average Salary**	**Top Performer**
Chef	AA degree or 3-year paid apprenticeship	35,000	200,000
Health-care cost manager	MBA plus related exp.	75,000	200,000+
Computer graphics artist	BA in art/design plus computer courses	30,000-60,000	75,000-150,000
Environmental engineer	BS and MS in environ-mental engineering	40,000-55,000	100,000+
Software developer	BS in applied math, engineering, or computer science	50,000-60,000	100,000
International lawyer	Law degree	75,000-150,000	200,000+
Industrial designer	BA in industrial design or architecture	55,000	90,000+
Physical therapist	BS or MS in physical therapy	30,000-42,000	100,000+
Management consultant	MBA + 2 years experience	100,000-120,000	250,000+

4. Enter the following article. Use tabular columns to create the table. Enter the column headings with tab stops set at 1.5 (left aligned) and 4.5 (center aligned). Enter the data in the columns with tab settings of 1.5 (left aligned) and 4.5 (decimal-aligned). Format the article as it appears below. Spell check the document. Save it as COMPETE. Enter your name and the current date on the first line of the document. Print the document.

Convenience Store Competition

Today, there are nearly 70,000 convenience stores across the country, according to the National Association of Convenience Stores. The average store stocks 3,350 different items and handles 4,450 customers a week. The average sale is $3.20. A percentage of the breakdown of what stores sell is shown in the table below.

Category	Percent
Tobacco	16.5
Soft drinks	12.7
Dairy	9.3
Beer/wine	9.1
Groceries	7.7
Candy	6.0
Bakery	4.6
Snack foods	4.5
Other	29.6

Command Summary

Command	Shortcut key	Action	Page
Print>**H**eaders and Footers		Creates headers/footers	111
Forma**t**>**P**lain Text		Restores text to normal display	110
Forma**t**>**B**old	CTRL - B	Bolds text	94
Forma**t**>**U**nderline	CTRL - U	Underlines text	99
Forma**t**>**L**eft	CTRL - L	Aligns text against left margin	107
Forma**t**>**C**enter	CTRL - C	Centers text	107
Forma**t**>**R**ight	CTRL - R	Aligns text against right margin	107
Forma**t**>**J**ustified	CTRL - J	Aligns text against right and left margins	106
Forma**t**>**S**ingle Space	CTRL - 1	Single spaces text	107
Forma**t**>**D**ouble Space	CTRL - 2	Double spaces text	107
Forma**t**>**T**abs		Set Tabs/styles	101
	SHIFT - ↵	End-of-line mark	104
Options>**W**orks Settings>Te**x**t		Changes screen mode to text	109
Options>**W**orks Settings>**G**raphics		Changes screen mode to graphics	109
Options>Check **S**pelling		Check spelling	124
Window>**M**ove		Moves window on screen	119
Window>**S**ize		Changes size of window	120
Window>**M**aximize		Toggles between enlarged and initial window size	118
Window>**A**rrange All		Displays all open files on screen at the same time	117

CONTENTS
Electronic Spreadsheets

OVERVIEW

Electronic Spreadsheets

In contrast to a word processor, which manipulates text, an electronic spreadsheet manipulates numerical data. The first electronic spreadsheet software program (VisiCalc) was offered on the market in 1979. Since then more than 5 million electronic spreadsheet programs of differing brands have been sold. In a ten-year period, spreadsheets have revolutionized the business world.

Definition of Electronic Spreadsheets

The electronic spreadsheet, or worksheet, is an automated version of the accountant's ledger. Like the accountant's ledger, it consists of rows and columns of numerical data. Unlike the accountant's ledger, which is created on paper using a pencil and a calculator, the electronic spreadsheet is created using a computer system and an electronic spreadsheet applications software program.

The electronic spreadsheet eliminates the paper, pencil, and eraser. With a few keystrokes the user can quickly change, correct, and update the data. Even more impressive is the spreadsheet's ability to perform calculations—from very simple sums to the most complex financial and mathematical formulas. The calculator is replaced by the electronic spreadsheet. Analysis of data in the spreadsheet has become a routine business procedure. Once requiring hours of labor and/or costly accountants' fees, data analysis is now available almost instantly using electronic spreadsheets.

Nearly any job that uses rows and columns of numbers can be performed using an electronic spreadsheet. Typical uses of electronic spreadsheets are for budgets and financial planning in both business and personal situations.

Advantages of Using an Electronic Spreadsheet

Like a word processor, the speed of entering the data into the worksheet using the keyboard is not the most important advantage gained from using an electronic spreadsheet. This is because the speed of entering data is a function of the typing speed of the user and the user's knowledge of the software program. The advantages are in the ability of the spreadsheet program to quickly edit and format data, perform calculations, create graphs, and print the spreadsheet.

The data entered in an electronic spreadsheet can be edited and revised using the program commands. Numeric or text data is entered into the worksheet in a location called a cell. These entries can then be erased, moved, copied, or edited. Formulas can be entered that perform calculations using data contained in specified cells. The results of the calculations are displayed in another cell.

The design and appearance of the spreadsheet can be enhanced in many ways. There are several commands that control the format or display of a numeric entry in a cell. For instance, numeric entries can be displayed with dollar signs or with a set number of decimal places. Text or label entries in a cell can be displayed centered or left- or right-justified (aligned) to improve the spreadsheet appearance. Columns and rows can be inserted and deleted. The cell width can be changed to accommodate entries of varying lengths.

You have the ability to "play" with the values in the worksheet, to see the effect of changing specific values on the worksheet. This is called "what-if," or sensitivity, analysis. Questions that once were too expensive to ask or took too long to answer can now be answered almost instantly, and with little cost. Planning that was once partially based on instinct has been replaced to a great extent with facts. However, any financial planning resulting from the data in a worksheet is only as accurate as that data and the logic behind the calculations. Incorrect data and faulty logic produce worthless results.

Most electronic spreadsheets also have the ability to produce a visual display of the data in the form of graphs. As the values in the worksheet change, a graph referencing those values automatically reflects the new values. The graphs produced by most spreadsheet programs are a tool for visualizing the effects of changing values in a worksheet. Thus, they are analytic graphs. An electronic spreadsheet program is not designed to produce graphs exclusively, as many presentation graphics programs are. As a result the graphs may appear crude compared to those produced by a pure graphics software program.

Electronic Spreadsheet Terminology

Absolute cell address: The cell address in a formula does not change when the formula is copied to another cell. A $ character entered before the row number and/or column letter causes absolute addressing.

Absolute cell reference: The cell reference in a formula does not change when the formula is copied to another cell. A $ character entered before the row number and/or column letter causes absolute cell referencing.

Arithmetic operators: Special characters assigned to basic numerical operations (e.g., + for addition, * for multiplication).

Automatic recalculation: The recalculation of all formulas in a worksheet whenever a value in a cell changes.

Cell: The space created by the intersection of a horizontal row and a vertical column. It can contain a label, value, or formula.

Chart: The visual representation of ranges of data in the worksheet as a chart or graph. Some graph types are a line, bar, stacked-bar, or pie chart.

Circular reference: A formula in a cell that directly or indirectly references itself.

Column: The vertical line on the spreadsheet identified by letters.

Copy: A spreadsheet command that duplicates the contents of a cell or range of cells to another location in the worksheet.

Format: The feature that controls how values in the spreadsheet are displayed (currency, percent, number of decimal places, etc.).

Formula: A numeric computation containing cell references and arithmetic operators.

Freeze: A spreadsheet feature that stops the scrolling of specified rows and/or columns on the display.

Function: A set of built-in or preprogrammed formulas.

Global: Command that affects all rows and columns in the spreadsheet.

Justification: The alignment of a label in a cell to the left, centered, or right in the cell space.

Label: A text entry in a cell used to describe the data contained in the row or column.

Manual recalculation: Recalculation of the formulas in a worksheet is performed only when specified by the user.

Move: The command that relocates the contents of a cell(s) to another area in the worksheet.

Range: A cell or rectangular group of adjoining cells.

Relative cell reference: The adjustment of the cell address in a formula to reflect its new location in the spreadsheet when copied.

Row: The horizontal line on the worksheet identified by numbers.

Value: A number displayed in a cell.

What-if analysis: A process of evaluating the effect of changing the contents of one or more cells in the spreadsheet to help in decision making and planning.

Case Study for Labs 5–8

Paula Nichols is the manager of the Courtside Cafe at the Sports Club. She has proposed expanding the menu of the cafe and has been asked by the board of directors to prepare a budget for the first six months of operation.

In Lab 1, Paula learns how to use a spreadsheet program to assist her in preparing this budget. She enters descriptive row and column titles and enters the values for the expected sales for food and beverages. She also enters a formula to compute a total value.

Lab 2 continues the building of the cafe budget by entering the values for expenses using copying. Functions are introduced. The worksheet is formatted to display currency.

In Lab 3, Paula expands the cafe budget to cover a one-year period. The problems of managing a large worksheet are handled in this lab by freezing titles and creating windows. What-if analysis on the worksheet is used to achieve the objectives of a 20 percent profit margin by the end of a year of operation.

Lab 4 deals exclusively with creating graphs. It requires that the computer can display and print graphs. The case used in this lab follows Fred Morris as he prepares several graphs to show trends in membership growth of the Sports Club over five years. A line, bar, stacked-bar, and pie chart are created.

LAB

Creating a Spreadsheet: Part 1

5

OBJECTIVES

In this lab you will learn how to:

1. Move around the spreadsheet.
2. Enter labels.
3. Edit spreadsheet entries.
4. Enter values.
5. Enter formulas.
6. Recalculate the spreadsheet.
7. Save a spreadsheet file.
8. Print a spreadsheet.

CASE STUDY

Paula Nichols is the manager of the Courtside Cafe at the Sports Club. She has proposed that the menu of the Courtside Cafe be expanded. The board of directors, before approving the expansion, want her to prepare a budget for the first six months of the proposed cafe expansion. During the next three labs, you will follow Paula as she uses Works to create a spreadsheet for the proposed cafe budget.

In this lab, you will follow Paula as she learns to move around a spreadsheet, enter and edit labels, numbers, and formulas, and print the spreadsheet.

Examining the Spreadsheet Window

Turn on the computer and load Works. Your data disk should be in the appropriate drive for your computer system. The Works opening screen should be displayed and the File menu should be open.

Select: Create **N**ew File>New **S**preadsheet

Your display should be similar to Figure 5-1.

FIGURE 5-1

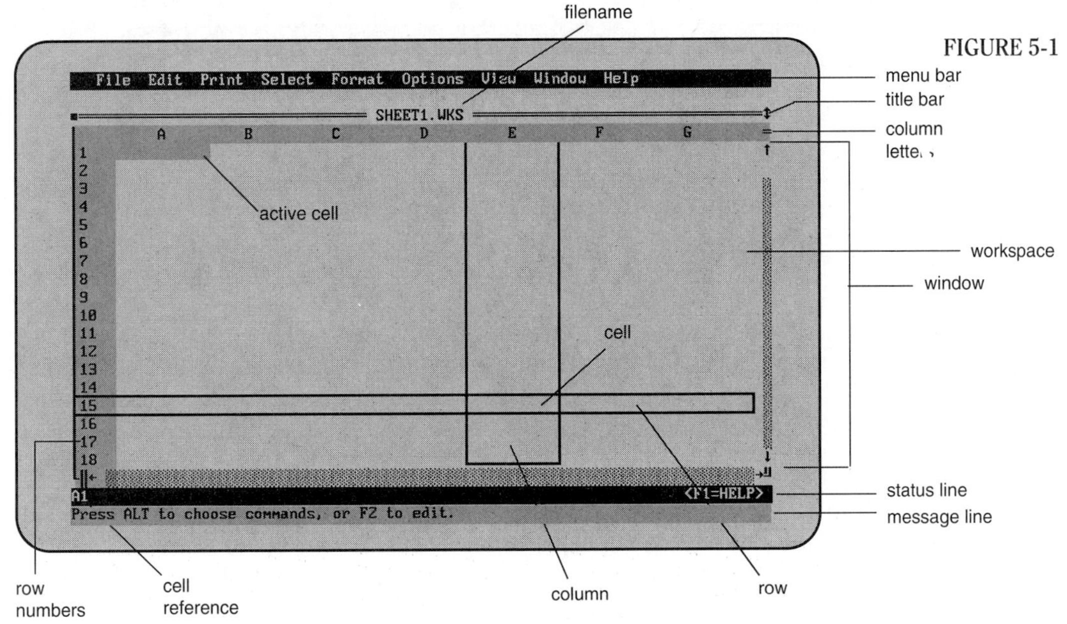

This is a blank Works 2.0 **spreadsheet.** It is similar to a financial spreadsheet in that it consists of a rectangular grid of rows and columns used to enter data.

The spreadsheet screen is divided into three areas: the **menu bar** at the top of the screen, the spreadsheet **window** in the middle, and the **status** and **message lines** at the bottom. The menu bar and the status and message lines perform just like they did in the word processing tool. The spreadsheet title SHEET1.WKS is displayed in the title bar. This is the default filename.

The **workspace** is where your work is displayed. In a spreadsheet, it consists of a rectangular grid of **rows** and **columns.** The **row numbers** along the left side of the workspace identify each row in the spreadsheet. The **column letters** across the top of the workspace identify the columns.

The intersection of a row and column creates a **cell.** The cell that is highlighted on your display is called the **active cell.** This is the cell that your next entry or procedure affects.

Each cell has a unique name consisting of a column letter followed by a row number. This is called the **cell reference.** The cell reference of the active cell is A1. The cell reference of the active cell is always displayed in the status line.

The scroll bars and other mouse symbols are the same as those described in the word processing tool.

Moving Around the Spreadsheet

The direction keys, (HOME), (END), (PGUP), (PGDN), and (TAB) keys allow you to move the highlight around the spreadsheet to different cells. The direction keys on the numeric keypad move the highlight in the direction indicated by the arrow.

To move the highlight to cell E3,

Press: (→) (4 times)
Press: (↓) (2 times)

Your display screen should be similar to Figure 5-2.

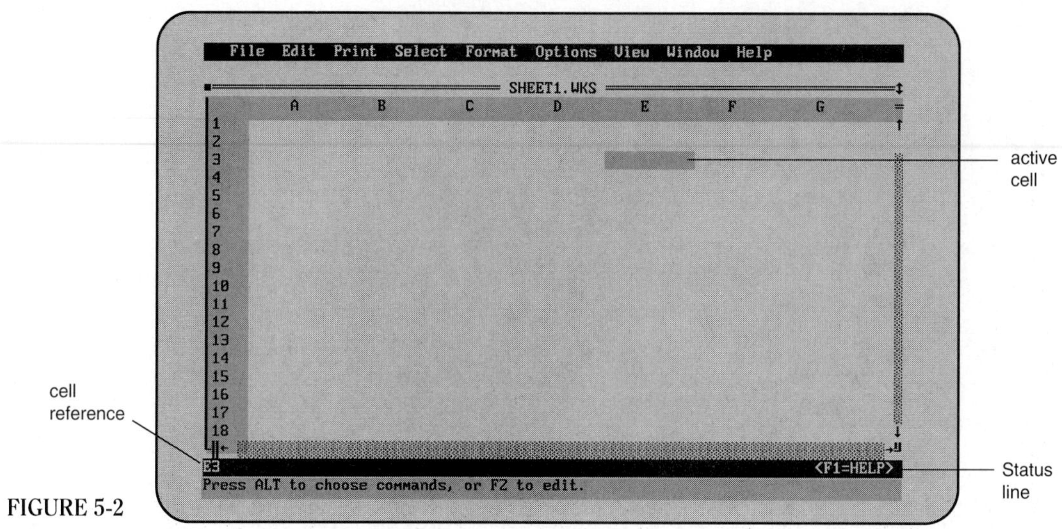

FIGURE 5-2

The highlight is in cell E3, making this cell the active cell. The status line reflects the new location of the highlight in the spreadsheet by displaying the cell reference E3 (column E, row 3).

Press: ← (5 times)

Even though you pressed the left arrow five times, the highlight only moved four cells to the left. This is because the highlight cannot be moved beyond the limits of the row border. This is also true for the column border at the top of the workspace.

To practice moving around the spreadsheet using the four directional keys,

Move to: E10
Move to: C6
Move to: G16

To return quickly to the first cell of the row,

Press: HOME

The highlight should be in cell A16.

No matter where you are in the spreadsheet, pressing CTRL - HOME will move the highlight to the upper-left corner.

Press: CTRL - HOME

The highlight should be in cell A1.

The spreadsheet is much larger than the part you are viewing in the window. It actually extends many columns to the right and many rows down. The spreadsheet in Works 2.0 has 256 columns and 4,096 rows. Currently, rows 1 through 18 and columns A through G are displayed in the window.

To move down one full window on the spreadsheet,

Press: (PGDN)

Your display screen should be similar to Figure 5-3.

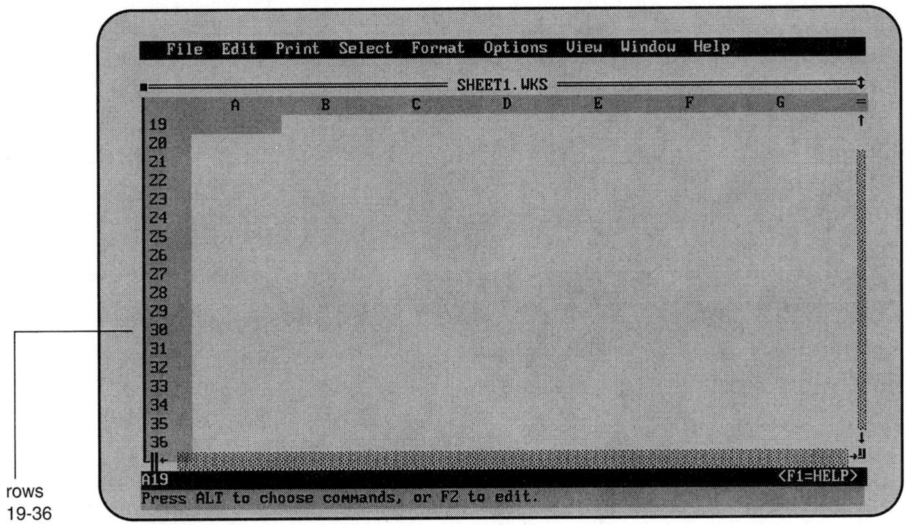

FIGURE 5-3

The window is positioned over rows 19 through 36 of the spreadsheet. Columns A through G have remained the same.

To move up a window on the spreadsheet,

Press: (PGUP)

The window is positioned over rows 1 through 18 of the spreadsheet again.

To move one full window to the right of the current window,

Press: (CTRL) - (PGDN)

Your display screen should be similar to Figure 5-4.

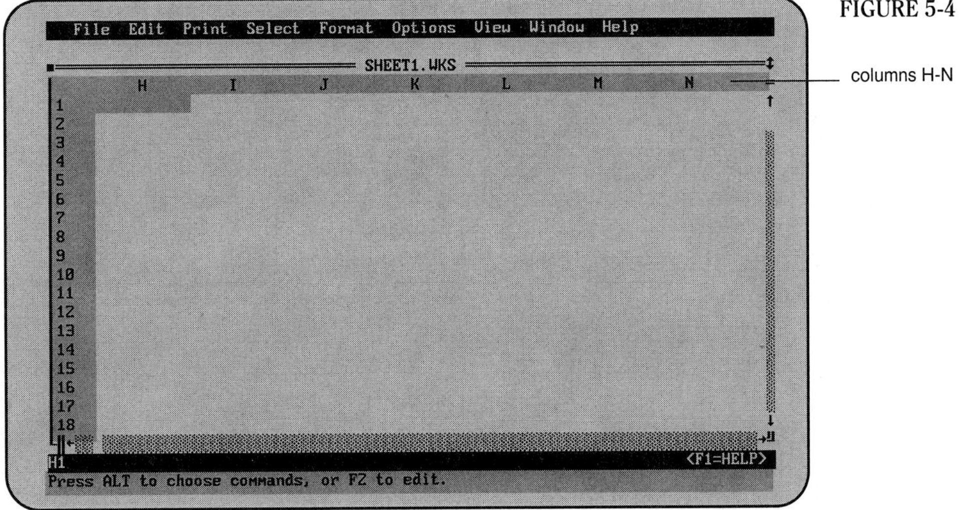

FIGURE 5-4

The window is now positioned over columns H through N and rows 1 through 18 of the spreadsheet. Columns are labeled A to Z, AA to AZ, BA to BZ, and so forth, through IA to IV.

To return to the previous window,

Press: (CTRL) - (PGUP)

The window is now positioned over columns A through G again.

If you hold down the directional keys, the (CTRL) - (PGUP) or (CTRL) - (PGDN) keys, or the (PGUP) or (PGDN) keys, you can quickly move through the spreadsheet. This is called **scrolling.** You will try this by holding down (CTRL) - (PGDN) for several seconds. Watch your display screen carefully as the columns quickly change window by window.

Press: (CTRL) - (PGDN) (Hold down for several seconds)

To quickly return to cell A1,

Press: (CTRL) - (HOME)

To move to a location in the spreadsheet several windows away, you could press (PGUP), (PGDN), (CTRL) - (PGUP), or (CTRL) - (PGDN) several times to move window by window. Alternatively, you could use the Select>Go To command. To move the highlight to a specific cell in a spreadsheet,

Select: Select

The Select menu commands in the spreadsheet tool perform functions similar to the word processor tool's Select menu. The command names, however, reflect the structure of the spreadsheet tool. For example, instead of selecting text, you select cells. You will be using many of these commands in the next lab.

The command that will move the highlight to a specific cell is Go To.

Select: Go To

Your screen should be similar to Figure 5-5.

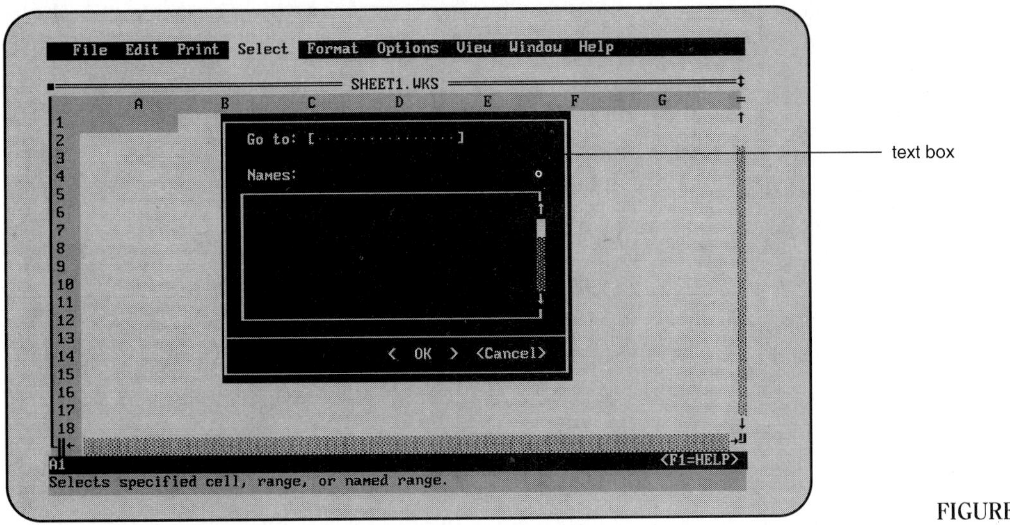

FIGURE 5-5

The Go To dialog box is displayed. In the text box you need to enter the cell reference that you want to move the highlight to. The cell reference can be entered in either upper- or lowercase letters. To move the highlight to cell AL55,

Type: **AL55**

To complete the command by selecting OK,

Press: ↵

Your display screen should be similar to Figure 5-6.

FIGURE 5-6

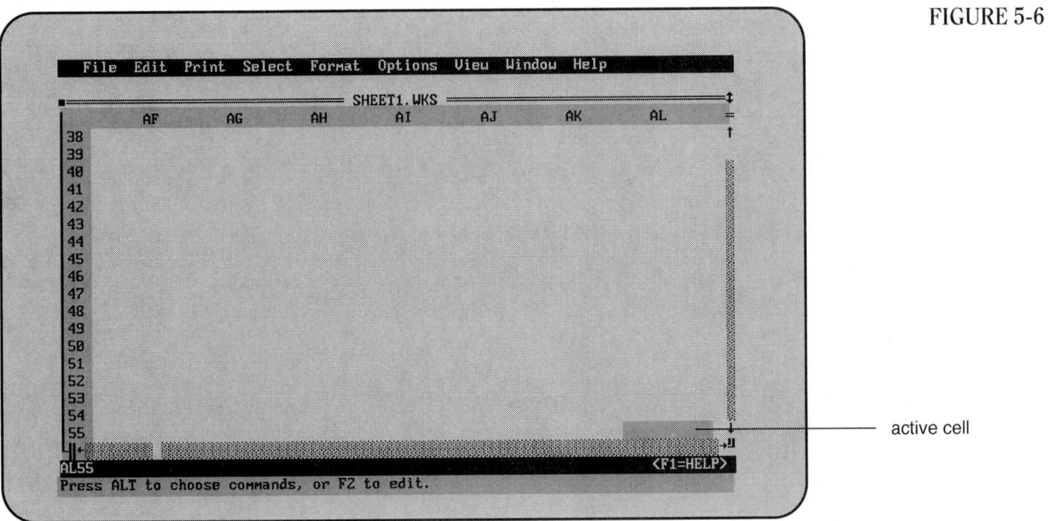

The highlight is positioned in cell AL55.

The shortcut key for the Select>Go To command is (F5). This is the same as in the word processing tool. This time, move the highlight to the last spreadsheet cell, IV4096, using the shortcut key (F5).

To review, the following keys are used to move around the spreadsheet:

Keys	***Action***
Arrow keys	Move the highlight one cell in the direction of the arrow
(CTRL) - (PGDN)	Moves the highlight right one full window
(CTRL) - (PGUP)	Moves the highlight left one full window
(PGDN)	Moves the highlight down one full window
(PGUP)	Moves the highlight up one full window
(CTRL) - (HOME)	Moves the highlight to the cell in the upper-left corner of spreadsheet
(HOME)	Moves the highlight to the left end of row
Select>**G**o To or (F5)	Moves the highlight to the specified cell

Practice moving the highlight around the spreadsheet using each of the keys presented above.

When you are ready to go on,

Move to: A1

Moving Around the Spreadsheet with the Mouse

Note: If you do not have a mouse, skip to the next section, "Entering Labels."

To move from cell to cell within the window, position the mouse pointer on the cell and click the left button.

Move to: D10
Move to: G16
Move to: B4

You may find that using the mouse to move the highlight in a blank spreadsheet is difficult because you cannot tell the exact location of the mouse pointer. When the spreadsheet contains data, it is much easier to position the mouse pointer accurately.

To use the mouse to scroll the spreadsheet one row or column at a time, click on a scroll arrow in the direction you want to move. The scroll arrows are located at the ends of the scroll bars.

To move down three rows, position the mouse pointer on the down arrow and click three times. Rows 4 through 21 should be on the screen.

To scroll continuously, click and hold down the mouse button on a scroll arrow.

To move down continuously by rows, with the mouse pointer on the down scroll arrow, hold down the left button until row 45 comes into view in the window.

To move one window to the left or right, position the mouse pointer on either side of the scroll box in the scroll bar and click the left mouse button.

To move one window to the right, position the mouse pointer to the right of the scroll box in the bottom scroll bar and click the left mouse button.

Columns H through N should be in the window.

To scroll to an approximate location in the file, drag the scroll box. Position the mouse pointer on the scroll box in the right scroll bar and drag it to the middle of the scroll bar.

Rows numbered in the 1900s to 2000s should be displayed on your screen.

To return to row 1, drag the scroll box to the top of the scroll bar.

To review, the following mouse features are used to move around the spreadsheet:

Mouse	**Action**
Click cell location	Moves the highlight to the cell
Click arrow	Moves one row/column in the direction of the arrow
Click above/below scroll box	Moves one window
Click right/left scroll box	Moves one window right/left
Drag scroll box	Moves multiple screens up/down or right/left

Practice moving the highlight around the spreadsheet using each of the mouse procedures presented above.

When you are ready to go on,

Move to: A1

Entering Labels

Now that you know how to move around the spreadsheet, you will begin creating the budget for the Courtside Cafe. By the end of this lab, you will have entered part of the cafe budget as shown in Figure 5-7.

Entries into a spreadsheet are either text or numbers. Text entries are called

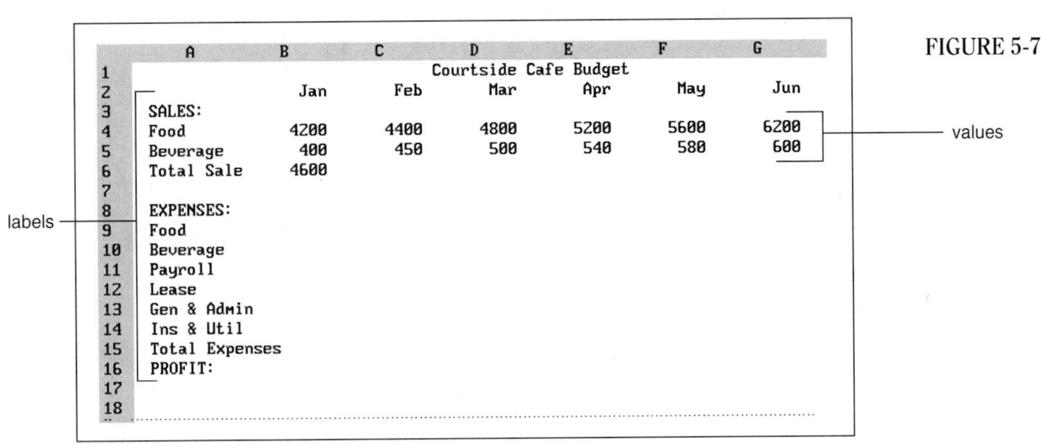

	A	B	C	D	E	F	G
1				Courtside Cafe Budget			
2		Jan	Feb	Mar	Apr	May	Jun
3	SALES:						
4	Food	4200	4400	4800	5200	5600	6200
5	Beverage	400	450	500	540	580	600
6	Total Sale	4600					
7							
8	EXPENSES:						
9	Food						
10	Beverage						
11	Payroll						
12	Lease						
13	Gen & Admin						
14	Ins & Util						
15	Total Expenses						
16	PROFIT:						
17							
18							

FIGURE 5-7

labels and numeric entries are called **values.** Labels create the structure of the spreadsheet and describe other spreadsheet entries. Labels are commonly used for the spreadsheet title and row and column headings. The entries in column A are labels. Values are numbers (data) or results of formulas or functions. The entry in cell B4, 4200, is a value.

The row labels in Column A describe the following:

SALES:

Food	Income from sales of food items
Beverage	Income from sales of beverages
Total Sales	Sum of food and beverage sales

EXPENSES:

Food	Cost of food supplies
Beverage	Cost of beverage supplies
Payroll	Hourly personnel expenses
Lease	Monthly cost of space used by club
Gen & Admin	General and administrative costs
Ins & Util	Direct expenses such as insurance, utilities, etc.
Total Expenses	Sum of Food, Beverage, Payroll, Lease, General and Administrative, and Direct expenses

PROFIT:	Total Sales minus Total Expenses

To create the framework for this spreadsheet, you will begin by entering the row labels in column A. The first row label, SALES:, will be entered in cell A3. To enter the label in all capital letters,

Press: CAPS LOCK

Notice the indicator, CL, appears in the status line. This tells you the CAPS LOCK key is on. The CAPS LOCK key affects only the letter keys. To produce the characters above the number or punctuation keys, you must use SHIFT in combination with the character.

Move to: A3

Type the label exactly as it appears below.

Type: SALES:

Your display screen should be similar to Figure 5-8.

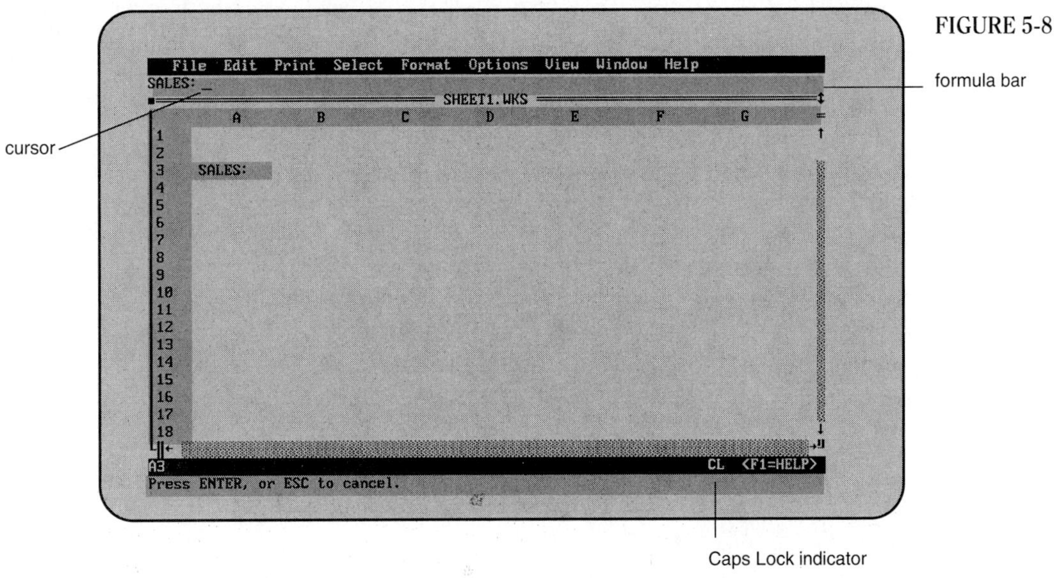

FIGURE 5-8

Several changes have occurred on the screen. As you type, the blank line below the menu bar displays each character. It should display SALES:. This line is called the **formula bar.** The blinking cursor marks your location on the line. Cell A3 displays the entry.

Note: If you made an error while typing the label, use the (Bksp) key (the left-facing arrow key located above the (↵) key) to erase the characters back to the error. Then retype the entry correctly.

Although the label is displayed in the formula bar and in the cell, it has not yet been entered into the cell. To actually enter the label into cell A3,

Press: (↵)

Your display screen should be similar to Figure 5-9.

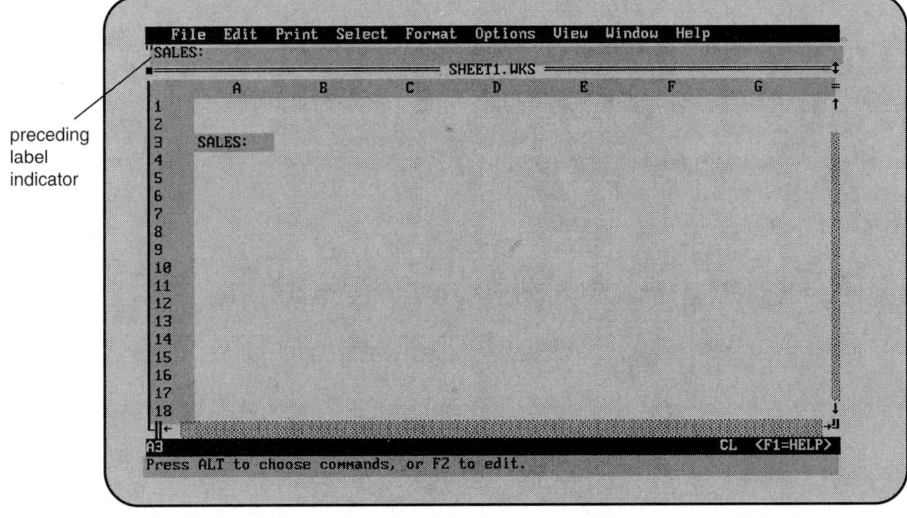

FIGURE 5-9

The label "SALES:" is displayed in cell A3. Notice that the label is still displayed in the formula bar. Whenever the highlight is positioned on a cell containing an entry, it is displayed in the formula bar. Notice the quotation marks (") before the label. The quotes are a **preceding label indicator.** They are entered automatically by Works to signify that the contents of the cell is a label. The preceding label indicator is displayed in the formula bar only. It is not displayed in the cell space.

Note: If you find that the entry in the cell is not correct or that it is in the wrong cell, to remove it, position the highlight on the cell and press (Bksp) and then press (↵). Then reenter the label correctly.

To turn off (CAPS LOCK),

Press: (CAPS LOCK)

To enter the next row heading,

Move to: A4
Type: **Food**

Another way to complete an entry is to move the highlight to any other cell. This will both enter the label or value into the cell and move the highlight in the direction of the arrow. Since the next entry you will make is one cell down,

Press: (↓)

Using (↓) entered the label into the cell. It also moved the highlight one cell down. You are now ready to enter the label "Drinks" into cell A5.

Type: **Drinks**
Press: (↓)

Editing an Entry

Paula wants to change the entry in cell A5 to "Beverages." An entry in a cell can be changed or edited by retyping the entry the way you want it to appear.

Move to: A5
Type: **Beverages**
Press: (↵)

Your display screen should be similar to Figure 5-10.

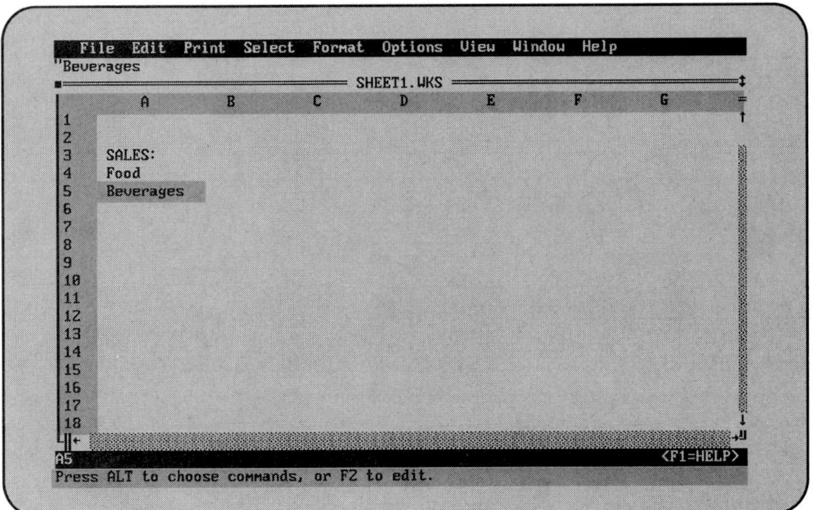

FIGURE 5-10

The new label "Beverages" replaces the cell contents.

Paula wants to change this entry to "Beverage." Rather than retype the entire label again, she can use the EDIT feature to delete the "s." The EDIT key is (F2). This is the same key you use in the word processing tool to turn on EDIT. To use EDIT,

Press: (F2)

Your display screen should be similar to Figure 5-11.

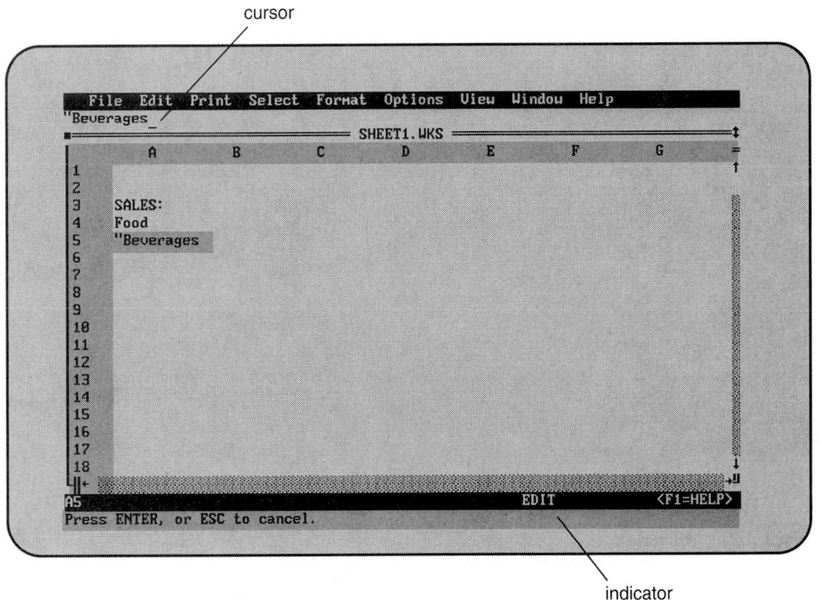

FIGURE 5-11

The status line displays EDIT to tell you this feature is on. The cursor is positioned at the end of the label in the formula bar.

In EDIT, the following keys can be used:

Key	*Action*
(HOME)	Moves the cursor to the beginning of the entry
(END)	Moves the cursor to the end of the entry
(DEL)	Erases the character at the cursor
(Bksp)	Erases the character to the left of the cursor
(→)	Moves the cursor one character right
(←)	Moves the cursor one character left

To delete the "s,"

Press: (Bksp)

The "s" is removed. To complete the edit,

Press: (↓)

You are now ready to enter the next label.

Type: **Total Sales**

Notice that the "T" in Total is not displayed in the cell. This is because the entry is longer than the 10 spaces in the cell, forcing the text to scroll in the cell highlight.

Press: (↵)

The entry is fully displayed even though it is longer than the ten spaces in cell A6. When a label is longer than the cell's column width, it is called a **long entry.** Works will display as much of a label entry as it can. If the cells to the right are empty, the whole label will be displayed. If the cells to the right contain an entry, the overlapping part of the label will not be displayed.

Continue by entering the next six labels in the cells specified. Enter the labels using capital letters where indicated. Use (↓) to complete each entry and move to the next cell.

Cell	Label
A8	**EXPENSES:**
A9	**Food**
A10	**Beverage**
A11	**Payroll**
A12	**Lease**
A13	**General and Administrative**

Paula decides the last entry is too long. To edit it,

Move to: A13
Press: (F2)

To shorten this label to "Gen and Admin"

Press: (HOME)

The cursor moves to the beginning of the cell entry.

Press: (→) (4 times)
Press: (DEL) (4 times)

The word "General" is shortened to "Gen."

Press: (END)
Press: (Bksp) (9 times)

The word "Administrative" is shortened to "Admin."

To complete the entry and see how it appears in the cell space,

Press: (↵)

Your display screen should be similar to Figure 5-12.

FIGURE 5-12

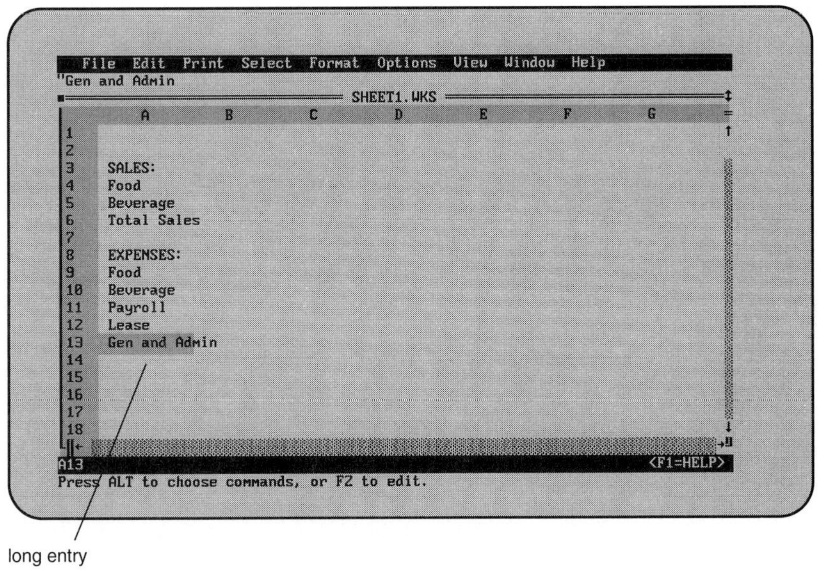

As you can see, editing is particularly useful with long or complicated entries.

Paula still does not like how the label appears. She wants to replace the word "and" with "&." To make this change,

Press: (F2)

To delete the word "and,"

Press: (←) (6 times)
Press: (Bksp) (3 times)

To enter the "&"

Type: **&**
Press: (↵)

The next label to be entered is "Insurance and Utilities." You will practice using the EDIT mode while entering this label in cell A14 as follows:

Move to: A14
Type: **Insurance and Utilities**

Again, Paula decides this label is too long. Even though it has not been entered into cell A14 yet, you can change the mode to Edit so you can use the editing keys to change the entry. To edit this label to "Ins & Util,"

Press: (F2)
Press: (Bksp) (5 times)
Press: (HOME)
Press: (→) (3 times)
Press: (DEL) (10 times)
Press: Space bar
Type: **&**
Press: (↓)

To complete the row labels, enter the following labels in the cells specified:

Cell	Label
A15	**Total Expenses**
A17	**PROFIT:**

Your display screen should be similar to Figure 5-13.

FIGURE 5-13

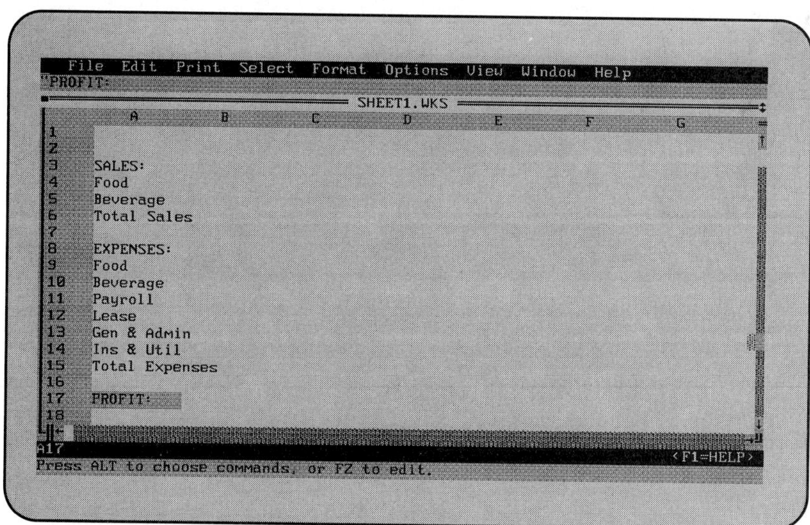

Above the headings, in row 1, Paula wants to enter a title for the spreadsheet.

Move to: D1
Type: **Estimated Budget for the Courtside Cafe**
Press: ↵

Paula decides to change the spreadsheet title.
Use EDIT to change the title in cell D1 to "Courtside Cafe Budget."

Entering the Month Label

The month labels for January through June need to be entered in cells B2 through G2 next.

Move to: B2
Type: **January**
Press: ↵

Your display screen should be similar to Figure 5-14.

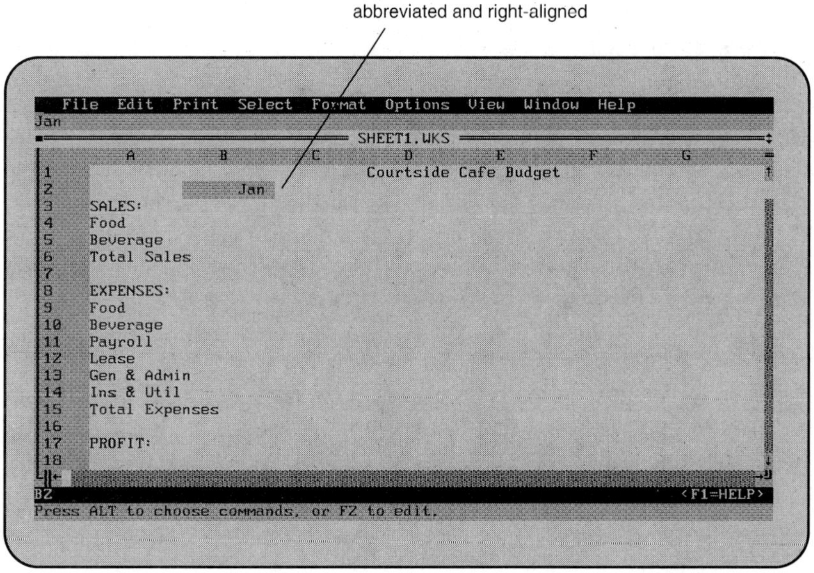

abbreviated and right-aligned

FIGURE 5-14

January has been shortened to the first three letters Jan. In addition, the entry is right-aligned (displayed to the right) in the cell space and there is no preceding label indicator in the formula bar. This is different from the other labels you entered as the row headings. These changes occurred because Works applies a special format to any text that is the name of a month.

Works automatically changes month labels to values by assigning each month a numerical value. This lets you include the cell in a mathematical calculation. If you wanted the month spelled out fully or if you wanted a different abbreviation, you would need to begin the entry with a preceding label indicator ("January). To try this for the February month label,

Move to: C2
Type: **"February**
Press: ↵

The month entry did not change and is displayed in the cell exactly as you entered it. The preceding label indicator you entered before the label forced Works to accept the entry as a label. The quotation marks are not displayed in the cell as part of the entry, just as they are not displayed when Works automatically inserts a preceding label indicator before a label entry.

However, Paula likes how Works displays the months by default and wants to enter the remaining months in this format. To remove the entry from cell C2, with the highlight on this cell,

Press: Bksp
Press: ↵

The entry is cleared from the cell.

Entering a Series

To enter the remaining month headings, Paula could type each one individually or use the Edit>Fill Series command. This command lets you automatically fill any number of cells with a series of numbers or dates.

To use this command, you must first enter the starting value or date into the cell. You have done this already by entering January in cell B2. Next, you need to select the cell with the starting value and the cells to the right or below in which you want the series entered.

The cell with the starting value is B2. The five cells to the right of cell B2 (C2 through G2) will hold the month labels for February through June.

The Select menu commands are used to select cells in the spreadsheet tool just as you use them to select text in the word processor. The highlight should be positioned on a cell at the upper-left or lower-right corner of the block of cells before you use the Select menu. To move to the first cell,

Move to: B2
Select: Select

The first four commands let you select specific cells, an entire row or column, or the entire spreadsheet file. You need to select specific cells in the spreadsheet. When selecting cells in a spreadsheet, you define a **range.** A range is a rectangular block of cells. It can be single cell or a row or column of cells. Figure 5-15, on the next page, shows valid and invalid ranges.

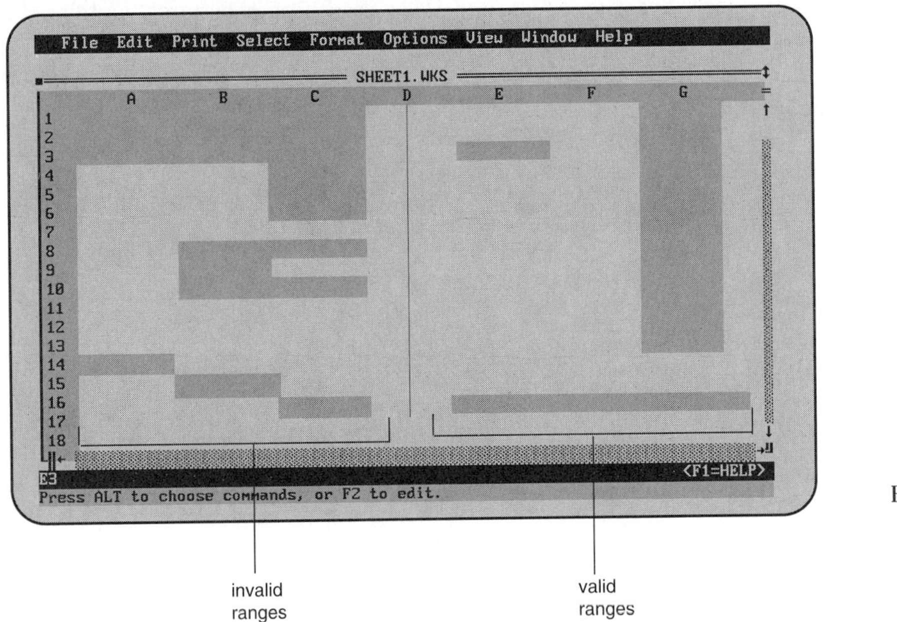

FIGURE 5-15

To select a range of cells,

Select: Cells

EXT (for "extend") appears in the status line to remind you this feature is on. To extend the highlight to the right through cell G2,

Press: (→) (5 times)

Your screen should be similar to Figure 5-16.

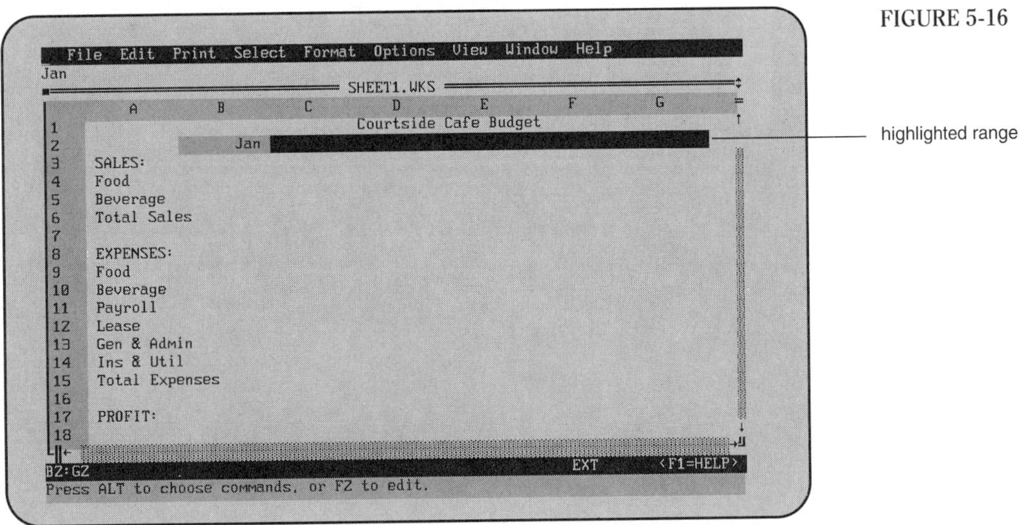

FIGURE 5-16

The range B2 through G2 is highlighted.

The shortcut key for this command is (F8). This is the same as in the word processing tool. Unlike the word processing tool, however, pressing (F8) repeatedly does not extend the highlight. The highlight must be extended using the directional keys. Pressing (F8) simply turns the Select command on and off.

Mouse Note: You can turn on the Select command and specify the range at the same time by clicking on the beginning cell of the range and dragging the mouse pointer to the ending cell of the range.

To fill the selected range with a series of months,

Select: Edit

The spreadsheet tool's Edit menu commands are also similar to the word processing tool's Edit menu. The Edit menu lets you copy, move, and delete entries. Notice, however, in the spreadsheet Edit menu that there is no Undo command.

Select: Fill Series

Your screen should be similar to Figure 5-17.

FIGURE 5-17

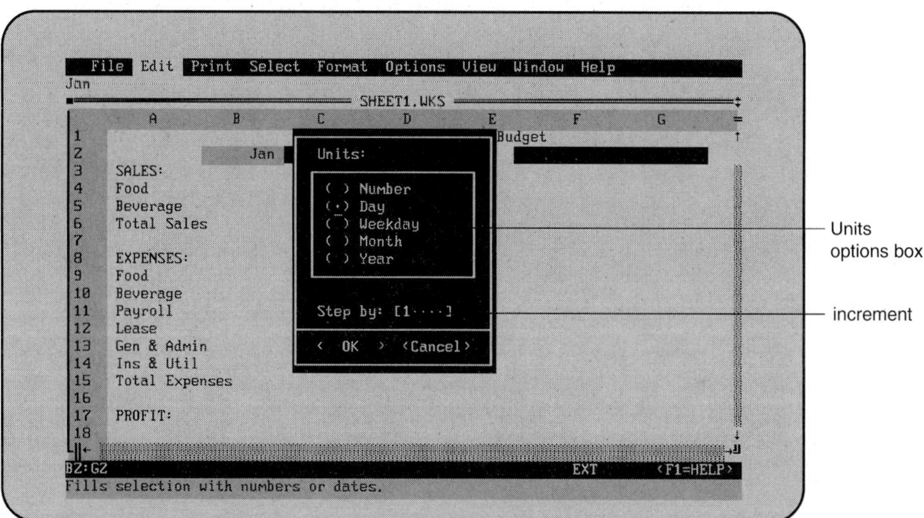

A Units options box is displayed. To specify the type of series to be months, you need to select the Month option. Using (TAB) to move the bullet or pressing (ALT) - M,

Select: Month

If you wanted Works to increase the series by an increment other than one, you would need to specify the number in the Step By: box. In this case, you want to increase the months one month at a time and you do not need to enter a value. To complete the command,

Press: (↵)

Your display screen should be similar to Figure 5-18.

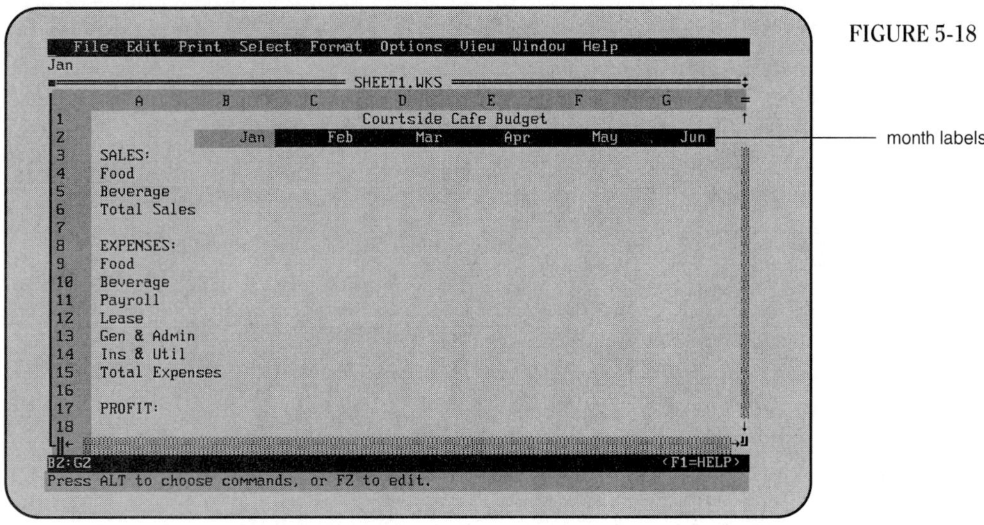

FIGURE 5-18

The selected cells have been filled with a series of consecutive months. To clear the highlight, you can press any directional key.

Press: ↓

Entering Values

The next step is to enter the data or values into the cells.

Paula has estimated that the sales of food items during the month of January will be $4,200. To enter the value 4200 into cell B4,

Move to: B4
Type: **4200**
Press: ↵

Your display screen should be similar to Figure 5-19.

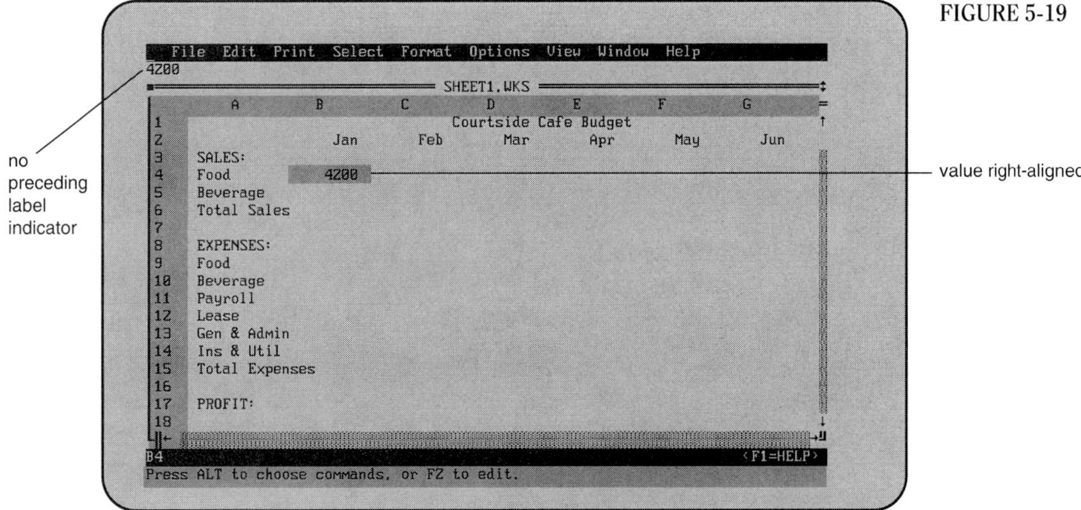

FIGURE 5-19

The value in the formula bar does not begin with the preceding label indicator. This is because Works interpreted this entry as a value. The value 4200 is displayed in cell B4. The value is displayed to the right side of the cell space. One space to the right of the value is left blank. It is reserved for special numeric displays, such as a percent (%) sign. All values are automatically displayed flush right in their cell space, unlike labels, which are flush left.

To complete the data for food sales (row 4), enter the following values into the cells indicated. Use (→) to enter the value and move to the next cell. Use (↵) to enter the last value in the row.

Cell	Value
C4	**4400**
D4	**4800**
E4	**5200**
F4	**5600**
G4	**6200**

Your display screen should be similar to Figure 5-20.

FIGURE 5-20

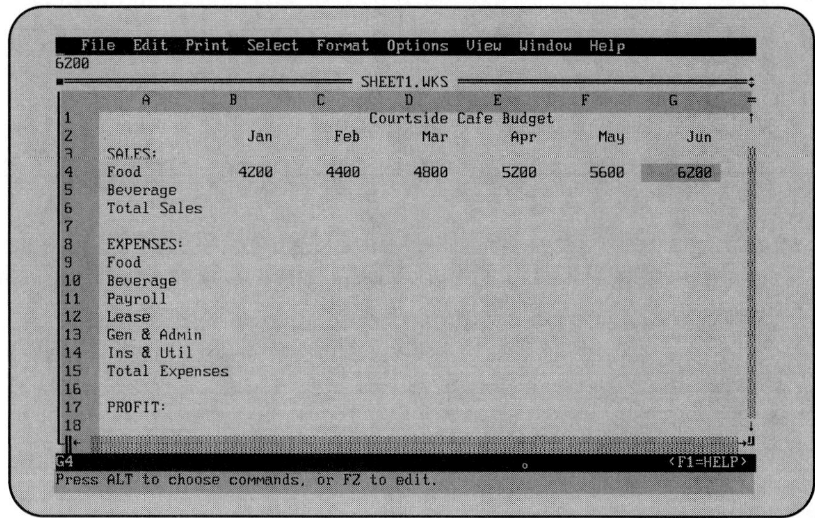

The values for beverage sales need to be entered into cells B5 through G5 next. Use (→) to enter the value and move to the next cell. Use (↵) to enter the last value in the row.

Cell	Value
B5	**350**
C5	**450**
D5	**500**
E5	**540**
F5	**580**
G5	**600**

Your screen should be similar to Figure 5-21.

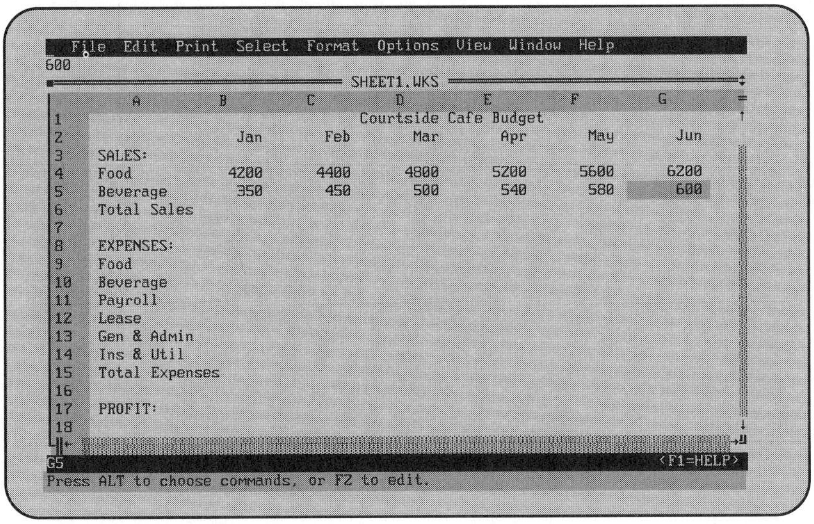

FIGURE 5-21

```
  File  Edit  Print  Select  Format  Options  View  Window  Help
600
                         SHEET1.WKS
        A          B          C          D          E          F          G
1                                   Courtside Cafe Budget
2                 Jan        Feb        Mar        Apr        May        Jun
3   SALES:
4   Food         4200       4400       4800       5200       5600       6200
5   Beverage      350        450        500        540        580        600
6   Total Sales
7
8   EXPENSES:
9   Food
10  Beverage
11  Payroll
12  Lease
13  Gen & Admin
14  Ins & Util
15  Total Expenses
16
17  PROFIT:
18
G5                                                                <F1=HELP>
Press ALT to choose commands, or F2 to edit.
```

Entering Formulas

A **formula** is an entry that performs a calculation. The result of the calculation is displayed in the spreadsheet cell. Numeric values or cell references can be used in a formula. If cell references are used, the calculation is performed using the contents of the cell references. As the values in the referenced cell(s) change, the value calculated by the formula is automatically recalculated. Formulas are the power behind the spreadsheet.

You will enter a formula to calculate the total sales for January. A formula must begin with an equals (=) symbol, which defines the entry as a formula. It can contain any of the following **arithmetic operators:**

+	for addition
-	for subtraction
/	for division
*	for multiplication
^	for exponentiation

Cell references can be typed in either upper- or lowercase letters. If you enter a formula using the wrong format, Works will display a message and change to EDIT to let you correct your entry.

The cells containing the sales values for January are B4 and B5. To sum the values in these cells, enter the following formula in cell B6.

Move to: B6
Type: **=B4+B5**
Press: ↵

Note: If you forget to begin a formula with an = symbol, Works interprets the entry as a label and displays the formula in the cell.

Your display screen should be similar to Figure 5-22.

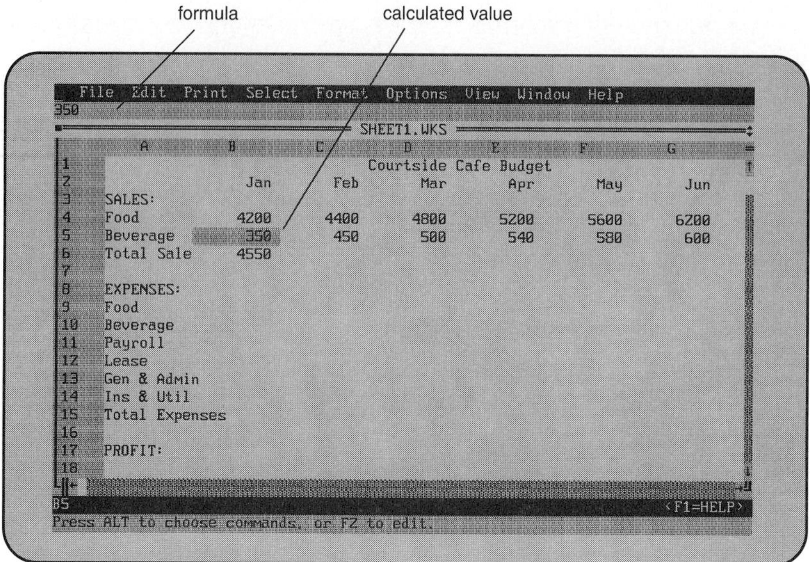

FIGURE 5-22

The formula appears in the formula bar. The result of the formula, "4550," is displayed in cell B6.

Notice that the label in cell A6 is now displayed as "Total Sale." This is because the label exceeds the cell width of 10 spaces. The new entry in cell B6 causes the label to be interrupted after 10 characters.

Move to: A6

The formula bar shows the complete row label as entered into the cell. Only the display of the label in cell A6 has been interrupted. You will learn how to change the width of a column in the next lab so that the entire label can be displayed.

Recalculating the Spreadsheet

Paula feels that she has underestimated the January beverage sales. She wants to change this value to 400.

Move to: B5
Type: **400**
Press: ↵

The formula in cell B6 has been automatically recalculated. The value displayed is now "4600." The **automatic recalculation** of a formula whenever a value in a referenced cell in the formula changes is one of the most powerful features of electronic spreadsheets.

In the next lab you will complete the spreadsheet by entering the remaining values and formulas.

Before saving the spreadsheet, enter your first initial and last name in cell A1. Put the date in cell A2 (for example, 9-9-93).

Saving the Spreadsheet

To save the current spreadsheet in a file on the your data diskette, the File>Save As command is used. The procedure is the same as saving a word processing file.

Select: File>Save As

The Save dialog box is displayed so that you can assign the file another filename. The default filename SHEET.WKS is displayed in the "Save file as:" text box.

Select the appropriate drive for your system where you want Works to save the file.

Next, you need to specify a new filename. To save the spreadsheet as it appears on the display in a new file named CAFE,

Type: CAFE
Press: ↵

The spreadsheet data that was on your screen and in the computer's memory is now saved on your data diskette in a new file called CAFE.WKS. The file is automatically saved with the file extension .WKS. This file extension identifies this file as a spreadsheet file. The new filename is displayed in the title bar.

Printing the Spreadsheet

If you have printer capability, you can print a copy of the spreadsheet. If necessary, turn the printer on and check to see that it is on-line. Adjust the paper so that the perforation is just above the printer scale (behind the ribbon).

Select: Print>Page Setup & Margins

Your screen should be similar to Figure 5-23.

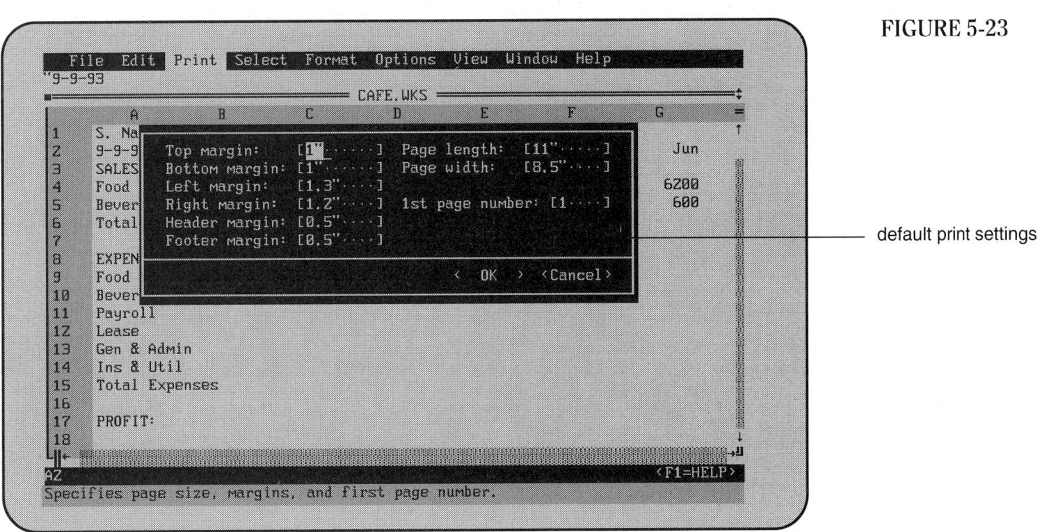

FIGURE 5-23

The dialog box displays Works' preset page setup. The default settings are displayed to the right of each option. For example, Works is preset to print on letter-size 8.5-

inch by 11-inch paper. The default setting for this paper size is displayed to the right of the Page length and Page width options. You do not need to change the paper size unless you want to print on paper of a different size, such as legal paper.

The settings Paula wants to change are the right and left margin sizes. The **margins** are the spaces between the edges of the paper and the printed area. The top and bottom margins are preset at 1 inch each. These settings are acceptable. However, the left and right margin settings are preset at 1.3 inches and 1.2 inches, respectively. She wants to reduce the size of each of these margins to .5 inch. This will allow more text to be printed on a line. To change the left margin setting first,

Select: Left (use TAB to move to the Left margin option or press ALT - E)
Type: .5

You do not need to enter the inches symbol ("). Works assumes the setting you enter is in inches. To change the right margin,

Select: **R**ight
Type: .5

To complete the command,

Press: ↵

Now you are ready to print the spreadsheet.

Select: Print>**P**rint

The Print dialog box is displayed. You will use the default print options and do not need to specify any settings.

If you are using a floppy disk system, when directed, insert the Accessories disk and the Working Copy disk.

To complete the command by selecting the default Print command button,

Press: ↵

Your printer should be printing out the spreadsheet. Your printed output should look like Figure 5-24.

FIGURE 5-24

```
S. Name                               Courtside Cafe Budget
9-9-93          Jan        Feb        Mar        Apr        May        Jun
SALES:
Food            4200       4400       4800       5200       5600       6200
Beverage         400        450        500        540        580        600
Total Sale      4600

EXPENSES:
Food
Beverage
Payroll
Lease
Gen & Admin
Ins & Util
Total Expenses

PROFIT:
```

The full width of the spreadsheet is printed on a single page. If you had not made the left and right margins smaller, the spreadsheet would have printed on two pages, with the June column of data on the second page.

If you want to quit or exit the Works 2.0 program at this time,

Select: File>Exit

Works prompts you to specify whether you want to save the changes to the file before exiting the program. The only changes made to the file since last saving it were to specify the new margin settings. To save these settings with the file,

Select: Yes

If you plan to continue using Works, close and save the CAFE file. To do this,

Select: File>Close>Yes

Key Terms

spreadsheet	row number	formula bar
menu bar	column letter	preceding label indicator
window	cell	long entry
status line	active cell	range
message line	cell reference	formula
workspace	scrolling	arithmetic operator
row	label	automatic recalculation
column	value	margins

Matching

1. CTRL - PGDN	_____	**a.**	moves the highlight to a specified cell
2. *	_____	**b.**	turns EXT on and off
3. F5	_____	**c.**	moves the window one full window right
4. "123	_____	**d.**	a label entry
5. .WKS	_____	**e.**	a cell reference
6. F2	_____	**f.**	a number or result of a formula or function
7. C19+A21	_____	**g.**	an arithmetic operator
8. F8	_____	**h.**	accesses EDIT mode
9. D11	_____	**i.**	a formula summing the values in two cells
10. value	_____	**j.**	a spreadsheet file extension

Practice Exercises

1. Identify the parts of the spreadsheet screen shown below. The first one has been completed for you.

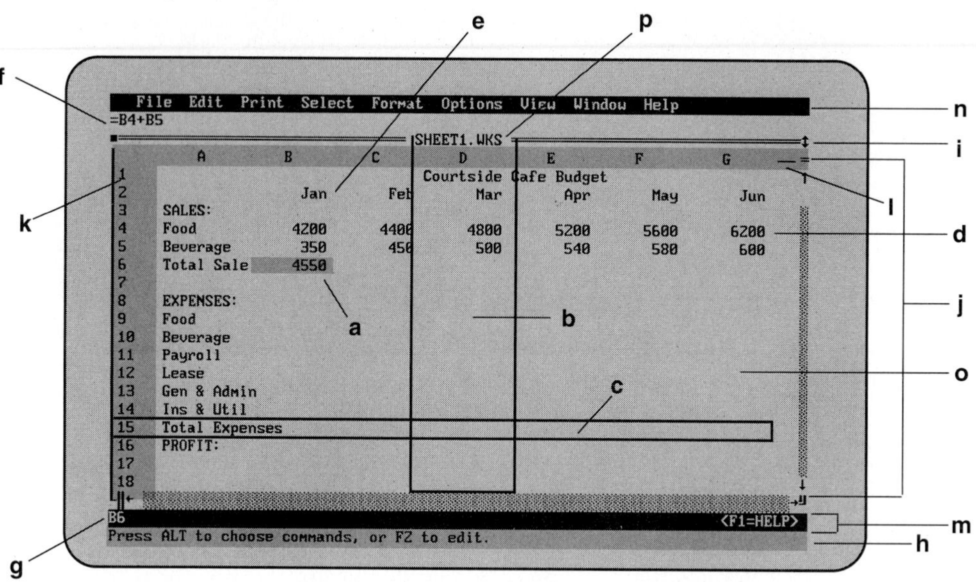

a. **highlight** ____________

b. ____________

c. ____________

d. ____________

e. ____________

f. ____________

g. ____________

h. ____________

i. ____________

j. ____________

k. ____________

l. ____________

m. ____________

n. ____________

o. ____________

p. ____________

2. Retrieve the spreadsheet file SURVEY.WKS. This spreadsheet contains data from a survey conducted over the years 1978 to 1990. It shows the percentage of college freshmen who expressed interest in careers in computers, education, and business. It contains many errors that you will correct as follows:

- Change the title in cell D2 to all uppercase characters.
- Change the title in cell D4 to "Percent of College Freshmen."
- Enter the years (1978-1990) in columns C through G of row 8. Use the Edit>Fill Series command to enter the series of numbers with an increment of 3.

- Change the values in the following cells:

Cell	**Value**
D10	**5**
C14	**19**
F12	**5.5**
G14	**24**

- Check the formulas in row 16. Correct as needed.
- Enter your name in cell A1. Enter the date in cell A2.
- Save the file as SURVEY1.
- Print a copy of the file, using 1" left and right margins.

3. You have just finished paying off the loan on your old car and you are considering purchasing a new 1992 model car. The new car costs $12,300 and the trade-in value on your old car is $3,700. You can borrow the difference with a four-year loan of 8.9%. You decide to create a spreadsheet to help you analyze whether you should keep the old car or trade it in on a new one.

- Create the spreadsheet shown below by entering the labels and values in the cells indicated.

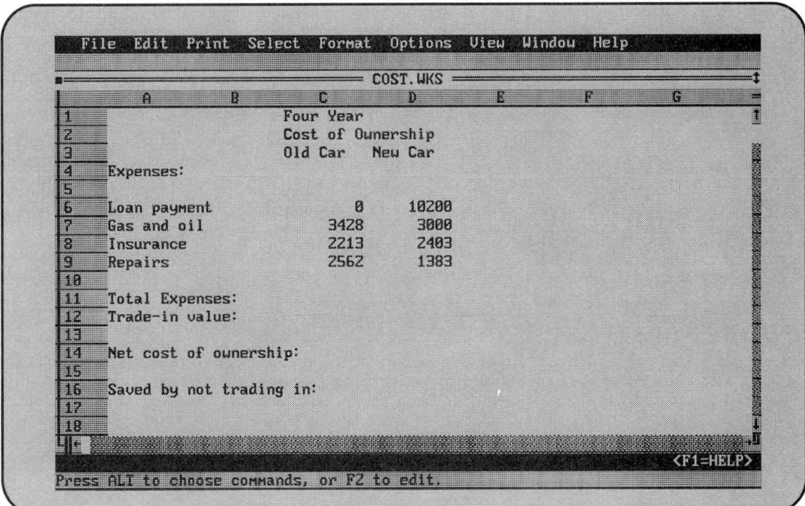

- Enter the formula to calculate the Total expenses for the old and new car.
- Enter your name in cell A1 and the date in cell A2.
- Save the spreadsheet as COST.
- Print the spreadsheet.

You will complete this spreadsheet as a practice exercise in the next lab.

4. You are the manager of Fine Things Jewelry Store. You are having a sales campaign that will reward the salesperson who has the highest average sales over a four-week period. The campaign has already been in progress for two weeks.

- Create the spreadsheet shown below by entering the labels and values in the cells indicated.

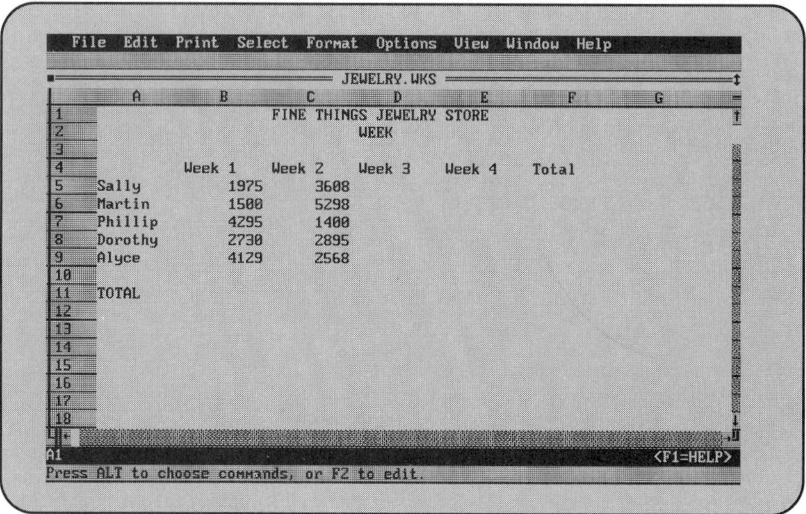

- Enter the formula to calculate the total sales for the two weeks.
- Enter your name in cell A1 and the date in cell A2.
- Save your completed spreadsheet as JEWELRY.
- Print a copy of the spreadsheet.

You will complete the spreadsheet as a practice exercise in the next lab.

5. The Assistant Director of the Zoo wants to prepare a financial summary for the years 1990, 1991, and 1992.

- Create the spreadsheet shown below by entering the labels and values in the cells indicated.

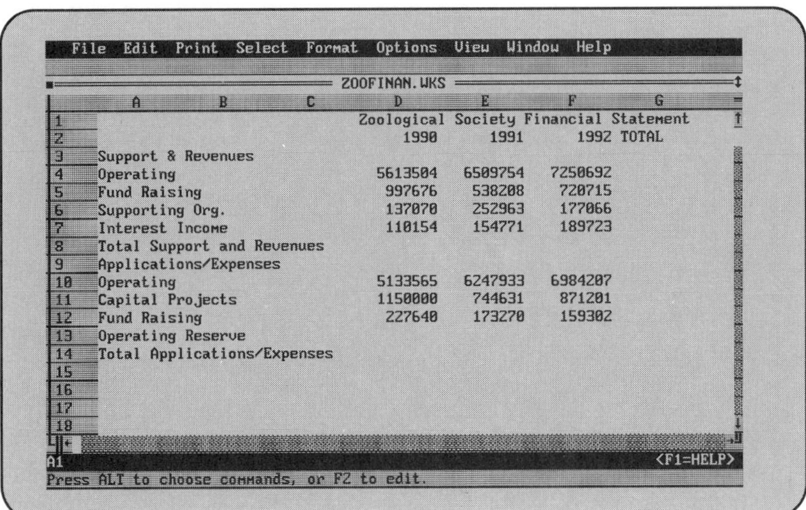

	A	B	C	D	E	F	G
1				Zoological	Society	Financial	Statement
2				1990	1991	1992	TOTAL
3	Support & Revenues						
4	Operating			5613504	6509754	7250692	
5	Fund Raising			997676	538208	720715	
6	Supporting Org.			137070	252963	177066	
7	Interest Income			110154	154771	189723	
8	Total Support and Revenues						
9	Applications/Expenses						
10	Operating			5133565	6247933	6984207	
11	Capital Projects			1150000	744631	871201	
12	Fund Raising			227640	173270	159302	
13	Operating Reserve						
14	Total Applications/Expenses						
15							
16							
17							
18							

- Edit the row labels indicated:

  A3: All capital letters

  A4 through A7: Enter five blank spaces before each label

  A8: TOTAL S & R

  A9: All capital letters

  A10 through 13: Enter five blank spaces before each label

  A14: TOTAL A/E

- Enter formulas to calculate the TOTAL S&R (D8) and TOTAL A/E (D14) for 1990 only.
- Enter the formula to calculate the Operating Reserve for 1990 in cell D13. This value is calculated by subtracting the operating (D10), capital projects (D11), and fund-raising expenses (D12) from the total support and revenues (D8).
- Enter your name in cell A1 and the date in cell A2.
- Save the spreadsheet as ZOOFINAN.
- Print the spreadsheet using left and right margin settings of .5 inch.

You will continue working on this spreadsheet as a practice exercise in the next lab.

6. The income statement is a thermometer by which a business measures its financial health. The income statement is usually prepared at regular intervals (monthly, quarterly, and yearly) to show profitability and cost of operation.

- Create the spreadsheet for the income statement shown below by entering the labels in the cells indicated.

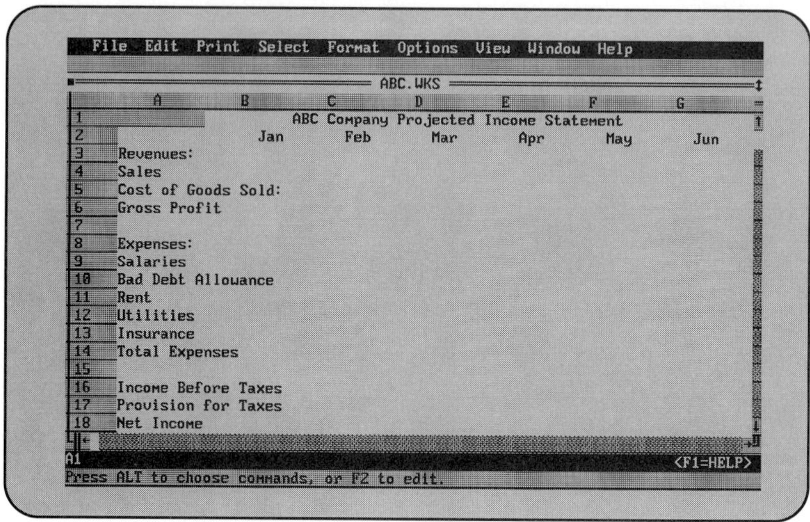

- Edit the row labels indicated:

  C1: ABC Semi-Annual Income Statement

  A3: All capital letters

  A4: Enter three blank spaces before label

  A8: All capital letters

  A9 through A13: Enter three blank spaces before each label

- Enter the following sales and cost of goods sold values in the appropriate cells for the months indicated:

	Sales	Cost of Goods Sold
Jan	68572	47355
Feb	72439	49782
Mar	67492	46978
Apr	72905	51025
May	77589	53112
Jun	78213	53475

- Enter a formula to calculate the Gross Profit (B6) for January only. This value is calculated by subtracting the cost of goods sold (B5) from the sales value (B4).

- Enter the January expenses as follows:

Salaries	10% of sales
Bad Debt Allowance	500
Rent	1000
Utilities	300
Insurance	225

- Enter the formula to calculate the total expenses for January in cell B14.
- Enter your name in cell A1 and the date in cell A2.
- Save your completed spreadsheet as ABC.
- Print a copy of the spreadsheet using left and right margin settins of .5 inch.

You will continue working on this spreadsheet as a practice exercise in the next lab.

Command Summary

Keys	Action
Arrow keys	Move highlight one cell in direction of arrow
CTRL - PGDN	Moves highlight right one full window
CTRL - PGUP	Moves highlight left one full window
PGDN	Moves highlight down one full window
PGUP	Moves highlight up one full window
CTRL - HOME	Moves highlight to cell in upper-left corner of spreadsheet
HOME	Moves highlight to left end of row
CAPS LOCK	Produces capital letters

Command	Shortcut	Action	Page
File>**C**reate New File>New **S**preadsheet		Opens new spreadsheet	136
File>Save**A**s		Saves file to disk with new filename	159
File>**C**lose		Closes file	161
File>E**x**it		Exits Works	161
Edit>Fi**l**l Series		Fills range with series	152
Print>Page Setup & **M**argins		Sets printed page formats	159
Select>C**e**lls	F8	Selects range	153
Select>**G**o To	F5	Moves highlight to specified cell	140
	F2	Edits cell entry	147

LAB

Creating a Spreadsheet: Part 2

6

OBJECTIVES

In this lab you will learn how to:

1. Copy cell contents.
2. Use the POINT mode.
3. Enter functions.
4. Erase cell contents.
5. Change column widths.
6. Insert and delete rows.
7. Insert and delete columns.
8. Set cell display format.
9. Save and replace a file.

CASE STUDY

During Lab 5, Paula Nichols, the manager of the Courtside Cafe at the Sports Club, defined the row and column labels for the cafe budget spreadsheet. She entered the expected food and beverage sales figures. She also entered a formula to calculate the total sales for food and beverages for January.

In Lab 6, you will continue to build the spreadsheet for the cafe. The data for the expenses needs to be entered into the spreadsheet. The formulas to calculate the total sales, expenses, and profit also need to be entered. The physical appearance of the spreadsheet will be improved. This will be done by adjusting column widths, inserting and deleting rows and columns, and underlining the column labels.

Copying a Cell

Load the Works 2.0 program. Your data diskette should be in the drive appropriate for your computer system.

Open the spreadsheet CAFE1.WKS.

Your display screen should be similar to Figure 6-1.

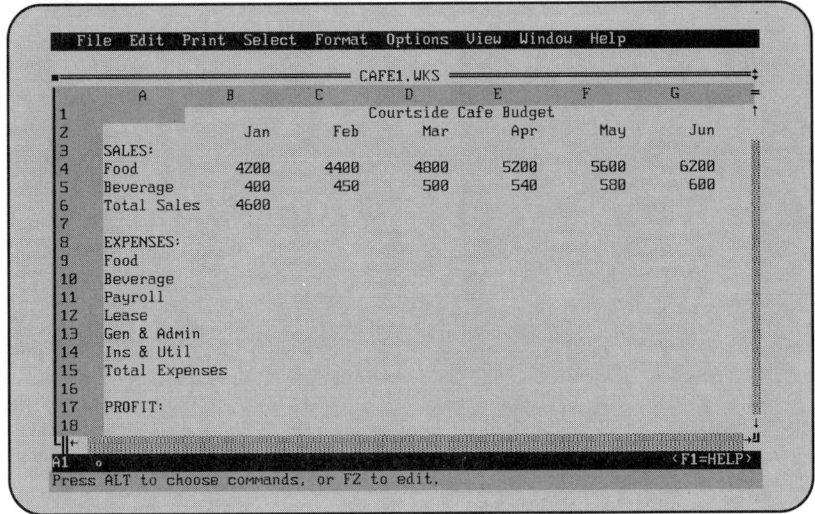

FIGURE 6-1

This spreadsheet should be the same as the spreadsheet you created in Lab 5 and saved as CAFE.WKS on your data diskette.

Paula needs to enter the values for the expenses (rows 9 through 14) into the spreadsheet. The food and beverage costs are estimated by using a formula to calculate the value as a percent of sales. The remaining expenses are estimated over the six-month period. They are the same for each month.

In Lab 5, the food and beverage sales values for January through June were entered individually into each cell because the value changed from month to month. But sometimes a value or formula in a cell is the same across several cells. Then it is faster to enter the information by using the Edit>Copy command.

Paula will begin by entering the estimated expenses for Payroll first. She estimates that payroll expenses, based on the average hourly rate of pay and the number of hours needed per month to operate the cafe, will be $2,250 per month.

Move to: B11
Type: **2250**
Press: (↵)

The value in cell B11 is the same value that needs to be entered in cells C11 through G11 for February through June. You could type the same amount into each month or **copy** the value in B11 into the other cells by using the Edit>Copy command. The shortcut key for this command is (SHIFT) - (F3). This is the same as in the word processing tool.

To use the Edit>Copy command, with the cell pointer in cell B11,

Select: Edit>Copy
⋙ (SHIFT) - (F3)

Your display screen should be similar to Figure 6-2.

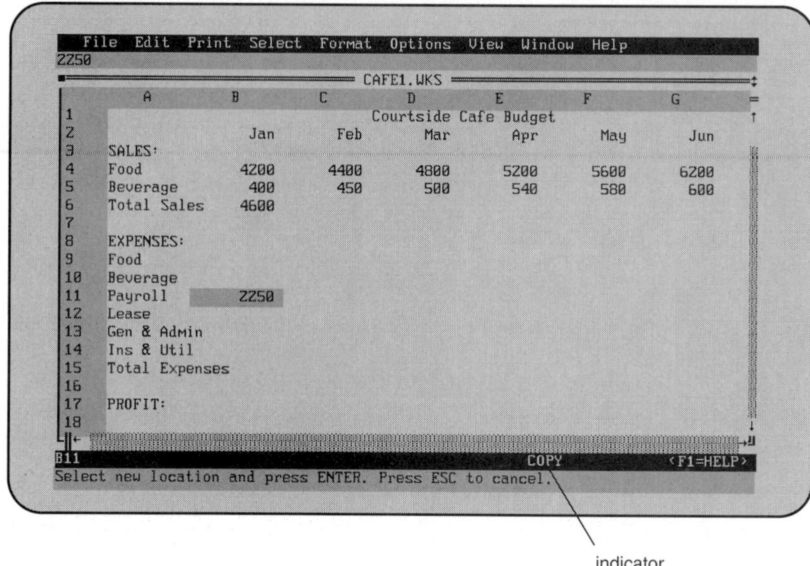

FIGURE 6-2

The status line displays the indicator "COPY" and the message line displays the message "Select new location and press ENTER. Press ESC to cancel."

To specify the new location, C11,

Press: →
Press: ↵

The value 2250 is entered into cell C11. One of the major advantages to using the Copy command is that it eliminates the possibility of typing errors.

Using the same procedure, enter the value 2250 in cells D11 through G11. When you are done, your screen should be similar to Figure 6-3.

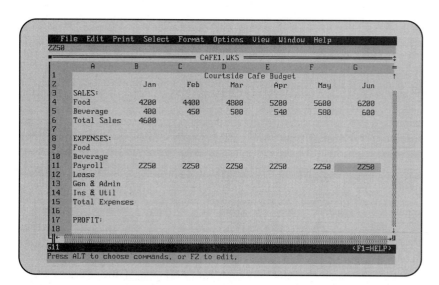

FIGURE 6-3

```
 File  Edit  Print  Select  Format  Options  View  Window  Help
2250
                         CAFE1.WKS
         A          B         C         D         E         F         G
1                                Courtside Cafe Budget
2                  Jan       Feb       Mar       Apr       May       Jun
3  SALES:
4  Food           4200      4400      4800      5200      5600      6200
5  Beverage        400       450       500       540       580       600
6  Total Sales    4600
7
8  EXPENSES:
9  Food
10 Beverage
11 Payroll        2250      2250      2250      2250      2250      2250
12 Lease
13 Gen & Admin
14 Ins & Util
15 Total Expenses
16
17 PROFIT:
18
G11                                                         <F1=HELP>
Press ALT to choose commands, or F2 to edit.
```

Copying a Range

Next, you will enter the value 500 for the Lease expense for January in cell B12 and copy it across row 12 for February through June. To do this,

Move to: B12
Type: **500**
Press: ⏎

You could copy the value in B12 to C12 and then from C12 to D12 as you just did using Copy>Edit. However, there is a faster way to copy cell contents when you are copying to adjacent cells in the spreadsheet. The Edit>Fill Right or Edit>Fill Down command is used to do this. First, you need to select the cell you want to copy and the cells where you want to copy to. With the highlight on cell B12,

Select: Select>C**e**lls
⋙ F8

"EXT" appears in the status line. The cell whose contents you want to copy is highlighted. To extend the selection to include the cells you want to copy to,

Press: → (5 times)

The range B12 through G12 should be highlighted.

Next, to fill the cells to the right of the cell whose contents you want to copy,

Select: Edit>Fill **R**ight

Your screen should be similar to Figure 6-4.

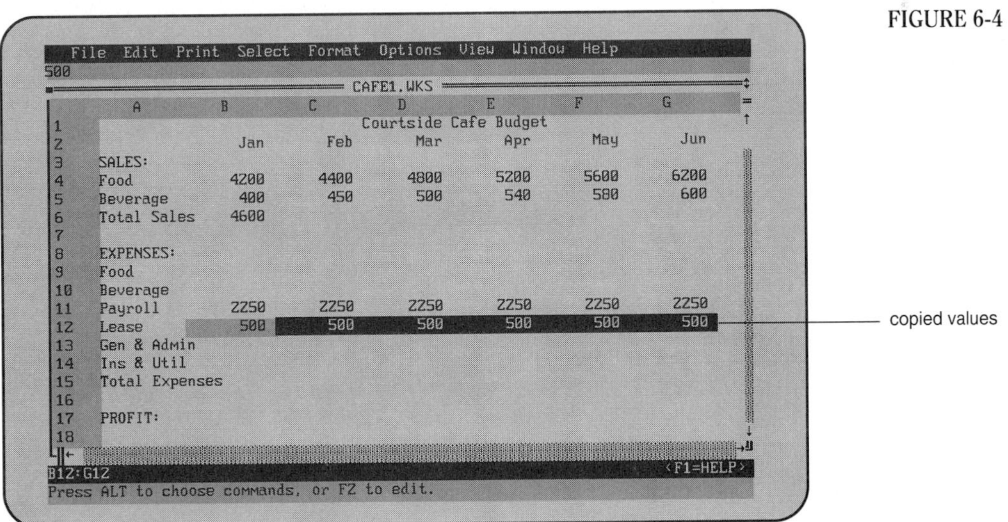

FIGURE 6-4

The value 500 is quickly copied into cells C12 through G12. Using the Edit>Fill Right command is much faster than using Edit>Copy repeatedly, especially when you have a large spreadsheet. The Edit>Copy command is used when you want to copy to nonadjacent cells.

Like the Edit>Copy command, this command also improves the accuracy of your work by eliminating the entry of incorrect data due to typing errors.

The values for General & Administrative (Gen & Admin) and the Insurance and Utility (Ins & Util) expenses need to be entered next. For January, enter the values of 175 for General & Administrative expense and 975 for Insurance and Utility expenses as follows:

Move to: B13
Type: **175**
Move to: B14
Type: **975**
Press: ↵

To copy the contents of cells B13 and B14 to two rows at the same time,

Press: F8

A range can be selected from any direction, as long as you begin the range on a corner cell. To highlight the range B14 through G13,

Move to: G13
Select: **E**dit>Fill **R**ight

Your display screen should be similar to Figure 6-5.

FIGURE 6-5

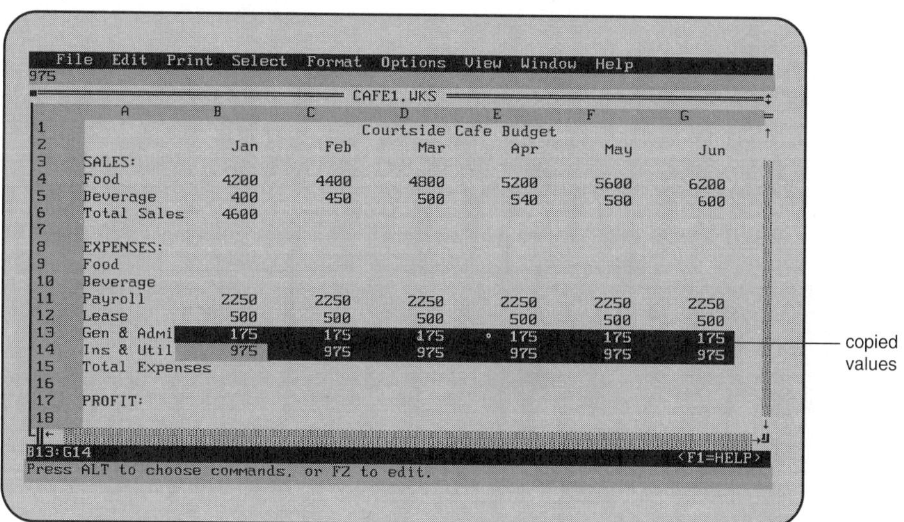

The values for the Gen & Admin and Ins & Util expenses for January (cells B13 and B14) were quickly copied into the February through June cells (C13 through G13 and C14 through G14.)

Pointing Formulas

The final two expenses that need to be entered into the spreadsheet are for Food and Beverage expenses. Paula has estimated that the cost of food and beverage supplies will be 30 percent of food and beverage sales each month.

The formulas to calculate these values are:

Food expense = monthly food sales * 30%
Beverage expense = monthly beverage sales * 30%

Instead of typing the cell reference in this formula as you did in Lab 5, you will **point** to the cell. To do this,

Move to: B9
Type: =
Press: ↑

The indicator in the status line displays POINT. When POINT is displayed, you can move the highlight to any spreadsheet cell. Works will enter the cell reference of the highlighted cell into the cell containing the formula. Because the highlight is on cell B8, the formula displays the cell reference, B8, in the formula bar and the beginning cell. As you move the highlight, the cell reference in the formula will change to the cell reference of the cell the highlight is on. To point to the cell containing the January food sales, cell B4,

Press: ↑ (4 times)

Your screen should be similar to Figure 6-6.

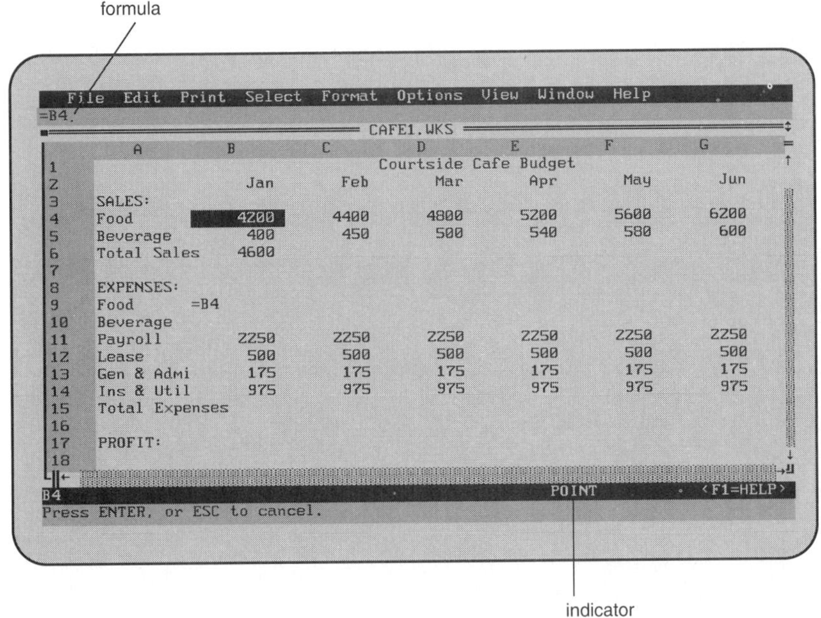

FIGURE 6-6

The cell reference, B4, is entered following the = sign in the formula. To continue building the formula by entering the arithmetic operator for multiplication,

Type: *

The cell highlight returns to the beginning cell in which you entered the formula and POINT is no longer displayed in the status line. To continue building the formula by multiplying the value in the referenced cell (B4) times 30 percent,

Type: 30%
Press: ⏎

The calculated value of 1260 is displayed in cell B9 and the formula is displayed in the formula bar. Works automatically converts the percentage in the formula to its decimal equivalent. You could also have entered .30 instead of 30% and the same result would be calculated.

Using the POINT feature to enter cell references in a formula lets you see the cell being used in the formula, making the entry more accurate and less prone to typing errors. Also, for large formulas pointing is faster than typing the cell references.

Copying Formulas

The formulas to calculate the February through June food expenses (C9 through G9) need to be entered next.

Copy the formula from the January expense cell (B9) to make these calculations using the Edit>Fill Right command. The calculated values are displayed in the specified cell range.

Let's look at the formulas as they were copied into the cells.

Move to: C9

Your display screen should be similar to Figure 6-7.

FIGURE 6-7

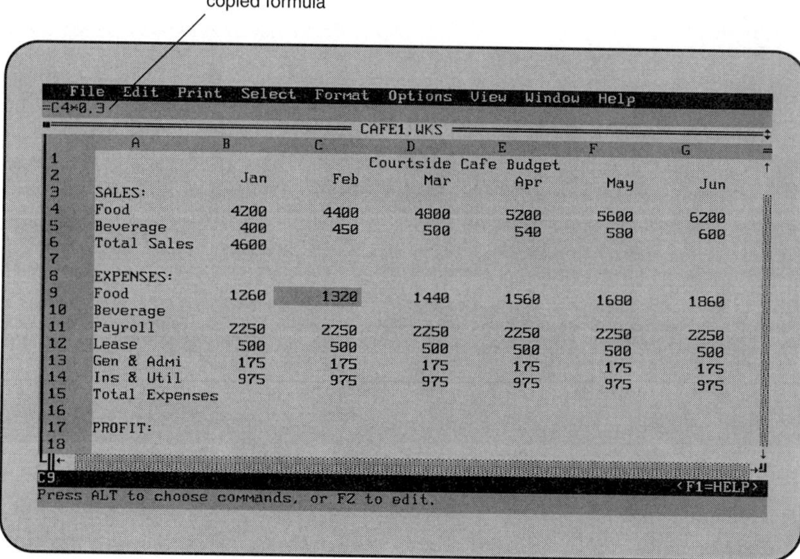

The value “1320” is displayed in the cell. Look at the formula displayed in the formula bar. It is =C4*0.3. The formula to calculate the February food expense is not an exact duplicate of the formula used to calculate the January food expense (=B4*0.3). Instead, the cell address referenced in the formula has been changed to reflect the new column location. This is because the formula uses a **relative cell reference.** A relative cell reference is a cell or range address in a formula whose location is interpreted by Works as relative to the cell that contains the formula. When the formula in B9 was copied, the referenced cell in the formula was automatically adjusted to reflect the new column location, so that the relative relationship between the referenced cell and the new column location is maintained.

Look at the formulas as they appear in the formula bar as you move to cells D9 through G9. The formula has changed to reflect the new column location in each, and it appropriately calculates the value based on the food sales for each month.

The formula to calculate Beverage expenses needs to be entered next. This formula will take the monthly beverage sales values in row 5 and multiply them by 30%.

Enter the formula =B5*.30 using pointing in cell B10. Copy it across the row through column G.

Move across the row and look at how the formulas have been adjusted to reflect the new column location.

Finally, copy the formula to calculate Total Sales in cell B6 across the row through H6. Examine the formulas to see how the cell references adjusted.

When you are done, your screen should be similar to Figure 6-8.

FIGURE 6-8

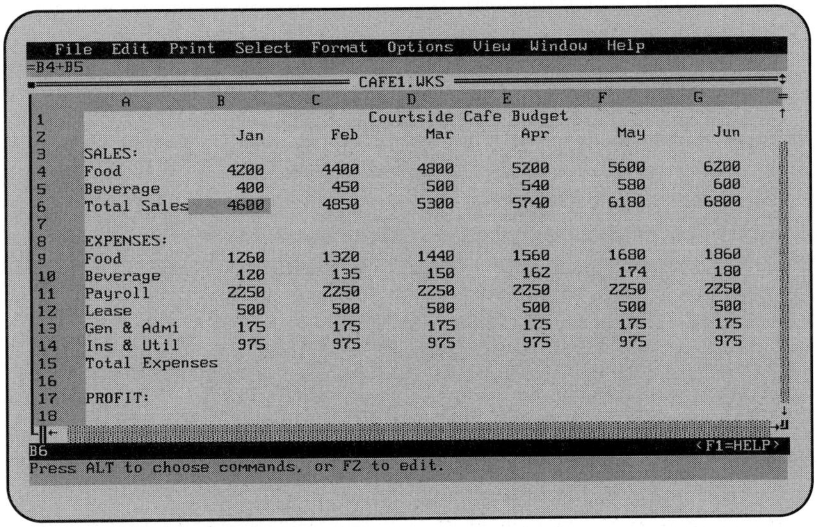

File Edit Print Select Format Options View Window Help
=B4+B5
CAFE1.WKS

	A	B	C	D	E	F	G
1				Courtside Cafe Budget			
2		Jan	Feb	Mar	Apr	May	Jun
3	SALES:						
4	Food	4200	4400	4800	5200	5600	6200
5	Beverage	400	450	500	540	580	600
6	Total Sales	4600	4850	5300	5740	6180	6800
7							
8	EXPENSES:						
9	Food	1260	1320	1440	1560	1680	1860
10	Beverage	120	135	150	162	174	180
11	Payroll	2250	2250	2250	2250	2250	2250
12	Lease	500	500	500	500	500	500
13	Gen & Admi	175	175	175	175	175	175
14	Ins & Util	975	975	975	975	975	975
15	Total Expenses						
16							
17	PROFIT:						
18							

B6 <F1=HELP>
Press ALT to choose commands, or F2 to edit.

Entering a Function

Now that all the expenses have been entered into the spreadsheet, the monthly total expenses can be calculated.

Move to: B15

You could use a formula similar to the formula used to calculate the total food and beverage sales for January in cell B6 (=B4+B5). The formula in cell B15 would be =B9+B10+B11+B12+B13+B14.

However, Works has a set of built-in formulas called **functions** that perform certain types of calculations automatically. There are 57 financial, statistical, and scientific functions. Functions help you enter complex calculations quickly and easily. They are a shorthand for most common calculations.

The structure or **syntax** of a function is:

=Function name(argument1,argument2...)

All functions begin with the = symbol followed by the function name. Most require that you enter one or more **arguments** following the function name. An argument is the data the function uses to perform the calculation. It can be a number, a cell address, or a range of cells. The argument is enclosed in parentheses. Multiple arguments are separated by commas. Do not enter a space between the function name and arguments.

The function you will use to calculate a sum of a range of cells is SUM(Range Reference0,Range Reference1,...). A range reference is one of many different arguments that may be required by the function. **Range references** may be numbers, cell references, cell ranges, formulas, or a combination of these, each separated by a comma.

You can enter a function in either upper- or lowercase characters. As with formulas, if you incorrectly enter a function, Works 2.0 will display a message and change to EDIT to allow you to correct your entry. Alternatively, you could press (ESC) to clear the entry and then retype it correctly.

To enter the function to calculate the total expenses for January in cell B15,

Type: **=SUM(**

Next, you need to enter the range reference. You can type the cell reference or specify the cell or range by pointing. To use pointing,

Move to: B9

Next, you need to enter a colon (:). This tells Works to include all cells selected from the first cell to the last cell.

Mouse Note: Instead of typing a colon, you can click on the first cell and drag to the last cell of the range. Works will enter the colon automatically for you.

Type: **:**
Move to: B14

Your screen should be similar to Figure 6-9.

FIGURE 6-9

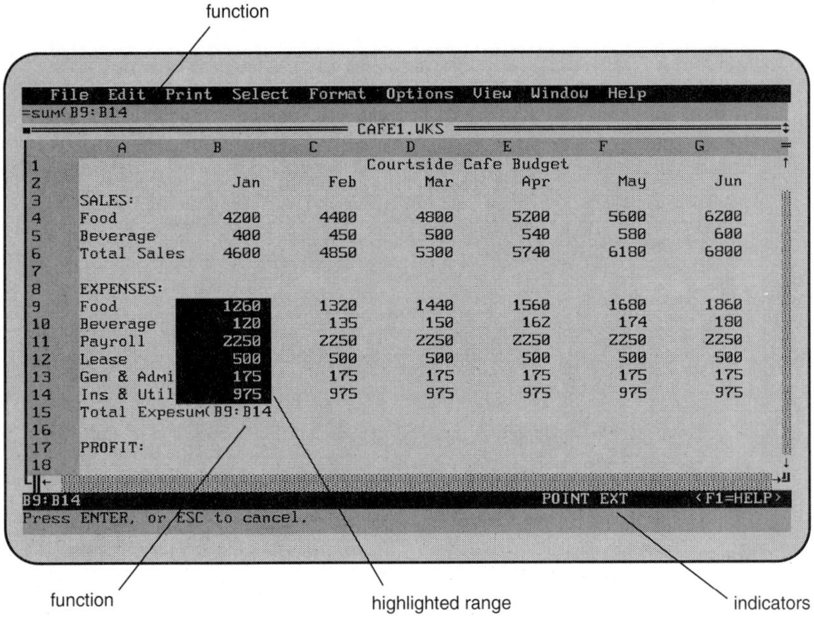

function

```
 File  Edit  Print  Select  Format  Options  View  Window  Help
=SUM(B9:B14
                        CAFE1.WKS
        A          B          C          D          E          F          G
1                                  Courtside Cafe Budget
2                 Jan        Feb        Mar        Apr        May        Jun
3   SALES:
4   Food         4200       4400       4800       5200       5600       6200
5   Beverage      400        450        500        540        580        600
6   Total Sales  4600       4850       5300       5740       6180       6800
7
8   EXPENSES:
9   Food         1260       1320       1440       1560       1680       1860
10  Beverage      120        135        150        162        174        180
11  Payroll      2250       2250       2250       2250       2250       2250
12  Lease         500        500        500        500        500        500
13  Gen & Admi    175        175        175        175        175        175
14  Ins & Util    975        975        975        975        975        975
15  Total ExpesUM(B9:B14
16
17  PROFIT:
18
B9:B14                                      POINT EXT          <F1=HELP>
Press ENTER, or ESC to cancel.
```

function   highlighted range   indicators

The range of cells is highlighted. Notice that the status line displays both POINT and EXT and that the function as it is being built by Works is displayed in the formula bar and in cell B15. Cell B14 is the last cell in the range reference. To end the formula,

Type:)
Press: ↵

The function =SUM(B9:B14) is displayed in the formula bar and the calculated value, 5280, is displayed in cell B15. You could also have entered this function by typing the range references directly.

Copy the function in the January total expense cell to the February through June total expense cells using the Edit>Fill Right command.

The calculated values for the total expenses for January through June are displayed in cells C15 through G15 as specified.

Move to: C15

Your screen should be similar to Figure 6-10.

FIGURE 6-10

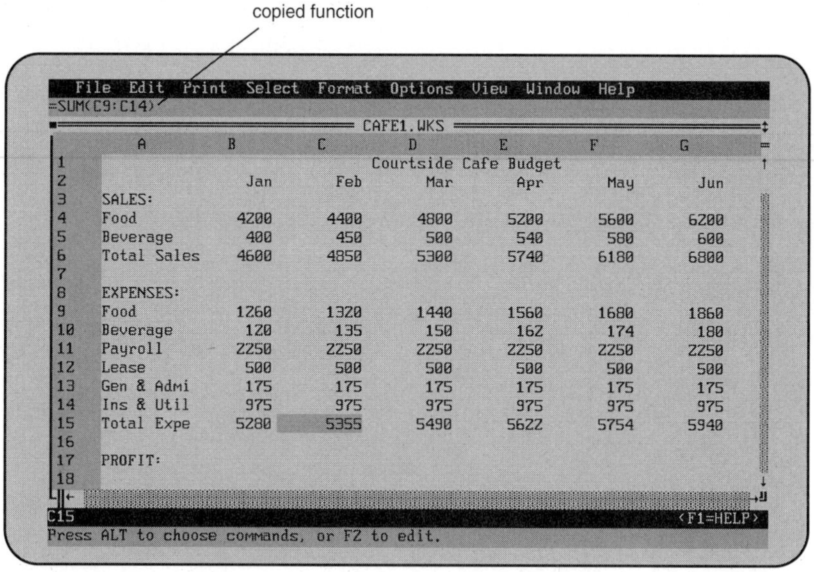

copied function

```
 File  Edit  Print  Select  Format  Options  View  Window  Help
=SUM(C9:C14)
                              CAFE1.WKS
        A            B          C          D          E          F          G
 1                                  Courtside Cafe Budget
 2                  Jan        Feb        Mar        Apr        May        Jun
 3   SALES:
 4   Food          4200       4400       4800       5200       5600       6200
 5   Beverage       400        450        500        540        580        600
 6   Total Sales   4600       4850       5300       5740       6180       6800
 7
 8   EXPENSES:
 9   Food          1260       1320       1440       1560       1680       1860
 10  Beverage       120        135        150        162        174        180
 11  Payroll       2250       2250       2250       2250       2250       2250
 12  Lease          500        500        500        500        500        500
 13  Gen & Admi     175        175        175        175        175        175
 14  Ins & Util     975        975        975        975        975        975
 15  Total Expe    5280       5355       5490       5622       5754       5940
 16
 17  PROFIT:
 18
C15                                                                  <F1=HELP>
Press ALT to choose commands, or F2 to edit.
```

The value "5355" is displayed in the cell. Look at the function as displayed in the formula bar. It is =SUM(C9:C14). When a function is copied, it is adjusted relative to the new cell location just like a formula.

Now that the total sales and expenses are calculated, the formula to calculate profit can be entered in cell B17 and copied across the row through G17. The formula to calculate profit is the difference between monthly total expenses and monthly total sales.

In the January Profit cell (B17), enter the formula to calculate Total Sales minus Total Expenses using pointing. Then copy the formula to calculate the February through June profits using Edit>Fill Right.

To clear the highlight,

Press: ←

Your display screen should be similar to Figure 6-11.

FIGURE 6-11

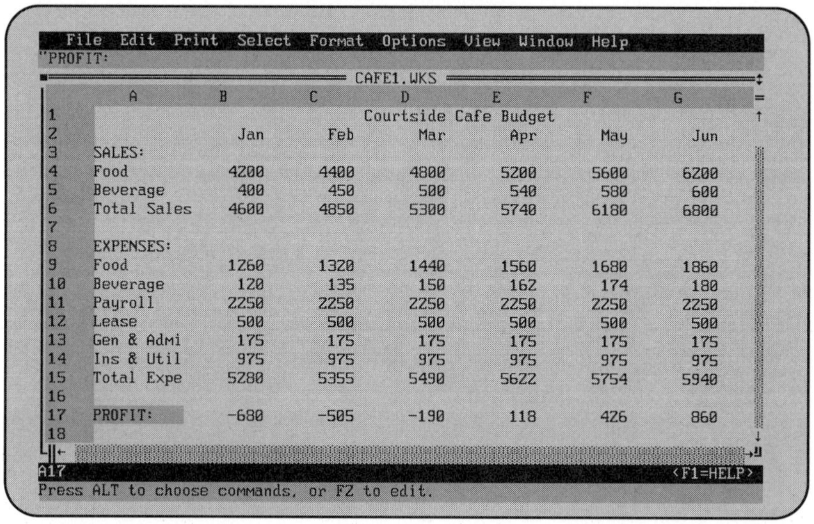

```
 File  Edit  Print  Select  Format  Options  View  Window  Help
"PROFIT:
                              CAFE1.WKS
        A            B          C          D          E          F          G
 1                                  Courtside Cafe Budget
 2                  Jan        Feb        Mar        Apr        May        Jun
 3   SALES:
 4   Food          4200       4400       4800       5200       5600       6200
 5   Beverage       400        450        500        540        580        600
 6   Total Sales   4600       4850       5300       5740       6180       6800
 7
 8   EXPENSES:
 9   Food          1260       1320       1440       1560       1680       1860
 10  Beverage       120        135        150        162        174        180
 11  Payroll       2250       2250       2250       2250       2250       2250
 12  Lease          500        500        500        500        500        500
 13  Gen & Admi     175        175        175        175        175        175
 14  Ins & Util     975        975        975        975        975        975
 15  Total Expe    5280       5355       5490       5622       5754       5940
 16
 17  PROFIT:       -680       -505       -190        118        426        860
 18
A17                                                                  <F1=HELP>
Press ALT to choose commands, or F2 to edit.
```

The profit for January, February, and March shows a loss. Paula is not too concerned about this. In the first few months of operation of the new cafe she does not expect to make a profit.

Changing Column Widths

Next, Paula wants to improve the appearance of the spreadsheet. After entering the values for January in column B, many of the long label entries in column A were truncated or shortened because they were longer than the 10 spaces available. To allow the long entries to be fully displayed, you can increase the width of column A.

Begin by positioning the highlight on the longest label in the column whose width you want to change. In this spreadsheet, "Total Expenses" is the longest label in column A.

Move to: A15

With the highlight positioned over the entry, you can see that the label is four characters longer than the preset column width of 10 spaces. The column width needs to be increased to 14.

To change the width of a column, the Format>Column Width command is used.

Select: Format

As in the word processing tool, the Format menu contains commands that enhance the appearance of your file. However, the commands are very different in the spreadsheet Format menu. You will be using many of these commands later in this lab.

To change the column width,

Select: Column **W**idth

A dialog box is displayed. The preset column width of 10 is displayed in the text box. To enter the new width,

Type: **14**
Press: ↵

Your display screen should be similar to Figure 6-12.

FIGURE 6-12

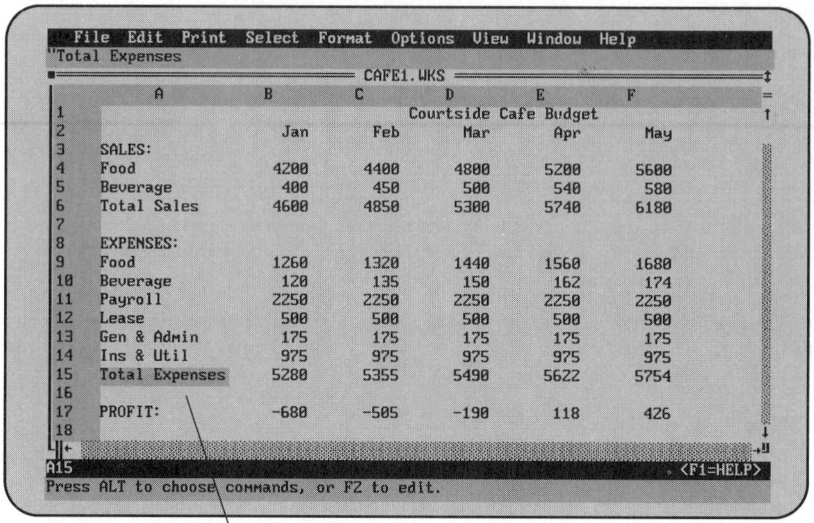

	A	B	C	D	E	F
1				Courtside Cafe Budget		
2		Jan	Feb	Mar	Apr	May
3	SALES:					
4	Food	4200	4400	4800	5200	5600
5	Beverage	400	450	500	540	580
6	Total Sales	4600	4850	5300	5740	6180
7						
8	EXPENSES:					
9	Food	1260	1320	1440	1560	1680
10	Beverage	120	135	150	162	174
11	Payroll	2250	2250	2250	2250	2250
12	Lease	500	500	500	500	500
13	Gen & Admin	175	175	175	175	175
14	Ins & Util	975	975	975	975	975
15	Total Expenses	5280	5355	5490	5622	5754
16						
17	PROFIT:	-680	-505	-190	118	426
18						

File Edit Print Select Format Options View Window Help
"Total Expenses
CAFE1.WKS
A15 <F1=HELP>
Press ALT to choose commands, or F2 to edit.

14 spaces

Column A can now fully display all the labels. Also notice that the June column, column G, is no longer visible in the window. It was pushed to the right to make space for the increased width of column A.

To bring this column back into view in the window, you will decrease the column widths of all other columns in the spreadsheet. To change the column widths of several columns, you must first select the range.

Move to: B15
Press: (F8)

Select cells B15 through G15.

Select: Format>Column **W**idth

To decrease the column width to 7 and see the effect on the spreadsheet display,

Type: **7**
Press: (↵)
Press: (HOME)

Column G is now visible in the window. Column H is also visible; however, its column width is still at the default setting of 10 spaces. Column A is still set at 14 spaces.

Paula realizes she needs to add a column to sum the sales and expenses for the six months. To enter the column heading,

Move to: H2
Type: **TOTAL**
Press: (↵)

The label is displayed left-aligned in the cell space. Paula wants to change the label so that it is displayed to the right in the cell. This way it will be aligned with the values in the column. To change the alignment of a label,

Select: Format>**S**tyle

Your screen should be similar to Figure 6-13.

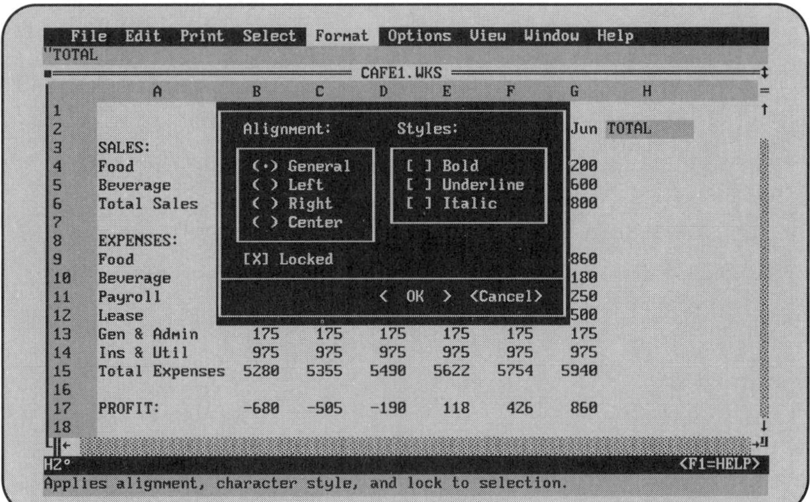

FIGURE 6-13

The Style dialog box lets you change the alignment of labels and their style or appearance. Paula wants the label to be aligned to the right side of the cell space. The Alignment options box displays four choices that have the following effects:

General	Left-aligns labels and right-aligns values
Left	Left-aligns the label or value entry
Right	Right-aligns the label or value entry
Center	Centers the label or value entry

General is the default setting. To change the alignment of the entry in this cell to Right,

Select: **R**ight

Reminder: To select an option, you can press (TAB) to move to the option and then press the bold letter, or you can press (ALT) and type the bold letter of the option.

Mouse Note: You can click on the option to select it.

A dot appears to the left of the selected alignment setting to tell you the option has been selected. Only one option can be selected from an option box.

Paula would also like the label to be bold to separate it from the month labels. To select the bold style from the Styles check box,

Select: **B**old

An X appears in the Styles box next to the selected option. You can select more than one setting from a check box. To clear a selected style setting, select the option again. The X will be removed and the cell display will return to normal.

To complete the command,

Press: ↵

Your screen should be similar to Figure 6-14.

FIGURE 6-14

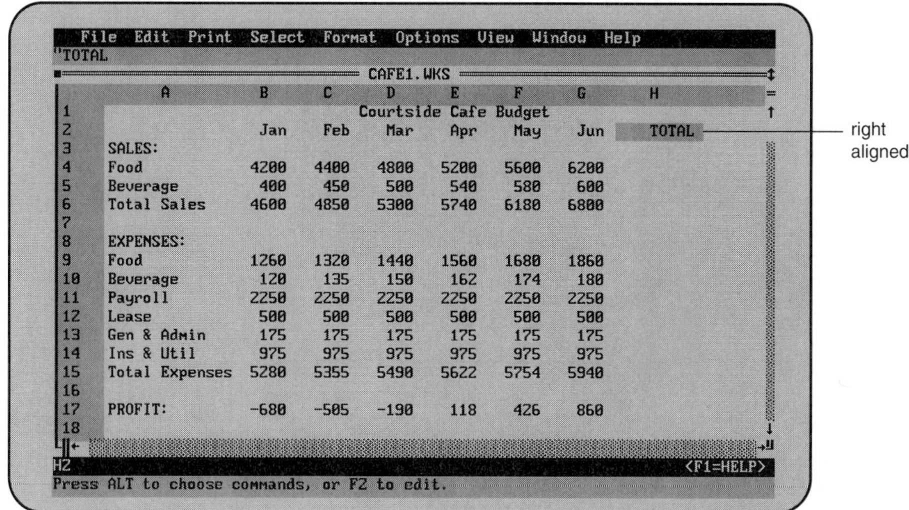

The label is displayed right-aligned in the cell space and in bold.

Note: In many Works dialog boxes, you can simply type the bold letter to select an option. In many other cases, however, you need to hold down ALT while pressing the bold letter. The second method will work in all situations, whereas the first will not. Therefore, it is generally safer to use the ALT - bold letter combination to select options.

Using the Delete Command

The functions that calculate the totals for the six months for sales and expenses need to be entered next. To enter the function to calculate the total food sales for January through June,

Move to: H4

Using pointing, enter the function to sum the January through June Food sales.

Copy this function to cells H5 through H17 using the Edit>Fill Down command. This command operates just like the Edit>Fill Right command, except that the selected cells are filled down a column rather than across a row.

Move to: H7

Your display screen should be similar to Figure 6-15.

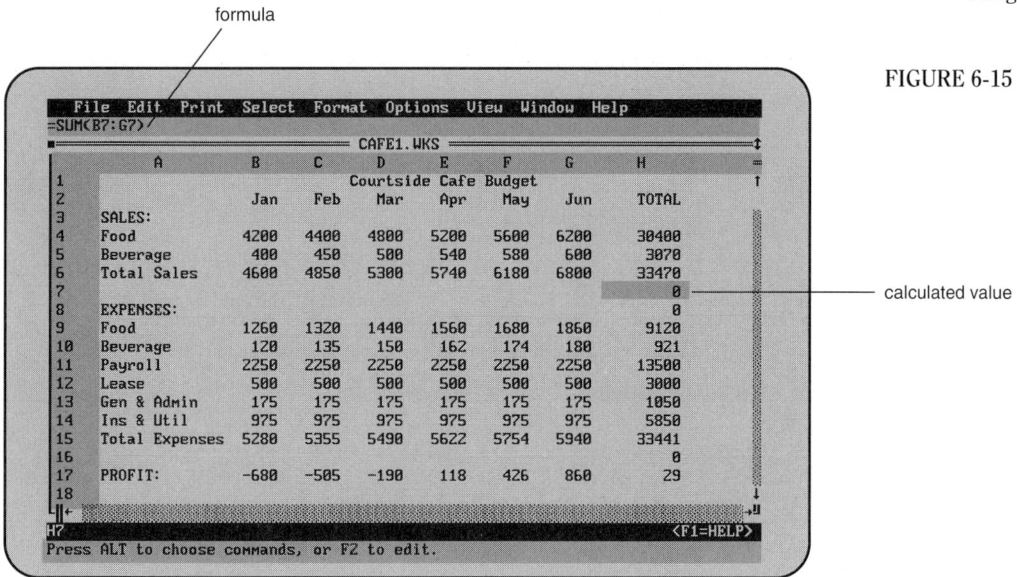

	A	B	C	D	E	F	G	H
1				Courtside Cafe Budget				
2		Jan	Feb	Mar	Apr	May	Jun	TOTAL
3	SALES:							
4	Food	4200	4400	4800	5200	5600	6200	30400
5	Beverage	400	450	500	540	580	600	3070
6	Total Sales	4600	4850	5300	5740	6180	6800	33470
7								0
8	EXPENSES:							0
9	Food	1260	1320	1440	1560	1680	1860	9120
10	Beverage	120	135	150	162	174	180	921
11	Payroll	2250	2250	2250	2250	2250	2250	13500
12	Lease	500	500	500	500	500	500	3000
13	Gen & Admin	175	175	175	175	175	175	1050
14	Ins & Util	975	975	975	975	975	975	5850
15	Total Expenses	5280	5355	5490	5622	5754	5940	33441
16								0
17	PROFIT:	-680	-505	-190	118	426	860	29
18								

FIGURE 6-15

Look at the contents of cells H7 and H8. They both display a zero. The function was copied into cells that reference empty cells. The command to erase, or clear, the contents of a cell or range of cells is an option under the Edit menu. To erase the function from cells H7 and H8,

Press: (F8)

Highlight cells H7 and H8.

Select: **E**dit>Cle**a**r

The function is erased from the cells and consequently the value 0 is no longer displayed.

The next cell that needs to be cleared is H16.

Move to: H16

To clear the contents of an individual cell, you could select Edit>Clear. Alternatively, you can simply press (DEL) or (Bksp).

Press: (DEL) or (Bksp)
Press: (↵)

Paula wants to change the width of this column to the same width as the month columns. To do this,

Select: Forma**t**>Column **W**idth
Type: **7**
Press: (↵)

To further improve the appearance of the spreadsheet, bold the SALES, EXPENSES, and PROFIT row headings in cells A3, A8, and A17.

Next, Paula wants to underline rows 5 and 14. This will visually separate the Total Sales and Total Expense rows from the rows above them. To do this,

Move to: A6
Press: (F8)

Highlight A5 through H5.

Note: A quick way to extend the highlight to the end of a row or column of data is to press (END).

Select: Forma**t**>**S**tyle>**U**nderline>(↵)

The selected row appears in color, highlighted, or underlined on your screen, depending on your monitor. It will be underlined when you print the spreadsheet.

Underline row 14 (columns A through H).

Formatting Values

Next, Paula wants the values to be displayed with dollar signs and commas. You can change the format of values by using the Format command. The cell or range of cells you want to format must be selected first.

Paula wants to format values in the Food Sales (row 4) and Profit (row 17) rows as currency. To format the Food Sales row first,

Move to: B4
Press: (F8)

Highlight row 4, columns B through H.

Select: Forma**t**

The eight Format menu commands in the upper section of the menu box affect values. Although you can also change the alignment and style of values, typically values in a spreadsheet remain right-aligned. The default format is General. This format displays numbers as precisely as possible using either an integer (123), a decimal fraction (1.23), or scientific notation (1.23E+75). In most cases, financial information is formatted to display in either currency or comma format. The Currency command will display a dollar sign in front of the value and commas where appropriate. Comma format will not display the dollar sign.

Select: C**u**rrency

A text dialog box is displayed. It lets you specify the number of decimal places you want displayed following the decimal point. Since all the values in this spreadsheet are whole numbers, to change the setting from the default of 2 to 0,

Type: 0
Press: (↵)

Your display screen should be similar to Figure 6-16.

FIGURE 6-16

```
 File  Edit  Print  Select  Format  Options  View  Window  Help
4200
                               CAFE1.WKS
             A          B      C      D      E      F      G      H        I
1                                  Courtside Cafe Budget
2                      Jan    Feb    Mar    Apr    May    Jun   TOTAL
3    SALES:
4    Food           $4,200 $4,400 $4,800 $5,200 $5,600 $6,200 ########
5    Beverage          400    450    500    540    580    600    3070
6    Total Sales      4600   4850   5300   5740   6180   6800   33470
7
8    EXPENSES:
9    Food             1260   1320   1440   1560   1680   1860    9120
10   Beverage          120    135    150    162    174    180     921
11   Payroll          2250   2250   2250   2250   2250   2250   13500
12   Lease             500    500    500    500    500    500    3000
13   Gen & Admin       175    175    175    175    175    175    1050
14   Ins & Util        975    975    975    975    975    975    5850
15   Total Expenses   5280   5355   5490   5622   5754   5940   33441
16
17   PROFIT:          -680   -505   -190    118    426    860      29
18
B4:H4                                                        <F1=HELP>
Press ALT to choose commands, or F2 to edit.
```

cell width too small

The values in columns B through G are displayed with dollar signs and commas. However, a series of number symbols (#####) is displayed in cell H4. This is how Works tells you that the width of a cell is too small to display the entire value in that cell, including the format. To increase the column width of this column to 8,

Move to: H4
Select: Forma**t**>Column **W**idth>**8**>(↵)

Now the value is fully displayed in the cell.

In the same way, format the values in cells B17 through H17 to be displayed with dollar signs and 0 decimal places. Begin with the highlight in cell H17.

Notice the use of parentheses in cells B17, C17, and D17 to show that they contain negative values.

Next, you will change the format of the remaining values in the spreadsheet to Comma. This command will display commas and decimal places only.

Move to: H15

Select the range of cells H15 through B5.

Select: Forma**t**>**C**omma>**0**>(↵)

To clear the highlight,

Press: (↑)

Your screen should be similar to Figure 6-17.

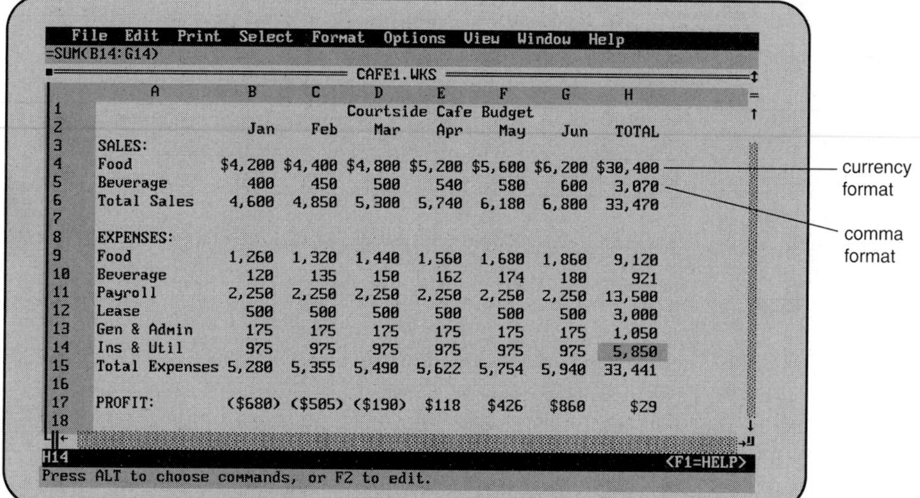

FIGURE 6-17

Now the spreadsheet displays commas where appropriate.

Inserting Rows

The appearance of the spreadsheet is greatly improved already. However, Paula still feels that it looks crowded. She wants a blank row entered below the spreadsheet title as row 2.

To insert a blank row into the spreadsheet, begin by moving the cell highlight to the row where the new blank row will be inserted.

Move to: H2
Select: **E**dit>**I**nsert Row/Column

In the Insert dialog box you need to specify whether you want a row or a column inserted at the location of the highlight. Row is the default setting. To accept it and complete the command,

Press: ↵

Your display screen should be similar to Figure 6-18.

FIGURE 6-18

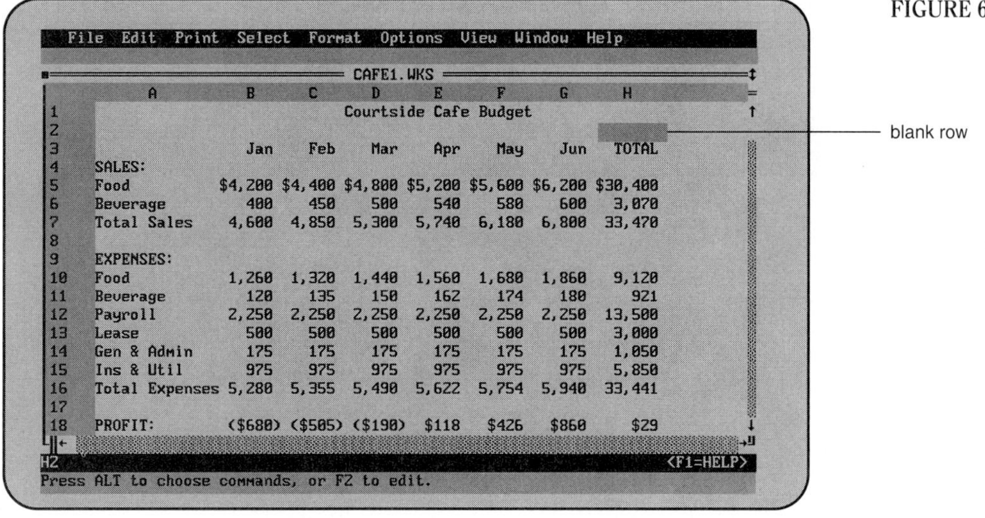

	A	B	C	D	E	F	G	H
1				Courtside Cafe Budget				
2								
3		Jan	Feb	Mar	Apr	May	Jun	TOTAL
4	SALES:							
5	Food	$4,200	$4,400	$4,800	$5,200	$5,600	$6,200	$30,400
6	Beverage	400	450	500	540	580	600	3,070
7	Total Sales	4,600	4,850	5,300	5,740	6,180	6,800	33,470
8								
9	EXPENSES:							
10	Food	1,260	1,320	1,440	1,560	1,680	1,860	9,120
11	Beverage	120	135	150	162	174	180	921
12	Payroll	2,250	2,250	2,250	2,250	2,250	2,250	13,500
13	Lease	500	500	500	500	500	500	3,000
14	Gen & Admin	175	175	175	175	175	175	1,050
15	Ins & Util	975	975	975	975	975	975	5,850
16	Total Expenses	5,280	5,355	5,490	5,622	5,754	5,940	33,441
17								
18	PROFIT:	($680)	($505)	($190)	$118	$426	$860	$29

A new blank row has been inserted into the spreadsheet at the cell highlight location. Everything below row 2 has moved down one row. All formulas and functions have been automatically adjusted to their new row location.

To delete a row, use the same procedure, except select Delete Row/Column rather than Insert Row/Column. Be very careful when using the Delete command, because any information in the row or column will be deleted.

If you need to insert or delete multiple rows, select the range before using the Edit>Insert or Delete command.

Inserting Columns

Next, Paula wants to separate the row labels from the months by inserting a blank column between column A and column B. The blank column will be column B.

Move to: B2
Select: **E**dit>Insert Row/Column>**C**olumn>↵

Your display screen should be similar to Figure 6-19.

FIGURE 6-19

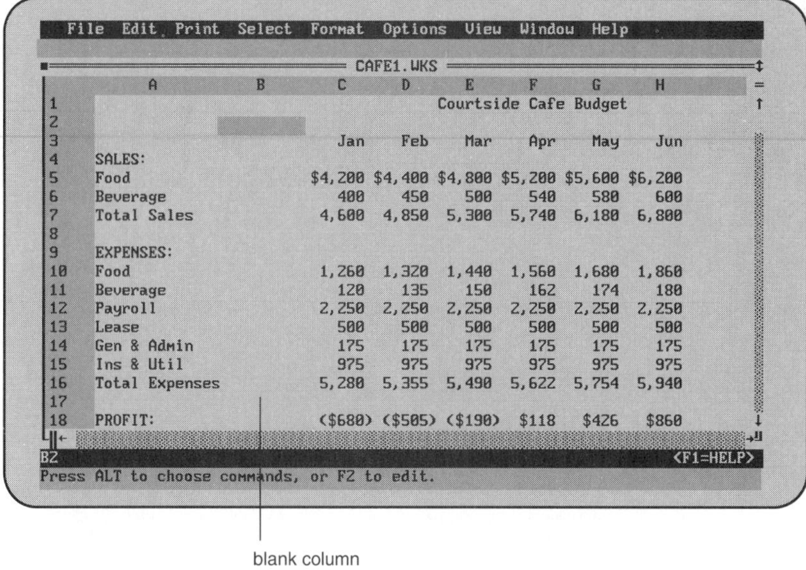

File Edit Print Select Format Options View Window Help

CAFE1.WKS

	A	B	C	D	E	F	G	H
1					Courtside Cafe Budget			
2								
3			Jan	Feb	Mar	Apr	May	Jun
4	SALES:							
5	Food		$4,200	$4,400	$4,800	$5,200	$5,600	$6,200
6	Beverage		400	450	500	540	580	600
7	Total Sales		4,600	4,850	5,300	5,740	6,180	6,800
8								
9	EXPENSES:							
10	Food		1,260	1,320	1,440	1,560	1,680	1,860
11	Beverage		120	135	150	162	174	180
12	Payroll		2,250	2,250	2,250	2,250	2,250	2,250
13	Lease		500	500	500	500	500	500
14	Gen & Admin		175	175	175	175	175	175
15	Ins & Util		975	975	975	975	975	975
16	Total Expenses		5,280	5,355	5,490	5,622	5,754	5,940
17								
18	PROFIT:		($680)	($505)	($190)	$118	$426	$860

B2 <F1=HELP>
Press ALT to choose commands, or F2 to edit.

A blank column has been inserted into the spreadsheet as column B.

Notice that the Total column, I, is no longer visible on the display. The inserted column forced it to the right of the window.

To see the rest of the spreadsheet, using the (→) key,

Move to: I2

Your display screen should be similar to Figure 6-20.

FIGURE 6-20

File Edit Print Select Format Options View Window Help

CAFE1.WKS

	B	C	D	E	F	G	H	I	J
1				Courtside Cafe Budget					
2									
3		Jan	Feb	Mar	Apr	May	Jun	TOTAL	
4									
5		$4,200	$4,400	$4,800	$5,200	$5,600	$6,200	$30,400	
6		400	450	500	540	580	600	3,070	
7		4,600	4,850	5,300	5,740	6,180	6,800	33,470	
8									
9									
10		1,260	1,320	1,440	1,560	1,680	1,860	9,120	
11		120	135	150	162	174	180	921	
12		2,250	2,250	2,250	2,250	2,250	2,250	13,500	
13		500	500	500	500	500	500	3,000	
14		175	175	175	175	175	175	1,050	
15		975	975	975	975	975	975	5,850	
16		5,280	5,355	5,490	5,622	5,754	5,940	33,441	
17									
18		($680)	($505)	($190)	$118	$426	$860	$29	

I2 <F1=HELP>
Press ALT to choose commands, or F2 to edit.

Column I is now visible on the display, but the row labels in column A are not. This makes reading the spreadsheet difficult, since it is hard to know what the figures mean. You will learn how to manage a spreadsheet that is larger than a window in the next lab.

A column can also be deleted using the same procedure, except the Delete option is selected rather than Insert. Again, be careful when deleting a column that you do not accidentally delete a column of important information.

Moving Cell Contents

The spreadsheet is just about complete. The last change Paula wants to make is to move the title in cell E1 so that it is better centered over the spreadsheet.

Move to: E1
Select: **E**dit>**M**ove

To specify the new location,

Move to: D1
Press: ↵

The label has been removed from cell E1 and moved to cell D1. If you need to move a range, select the cells before using the Move command. You can also use the Move command to move values. When you do, Works adjusts all references to the moved cells if needed. However, if the new location contains information, it will be replaced by the information you are moving.

Before saving and printing the spreadsheet, enter your name in cell A1 and the date in cell A2.

Saving and Replacing a File

Whenever you are finished working on a file, be sure to save the current version of the file displayed on the screen. If you leave the Works program without saving the current version of the spreadsheet, you will lose all your hard work.

When you save a spreadsheet file, you will either give the spreadsheet a new filename or write over the contents of an existing spreadsheet file using an old filename. When you use the File>Save command, Works automatically replaces the disk file with the current file. When you select File>Save As, Works displays a dialog box that lets you enter a different filename.

You no longer need the file you created at the end of Lab 5, CAFE.WKS. So you will reuse the filename and replace the file contents with the current spreadsheet.

Select: **F**ile>Save **A**s

The current spreadsheet filename, CAFE1.WKS, is displayed in the text box. If the directory displayed is not the directory where you want to save the file, select the appropriate directory.

To enter a different filename,

Type: **CAFE**
Press: 

The program checks the diskette and finds that another file already exists with the filename CAFE.WKS. The prompt in the dialog box asks you if you want to replace the existing file. This is a protection against accidentally writing over a file with the same name. To confirm that you do,

Press: ↵

The file is saved as CAFE.WKS.

Printing a File

If you have printer capability, you can print a copy of the spreadsheet. First, turn the printer on and check to see that it is on-line. Adjust the paper so that the perforation is just above the printer scale.

Select: Print>**P**rint>**P**rint

If you are ready to leave Works 2.0, issue the File>Exit command. If you are going to continue using Works, close the file before continuing.

Key Terms

copy
point
relative cell reference
function
syntax
argument
range references

Matching

1. Edit>Copy ______ **a.** lets you right-align an entry

2. DEL ______ **b.** inserts a column

3. pointing ______ **c.** erases contents of a single cell

4. Format>Style ______ **d.** indicates insufficient cell width

5. Edit>Insert Row/Column ______ **e.** method of entering a cell range

6. =SUM(B4:B9) ______ **f.** tells Works to include all cells selected from the first to the last cell

7. Edit>Fill Right ______ **g.** moves cursor to the last used cell in a row

8. : ______ **h.** copies the contents of a cell to adjacent cells to the right

9. ##### ______ **i.** sums a range of cells

10. END ______ **j.** copies the contents of a cell to a new location

Practice Exercises

1. To complete this problem, you must have created the spreadsheet in Lab 5, problem 4. If you have done so, open the file JEWELRY.WKS. You will continue to build the spreadsheet for the jewelry store sales campaign.

- Enter the following sales figures:

	Week 3	Week 4
Sally	2275	3602
Martin	1898	5900
Philip	3342	4688
Dorothy	4198	4975
Alyce	3604	2800

- Enter the column heading "Average" in cell G4 and "Percent" in cell H4.
- Right-align, bold, and underline the column labels.
- Insert a blank row below the spreadsheet title and below the column heads.
- Enter functions to calculate the total sales (=SUM) and average (=AVG) sales for each salesperson.
- Format the average values as Fixed with 0 decimal places.

The winner of the contest is the salesperson with the highest average sales over the four weeks. That person will earn 15 percent on their total sales. All other salespersons will earn 10 percent on their total sales.

- Enter the formulas to calculate the appropriate percent earned for each salesperson in column H.
- Format the percent earned values as Fixed with 0 decimal places.
- Enter seven double dashed underline characters (=====) in cell B12. Right-align the entry. Use the equals sign to create the characters. Copy the entry to cell C12 through H12.
- Copy the TOTAL formula in cell C13 to cells D13 through H13.
- Format the values in rows 7 and 13 to display as Currency with 0 decimal places.
- Erase the date from cell A3 and enter the current date in cell A2.
- Save the spreadsheet as CONTEST.
- Print the spreadsheet.

2. To complete this problem, you must have created the spreadsheet in practice exercise 3 of Lab 5. Open the file COST. You will continue to build the spreadsheet for the cost analysis of purchasing a new car versus keeping the old car.

- Right-align and bold the column labels.
- Enter the trade-in value for the old car as 924 and for the new car as 4637 after four years of ownership.
- Enter the formula to calculate the Net Cost of Ownership for the old car. This formula is the difference between the Total Expenses and the Trade-in value. Copy this formula to calculate the Net Cost of Ownership for the new car.
- Enter a formula to calculate the "Saved by not trading in" value. This formula is the difference between the Net Cost of Ownership for the old and new car. This value should be displayed in the old car column.
- Format all values to be displayed as Currency with 0 decimal places.
- Insert one blank row below the spreadsheet title and another below the column headings.
- Increase the column width of A to 15.
- Right-align the labels in cells A8 through A11.
- Underline cells C10 and D10.
- Enter six double dashed underline characters (=====) in cells C15 and D15. Use the equals sign to create the characters. Right-align the entry.
- Enter the current date in cell A2.
- Save the spreadsheet using the filename COST2.
- Print the spreadsheet.

3. To complete this problem, you must have created the spreadsheet in practice exercise 5 of Lab 5. Open the file ZOOFINAN. You will continue to build the spreadsheet for the three-year financial statement for the zoo.

- To make the spreadsheet easier to read, you will insert blank rows and columns. Insert a blank row between the spreadsheet title and the column headings. The blank row will be row 2.
- Insert a blank row below the column headings (row 4).
- Enter blank rows as rows 10, 12, and 18 (in that order).
- Delete column C.
- Increase the width of column A to completely display all row labels.
- Decrease the column width of column B to 4 spaces.
- Copy the formulas used to calculate TOTAL S&R and TOTAL A/E for 1990 to calculate these values for 1991 and 1992.
- Copy the formula used to calculate the operating reserve for 1990 to 1991 and 1992.
- Enter the column heading "AVERAGE" in cell G3.
- Right-align the TOTAL and AVERAGE column headings.

- Enter a function to calculate the TOTAL and AVERAGE operating revenue in cells F6 and G6, respectively. The function for calculating averages is entered just like the SUM function, except that the function name is AVG and it calculates the average of a range of values. Copy the functions down the columns. Clear the function from those cells that reference empty cells.
- Format the values in rows 6, 11, and 19 to display as currency with 0 decimal places. Increase the column widths to fully display the formatted values.
- Format all other worksheet values (those that are not formatted as currency) as Comma with 0 decimal places.
- Enter double dashed lines (===) in rows 10 and 18, columns D through G. Use the equals sign to create the double dashed line. Fill the cell space with one less character than there are spaces.
- Underline and bold the column headings.
- Clear the old date from cell A3 and enter the current date in cell A2.
- Save the spreadsheet using the filename ZOOFIN2.
- Print the spreadsheet.

4. The Scholastic Aptitude Test (SAT) taken by 1.03 million college-bound students is a two-part multiple-choice exam, each scored on a scale of 200 to 800. The average scores for the years 1969 through 1990 are displayed below. Create a spreadsheet of this data, leaving a blank row between each row.

	1969	1973	1977	1981	1985	1990
Math	492	485	470	466	473	476
Verbal	462	445	429	423	430	424

Source: The Arizona Republic

- Enter a third row of data that calculates the average of the verbal and math sections of the test for each year. Enter the row label "Average."
- Underline the column labels.
- Bold the row labels.
- Enter the spreadsheet title "SAT SCORES" centered over the spreadsheet. Enter a second title "by [Your Name]." Leave two blank rows below the second title line.
- Bold the titles.
- Decrease the column widths for the years to seven spaces. Change the column width of A to 8.
- Enter a sixth column that calculates the average for the math and verbal scores. Enter the column head "Average." Right-align it. Underline the column head. Make this column nine spaces wide.
- Format the row and column average values to display 0 decimal places.
- Save the spreadsheet as SCORES.
- Print the spreadsheet.

5. Open the file ABC.WKS you created in practice exercise 6 in Lab 5. You will continue to build the income statement spreadsheet.

- Copy the January expenses (rows 9–13) across the row through June.
- Copy the formula to calculate the Gross Profit for January across the row through June.
- Enter a function to calculate the total February expenses. Copy the function across the row through June.
- Enter formulas to calculate the following for January:

  Income Before Taxes (Gross Profit - Total Expenses)

  Provision for Taxes (33% of Income Before Taxes)

  Net Income (Income Before Taxes - Provision for Taxes)

- Copy these formulas across the row through June.
- Insert a blank row below the spreadsheet title.
- Increase the column width of A to completely display all row labels.
- Format the values for Sales (row 5), Gross Profit (row 7), Income Before Taxes (row 17), and Net Income (row 19) as Currency with 0 decimal places.
- Format the remaining rows of values as Comma with 0 decimal places.
- Decrease the column widths of columns B through G to nine spaces.
- Underline rows 6, 14, and 18; columns B through G.
- Bold the month column headings.
- Clear the old date from cell A3 and enter the current date in cell A2.
- Save the spreadsheet using the filename ABC2.
- Print the spreadsheet.

Command Summary

Command	**Shortcut**	**Action**	**Page**
File>Save **A**s		Saves file with new name	189
Edit>**M**ove	(F3)	Moves cell contents	189
Edit>**C**opy	(SHIFT) - (F3)	Copies cell contents to new location	169
Edit>Cl**e**ar	(DEL) or (Bksp)	Erases contents of cell	183
Edit>**D**elete Row/Column		Deletes row/column	187
Edit>**I**nsert Row/Column		Inserts blank row/column	186
Edit>Fill **R**ight		Copies to adjacent cells to right	171
Edit>**F**ill Down		Copies to adjacent cells down	171
Select>C**e**lls	(F8)	Selects cells	171
Forma**t**>**G**eneral		Displays values as integer, decimal fraction, or scientific notation	184
Forma**t**>C**u**rrency		Displays values with $, and decimal place	184
Forma**t**>**C**omma		Displays values with, and decimal place	184
Forma**t**>**S**tyle		Changes alignment/style of label entries	181
Forma**t**>Column **W**idth		Changes column width	179

LAB 7
Managing a Large Spreadsheet

OBJECTIVES

In this lab you will learn how to:

1. Correct a circular reference.
2. Freeze row and column titles.
3. Create and use panes.
4. Perform what-if analysis.
5. Use absolute cell references.
6. Enter the system date.

CASE STUDY

Paula Nichols, the manager of the Courtside Cafe at the Sports Club, presented the completed spreadsheet of the estimated operating budget for the proposed Courtside Cafe expansion to the board of directors. Although the board was pleased with the six-month analysis, it asked her to extend the budget to cover a full year.

The board also wants her to calculate the profit margin for the proposed cafe expansion over the 12 months. At the end of 12 months the profit margin should be 20 percent. You will follow Paula as she makes the adjustments in the budget.

Locating and Correcting a Circular Reference

After presenting the budget to the board, Paula revised the spreadsheet, making several of the changes requested.

Turn your computer on and load DOS. When responding to the DOS date prompt, be sure to enter the current date. Load Works. The data diskette should be in drive B (or the appropriate drive for your computer system). To see what Paula has done so far, open the file CAFE2.WKS.

Your display screen should be similar to Figure 7-1.

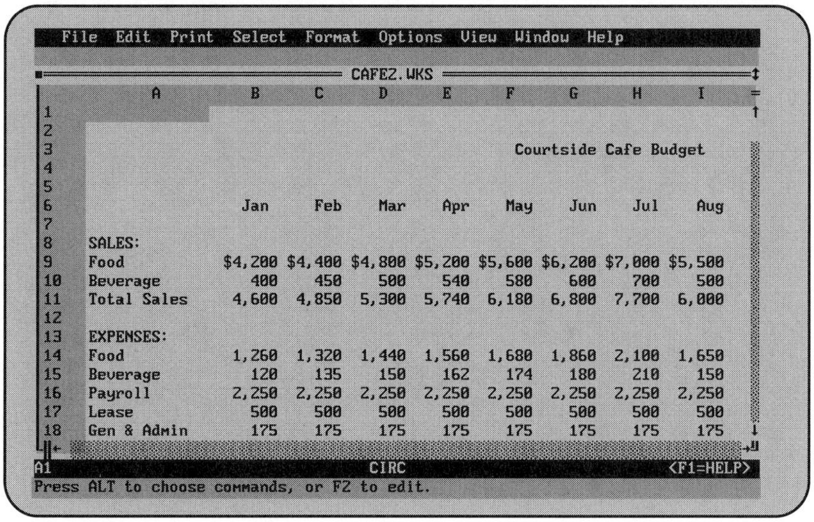

```
 File  Edit  Print  Select  Format  Options  View  Window  Help
                           CAFE2.WKS
          A              B      C      D      E      F      G      H      I
1
2
3                                               Courtside Cafe Budget
4
5
6                       Jan    Feb    Mar    Apr    May    Jun    Jul    Aug
7
8    SALES:
9    Food           $4,200 $4,400 $4,800 $5,200 $5,600 $6,200 $7,000 $5,500
10   Beverage          400    450    500    540    580    600    700    500
11   Total Sales     4,600  4,850  5,300  5,740  6,180  6,800  7,700  6,000
12
13   EXPENSES:
14   Food            1,260  1,320  1,440  1,560  1,680  1,860  2,100  1,650
15   Beverage          120    135    150    162    174    180    210    150
16   Payroll         2,250  2,250  2,250  2,250  2,250  2,250  2,250  2,250
17   Lease             500    500    500    500    500    500    500    500
18   Gen & Admin       175    175    175    175    175    175    175    175
A1                            CIRC                              <F1=HELP>
Press ALT to choose commands, or F2 to edit.
```

FIGURE 7-1

The spreadsheet now contains values for 12 months and a new row label for profit margin. The spreadsheet extends beyond column I and below row 18.

Note: Although there are quicker ways to move to cells in the spreadsheet, use the arrow keys when directed. Your display will then show the same rows and columns as the figures in the text.

To see the rest of the row labels, using (↓),

Move to: A24

The row label "PROFIT MARGIN:" is now visible on the display. The formula to calculate this value still needs to be entered into the spreadsheet. Notice that the column headings are no longer visible on the screen. This makes it difficult for you to know which column of data corresponds to which month.

To see the rest of the spreadsheet to the right of column I, using (→),

Move to: N24

Your display screen should be similar to Figure 7-2.

```
 File  Edit  Print  Select  Format  Options  View  Window  Help
                              CAFE2.WKS
        E      F      G      H      I      J      K      L      M      N
 7
 8
 9   $5,200 $5,600 $6,200 $7,000 $5,500 $6,400 $5,500 $6,500 $7,520 $68,820
10      540    580    600    700    500    750    800    650    775   7,245
11    5,740  6,180  6,800  7,700  6,000  7,150  6,300  7,150  8,295  76,065
12
13
14    1,560  1,680  1,860  2,100  1,650  1,920  1,650  1,950  2,256  20,646
15      162    174    180    210    150    225    240    195    233   2,174
16    2,250  2,250  2,250  2,250  2,250  2,250  2,250  2,250  2,250  27,000
17      500    500    500    500    500    500    500    500    500   6,000
18      175    175    175    175    175    175    175    175    175   2,100
19      975    975    975    975    975    975    975    975    975  11,700
20    5,622  5,754  5,940  6,210  5,700  6,045  5,790  6,045  6,389  69,620
21
22     $118   $426   $860 $1,490   $300 $1,105   $510 $1,105 $8,295 $12,834
23
24
N24                            CIRC                               <F1=HELP>
Press ALT to choose commands, or F2 to edit.
```

circular reference indicator

FIGURE 7-2

The TOTAL column and the values for the months of April through December are now visible. Looking at the values in the spreadsheet, you may find it difficult to remember what the values stand for when the row labels in column A and the column labels in row 6 are not visible on the display screen. For example,

Move to: M19

The value in this cell is 975. Is this value a lease expense or a beverage expense or a direct expense? Without seeing the row labels, it is difficult for you to know. You will learn shortly how to manage a spreadsheet that extends beyond a single window.

Notice the indicator CIRC displayed in the status line. This message is a warning that a **circular reference** has been located in the spreadsheet. This means that a formula in a cell either directly or indirectly references itself. For some special applications, a formula containing a circular reference may be valid. These cases, however, are not very common. Whenever this message is displayed, stop and locate the cell or cells containing the reference.

Locating the formula containing a circular reference in a spreadsheet can be very difficult. Each formula needs to be checked. Sometimes a value in a cell that is much larger or smaller than other values in the same category can point you to the location of the error.

Move to: M22

The value in this cell is 8295. It is much larger than the other values in this row. Look at the formula in the formula bar. It is =M11-M22. The formula in cell M22 incorrectly references itself, M22, as part of the computation.

The formula in this cell should calculate the profit for December using the formula =M11-M20.

Correct the formula in cell M22 to be =M11-M20.

Your display screen should be similar to Figure 7-3.

```
  File  Edit  Print  Select  Format  Options  View  Window  Help
=M11-M20
                                 CAFE2.WKS
        E      F      G      H      I      J      K      L      M      N
7
8
9    $5,200 $5,600 $6,200 $7,000 $5,500 $6,400 $5,500 $6,500 $7,520 $68,820
10      540    580    600    700    500    750    800    650    775   7,245
11    5,740  6,180  6,800  7,700  6,000  7,150  6,300  7,150  8,295  76,065
12
13
14    1,560  1,680  1,860  2,100  1,650  1,920  1,650  1,950  2,256  20,646
15      162    174    180    210    150    225    240    195    233   2,174
16    2,250  2,250  2,250  2,250  2,250  2,250  2,250  2,250  2,250  27,000
17      500    500    500    500    500    500    500    500    500   6,000
18      175    175    175    175    175    175    175    175    175   2,100
19      975    975    975    975    975    975    975    975    975  11,700
20    5,622  5,754  5,940  6,210  5,700  6,045  5,790  6,045  6,389  69,620
21
22     $118   $426   $860 $1,490   $300 $1,105   $510 $1,105 $1,907  $6,446
23
24
M22                                                          <F1=HELP>
Press ALT to choose commands, or F2 to edit.
```

FIGURE 7-3

The CIRC indicator has disappeared, and the affected spreadsheet formulas were recalculated. The new calculated value, "1907," is displayed in cell M22. This was a simple example of a circular reference error; others may be much more complex. In any case, whenever this indicator appears, locate the circular reference and determine whether it is valid or not.

Freezing Titles

As noted earlier, the spreadsheet is difficult to understand because the row labels in column A and the column heading in row 6 are not visible on the display screen. To see the row labels in column A,

Press: (HOME)

To bring the column labels into view using (↑),

Move to: A6

Although the row labels are visible again, you cannot see the values in columns J through N or the row containing the profit margin. To keep the row labels visible in the window all the time while viewing the values in columns J through N, you will **freeze** column A in the window.

Works lets you fix, or freeze, specified rows or columns (or both) on the window while you scroll to other areas of the spreadsheet. The "titles" can consist of any number of columns or rows along the top or left edge of the window.

To freeze a column of titles, move the highlight to the top-most visible cell in the column to the right of the columns you want to freeze. Since you want to freeze column A on the window,

Move to: B6

The command to freeze titles is in the Options menu.

Select: Options

The commands in the top box of the Options menu are the same as in the word processing tool. The other commands, however, are specific to the spreadsheet. To freeze the title in column A,

Select: Freeze **T**itles

Nothing appears different on the display screen until you move the highlight.

Press: (←)

Works will not let you move the highlight into column A because it is frozen.

Watch the movement of the columns on the display screen as you use (→) to

Move to: N6

Your display screen should be similar to Figure 7-4.

FIGURE 7-4

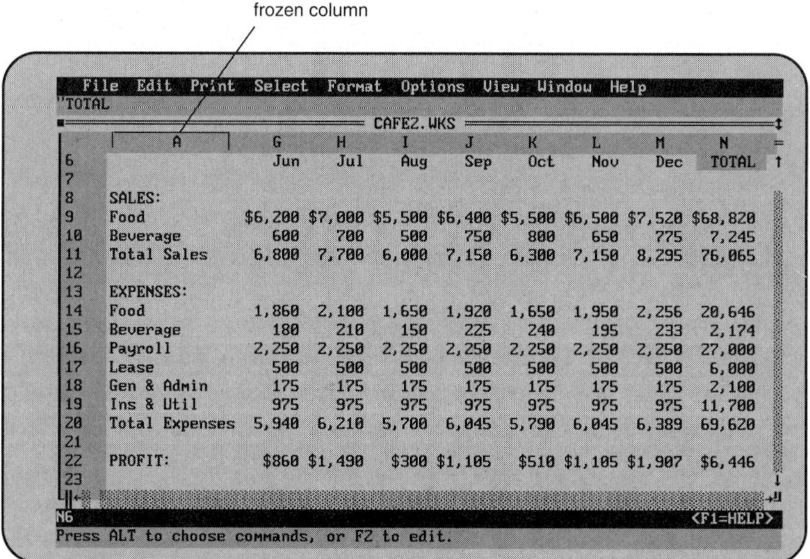

Column A has remained fixed in the window while columns G through N scroll into view. This makes reading the spreadsheet much easier.

To unfreeze, or clear, the frozen column,

Select: Options> Unfreeze **T**itles

Columns A through I are displayed again. The highlight, however, is still in cell N6, as you can see from the cell reference in the status line. To confirm that column A is unfrozen,

Press: (HOME)

Column A is no longer frozen and the highlight is positioned in cell A6.

Titles can also be frozen across a row as easily as they are frozen down a column. To indicate the row to freeze, move the highlight one row below the row to be frozen. To freeze the column labels in row 6,

Move to: A7
Select: **O**ptions>Freeze **T**itles
Press: (↑)

Again the highlight movement is restricted to unfrozen cells.

Using (↓),

Move to: A29

Your display screen should be similar to Figure 7-5.

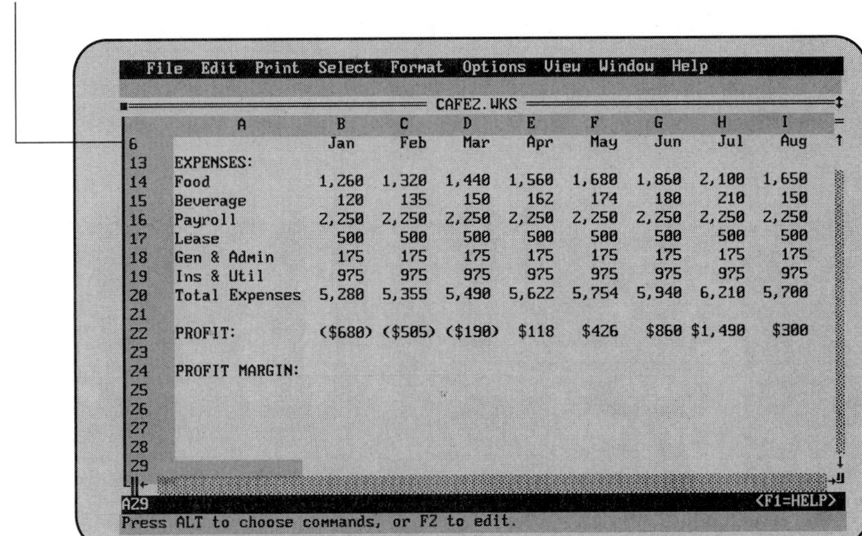

FIGURE 7-5

Row 6 remained stationary in the window as you scrolled down through the spreadsheet.

Using (→),

Move to: N29

Although the month labels have remained stationary in the window with the row labels unfrozen, it is again difficult to read the spreadsheet. Conveniently, both column and row titles can be frozen at the same time.

Press: (CTRL) - (HOME)

Notice that the Home position is the upper-left corner of the unfrozen spreadsheet cells rather than cell A1, which is frozen.

Clear the frozen horizontal titles.

To freeze both the row and column titles at the same time, move the highlight one row below the rows to be frozen and one column to the right of the columns to be frozen.

Move to: B7
Select: Options>Freeze Titles
Press: (←)
Press: (↑)

The rows above and the column to the left of the highlight position are frozen. Watch your display carefully as you use your arrow keys to

Move to: N7
Move to: N29

Your display screen should be similar to Figure 7-6.

FIGURE 7-6

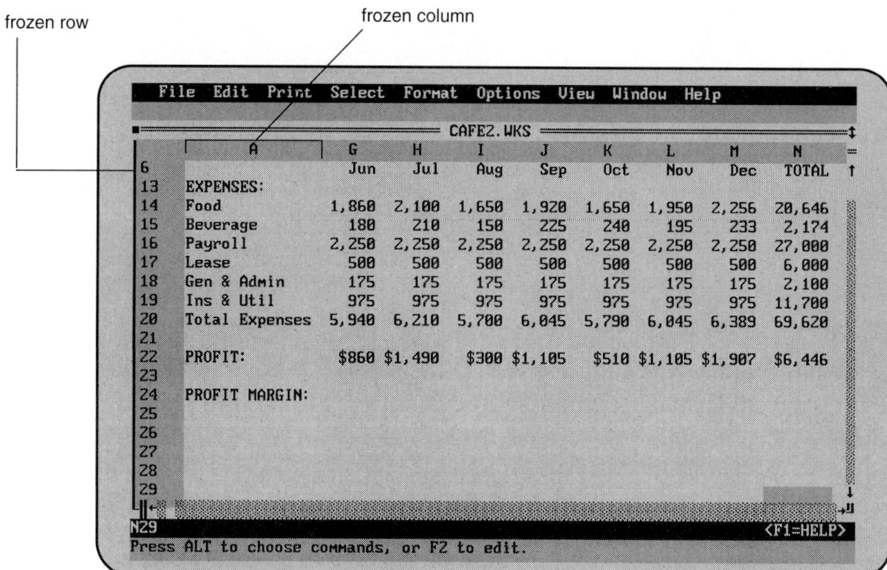

Both the row and column titles remain stationary in the window as you scroll through the spreadsheet.

Press: (CTRL) - (HOME)

The Home position is now the upper-left corner of the unfrozen rows and columns, cell B7.

Splitting Windows

The frozen titles greatly improve the readability of the spreadsheet. However, it is still difficult to compare the values in columns that cannot be viewed in the same window. For example, to compare the values in each month to the values in the TOTAL column or to certain other months is difficult. This is because as one column comes into view on the display screen, the other may scroll off because of lack of space in the window.

You could freeze the leftmost column you want to compare and then scroll the spreadsheet until the column on the right comes into view. But then you would not be able to make any changes or see the other columns to the left of the frozen column. The solution is to divide the window into different parts so you can view different areas of the spreadsheet at the same time.

The Window>Split command lets you split the window horizontally and vertically into **panes.** You can divide the window into two side-by-side panes, two upper and lower panes, or four panes.

To easily compare the values in each month to the values in column N, TOTAL, you will split the window into two side-by-side panes.

Select: Window

For Help information about this feature,

Highlight: Split
Press: F1

Read the three pages of Help information about this feature. When you are done, to leave Help,

Press: ESC

To select the Split command,

Press: ↵

Your display screen should be similar to Figure 7-7.

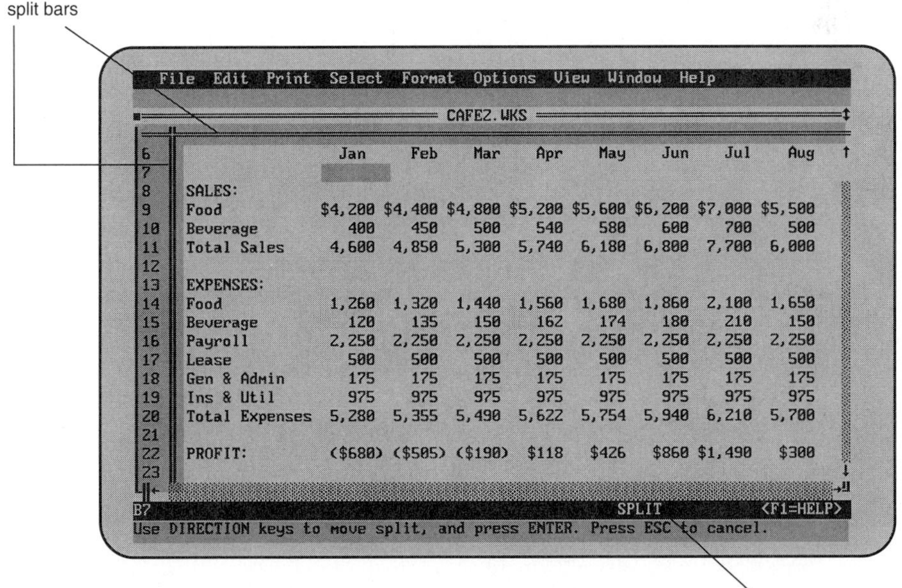

FIGURE 7-7

A split bar appears along the upper and left border of the workspace. The status line displays SPLIT to remind you that you are using this feature. You move the horizontal split bar by using the up and down arrow keys and the vertical split bar by using the right and left arrow keys.

Press: (↓) (2 times)
Press: (→) (5 times)

The horizontal split bar has moved down two rows and the vertical split bar has moved character by character five spaces to the right.

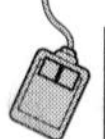

Mouse Note: You can move the split by dragging the split bar (= or ||) in the scroll bar to where you want the split.

You can also position the split bars on the opposite border of the workspace using the (END) key.

Press: (END)

The horizontal split bar is now on the bottom of the workspace and the vertical split bar is on the right edge of the workspace.

To position the vertical split bar two columns from the left edge of the workspace,

Press: (←) (16 times)

The vertical split bar should be between the June and July columns on the screen. To complete the command,

Press: (↵)

Your screen should be similar to Figure 7-8.

FIGURE 7-8

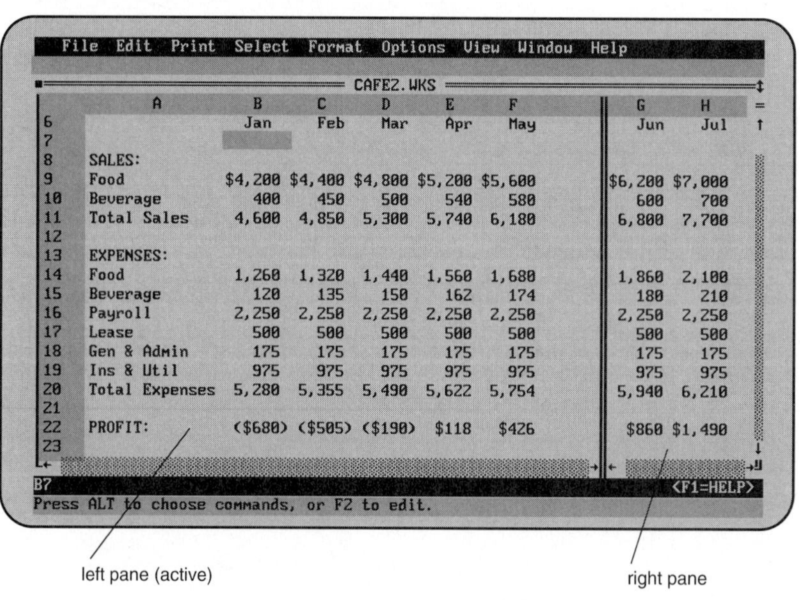

The highlight is positioned in the left pane. This is the **active pane**.

Watch your display screen carefully as you use (→) to

Move to: N7

The columns in the left pane move into view as the highlight moves across the row. The right pane does not change. Now the values for September through Total are visible.

Using (↓),

Move to: N29

Your display screen should be similar to Figure 7-9.

FIGURE 7-9

```
 File  Edit  Print  Select  Format  Options  View  Window  Help
                           CAFE2.WKS
           A             J      K      L      M      N        G      H
6                      Sep    Oct    Nov    Dec   TOTAL      Jun    Jul
13  EXPENSES:
14  Food              1,920  1,650  1,950  2,256  20,646    1,860  2,100
15  Beverage            225    240    195    233   2,174      180    210
16  Payroll           2,250  2,250  2,250  2,250  27,000    2,250  2,250
17  Lease               500    500    500    500   6,000      500    500
18  Gen & Admin         175    175    175    175   2,100      175    175
19  Ins & Util          975    975    975    975  11,700      975    975
20  Total Expenses    6,045  5,790  6,045  6,389  69,620    5,940  6,210
21
22  PROFIT:          $1,105   $510 $1,105 $1,907  $6,446     $860 $1,490
23
24  PROFIT MARGIN:
25
26
27
28
29
N29                                                          <F1=HELP>
Press ALT to choose commands, or F2 to edit.
```

The rows scrolled together in both panes. When you scroll vertically through a vertical pane, the rows in the other pane will scroll at the same time, keeping the rows even in both panes.

Press: (CTRL) - (HOME)

You can move the highlight from one pane to the other by using (F6) to move to the next pane or (SHIFT) - (F6) to move to the previous pane. When there are only two panes, (F6) will move the highlight back and forth between the two panes.

Press: (F6)

The highlight is positioned in cell G7 in the right pane.

Press: (END)

The TOTAL column is visible in the pane. Now the January through May data displayed in the left pane can easily be compared to the total values displayed in the right pane. Splitting the window into panes lets you view different parts of the same spreadsheet. Any changes made in one pane are made to the entire spreadsheet and will be seen in either pane.

Displaying a Percent

Now that Paula knows how to move around and manage a large spreadsheet, she needs to enter the formula to calculate the profit margin in cell B24. To switch back to the left window,

Press: (F6)

Using (↓),

Move to: B24

The formula to calculate profit margin is:

Profit/Total Sales*100%

Enter the formula in cell B24 to calculate the profit margin (January profit divided by the January Total Sales) using pointing. Do not multiply it times 100 percent.

Your display screen should be similar to Figure 7-10.

FIGURE 7-10

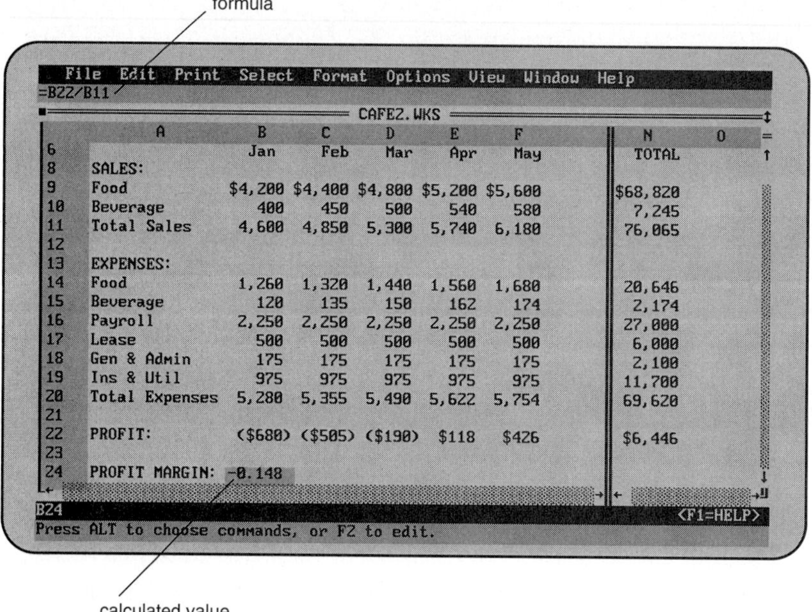

The formula =B22/B11 should be displayed in the formula bar and the value "-0.148" displayed in cell B24.

To display the value in this cell as a percent, you need to change the cell format to a percent with zero decimal places. Setting the cell format to Percent will also multiply the formula in the cell times 100.

Select: Format>**P**ercent>**0**>(↵)

Your display screen should be similar to Figure 7-11.

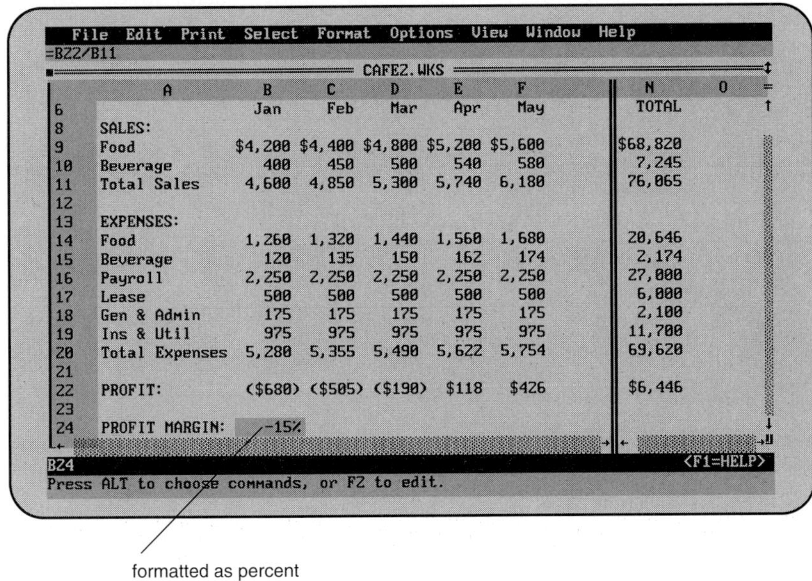

FIGURE 7-11

The profit margin for January is "-15%."

Setting the cell format to a percent takes the value in the cell and multiplies it by 100. The value is displayed with a percent sign (%).

Copy the formula in cell B24 across the row through N24 using the Edit>Fill Right command.

To clear the highlight,

Press: (←)

Your screen should be similar to Figure 7-12.

FIGURE 7-12

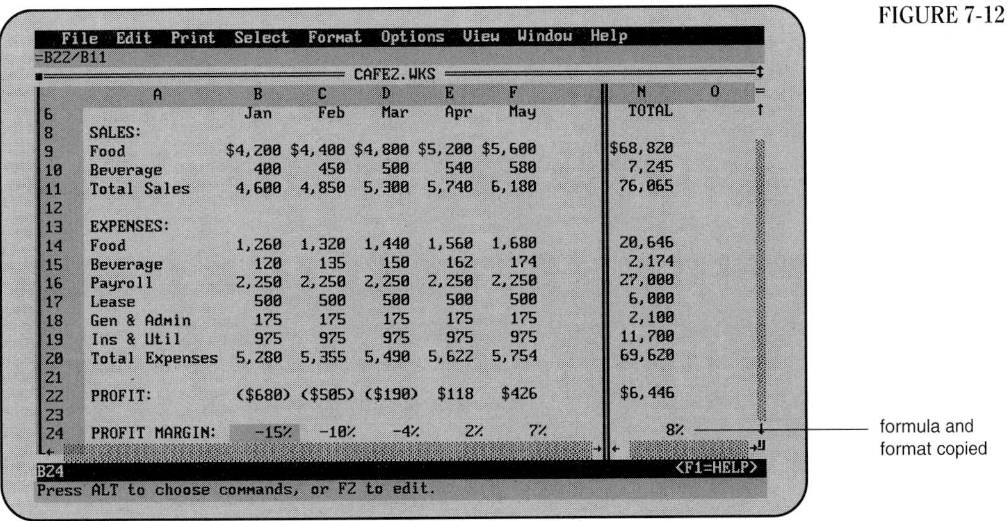

Notice that not only was the formula copied, but also the cell format. Also, you can see that the Total Profit margin in cell N24 in the right pane for the year is "8%." The board of directors wants the proposed cafe expansion to show a 20 percent total profit margin during the first year of operation. The total profit margin, using the figures as budgeted for the year, is much below this objective.

Using What-If Analysis

After some consideration, Paula decides that the only way to increase the total profit margin is to reduce expenses. She thinks she can reduce payroll by more carefully scheduling the number of hours the employees work. She can decrease the number of employee work hours by scheduling fewer employees to work during slow periods.

The process of evaluating what effect reducing the payroll expenses will have on the total profit margin is called **what-if analysis.** What-if analysis is a technique used to evaluate the effects of changing selected factors in a spreadsheet. Paula wants to know what would happen if payroll expenses decreased a set amount each month.

First, Paula would like to see the effect of reducing the payroll expenses to $2,100 per month.

Move to: B16
Type: **2100**
Press: ⏎

The profit margin for January (B24) changed from -15 to -12 percent.

To see the effect of reducing the payroll expenses to $2,100 for each month on the total profit margin, copy the January payroll value to the February through December payroll cells using Edit>Fill Right.

The spreadsheet has been recalculated. The new total profit margin is displayed in cell N24 in the right pane. Reducing the payroll expenses to 2100 per month has increased the total profit margin from 8 to 11 percent. This is still not enough.

Paula realizes that it may take her several tries before she reduces the payroll expenses enough to arrive at a total profit margin of 20 percent. Each time she changes the payroll expense, she has to copy the values across the entire row. A quicker way to enter different payroll expense values into the spreadsheet is by using a work cell. Any blank cell outside the spreadsheet area can be used as a work cell.

Paula will use cell O16 in the right pane as the work cell. To switch windows,

Press: F6

The highlight should be in cell O16 in the right pane.

This time, Paula will decrease payroll expenses to $1,900 per month.

Type: **1900**
Press: ⏎

The value in the work cell needs to be copied into the payroll expense cells in the spreadsheet. To do this, a formula referencing the work cell is entered in the payroll expense cells. This formula will tell the program to add the value in cell O16 to the cell contents.

Press: F6

The highlight should be in cell B16. To enter the formula =O16 in cell B16 using pointing,

Type: =
Press: F6

The highlight should be in cell O16 in the right pane.

Press: ↵

Your display screen should be similar to Figure 7-13.

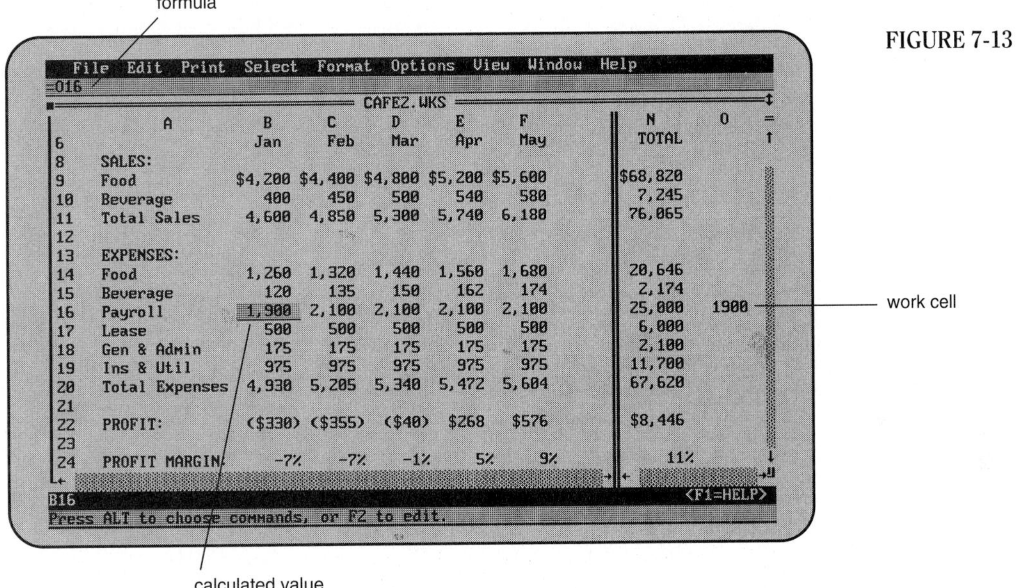

FIGURE 7-13

The value 1900 is entered in cell B16. The formula in B16 tells Works to add the value in cell O16 to cell B16.

Copy the formula in the January payroll cell to the February through December payroll cells using Edit>Fill Right.

To clear the highlight,

Press: ←

The spreadsheet again has been recalculated. However, there is something wrong. The value 1900 should appear in cells C16 through M16. Instead, the value 0 appears in those cells.

Move to: C16

Your display screen should be similar to Figure 7-14.

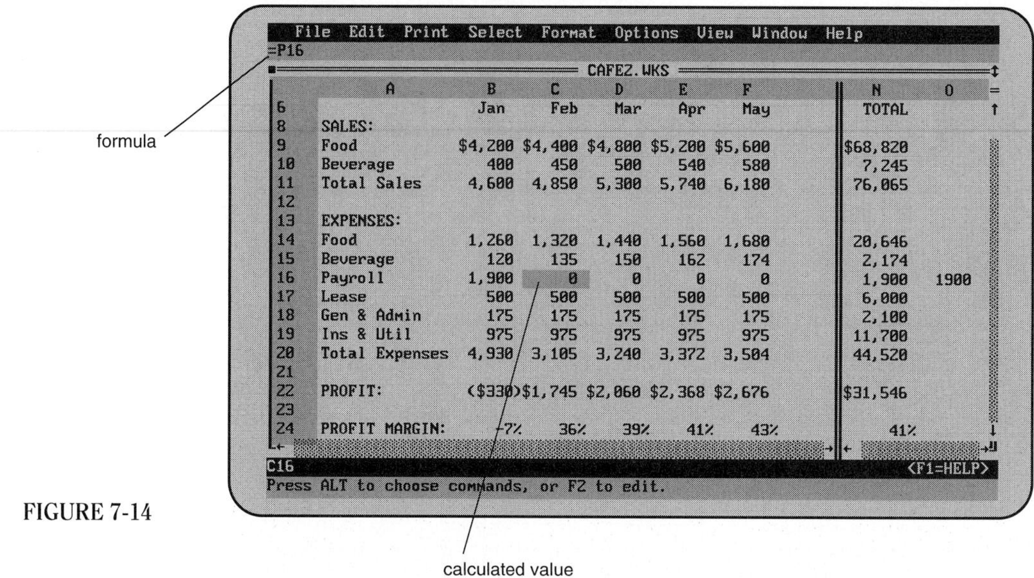

FIGURE 7-14

The formula bar shows the formula in this cell is =P16, which is a blank cell. Since it contains nothing, the value of zero is entered in C16.

Move to cells D16, E16, and F16. Look at how the formula changes from =P16 to =Q16, =R16, and =S16. The column letter has been adjusted relative to the new column location of the formula in row 16. Each of the formulas in the cells references the cell one column to the right of the previous formula. They were adjusted relative to their location in the spreadsheet. As you learned in Lab 6, the formulas contained relative cell references.

Using an Absolute Cell Reference

The formula in B16 needs to be entered so that the column in the referenced cell, O16, will not change when the formula is copied. To do this, you will use an **absolute cell reference.**

Move to: B16

To change the formula in B16 to have an absolute cell reference, enter a $ (dollar sign) character in front of the column letter. You can enter the dollar sign character by typing it in directly or you can use the (F4) key. Pressing (F4) repeatedly cycles a cell address through all possible combinations of cell reference types. When you use (F4), you must be using pointing to specify the cell reference in the formula. To reenter the formula

Type: =

To move the highlight to point to cell O16,

Press: (F6)

To change this cell reference in the formula bar to absolute,

Press: (F4)

The cell address now displays a $ character before both the column letter and row number (O16). Because a dollar sign is entered before both the column letter and row number, this cell address is absolute. If this formula were copied to another row and column location in the spreadsheet, the copied formula would be an exact duplicate of the original formula (O16).

Press: (F4)

The cell address has changed to display a dollar sign before the row number only (O$16). This is a **mixed cell reference** because only the row number is preceded by an absolute address, not the column letter. A mixed cell reference contains both relative and absolute cell references. If this formula were copied to another column and row, the column in the referenced cell in the formula would be adjusted relative to its new location in the spreadsheet, but the row number would not change. For example, if the formula in B16 (O$16) were copied from B16 to E12 (right three columns and up four rows), the formula in E12 would be R$16. The column letter increases three letters (O to R), but the row number does not change.

Press: (F4)

Again, this is a mixed cell reference. This time, the $ character precedes the column letter. Consequently, when this formula is copied to another row and column, the row in the referenced cell in the formula will be adjusted relative to its new location in the spreadsheet and the column will not change. For example, the formula in B16 ($O16) would change to $O12 if it were copied to cell B12. The column letter does not change, but the row number would decrease by 4 (16 to 12).

Press: (F4)

The formula returns to relative cell references. You have cycled the cell address through all possible combinations of cell references.

To stop the relative adjustment of the column in the formula when it is copied from one column location to another in the same row, the formula needs to be a mixed cell reference with the column letter absolute. To make this change,

Press: (F4) (3 times)

To accept the formula as displayed in the formula bar (=$O16),

Press: (↵)

Copy this formula from the January payroll cell to the February through December payroll cells using Edit>Fill Right.

To clear the highlight,

Press: (←)

The value 1900 appears in each cell in row 16.

Move to: C16

Your display screen should be similar to Figure 7-15.

FIGURE 7-15

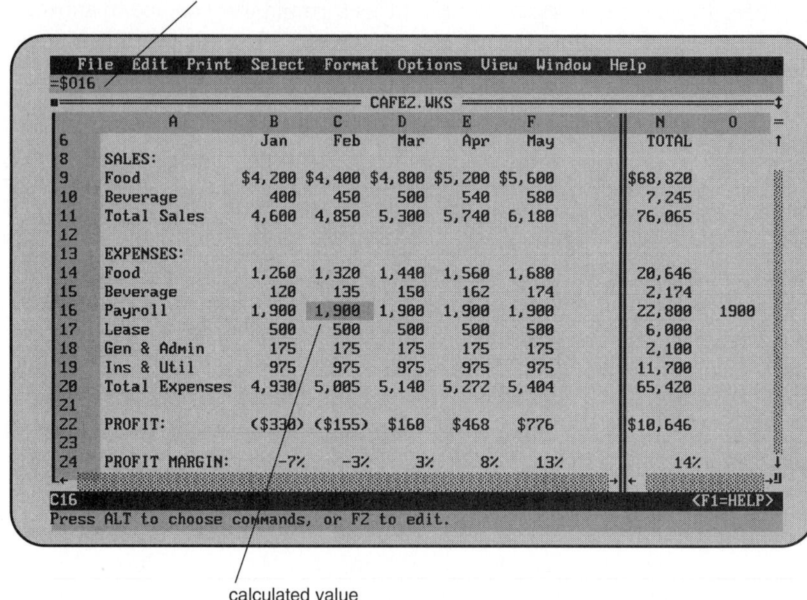

The formula displayed in the control panel is an exact duplicate of the formula in B16. It references the cell O16. Using an absolute cell reference in the formula easily solved the problem. It stopped the relative adjustment of the cells in the copied formula by maintaining the particular cell coordinates.

The result of decreasing the payroll expenses to $1,900 each month has increased the total profit margin to 14 percent (cell N24). This is closer to the 20 percent management objective. But it's still not good enough.

Decrease the payroll expense to $1,600 per month as follows:

Press: (F6)

The highlight should be in cell O16.

Type: **1600**
Press: (↵)

Your display screen should be similar to Figure 7-16.

FIGURE 7-16

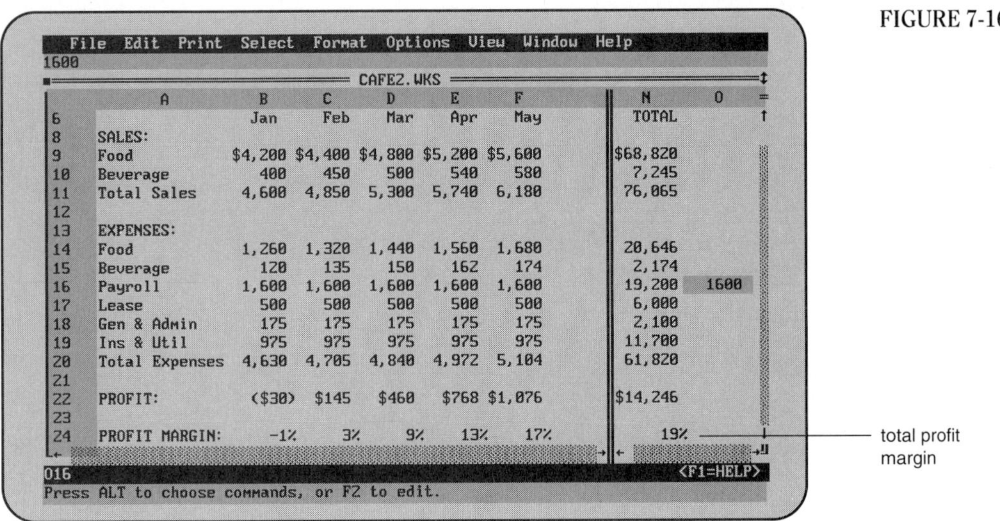
File Edit Print Select Format Options View Window Help
1600
CAFE2.WKS

	A	B	C	D	E	F	N	O
6		Jan	Feb	Mar	Apr	May	TOTAL	
8	SALES:							
9	Food	$4,200	$4,400	$4,800	$5,200	$5,600	$68,820	
10	Beverage	400	450	500	540	580	7,245	
11	Total Sales	4,600	4,850	5,300	5,740	6,180	76,065	
12								
13	EXPENSES:							
14	Food	1,260	1,320	1,440	1,560	1,680	20,646	
15	Beverage	120	135	150	162	174	2,174	
16	Payroll	1,600	1,600	1,600	1,600	1,600	19,200	1600
17	Lease	500	500	500	500	500	6,000	
18	Gen & Admin	175	175	175	175	175	2,100	
19	Ins & Util	975	975	975	975	975	11,700	
20	Total Expenses	4,630	4,705	4,840	4,972	5,104	61,820	
21								
22	PROFIT:	($30)	$145	$460	$768	$1,076	$14,246	
23								
24	PROFIT MARGIN:	-1%	3%	9%	13%	17%	19%	

O16 <F1=HELP>
Press ALT to choose commands, or F2 to edit.

The value in O16 was quickly entered into the payroll expense cells in row 16 for each month and the spreadsheet was recalculated.

By using a work cell and referencing it in a formula in the spreadsheet using absolute cell referencing, changing the what-if value becomes a simple process.

The total profit margin is now 19 percent. This is still not enough. Try 1400.

The total profit margin is now 22 percent. That's too high. You know the appropriate payroll expense level is between $1,700 and $1,400. Now try 1500.

Your display screen should be similar to Figure 7-17.

FIGURE 7-17

File Edit Print Select Format Options View Window Help
1500
CAFE2.WKS

	A	B	C	D	E	F	N	O
6		Jan	Feb	Mar	Apr	May	TOTAL	
8	SALES:							
9	Food	$4,200	$4,400	$4,800	$5,200	$5,600	$68,820	
10	Beverage	400	450	500	540	580	7,245	
11	Total Sales	4,600	4,850	5,300	5,740	6,180	76,065	
12								
13	EXPENSES:							
14	Food	1,260	1,320	1,440	1,560	1,680	20,646	
15	Beverage	120	135	150	162	174	2,174	
16	Payroll	1,500	1,500	1,500	1,500	1,500	18,000	1500
17	Lease	500	500	500	500	500	6,000	
18	Gen & Admin	175	175	175	175	175	2,100	
19	Ins & Util	975	975	975	975	975	11,700	
20	Total Expenses	4,530	4,605	4,740	4,872	5,004	60,620	
21								
22	PROFIT:	$70	$245	$560	$868	$1,176	$15,446	
23								
24	PROFIT MARGIN:	2%	5%	11%	15%	19%	20%	

O16 <F1=HELP>
Press ALT to choose commands, or F2 to edit.

total profit margin

That's it! The total profit margin is 20 percent if payroll expenses are reduced to $1,500 per month.

To remove the split pane from the window,

Select: Window>Split

The horizontal split bar needs to be moved out of the workspace. To do this quickly,

Press: (END)
Press: (↵)

The display screen returns to one window.
Unfreeze the titles.

Press: (CTRL) - (HOME)

Entering the System Date

You can enter the date into a spreadsheet either by typing the date in a format Works recognizes or by using a shortcut method, pressing (CTRL) in combination with the semi-colon key ((CTRL) - ;). Using this method displays the system date entered at the DOS prompt into the spreadsheet.

Move to: A2
Press: (CTRL) - ;
Press: (↵)

The current date is displayed in the formula bar and in the cell.
Your display screen should be similar to Figure 7-18.

FIGURE 7-18

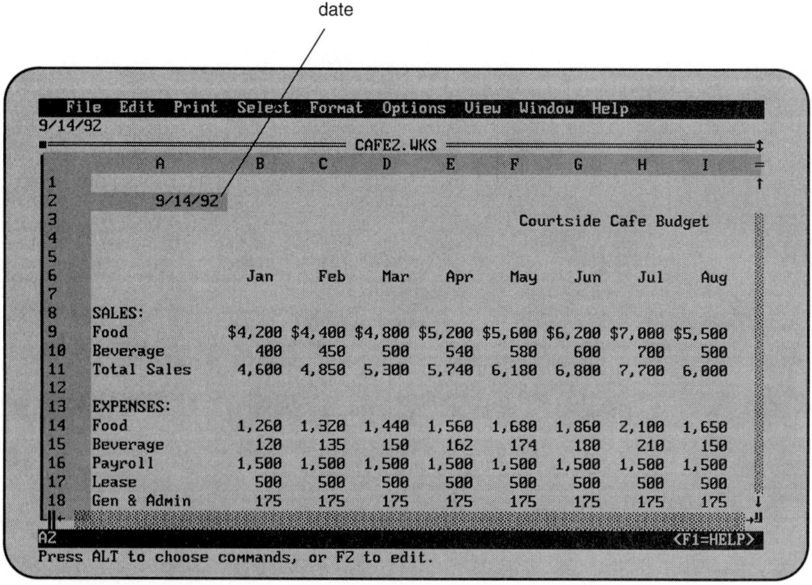

Note: The date displayed in this cell will differ, depending on the system date you entered at the DOS prompt.

The spreadsheet is ready to be printed.

Before saving and printing the spreadsheet, enter your name in cell A1. Save this spreadsheet using the filename CAFE3.

Printing a Range

When the spreadsheet is printed, Paula does not want the work cell, O16, included. To tell Works what area of the spreadsheet to print, select the range first.

Press: (F8)

Highlight cells A1 through N24.

Select: Print>Set Print **A**rea

The defined range is now ready to be printed. To clear the highlighted area,

Press: (↑)

Note for floppy disk users: Insert the appropriate disks as directed by the program.

Select: Print>**P**rint>**P**rint

Your spreadsheet should be printing. Your printed output should be similar to Figure 7-19.

FIGURE 7-19

Student Name
6/14/90

Courtside Cafe Budget

	Jan	Feb	Mar	Apr	May	Jun	Jul	Aug	Sep	Oct	Nov	Dec	TOTAL
SALES:													
Food	$4,200	$4,400	$4,800	$5,200	$5,600	$6,200	$7,000	$5,500	$6,400	$5,500	$6,500	$7,520	$68,820
Beverage	$400	$450	$500	$540	$580	$600	$700	$500	$750	$800	$650	$775	$7,245
Total Sales	$4,600	$4,850	$5,300	$5,740	$6,180	$6,800	$7,700	$6,000	$7,150	$6,300	$7,150	$8,295	$76,065
EXPENSES:													
Food	$1,260	$1,320	$1,440	$1,560	$1,680	$1,860	$2,100	$1,650	$1,920	$1,650	$1,950	$2,256	$20,646
Beverage	$120	$135	$150	$162	$174	$180	$210	$150	$225	$240	$195	$233	$2,174
Payroll	$1,500	$1,500	$1,500	$1,500	$1,500	$1,500	$1,500	$1,500	$1,500	$1,500	$1,500	$1,500	$18,000
Lease	$500	$500	$500	$500	$500	$500	$500	$500	$500	$500	$500	$500	$6,000
Gen & Admin	$175	$175	$175	$175	$175	$175	$175	$175	$175	$175	$175	$175	$2,100
Ins & Util	$975	$975	$975	$975	$975	$975	$975	$975	$975	$975	$975	$975	$11,700
Total Expenses	$4,530	$4,605	$4,740	$4,872	$5,004	$5,190	$5,460	$4,950	$5,295	$5,040	$5,295	$5,639	$60,620
PROFIT:	$70	$245	$560	$868	$1,176	$1,610	$2,240	$1,050	$1,855	$1,260	$1,855	$2,657	$15,446
PROFIT MARGIN:	2%	5%	11%	15%	19%	24%	29%	18%	26%	20%	26%	32%	20%

Displaying Formulas

Now that the spreadsheet is complete, Paula wants a copy of the formulas used in the spreadsheet for her files. Works can display the formulas a spreadsheet uses for calculations rather than the calculated values. This is useful to help someone better understand the structure of a spreadsheet and to locate errors in formulas. Using the Options>Show Formulas command is also helpful in locating the Formula containing the circular reference. To do this,

Select: Options>Show **F**ormulas

The formulas the spreadsheet uses for calcuations are displayed in the cells instead of the calculated values. Works automatically increases the column widths to allow long formulas to be fully displayed. To see the rest of the formulas in the spreadsheet,

Move to: N24

Your screen should be similar to Figure 7-20.

FIGURE 7-20

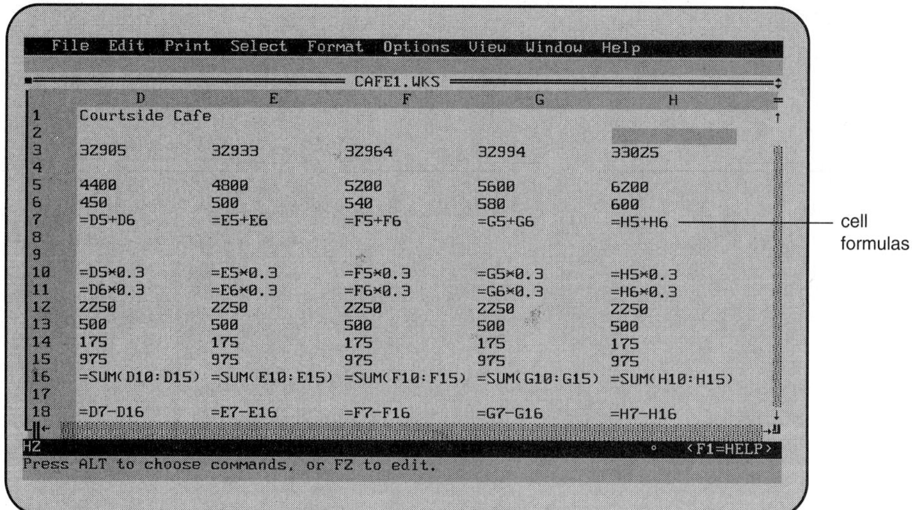

File Edit Print Select Format Options View Window Help

CAFE1.WKS

	D	E	F	G	H
1	Courtside Cafe				
2					
3	32905	32933	32964	32994	33025
4					
5	4400	4800	5200	5600	6200
6	450	500	540	580	600
7	=D5+D6	=E5+E6	=F5+F6	=G5+G6	=H5+H6
8					
9					
10	=D5*0.3	=E5*0.3	=F5*0.3	=G5*0.3	=H5*0.3
11	=D6*0.3	=E6*0.3	=F6*0.3	=G6*0.3	=H6*0.3
12	2250	2250	2250	2250	2250
13	500	500	500	500	500
14	175	175	175	175	175
15	975	975	975	975	975
16	=SUM(D10:D15)	=SUM(E10:E15)	=SUM(F10:F15)	=SUM(G10:G15)	=SUM(H10:H15)
17					
18	=D7-D16	=E7-E16	=F7-F16	=G7-G16	=H7-H16

H2 <F1=HELP>
Press ALT to choose commands, or F2 to edit.

Paula would like to keep a copy of the spreadsheet formulas in her files for future reference.

To print the spreadsheet formulas,

Select: Print>**P**rint

She also wants the row numbers and column letters printed so she can tell which cell each formula is in. To select the option that will print the row and column labels,

Select: Print row and column **l**abels>**P**rint

The spreadsheet should be printing. The row numbers and column letters are printed along with the displayed formulas.

To change the display back to values,

Select: Options>Show Formulas

The values are displayed in the spreadsheet cells again.

Exit Works or close the file if you plan to continue using Works.

Key Terms

circular reference
freeze
pane
active pane
what-if analysis
absolute cell reference
mixed cell reference

Matching

1. $R22	____	**a.**	absolute cell reference
2. (CTRL) - ;	____	**b.**	mixed cell reference
3. CIRC	____	**c.**	moves to the next pane
4. Options>Freeze Titles	____	**d.**	enters the system date
5. Window>Split	____	**e.**	cycles through cell reference types
6. (SHIFT) - (F6)	____	**f.**	displays a value as a percent
7. C25	____	**g.**	moves to the previous pane
8. (F6)	____	**h.**	freezes spreadsheet titles
9. (F4)	____	**i.**	divides the window into panes
10. Format>Percent	____	**j.**	status indicator for circular reference

Practice Exercises

1. Retrieve the file PETSHOP.WKS. This is a spreadsheet of an income statement for the Pet Supply Shop. The formulas in the spreadsheet are:

Row 11	Gross margin = Sales - Cost of goods sold
Row 17	Total expense = Marketing + Administrative + Miscellaneous expenses
Row 19	Net income before taxes = Gross margin - Total expense
Row 20	Federal taxes = Net income before taxes * .52
Row 22	Net income after taxes = Net income before taxes - Federal taxes

Column N Total = Sum over 12 months

- Locate and correct the formula or function causing the CIRC reference to be displayed in the spreadsheet (there may be more than one).

The owner of the Pet Supply Shop wants to change the spreadsheet to calculate the cost of goods sold as a percent of sales. He estimates that the cost of goods sold is about 45 percent of sales. You will use a work cell to hold the percent value and change the values in row 9 to be computed using this value as follows:

- Position the spreadsheet so that rows 6 through 23 are displayed in the window. Freeze everything above row 7 and to the left of column B.
- Create two side-by-side panes. The right pane should be large enough to display two columns of data. Display the Total column in the right pane.
- Switch to the left pane. Move to column B. Scroll rows 22 to 28 into view. Cell B25 is your work cell. A label has already been entered in cell A25 to identify the value you will enter in B25.
- Enter the value .45 in cell B25. Change the format of this cell to Fixed with two decimal places.
- Enter the formula using a mixed cell reference to calculate the cost of goods sold (Sales*Percent cost value) in cell B9.
- Copy the formula in B9 to C9 through M9. To see how this change has affected the total net income after taxes, look at the value in N22 (right pane). What is the value in cell N22?
- The manager feels he may have been too high in his estimate for the percent cost value. He wants to see the effect on the total of changing the value in cell B25. Change the value in cell B25 to .40. What is the value in cell N22 now?

Next, the manager would like to see the effect of changing the marketing, administrative, and miscellaneous expenses. By calculating these values as a percent of the gross margin, he feels he will be able to plan and budget better for the future.

- Enter the following values in the cells specified:

	Cell	**Value**
MKT	B26	.15
ADM	B27	.28
MISC	B28	.08

- Format cells B26, B27, and B28 to be displayed as Fixed with two decimal places.
- Change the contents of cells B13 through B15 to be calculated using a formula referencing cells B26 through B28. Copy the formulas from B13..B15 through C13..M15. What is the total net income after taxes (N22) now?
- Leave the percent value for cost at .40. Change the other percent values to arrive at a net total income (N22) value as close to 5500 as possible. What total net income after taxes did you get? What were the percentages used?
- Clear the split panes and titles.

- Enter your name in cell A1 and the date in cell A2. Save the spreadsheet as PETSHOP2.

- Print the spreadsheet. Set the print range so that the work cells are not included.
- Print the spreadsheet with the row and column displayed and showing spreadsheet formulas.

2. To complete this problem, you must have created the spreadsheet in practice exercise 3 of Lab 2. Retrieve the file ZOOFIN2. You will extend and expand the spreadsheet for the three-year financial statement for the zoo. The assistant director of the zoo would like to project the financial statement for the next three years, 1993, 1994, and 1995.

- Insert three columns between 1992 and TOTAL. These columns will hold the data for the projected years. Enter the column headings 1993, 1994, and 1995 in cells F3, G3, and H3, respectively. Underline the new headings.
- Insert another blank row above the column headings. Enter the heading "========Projected========" centered above the year headings for 1993 through 1995.
- Display rows 3 through 20 on the screen. Freeze everything to the left of column B and above row 4.
- Enter formulas to calculate the projected income values for the years 1993–1995. The Support & Revenues projections are: operating expenses increase 15 percent over the previous year, supporting organizations 20 percent, and interest income 22 percent. The fund-raising projected income is directly related to the amount of money allocated to fund-raising activities (cell F17). For each dollar allocated they expect to raise $4.25.
- Enter formulas to calculate the projected applications and expenses for the years 1993–1995. Operating expenses are expected to increase 17 percent each year over the previous year, capital projects 17 percent, and fund-raising 5 percent. The operating reserve is calculated using the same formula as in previous years.
- Format the values in the 1993–1995 columns to Currency or Comma, as appropriate.
- Copy the formula from the 1992 column for TOTAL S & R, and TOTAL A/E to calculate the values for the years 1993 through 1995.
- Copy the double underlines in rows 11 and 19 to columns F, G, and H.
- Change the formulas used to calculate the TOTAL and AVERAGE in columns I and J to include the new columns containing the projected values for 1993–1995.
- Display columns A, F, G, and H on the screen. Split the window vertically between columns G and H. The columns of data for the years 1993 and 1994 should be displayed in the left pane, and TOTAL in the right pane. Print your display screen ((SHIFT) - (PrtScr) on most keyboards).

  In 1996, the zoo plans to add a new jungle exhibit that will cost $1,500,000. After looking at the results of the projected income statement on the operating reserve, they realize that they will not have enough money for the new project. Currently the amount allocated toward fund-raising is based upon a 5 percent increase over the previous year.

- Use cell F22 as a work cell. Format this cell to display Fixed format with two decimal places. Enter the current percent value (1.05) in this cell.
- Change the formulas in cells F17, G17, and H17 to calculate the percentage increase for money allocated to fund-raising in the years 1993 to 1995 by referencing the percent value in cell F22. Adjust the percent value in cell F22 until the total operating reserve is at least $1,500,000 by the end of 1995.
- Clear the split windows and unfreeze the titles.
- Erase the old date from cell A3, enter the current date in cell A2, and save the spreadsheet as ZOOFIN3.
- Print the spreadsheet. Do not include the work cell.
- Display the spreadsheet formulas. Print the spreadsheet with the row and column labels.

3. Open the file SPORTING. This is a spreadsheet of an income statement for Tom's Sporting Goods Store. The formulas in the spreadsheet are:

Row 14	Total Sales = Camping sales + Sporting Equipment sales + Fishing sales + Miscellaneous sales
Row 22	Total Cost of Goods Sold = Camping COGS + Sporting Equipment COGS + Fishing COGS + Miscellaneous COGS
Row 24	Gross Margin = Total Sales - Total Cost of Goods Sold
Row 31	Total Expenses = Advertising + Administrative + Overhead expenses
Row 34	Net Income Before Taxes = Gross margin - Total expense
Row 35	Federal taxes = Net income before taxes * .52
Row 37	Net Income After Taxes = Net income before taxes - Federal taxes
Column N	Total = Sum over 12 months

Tom wants to change the spreadsheet to calculate the cost of goods sold as a percent of sales. He estimates that the cost of goods sold is about 45 percent of sales. You will use a work cell to hold the percent value and change the values in rows 17, 18, 19, and 20 to compute the cost of goods sold.

- Display rows 6 through 23 in the window. Freeze the titles above row 7 and to the left of column B.
- Move to column N. Split the window vertically between columns L and M and horizontally at row 19. There should be four panes in the window.
- Display column N in the upper-right pane, columns B-E in the upper-left pane, and rows 40-43 in the lower-left pane.
- Cell C40 (lower-left pane) will be the work cell. A descriptive label has already been entered in cell A40 to identify the value you will enter in cell C40. Enter the value .45 in cell C40.

- Switch to the upper-left pane. Enter the formula to calculate the cost of goods sold for camping (=B9*C40) in cell B17. Copy this formula into cells B18, B19, and B20 using Edit>Fill Down.
- Copy the formulas in cells B17 through B20 across the row through December. To see how this change has affected the total net income after taxes, look at cell N37 (upper-right pane). What is the value in cell N37?
- Tom feels he may have been too high in his estimate for the percent cost value. He wants to see what effect the changing of the value in Cell C40 to .40 has on the total net income after taxes. Change the value in cell C40 to .40. What is the value in cell N37 now?

  Next, Tom wants to see the effect of changing the advertising, administrative, and overhead expenses. By calculating these values as a percent of gross margin, he feels he will be able to plan and budget better for the future. He estimates that advertising will be 9 percent of gross, administrative 28 percent, and overhead 15 percent. Enter the values in the cells specified:

	Cell	Percent
Advertising	C41	.09
Administration	C42	.28
Overhead	C43	.15

- Enter formulas in cells B27, B28, and B29 to calculate each expense as a percent of gross using the percent values in cells C41, C42, and C43. Copy the formulas from B27 through B29 across the row through December. What is the total net income after taxes (N37) now?
- Leave the percent value for cost of goods sold (C40) at .40. Change the percent values in the other three work cells to arrive at a total net income after taxes (N37) value of 8464. What were the percentages you used?
- Clear the windows and titles.
- Enter your name in cell A1 and the current date in cell A2.
- Save the spreadsheet as SPORTS.
- Print the entire spreadsheet (set the left and right margins at .5 inch).
- Print the formulas only with the row and column labels.

4. Open the file ABC2. The values in an income statement can be used to calculate a number of vital state-of-income ratios. These ratios measure profitability. One of the most common of these ratios is the Net Profit Margin Ratio. This ratio calculates income as a percentage of sales. Income is the amount that remains after cost of goods and all other expenses have been deducted from total revenue. You will calculate the Net Profit Margin Ratio for this income statement using before- and after-tax income values. Then you will use what-if analysis to arrive at a monthly after-tax net profit margin of 14 percent.

- Split the window horizontally at row 9. The upper window should display rows 1 through 9. In the lower window, display rows 17 through 25.

- In cell A21 enter the label "Profit Margin (BT)." In cell B21 enter the formula to calculate the before-tax profit margin ratio. This formula is calculated by dividing the Income Before Taxes value by the Sales value. Use pointing to enter this formula.
- In cell A22 enter the label "Profit Margin (AT)." In cell B22 enter the formula to calculate the after-tax profit margin ratio. This formula is calculated by dividing the Net Income value by the Sales value. Use pointing to enter this formula.
- Format cells B21-B22 as percent with one decimal place.
- Copy the formulas in cells B21 and B22 across the row through June.
- The company objective is to have a monthly after-tax profit margin ratio of 14 percent. Adjust the sales value for each month until the profit margin is 14 percent.
- Clear the split window.
- Enter the current date in cell A2.
- Save the spreadsheet as ABC3.
- Print the entire spreadsheet.
- Print the formulas only with the row and column labels.

Command Summary

Command	Shortcut	Action	Page
Print>Set Print **A**rea		Prints a range	215
Print>**P**rint>Row and column **l**abels		Prints row numbers and column letters for the spreadsheet	216
Forma**t**>**P**ercent		Displays value as percent	206
	F4	Cycles cell reference through all cell reference types	210
	CTRL - ;	Enters system date	214
Options>Freeze **T**itles		Freezes specified rows/columns	200
Options>Unfreeze **T**itles		Unfreezes rows/columns	200
Options>Show **F**ormulas		Displays formulas in cells	
Window>Spli**t**		Divides window into panes	203
	F6	Switches to next pane	205
	SHIFT - F6	Switches to previous pane	205

LAB

8 Creating and Printing Charts

CASE STUDY

The Sports Club annual membership promotion month is January. In preparation, the board of directors has asked the membership coordinator, Fred Morris, to present a report on the membership growth over the last five years.

Fred has maintained the membership data for the past five years. He has entered the data into a spreadsheet using Works. Although the data in the spreadsheet shows the club's growth, Fred feels the use of several charts would make it easier for the board of directors to see the trends and growth patterns over the five years.

You will follow Fred as he creates several different charts of the membership data.

OBJECTIVES

In this lab you will learn how to:

1. Create a bar and stacked bar chart.
2. Specify the X-axis labels.
3. Specify data to be charted.
4. Enter chart titles and legends.
5. Name the chart.
6. Create a line and a mixed chart.
7. Create a pie chart.
8. Shade and explode the pie chart.
9. Print a chart.

Exploring Graphics

Turn on your computer and load DOS. Load Works. Your data diskette should be in drive B or in the drive appropriate for your system.

To see the spreadsheet of membership data, open the file GROWTH.WKS.

Your display screen should be similar to Figure 8-1.

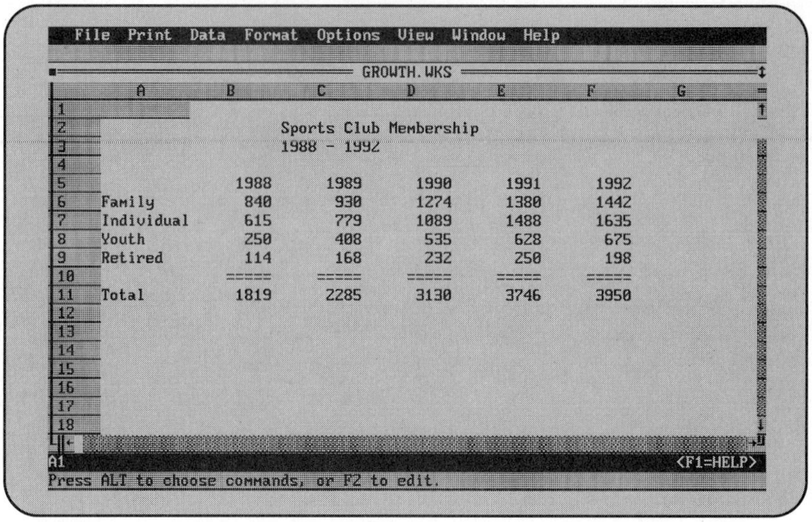

File Print Data Format Options View Window Help

GROWTH.WKS

	A	B	C	D	E	F	G
1							
2			Sports Club Membership				
3			1988 - 1992				
4							
5		1988	1989	1990	1991	1992	
6	Family	840	930	1274	1380	1442	
7	Individual	615	779	1089	1488	1635	
8	Youth	250	408	535	628	675	
9	Retired	114	168	232	250	198	
10		=====	=====	=====	=====	=====	
11	Total	1819	2285	3130	3746	3950	
12							
13							
14							
15							
16							
17							
18							

A1 <F1=HELP>
Press ALT to choose commands, or F2 to edit.

FIGURE 8-1

The spreadsheet lists the four Sports Club membership categories as row labels in cells A6 through A9. They are defined as follows:

Family	Spouse and dependent children
Individual	Single-person membership
Youth	Individual under 18 years of age
Retired	Individual over 55 years of age

The column labels in row 5 represent the years 1988 through 1992. The total for the four membership categories is displayed in row 11.

Although the spreadsheet shows the values for each membership category, it is hard to see how the different categories have changed over time. A visual representation of data in the form of a **chart** or graph would convey that information in an easy-to-understand and attractive way.

Works can produce eight types of charts: line, bar, stacked bar, 100% bar, area line, Hi-Lo-Close, X-Y, and pie. All types, except the pie, have some basic similarities. The basic parts of a line or bar chart are illustrated in Figure 8-2.

The bottom boundary of the chart is the **X-axis.** It is used to label the data being charted, such as a unit of time or a category.

The left boundary of the chart is the **Y-axis**. This axis is a numbered scale whose values are determined by the data used in the chart.

The spreadsheet data is visually displayed within the X- and Y-axis boundaries. It can be displayed as a line, bar, or markers. Each group of data that is displayed is represented by a symbol. A **legend** at the bottom of the chart describes the symbols used within the chart.

A chart can also contain several different titles. **Titles** are used to explain the contents of the chart. In Works, the two title lines at the top of the chart are called the chart title and subtitle. Titles can also be used to label the X- and Y-axes.

In pie charts there are no axes. Instead, the spreadsheet data that is charted is displayed as slices in a circle or pie. Each slice can be labeled. A chart title and subtitle line can be used; however, legends and X- and Y-axis titles are not used.

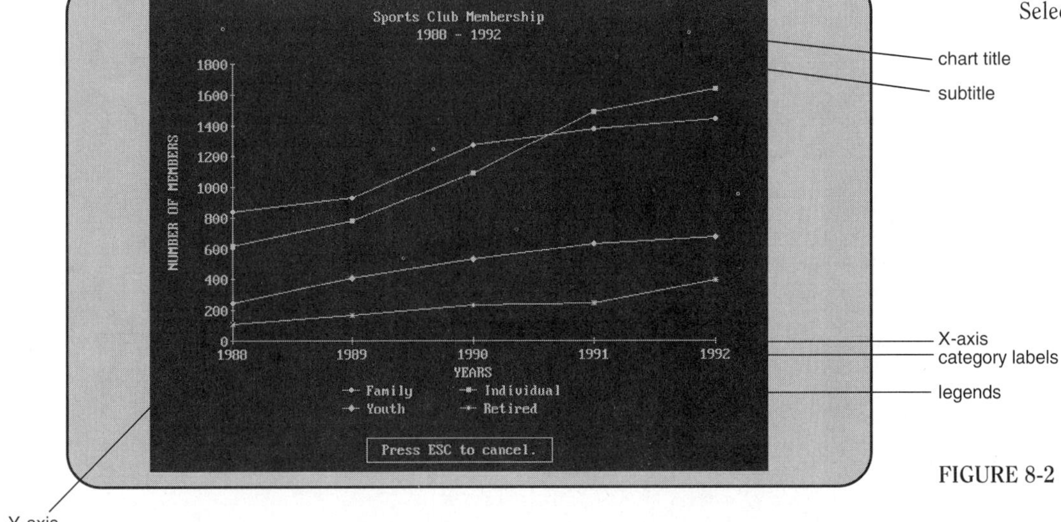

FIGURE 8-2

Selecting the Data to Chart

All charts are created from data contained in a spreadsheet. The first chart Fred would like to create is one of the membership growth for the four categories over the five years.

To create a chart in Works, you select the information from the spreadsheet that you want displayed as a chart. You can select up to six adjacent rows or columns of numbers plus any words that label each row and column. Works then translates the selected data into a chart.

The numbers to be charted are in cells B6 through F9. The year labels in cells B5 through F5 will label the X-axis, and the row labels in cells A6 through A9 will be the legends. The entire range, including the labels, must be selected. The range consists of the cells A5 through F9. Although cell A5 is empty, it is the corner cell of the range and must be included in order to correctly specify the range.

Move to: A5
Press: F8

Highlight the range A5 through F9.

Once the range is selected, you can view the chart Works has created. To do this,

Select: View

The View menu lets you switch between the Spreadsheet view and the Chart view of the spreadsheet tool. The Spreadsheet view, which is the default view, is the view you have been using throughout the labs. The Chart view is used to create and modify charts. To switch to the Chart view and instruct Works to create a new chart,

Select: New Chart

Note for floppy disk users: Insert the appropriate disk when directed by the program.

Note: To display charts, you must have a graphics adapter card that is supported by Works and the Works program must have been properly installed. See your instructor if your chart is not displayed.

Your screen should be similar to Figure 8-3.

FIGURE 8-3

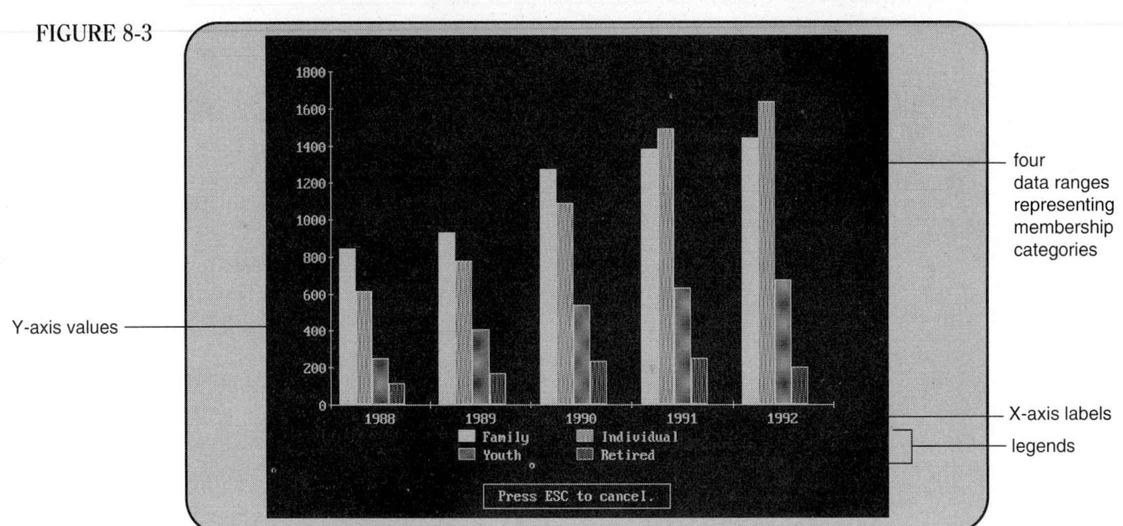

A **bar chart** of the data is displayed on the screen. Works creates a bar chart by default. A bar chart consists of a set of evenly spaced bars. Each bar represents one of the four membership categories in each year (B6 through F9). If you have a color monitor, the bars are displayed in different colors. If you have a monochrome monitor, the bars have different dot patterns.

The values on the Y-axis begin at 0 and end at 1800. The Y-axis is automatically set by Works as a scale of values determined by the lowest and highest values in the data range. The year labels in cells B5 through F5 label the X-axis, and the row labels in cells A6 through A9 are the legends. The legends add descriptive information to the chart. Without this information you would not understand what the data represent.

To clear the chart,

Press: (ESC)

Your screen should be similar to Figure 8-4.

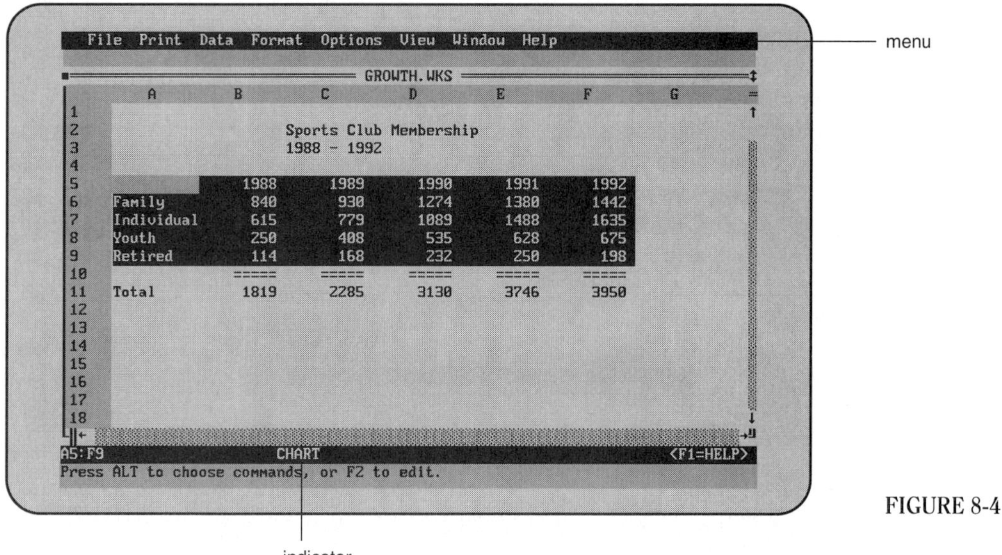

FIGURE 8-4

The spreadsheet is redisplayed.

Notice in the status line that the indicator CHART is displayed. This tells you that you are in the Chart view of the spreadsheet tool. Each view has its own menu. The Chart view menu bar lists eight menus. The commands in these menus allow you to modify charts you have created with Works. To briefly preview the Chart commands using the Help system,

Press: F1

Note for floppy disk users: Insert the appropriate disk when directed by the program.

Read the information on this and the next nine screens carefully; it describes many of the Chart commands you will be using in this lab. When you are done, to leave Help,

Press: ESC

Naming a Chart

Up to eight different charts can be created and stored in a spreadsheet. To create more than one chart in a spreadsheet, each chart is assigned a different name. Naming the chart allows the current chart settings to be stored in the spreadsheet and recalled for later use. The bar chart you just created was automatically assigned the name CHART1 by Works.

Select: View

Notice the name Chart1 below the Charts command. Works assigns a numbered name to each chart you create, just as it does to a file. And just as with a file, you can change the name to one that is more descriptive of the contents of the chart. To do this,

Select: Charts

Your screen should be similar to Figure 8-5.

FIGURE 8-5

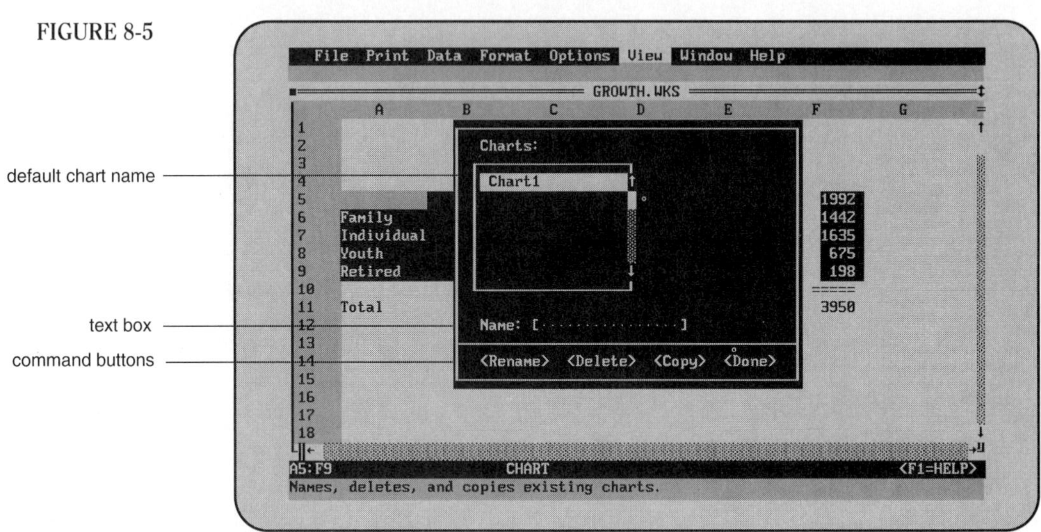

The Charts dialog box is displayed, showing the name of the chart you created. Since it is the only chart, it is also the selected chart. The Charts box lets you rename, copy, and delete charts. To rename this chart,

Select: Name

The cursor is positioned in the Name text box so you can type in a new name for the chart. A chart name can be up to 15 characters long and should be descriptive of the contents of the chart. It will appear exactly as you enter it, including upper- and lowercase characters. To rename the chart BAR,

Type: **BAR**
Select: Rename

The name Chart1 has been replaced by BAR in the chart box. To leave this command,

Select: Done

To view the chart again,

Select: View

The name of the chart is displayed. It is assigned the number 1 because it is the first chart created in this spreadsheet. The number is used to select the chart you want to view.

Select: 1 Bar

The chart is redisplayed. To clear the chart,

Press: (ESC)

The BAR chart settings are stored in the computer's memory for later use. The named chart is not permanently saved on the diskette until you save the spreadsheet file by using the File>Save command.

Changing the Chart Style

Once a chart is created, you can change or modify it. Fred would like to see how the same data displayed in the bar chart would look as a stacked bar chart. This can easily be done by changing the type of chart to stacked bar.

Select: Format

Your display screen should be similar to Figure 8-6.

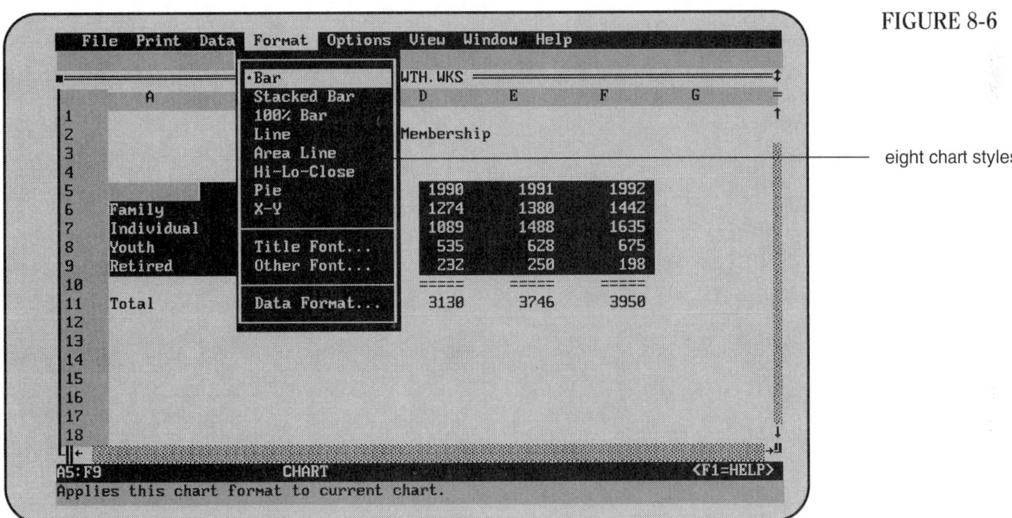

FIGURE 8-6

The eight styles or types of charts are listed in the Format menu. The Bar chart is the selected style. To change the current chart to a stacked bar chart,

Select: Stacked Bar

To see the change in the chart, you will use the View>Charts shortcut key, (SHIFT) - (F10).

Press: (SHIFT) - (F10)

Note: If you accidentally press (F10), you will be returned to the Spreadsheet view. To get back to the Chart view and view the chart, select View>1 Bar.

Your screen should be similar to Figure 8-7.

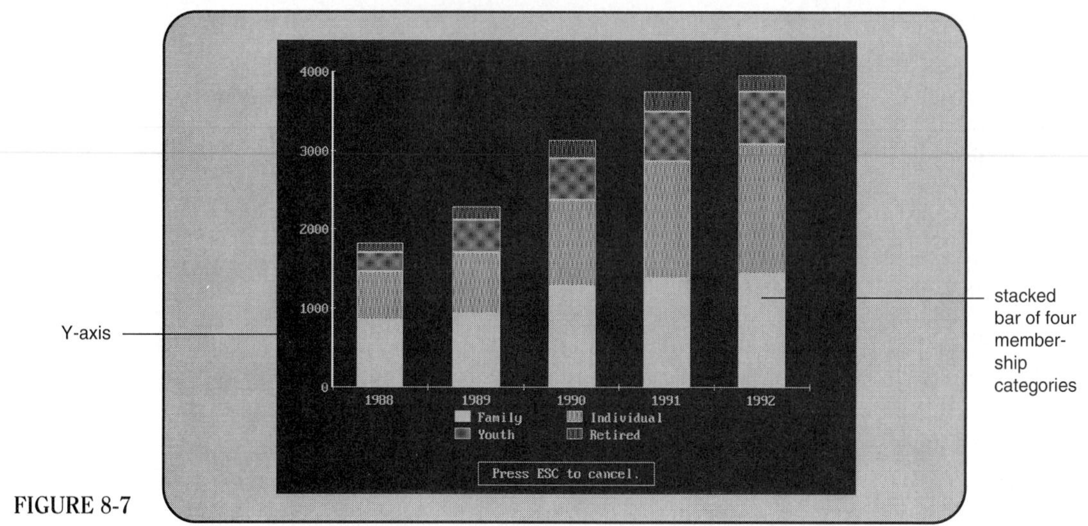

FIGURE 8-7

The same data displayed as a bar chart is displayed as a stacked bar chart. The **stacked bar chart** shows the proportion of each type of membership to the total membership in each year. Rather than the bars being displayed side by side, the bars are stacked upon each other. The Y-axis begins at 0 and ends at 4000. It is now easy to compare how much each membership category contributed to the total membership in each year.

Press: (ESC)

Entering Chart Titles

Chart titles help clarify the meaning of the data displayed in the chart. Titles can be entered at the top of the chart (two lines) and along the X- and Y-axes. The command to add titles is Data>Titles. Before using this command, look at the spreadsheet to see if any titles in the spreadsheet would be appropriate chart titles. The spreadsheet titles "Sports Club Membership" in cell C2 and "1988-1992" in cell C3 would be appropriate titles for this chart.

Select: Data>**T**itles

Your display screen should be similar to Figure 8-8.

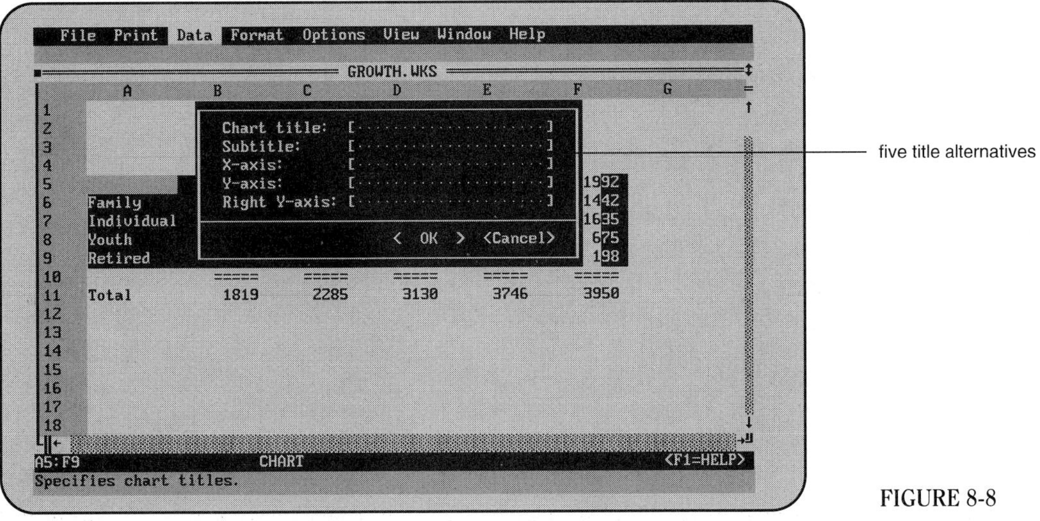

FIGURE 8-8

The five title alternatives are displayed in the Titles dialog box. They have the following effect:

Chart Title	Puts centered text at the top of the chart
Subtitle	Centers a second line of text at the top of the chart
X-axis	Places text along the horizontal axis
Y-axis	Places text along the vertical axis
Right Y-axis	Places a title along a vertical right axis

The cursor is ready for you to enter the chart title in the text box. You can type any title exactly as you want it to appear, or you can copy a title used in the spreadsheet. Each title can be a maximum of 37 characters long.

Rather than type the title in, you will enter the cell reference of the cell containing the label you want to use from the spreadsheet. Unfortunately, the dialog box covers up the location of the title in the spreadsheet.

As you noted earlier, however, the spreadsheet titles are located in cells C2 and C3. It is always a good idea to note the location of the titles in the spreadsheet before selecting the Titles command.

To enter the cell reference of the spreadsheet label you want to use as the chart title,

Type: **C2**

You can enter the subtitle next. The spreadsheet title "1988 - 1992" in cell D3 will be used as the chart subtitle.

Select: Subtitle
Type: **C3**

Next, you can enter titles for the X- and Y-axis. The X-axis shows the growth in membership over the five years. The Y-axis shows the number of members. You will label the X-axis "YEARS" and the Y-axis "NUMBER OF MEMBERS." The axis titles you want to use in the chart are not labels that are used in the spreadsheet. Therefore, the titles must be typed in the text box.

A title is displayed in the chart exactly as entered in the text box. You will enter the axis titles in all capital letters. If you make a mistake while typing the titles, use the (→) and (←) keys to move to the location of the error, delete it using (Bksp) or (DEL), and retype the entry correctly.

Select: X-axis
Type: **YEARS**

Select: Y-axis
Type: **NUMBER OF MEMBERS**

Your screen should be similar to Figure 8-9.

FIGURE 8-9

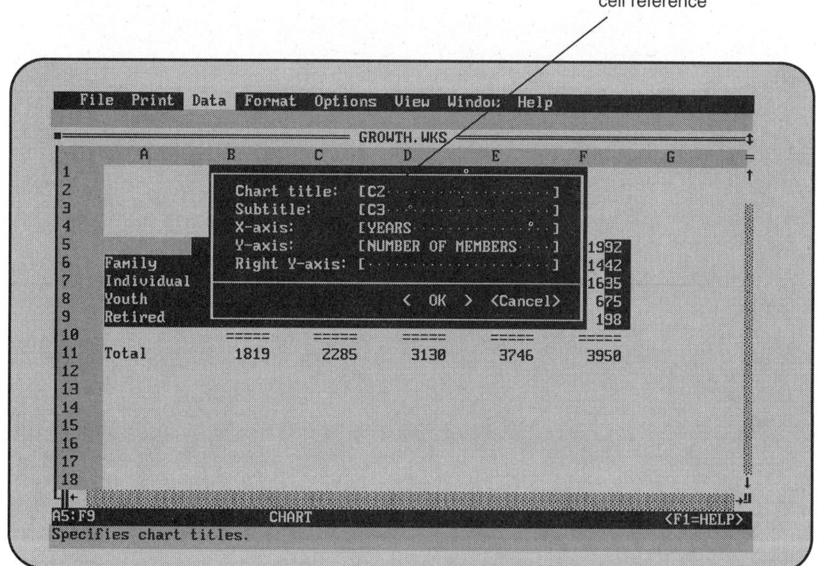

To complete the command,

Press: (↵)

To view the chart with the titles,

Press: (SHIFT) - (F10)

Your display screen should be similar to Figure 8-10.

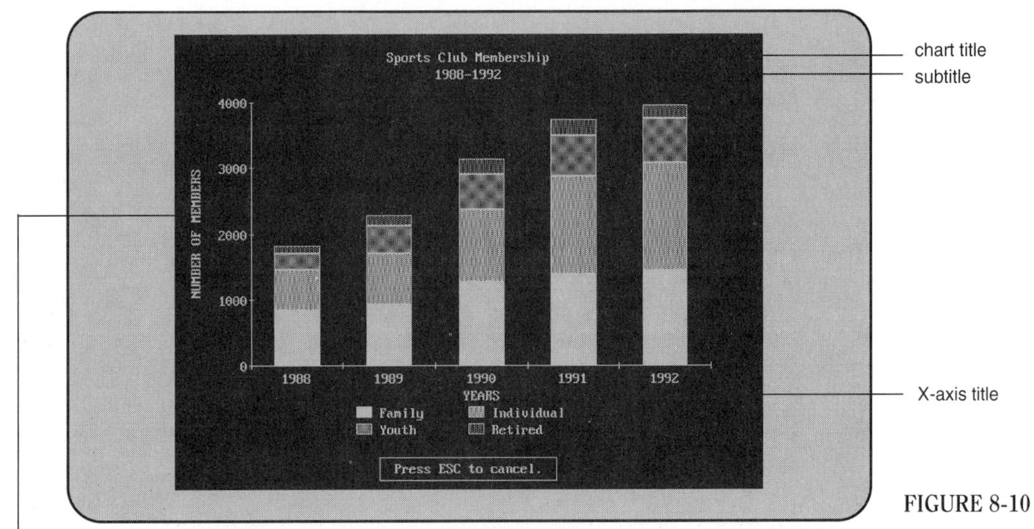

FIGURE 8-10

The chart title and subtitle lines are displayed centered above the chart. The title "YEARS" is displayed along the horizontal X-axis. The title "NUMBER OF MEMBERS" is displayed along the vertical Y-axis.

Using titles within the chart greatly improves its appearance and meaning.

To clear the chart,

Press: (ESC)

Creating Another Chart

So far you have created one chart in the spreadsheet. Fred would like to create another chart showing the total membership growth pattern over the five years. He thinks a line chart will display this data best. A **line chart** represents data as a set of points along a line.

The data for total membership is in cells B11 through F11. Again you must begin by selecting the data to be charted. This time, however, the labels for the years are not in adjacent cells and cannot be included in the range. In Chart view you can also select the data to be charted.

Move to: B11
Press: (F8)

Select the range B11 through F11.

To tell Works that you want to create a new chart using the highlighted data,

Select: View>New Chart

By default, a bar chart of the data is displayed. This chart is not very descriptive of the data. To clear the chart and change it to a line chart,

Press: (ESC)
Select: Format>**L**ine

To view the chart,

Press: (SHIFT) - (F10)

Your screen should be similar to Figure 8-11.

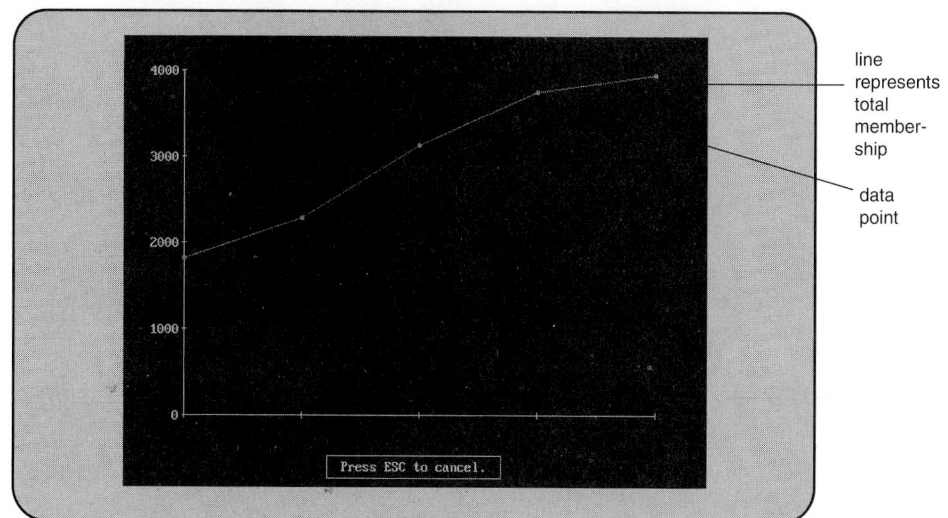

FIGURE 8-11

The data for total membership is displayed within the chart boundaries. Each data point is marked by a circle and connected by a line. The total membership growth pattern over the five years is now easy to see. The chart, however, is difficult to understand because it does not contain X-axis labels or titles. To clear the chart,

Press: (ESC)

Labeling the X-Axis

The next step is to specify the labels to be entered along the horizontal or X-axis of the chart. These labels are called **category labels**. In a line chart the category labels usually represent some block of time, such as days, weeks, months, or years. The category labels for Fred's line chart will display the year labels, 1988 through 1992, located in cells B5 through F5. To define the years as the category labels,

Move to: B5
Press: (F8)

Highlight B5 through F5.

Select: **D**ata

The top box of the Data menu displays the six possible data ranges you can specify in a chart. They are called the **Y-series**. The current chart has one range of data (B11 through F11), which Works automatically defined as the first Y-series when you created the new chart.

The **X-series** defines the range of cells containing the words or numbers you want to use as category labels for the the X-axis. To specify the highlighted range B5 through F5 as the X-series,

Select: **X**-series
Press: (SHIFT) - (F10)

Your screen should be similar to Figure 8-12.

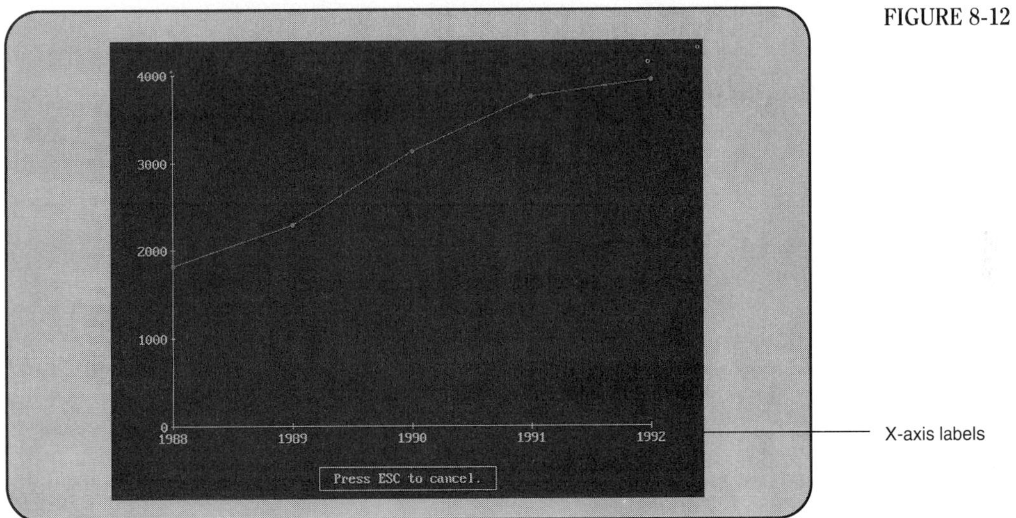

FIGURE 8-12

The years are displayed along the X-axis. However, the chart is still not very descriptive; it would benefit from the addition of titles.

Press: (ESC)

Add the following titles using the Data>Titles command:

Chart Title	**SPORTS CLUB GROWTH**
Subtitle	**For The Years 1988 - 1992**
X-axis	**YEARS**
Y-axis	**NUMBER OF MEMBERS**

To view the chart,

Press: (SHIFT) - (F10)

Your screen should be similar to Figure 8-13.

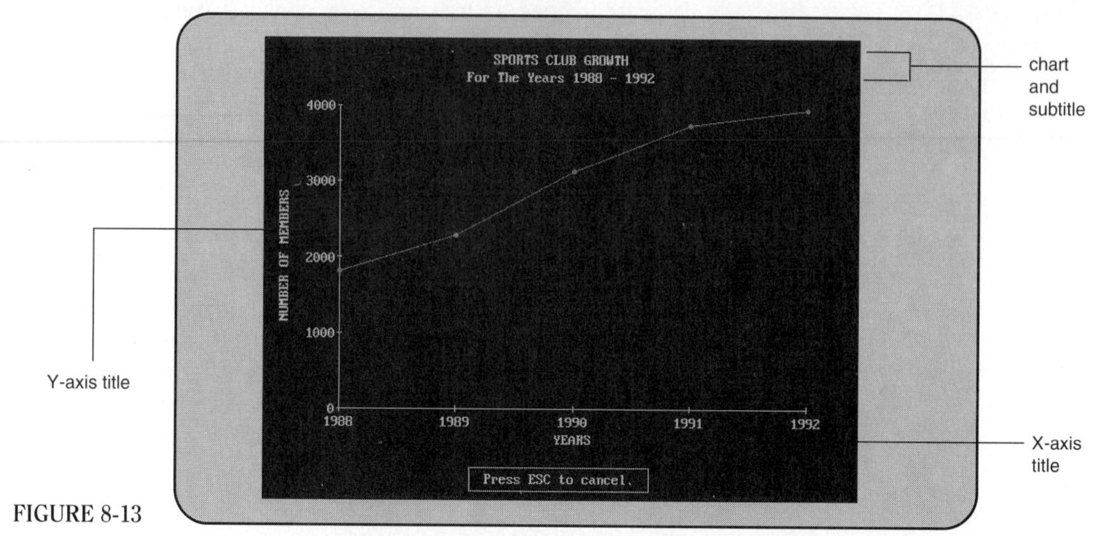

FIGURE 8-13

The titles greatly improve the meaning of the chart. To clear the chart,

Press: (ESC)

To rename the second chart,

Select: View

Notice the new chart has been named Chart1. The symbol next to the name tells you that it is the **active chart,** or the chart that will be displayed when you press (SHIFT) - (F10). Works uses the default name CHART1 again because you renamed the first chart. If you had not renamed the first chart, this chart would have been named CHART2. To change its name to LINE,

Select: Charts

The active chart is the selected chart.

Select: Name
Type: **Line**
Select: Rename>**D**one

Specifying Additional Data

Fred thinks it would be interesting to calculate and display the average membership growth in addition to the total membership growth as part of this chart. To calculate the average, the AVG function will be used.

Move to: B12

Enter the function =AVG(B6:B9) using pointing in cell B12.

Next, this function needs to be copied across the row through cell F12. The Chart menu does not contain a command to copy cell values. You need to switch back to the Spreadsheet view menu. To do this, you can use View>Spreadsheet or the shortcut key (F10).

Select: **V**iew>**S**preadsheet

➾ (F10)

The CHART indicator is no longer displayed in the status line and the spreadsheet menu is displayed in the menu bar.

To copy the average function,

Press: (F8)

Highlight cells B12 through F12.

Select: **E**dit>Fill **R**ight

Enter the label "Average" in cell A12.

Your screen should be similar to Figure 8-14.

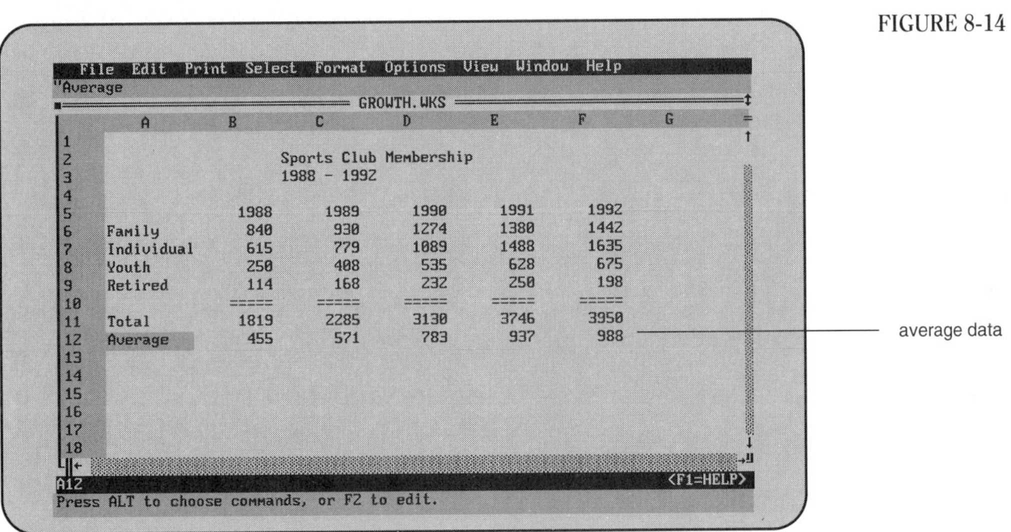

FIGURE 8-14

To return to the Chart view,

Select: **V**iew>**2** Line

The active chart is displayed. To clear it,

Press: (ESC)

Next, the average data needs to be added to the line chart. To select this data,

Move to: B12
Press: (F8)

Select cells B12 through F12.

The selected range of data needs to be added to the chart next. The Data command lets you do this.

Select: Data

The first Y-series data range has already been specified. It displays the total data (B11 through F11) in the current line chart. To enter a second Y-series to display the average data,

Select: 2nd Y-Series

The highlighted range is now defined as the second Y-series of data.

To view the chart,

Press: SHIFT - F10

Your screen should be similar to Figure 8-15.

FIGURE 8-15

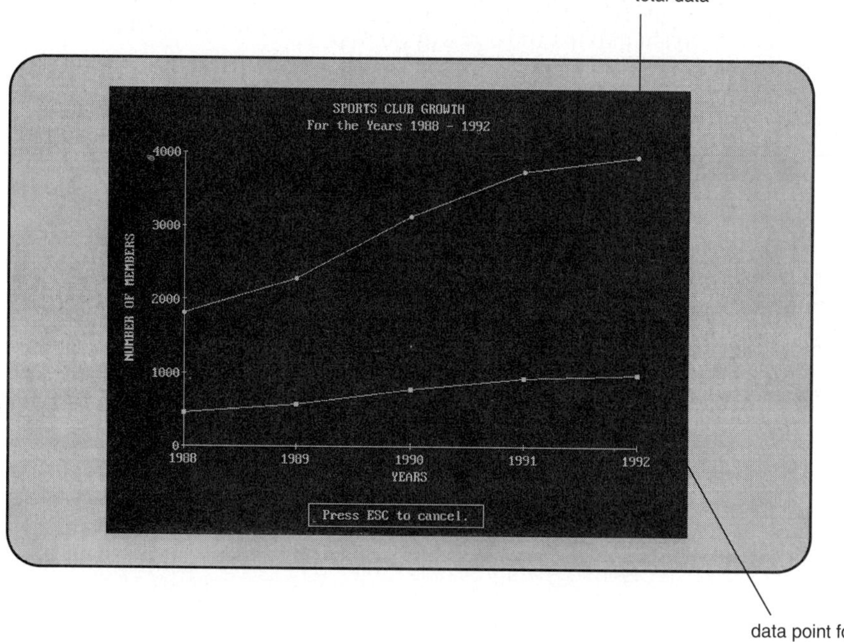

There are now two lines of data. If you have a color monitor, the lines are in different colors. If you have a monochrome monitor, the data points on the lines are different (circle and square).

Adding Legends

When only one category was charted, the chart was easy to understand. However, with the addition of the other category to the chart, it is hard to know which line represents which group.

Using color or a different symbol on each line helps differentiate the groups. But how do you know which pattern or color represents the Total and which represents the Average?

To identify or label each pattern, legends are used. Recall that a legend is a short descriptive label that helps identify the data symbols in a line chart or patterns that represent the Y-series of data.

Now that there are two lines of data, a legend needs to be added to the chart.

To clear the chart,

Press: ESC

To add legends,

Select: Data>Legends

Your screen should be similar to Figure 8-16.

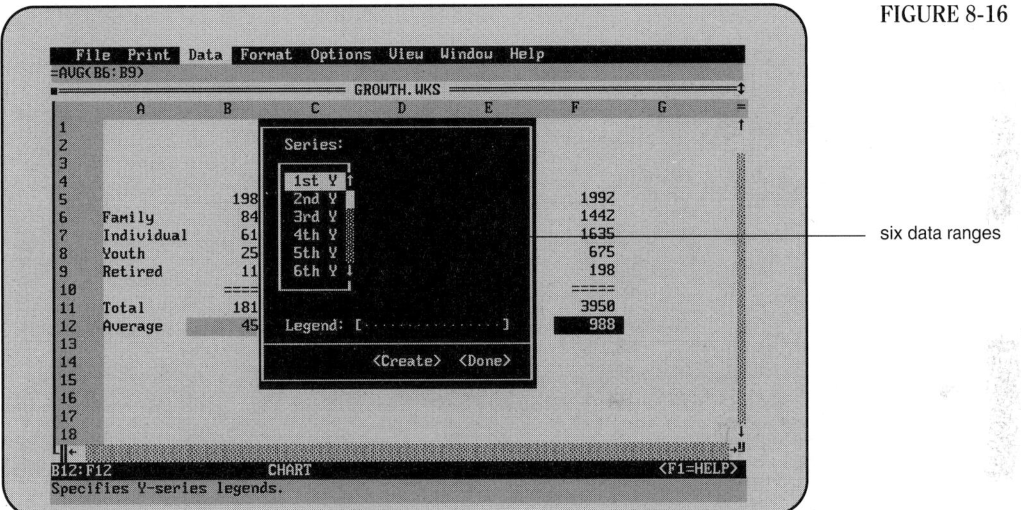

FIGURE 8-16

The first Y-series option should be highlighted. To enter the legend name,

Select: Legend

You can type a legend name of up to 19 characters or reference a cell in the spreadsheet containing a label you want to use as the legend. The label in cell A11, Total, would be an appropriate legend for this data.

Type: **A11**

To create this legend label by selecting the default command button, Create,

Press: ↵

You can now continue to specify a legend for the second Y-series. To do this,

Select: 2nd Y>Legend

The label in cell A12, Average, would be an appropriate legend label.

Type: A12
Press: ⏎

To complete the command,

Select: Done

To view the line chart,

Press: SHIFT - F10

Your screen should be similar to similar to Figure 8-17.

FIGURE 8-17

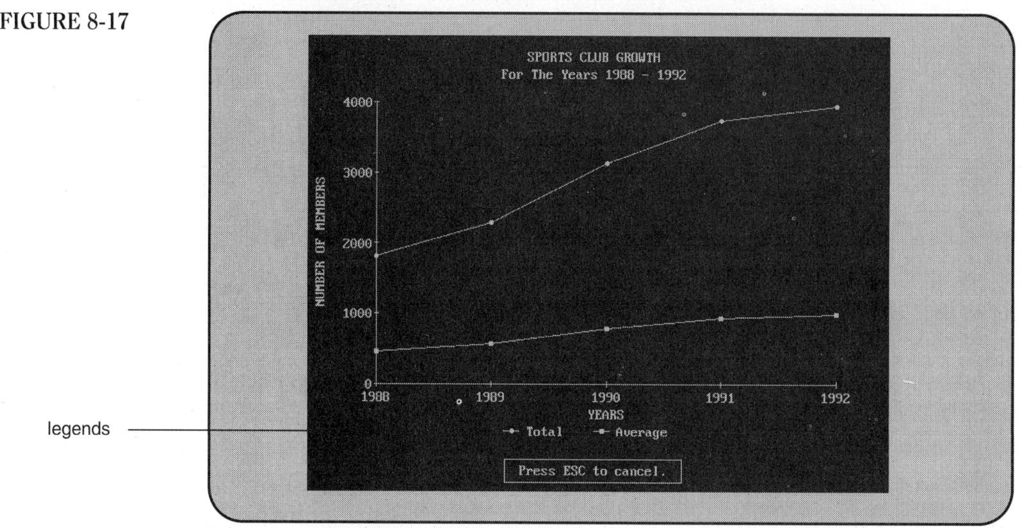

The two legends are displayed at the bottom of the chart to the right of the corresponding line symbol or color. Although Works will accept legends up to 19 characters long, it will wrap long legends to a second line if there is not enough space below the X-axis to display the legends on a single line.

The addition of legends to the chart makes reading and understanding the chart much easier. To clear the chart,

Press: ESC

Copying a Chart

Next, Fred wants to create a chart of the combined line and bar chart information. Rather than specifying the bar chart data again, he will copy the bar chart by giving it another name. To do this,

Select: View>Charts
Select: Bar

To assign this chart a new name,

Select: Name
Type: **Bar-Line**
Select: Copy

Your screen should be similar to Figure 8-18.

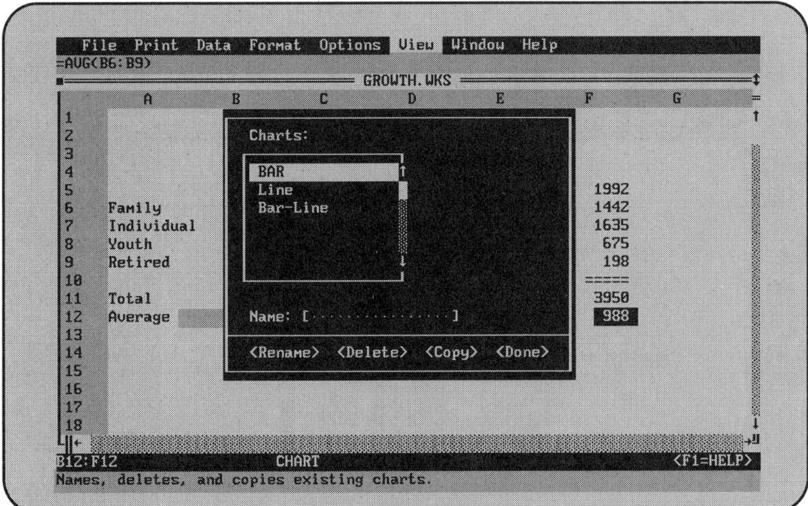

FIGURE 8-18

The copy of the bar chart is added to the list of charts in the dialog box under the new chart name.

Select: Done
Select: View

The copied chart, which is the third one you have created in the spreadsheet, is the active chart. To view it,

Select: **3** Bar-Line

The stacked bar chart you created earlier is displayed. This chart is a duplicate of the chart named Bar. It displays four Y-series of data. To clear the chart,

Press: (ESC)

Now you can modify this chart without affecting the original chart, BAR. First, Fred wants this chart to be a side-by-side bar chart rather than a stacked bar chart. To change the chart type,

Select: Format>Bar

Next, to specify the Total data in cells B11 through F11 as the fifth Y-Series,

Move to: B11
Press: (F8)

Highlight cells B11 through F11.

Select: **D**ata
Select: **5**th Y-Series

To view the change in the chart,

Press: (SHIFT) - (F10)

Your screen should be similar to Figure 8-19.

FIGURE 8-19

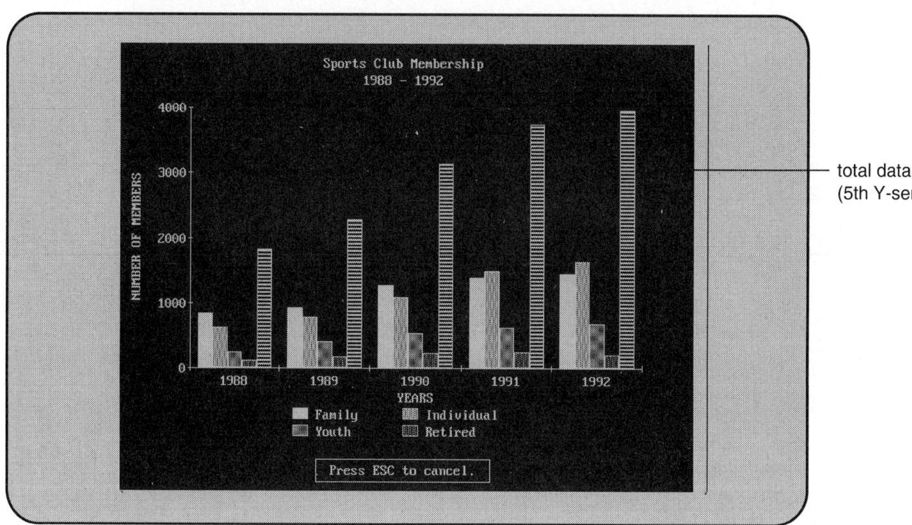

The data for the totals have been added to the chart as a fifth bar. Next, a legend identifying this data needs to be added. To clear the chart,

Press: (ESC)

To add a legend to identify the fifth Y-series of data,

Select: **D**ata>**L**egends>**5**th Y>**L**egend>**A11**>**C**reate>**D**one
Press: (SHIFT) - (F10)

The legend for the fifth Y-series of data is displayed below the chart.

After looking at the chart, Fred thinks it would be more interesting to display the fifth Y-series as a line rather than a bar. To clear the chart,

Press: (ESC)

Creating a Mixed Chart

Works lets you mix a line and bar chart in a single chart by defining how you want each Y-series displayed. To do this,

Select: Options>Mixed Line & Bar

Your screen should be similar to Figure 8-20.

FIGURE 8-20

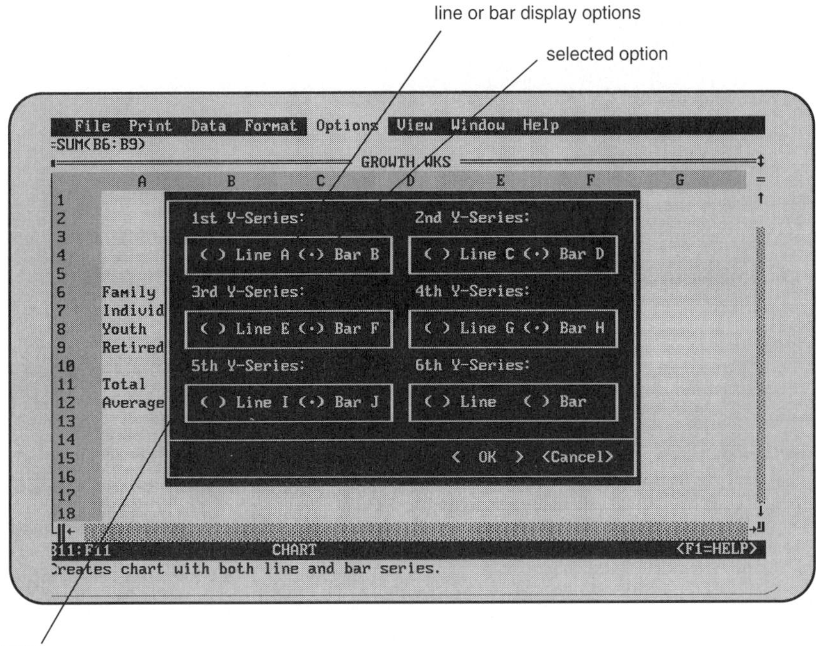

The six possible Y-series are displayed in the dialog box. Under each Y-series, two options, Line or Bar, are displayed. The Line or Bar option is selected by typing the highlighted letter under the Y-series you want to change. The option indicator (◆) to the left of the Bar option shows that the five defined Y-series are to be displayed as bars.

Look at the fifth Y-series box. The highlighted letter associated with the Line option is "I." The selected option is Bar. To change the display of the fifth Y-series to a line,

Select: Line **I**

The option indicator mark moves from the Bar to the Line category. The other four Y-series are still bars. To complete the command and view the chart,

Press: ↵
Press: SHIFT - F10

Your screen should be similar to Figure 8-21.

FIGURE 8-21

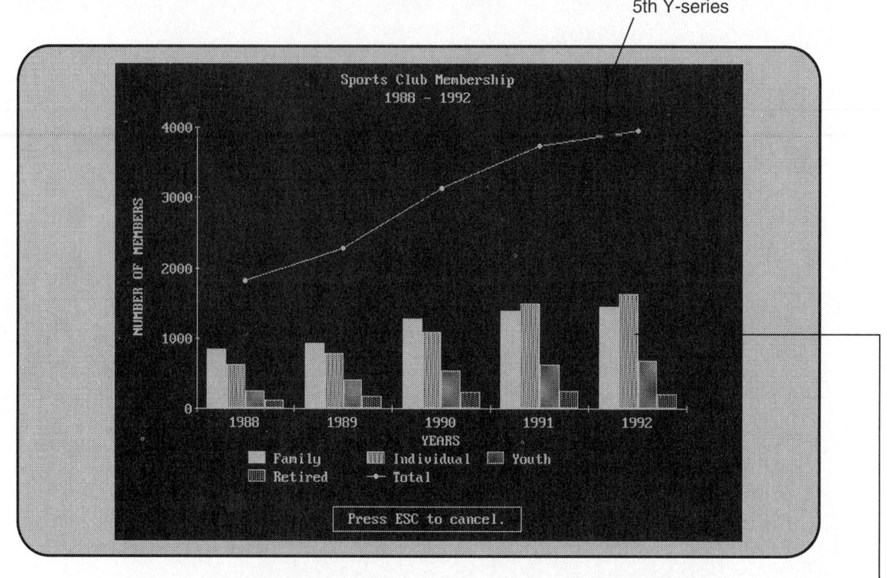

The four Y-series of data that represent the four membership categories are displayed as bars. The total membership data is represented as a line. The legend for the fifth Y-series has changed to identify the line. To clear the chart,

Press: ESC

Creating a Pie Chart

The final chart Fred would like to create using the spreadsheet data is a **pie chart.** A pie chart compares parts to the whole, in a similar manner to a stacked bar chart. However, each value in the range is a slice of the pie or circle displayed as a percentage of the total.

The use of X- and Y-series in a pie chart is different from their use in a bar or line chart. The X-series labels the slices of the pie rather than the X-axis. The Y-series is used to create the wedges or slices in the pie. Only one Y-series (1st) is defined in a pie chart.

Fred wants to compare the four membership categories for the year 1992. The labels for the slices (membership category) will be defined in the X-series as A6 through A9. The Y-series will be the values in cells F6 through F9.

To specify the values for 1992 as the first Y-series,

Move to: F6
Press: F8

Highlight F6 through F9.

Select: View>New Chart

By default, the data is displayed as a bar chart. To change it to a pie chart,

Press: (ESC)
Select: Format>**P**ie
Press: (SHIFT) - (F10)

Your screen should be similar to Figure 8-22.

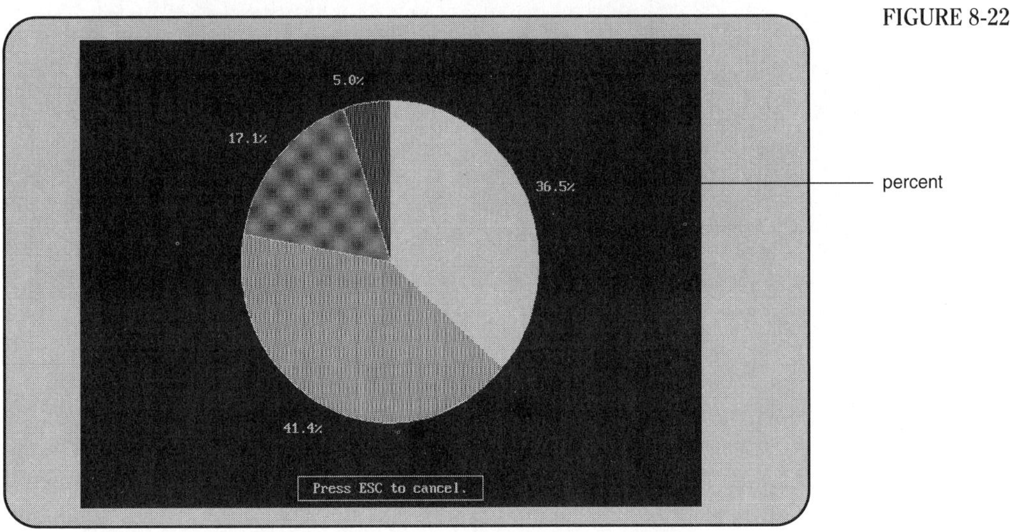

FIGURE 8-22

The percent each membership category is of the total membership for 1992 is displayed next to each slice. To clear the chart,

Press: (ESC)

Again, it is difficult to know what each slice stands for. The labels in cells A6 through A9 would be appropriate category labels to identify the slices of the pie. To select this range,

Move to: A6
Press: (F8)

Highlight cells A6 through A9.

To define the selected range as the X-series category labels for the pie chart,

Select: **D**ata>**X**-Series
Press: (SHIFT) - (F10)

Your display screen should be similar to Figure 8-23.

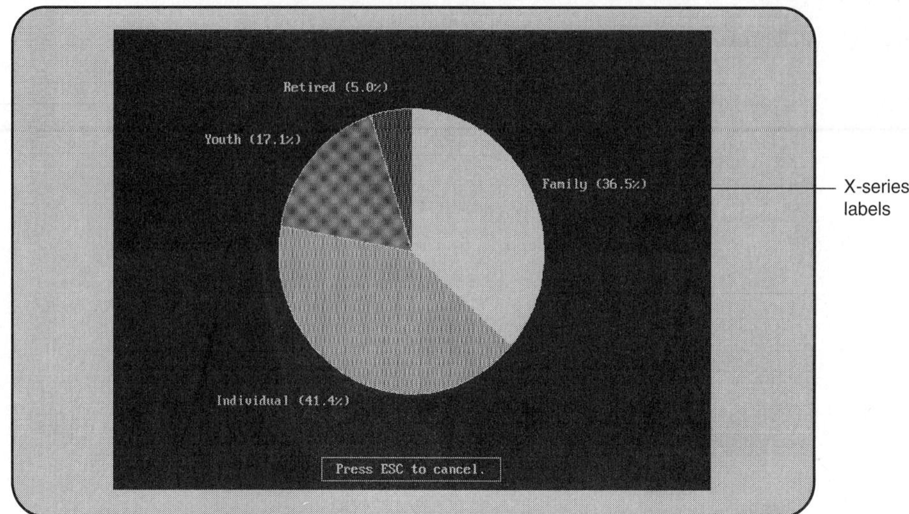

FIGURE 8-23

Each membership category label, defined as the X-series, labels each slice of the pie.

To complete this chart, a title needs to be entered. Since the pie chart compares the four membership categories for the year 1992 only, the same title as used in the spreadsheet would not be appropriate. To clear the chart,

Press: (ESC)

Enter the chart title line "1992 Membership Comparison" and a subtitle line "By [Your Name]"

View the chart.

The two title lines are displayed centered at the top of the chart. To clear the chart,

Press: (ESC)

Shading the Pie Slices

If you are viewing your charts in color, you will change the display to black and white. This way, if you are not using a color printer, it will appear on the screen as it will be printed. To change to black-and-white display,

Select: **O**ptions>**F**ormat For B&W
Press: (SHIFT) - (F10)

A different dot pattern replaces each color. When you are viewing charts in black and white, Works automatically decides what patterns to place in each bar or slice. The colors, patterns, markers, and line styles used in a chart are called **data formats**. When you create a chart, Works automatically assigns each Y-series a different data format.

If you are viewing the chart after changing the display to black and white, clear the chart.

You can refine the appearance of a chart by changing the data formats for individual Y-series of data. To change the data format for the pie chart,

Select: Format>Data Format

Your screen should be similar to Figure 8-24.

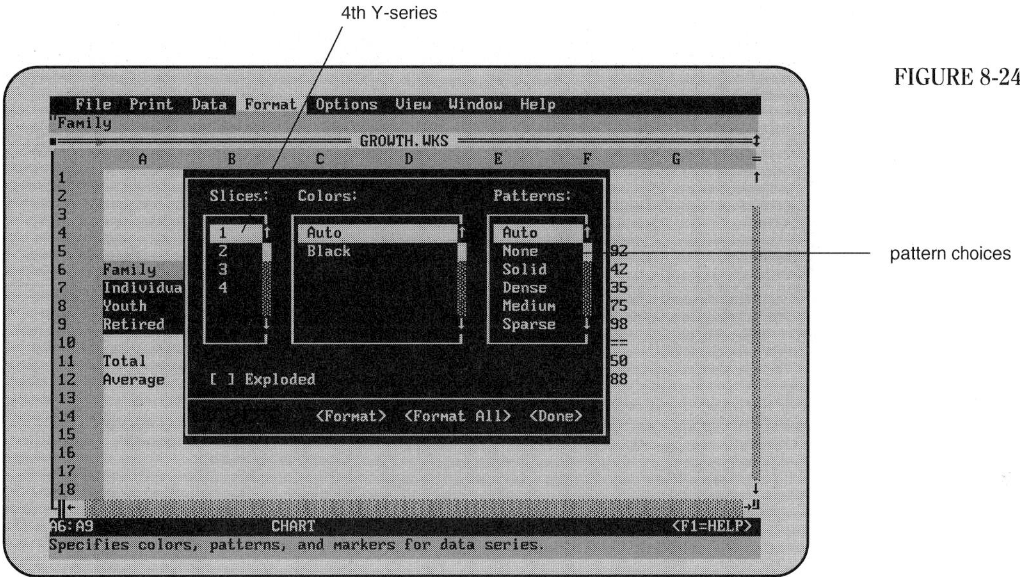

FIGURE 8-24

The Data Format dialog box is displayed. The Slices box lists the four Y-series of data in the current pie chart as 1, 2, 3, and 4. The Colors box shows the colors available, Auto and Black. The Auto setting is the settings Works automatically uses when you create a chart. Since you changed the display to black and white, the only color displayed is Black. The Patterns box shows the patterns available for bars, lines, or slices.

The current pattern setting is Auto. This means that Works automatically defined the patterns used in the chart. To change the patterns from Auto to a pattern you select from those listed in the Patterns box,

Select: Patterns

The Patterns box shows the first six patterns. To scroll the rest of the patterns into view in the box,

Press: ⓥ until the highlight is on "Light \\"

Mouse Note: If you have a mouse, you can drag on the scroll box to scroll the patterns.

To change the pattern of the first pie slice to this pattern by selecting the active button, Format,

Press: ↵

The cursor returns to the Slices box to let you select the next slice you want to change. To change the second slice pattern to "++,"

Select: 2
Select: **P**atterns>++
Press: ↵

To change the third slice to "\\," and the fourth slice to "Dark //"

Select: 3
Select: **P**atterns>\\
Press: ↵

Select: 4
Select: **P**atterns>Dark //
Press: ↵

To end the command,

Select: **D**one

To view the changes in the patterns,

Press: SHIFT - F10

Your screen should be similar to Figure 8-25.

FIGURE 8-25

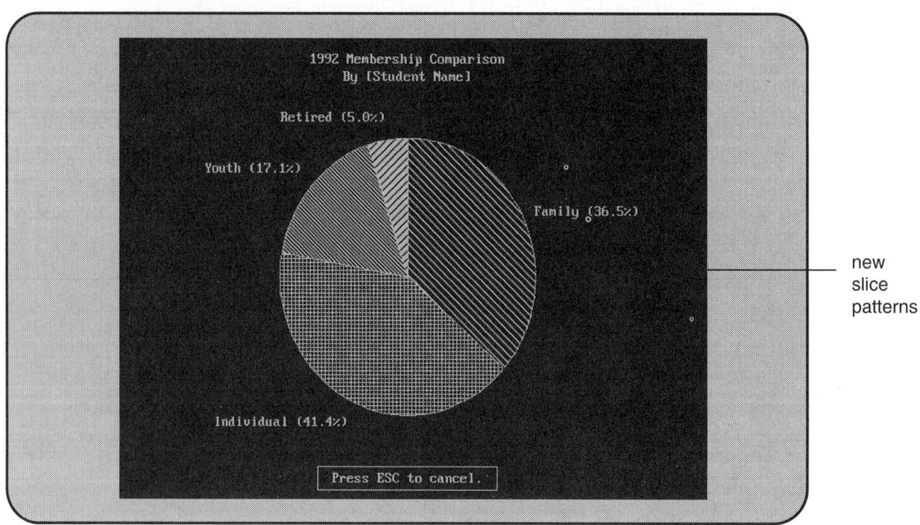

The patterns in the slices have changed to the patterns you selected in the Data Format dialog box. To clear the chart,

Press: ESC

Exploding a Slice of the Pie

A slice or several slices of a pie chart can be **exploded,** or separated slightly from the other slices in the pie. This lets you emphasize a particular part of the pie chart. To explode a slice,

Select: Format>Data Format

To explode the slice of the pie containing the data for the retired membership category (the fourth Y-series),

Select: Slices>4
Select: Exploded>Format>Done
Press: SHIFT - F10

Your display screen should be similar to Figure 8-26.

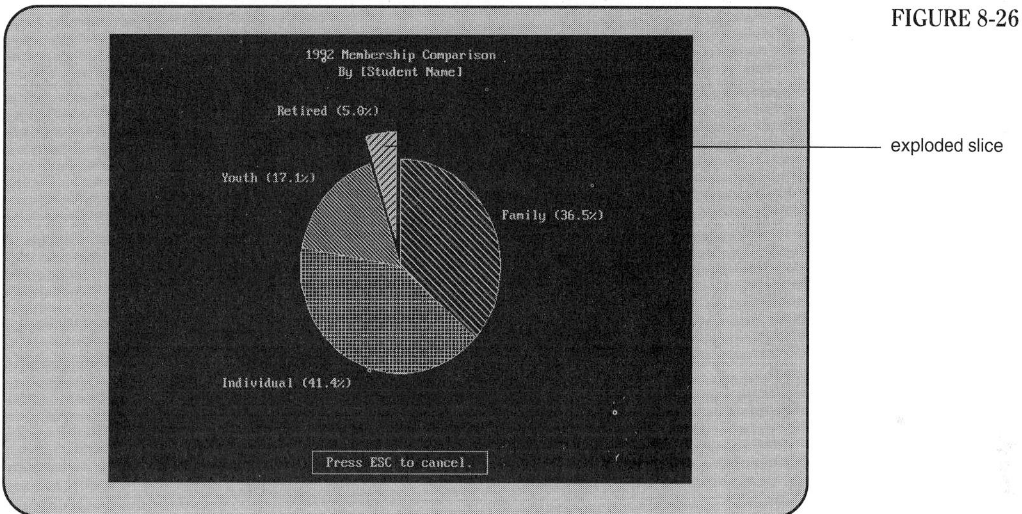

FIGURE 8-26

The slice of the pie representing the retired category is exploded or separated from the other slices of the pie chart.

Fred notices that the retired membership category represents only five percent of the total. He thinks this figure is a little low. To check the data entered in the spreadsheet for this category, return to the spreadsheet. To clear the chart,

Press: ESC

The value in cell F9 is 198. After checking his records, Fred sees that it was entered incorrectly into the spreadsheet. It should be 398. To change this figure in the spreadsheet,

Move to: F9
Type: **398**
Press: ↵

The spreadsheet has been recalculated. But what about the charts and pie chart using the value in this cell as part of a data range? Do they change to reflect the new value?

To view the current chart again,

Press: SHIFT - F10

The pie chart is redrawn to reflect the change in the spreadsheet value for the retired membership group. The retired membership category for 1992 is now 9.6 percent of the total membership. The other percentages have been adjusted accordingly.

Using charts to visually display the effects of performing what-if analysis in a spreadsheet is another powerful management tool. To clear the chart,

Press: ESC

Name the current pie chart settings PIE.

Recalling Named Charts

There are now four named charts stored in memory: Line, Bar, Bar-Line, and Pie.

To view the Bar chart again,

Select: View>**1** BAR

Your display screen should be similar to Figure 8-27.

FIGURE 8-27

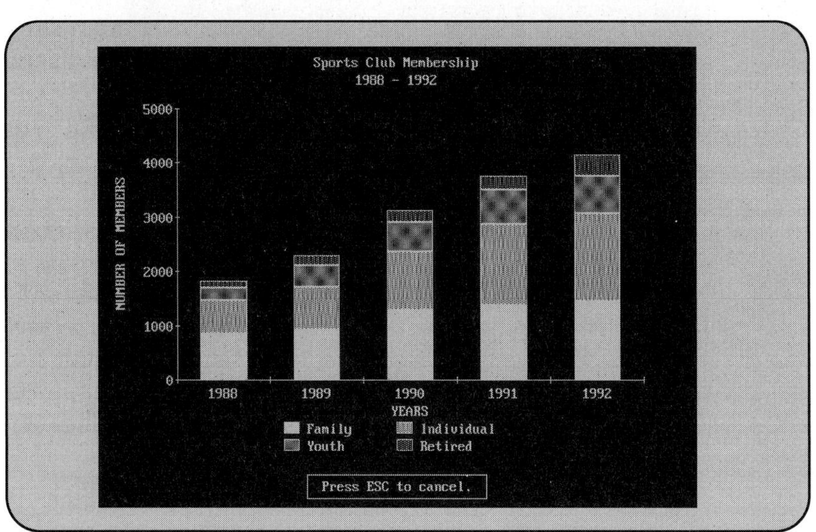

The stacked bar chart whose settings were named and stored in memory is displayed on the screen. Notice that this chart also reflects the change in the data in cell F9. The named chart stores only the settings, not the data in the spreadsheet. As a result, changes to the spreadsheet data are automatically reflected in the chart. The

BAR chart is now the active chart and any changes you might make to the chart settings would affect it only. To clear the chart,

Press: (ESC)

To view the other two charts (remember to erase the chart from the display after viewing it by pressing (ESC)),

Select: **V**iew>**2** Line
View>**3** Bar-Line

Each time you select a chart to view, it becomes the active chart.

If you have not cleared the chart from the screen,

Press: (ESC)

Printing a Chart

To print a chart, select it to make it active and then select the Print command. The active chart is the Bar-Line chart. To make the pie chart the active chart,

Select: **V**iew>**4** PIE
Press: (ESC)
Select: **P**rint>Page Setup and **M**argins

Your display screen should be similar to Figure 8-28.

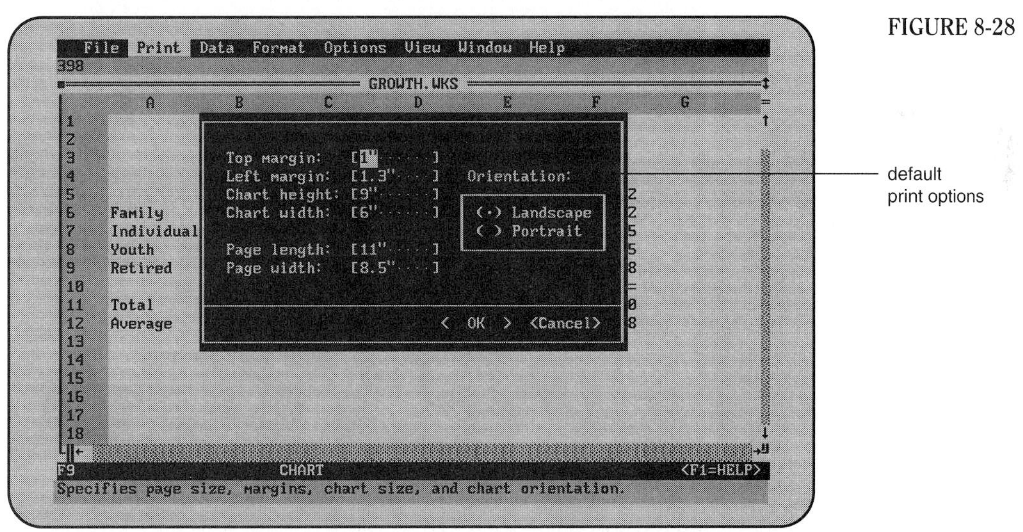

FIGURE 8-28

The default settings are displayed in the dialog box. The Orientation option lets you print a chart in landscape format (sideways across the length of the paper) or in portrait format (vertically on the paper). The chart height and width are set at 9 inches and 6 inches. These default settings can be changed just as you changed the Print settings in the Spreadsheet view. However, for our purposes, they look fine.

Press:  (ESC)

If necessary, turn the printer on and check to see that it is on-line and that the perforation in the paper is aligned with the printer scale.

Note for floppy disk users: Insert the appropriate disk when directed by the program.

Select: Print>**P**rint>**P**rint

After a few moments, your printed chart should be similar to Figure 8-29.

FIGURE 8-29

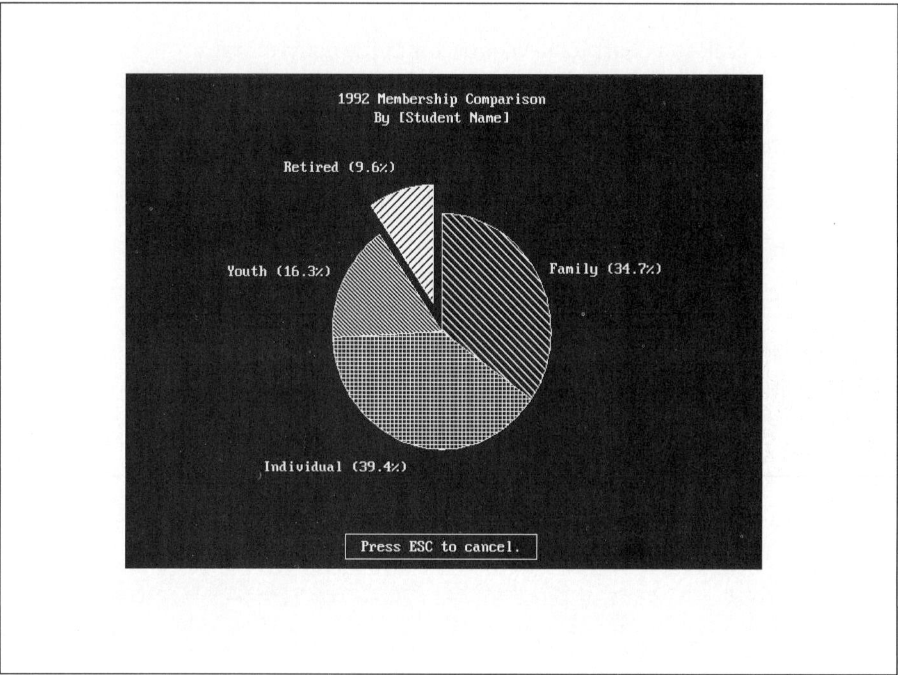

Note: If your instructor wants you to print the other charts you have created in this lab, change the subtitle line in each chart to "By [Your Name]" before printing them.

Saving the Spreadsheet

Before leaving Works, you should save your spreadsheet containing all the named chart settings. If you do not save the spreadsheet, the charts you created will be erased from memory when you leave the Works program.

To save the charts (currently stored only in memory) with the spreadsheet in a new file called CHARTS.WKS,

Select: File>Save **A**s>**CHARTS.WKS**>↵

Exit Works or close the file if you are going to continue using the program.

Key Terms

chart	category labels
X-axis	Y-series
Y-axis	X-series
legend	active chart
titles	pie chart
bar chart	data format
stacked bar chart	explode
line chart	

Matching

1. F10	_____	**a.** specifies the kind of chart
2. Pie	_____	**b.** changes the data patterns
3. data format	_____	**c.** defines the data ranges to chart
4. legend	_____	**d.** displays the active chart on the screen
5. X-series	_____	**e.** describes the chart
6. Y-series	_____	**f.** displays symbols and descriptive labels of the data
7. View	_____	**g.** separates pie slice
8. Title	_____	**h.** labels the horizontal axis
9. SHIFT - F10	_____	**i.** a type of chart
10. explode	_____	**j.** switch to Spreadsheet view

Practice Exercises

1. The American dream of owning your own home has become elusive, in part because the prices of homes in most places have risen faster than incomes. The following data shows the average price of a home and the average family income levels from 1976 to 1986.

HOUSING PRICES vs. PERSONAL INCOME
(in thousands of dollars)

	1976	1980	1986
Avg. Home	37	55	89
Personal Income	15	22	30

- Create a spreadsheet displaying this data. Do not leave blank cells between rows and columns of data or the row and column labels. Use the titles and row and column labels shown.
- Create a line chart showing the change in the average cost of a home and family income over the years 1976 to 1986. The chart should include the X-axis labels and legends.

- Enter a chart title line using the title displayed in the spreadsheet.
- Enter a subtitle line: "By [Your Name]."
- Label the X-axis "Years." Label the Y-axis "Dollars."
- Name the line chart HOUSING.
- Print the line chart.
- Save the spreadsheet as HOME.

2. Financial planners generally recommend that you allocate your capital into five categories: cash, fixed income producers (bonds), real estate, equities, and precious metals. They also recommend changing how much you allocate to each category as you reach different stages of life.

On the average, financial planners recommend that the following percentages of your capital be allocated to the five categories according to three age groups:

PERCENT ASSET ALLOCATION
(by student name)

	In your 20s	In your 40s	In your 60s
Cash	22	9	5
Fixed Income	25	33	45
Real Estate	0	15	25
Equities	53	33	20
Precious Metals	0	0	5

- Create a spreadsheet using the titles, row and column labels, and data shown above. Do not leave blank rows or columns between the spreadsheet data and the row and column labels.
- Create a bar chart of this data. Enter a chart title and subtitle line using the spreadsheet titles. Enter an X-axis title line, "ASSET," and a Y-axis title of "Percent Allocation." Name the bar chart BAR3.
- Create another chart of the same information, except displayed as a stacked bar chart (use Copy). Name the chart STACKED3.
- Create a pie chart to display the asset allocation for people in their twenties. Define the X-series using the ASSET category labels in the spreadsheet. Enter a chart and subtitle (use your name) line. Add patterns of your choice to the pie chart and explode the Cash slice. Name the pie chart PIE20S.
- Create two more pie charts showing the suggested asset allocation for people in their forties and sixties. Add patterns of your choice to the pie charts. Explode the Cash slice. Name them PIE40S and PIE60S.
- Print all the charts you have saved.
- Save the spreadsheet file with the charts as ASSETS.

3. The U.S. athletic footwear market has shown continued growth over the past five years. The data presented below shows this growth. Create a spreadsheet of this data. Enter the years as text entries.

U.S. Athletic Footwear Market
Retail Sales (in billions of dollars)

1983	4.03
1984	4.15
1985	5.01
1986	6.87
1987	8.12

- Create a bar chart of this data. It should have two title lines and an X- and Y-axis title. The subtitle line should contain your name. Add patterns of your choice to the bars. Name the chart SHOESB.
- Create a line chart of this data. It should have two title lines and an X- and Y-axis title. The subtitle line should contain your name. Name the chart SHOESL.
- In the same spreadsheet file, create a second spreadsheet of the following data showing the top five manufacturers of athletic footwear and their sales for first half of 1987 compared to first half of 1988. Enter the years as text entries.

1987 First Half Sales vs. 1988 First Half Sales
(In millions of dollars)

	1987	1988
Reebok	488.87	589
Nike	104.16	434
Converse	112.24	140.3
Avia	44.55	99
Adidas	70.52	82

- Create a bar chart of this data comparing the 1987 and 1988 sales figures. It should have two title lines. The subtitle line should contain your name. Create X- and Y-axis titles. Add patterns of your choice to the bars. Name the chart SALESB.
- Create two pie charts of this data, one for each year. The X-series should display the manufacturer's name. It should have two title lines. The subtitle line should contain your name. Add patterns of your choice to the pie charts. Explode the Adidas slice. Name the chart SALES87 and SALES88.
- Print the charts.

- Save the spreadsheet as SHOES.

4. It appears that the exercise boom is losing its strength. Since 1984 the number of Americans participating in athletic activities has plunged. The two activities that have shown an increase are Walking and Bicycling. The following data shows this change.

1984 vs. 1987 Fitness Comparison
(In millions of participants)

	1984	1987
Running	29.9	27.5
Swimming	74.6	66
Aerobics	23.2	22.8
Tennis	19.9	18.2
Walking	41.1	58.9
Bicycling	50.7	52.2

- Create a bar chart of this data. It should have two title lines and X- and Y-axis titles. The subtitle line should contain your name. Add patterns of your choice. Name the chart FITNESSB.
- Create a line chart of this data. It should have two title lines and X- and Y-axis titles. The subtitle line should contain your name. Name the chart FITNESSL.
- Create two pie charts of this data, one for each year. It should have two title lines. The subtitle line should contain your name. Add patterns of your choice to the pie charts. Explode the Tennis slice. Name the charts FITNESS84 and FITNESS87.
- Print the charts.
- Save the spreadsheet as DECLINE.

Command Summary

Command	Shortcut	Action	Page
Data>**Y**-Series		Specifies the data to chart	238
Data>**X**-Series		Labels the X-axis	245
Data>**T**itles>**C**hart Title		Enters main title line	230
Data>**T**itles>**S**ubtitle		Enters subtitle line	231
Data>**T**itles>**X**-axis		Enters X-axis title	232
Data>**T**itles>**Y**-axis		Enters Y-axis title	232
Data>**L**egends		Adds labels to identify data	239
Forma**t**>**B**ar		Creates a bar chart	241
Forma**t**>**S**tacked Bar		Creates a stacked bar chart	229
Forma**t**>**L**ine		Creates a line chart	234
Forma**t**>**P**ie		Creates a pie chart	245
Forma**t**>**D**ata Format		Changes data patterns	247
Forma**t**>**D**ata Format> **S**lices>#>**E**xploded		Explodes selected slice	249
Options>**M**ixed Line & Bar		Creates a mixed chart	243
Options>**F**ormat For B&W		Changes display to black and white	246
View>**S**preadsheet	F10	Switches to Spreadsheet view	237
View>**N**ew Chart		Switches to Chart view, displays chart	233
View>**C**harts>**N**ame> *chart name*>**R**ename		Assigns a new name to a chart	241
View>*chart name*	SHIFT - F10	Displays the selected chart	225
View>**C**harts>**C**opy		Creates a copy of a chart	241

CONTENTS
Database

OVERVIEW
Database

A word processor helps you enter and manipulate text. An electronic spreadsheet helps you enter and analyze numerical data. A computerized database helps you enter and manage information or data in record format.

Databases have been in existence for many years. Paper records organized in a filing cabinet by name or department are a database. The information in a telephone book, organized alphabetically, is a database. The records maintained by a school of teachers, classes, and students is a database.

Before computers, most database records were kept on paper. With computers, the same data is entered and stored on a diskette. The big difference is that an electronic database can manipulate—sort, analyze, and display—the data quickly and efficiently. What took hours of time to pull from paper files can be extracted in a matter of seconds using a computerized database.

Definition of a Database

A ***database*** is an organized collection of related data that is stored in a file. The data is entered as a record that consists of several fields of data. Each record contains the same fields. For example, a school has a database of student records. Each record may contain the following fields of data: name, address, Social Security number, phone number, classes, and grades. All the records for each student in the school are stored in a single file.

Some database programs only access and manipulate the data in a single file. Others allow you to access and relate several files at one time. For example, the school may have a second database file containing data for each student's current class schedule. At the end of the semester, the grades for each student are posted in this file. The data in one file can then be merged into the other file by using a common field, such as the student's name, to link the two files.

The database program contains commands that allow you to design the structure of the database records and enter the data for each record into the file. This is the physical storage of the data. How this data is retrieved, organized, and manipulated is the conceptual use of the data.

Advantages of Using a Database

A computerized database system does not save time by making data quicker to enter. This, as in most programs, is a function of your typing speed and your knowledge of the program.

One of the main advantages of using a computerized database system is the speed of locating the records, updating and adding records to the file, and organizing the records to meet varying needs.

Once data is entered into the database file, it can be located very quickly by record number or field data. In a manual system, a record can usually be located by knowing one key piece of information. For example, if the records are organized by last name, to find a record you must know the last name. In a computerized database, even if the records are organized by last name, the record can be located without knowing the last name. Any other field, such as address or Social Security number, can be used to locate the record. Because specific records can be located quickly, the data in the fields can easily be edited and updated.

A second advantage to a computerized database system is its ability to arrange the records in the file according to different fields of data. The records can be organized by name, department, pay, class, or whatever else is needed at a particular time. This ability to produce multiple file arrangements helps provide information in a more meaningful way. The same records can provide information to different departments for different purposes.

A third advantage is the ability to perform calculations on different fields of data. Instead of pulling each record from a filing cabinet, recording the piece of data you want to use, and then calculating a total for the field, you can simply have the database program sum all the values in the specified field. It can even selectively use in the calculation only those records that meet certain requirements. Information that was once costly and time-consuming to get is now quickly and readily available.

Finally, a database program can produce either very simple or complex professional-looking reports. A simple report can be created by asking for a listing of specified fields of data and restricting the listing to records meeting specified conditions. A more complex professional report can be created using the same restrictions or conditions as the simple report. But the data can be displayed in column format, with titles, headings, subtotals, and totals.

There are other advantages, too. Manual systems often have several files containing some of the same data, and eliminating this duplicate information in a computerized database saves space and time. In addition, a computerized database system can allow access by more than one department to the same data, and common updating of the data can be done by any department.

Database Terminology

Create: The process of defining the database file structure.

Delete: To remove a record from the database file.

Edit: To change or update the data in a field.

Field: A collection of related characters, such as last name.

File: A database of records.

Record: A collection of related fields, such as class time, class name, and grade.

Report: A listing of specified fields of data for specified records in the file.

Search: To locate a specific record in a file.

Sort: To arrange the records in a file in a specified order.

Case Study for Labs 9–11

Lab 9 The Sports Club is growing rapidly. Their current method of maintaining employee records consists of a filing system of 3 × 5 index cards. This system was fine when the club was small. But now that the club has grown so much, the system no longer works.

The membership coordinator, Fred Morris, recently purchased Microsoft Works. He will use the program to create a database file of employee records. You will follow Fred as he creates the database entry form and enters, edits, displays, and prints records.

Lab 10 Fred continues to work on the employee database by adding a new field to the entry form, moving fields, and formatting the display of the data. In addition, he sorts the database records and uses the search and query features to quickly locate and change specific records.

Lab 11 In this lab you follow Fred as he creates a report showing selected fields of data for the records in the database.

LAB 9 Creating a Database

CASE STUDY

Fred Morris is the asssistant manager for the Sports Club. As part of his responsibilities he maintains all employee records and produces employee status reports. Currently this information is stored on 5 × 7 note cards like the one shown below.

Employee Record

SS Number: ____________
First Name: ____________
Last Name: ____________ Department: ________
Street: ____________ Title: ________
City: ____________ Pay: ________
State: ____________ Hours: ________
Zipcode: ____________

This system was fine when the club was small. Now, however, the club is much larger and Fred is having problems with this manual database system.

To automate the employee records, Fred will use the Works database tool. You will follow him as he learns how to use Works to create an employee database, insert records, and print the database.

OBJECTIVES

In this lab you will learn how to:

1. Plan and create the database entry form.
2. Enter and edit records in a database.
3. Change field size.
4. View multiple records.
5. Change field width.
6. Print the database records.

Exploring the Database Screen

Load DOS and respond to the date and time prompts if necessary. Load Works. Your data disk should be in the appropiate drive for your computer sytem.

To create a new database file,

Select: Create New File>New **D**atabase

Your display should look similar to Figure 9-1.

FIGURE 9-1

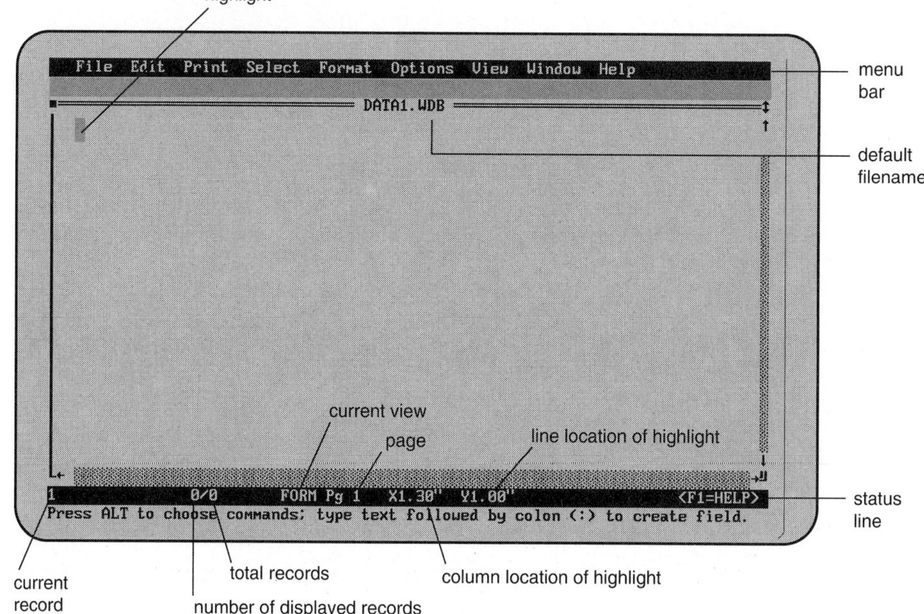

The database screen appears. The menu bar displays the nine menus associated with the database tool. They are the same menus as in the spreadsheet tool. You use the database menu in the same way as the word processing and spreadsheet tool menus.

The default database filename, DATA1.WDB, is displayed in the title line. The filename extension, .WDB, identifies this file as a Works database file. The workspace is currently empty except for the highlight showing your location on the screen. The highlight is one character-space wide.

The status line contains several new pieces of information. The number 1 on the left end indicates the record currently on the screen. In this case, the record you will enter will be the first record in the database. The 0/0 tells you two pieces of information. The first number tells you the number of records displayed in the database. As you will see in later labs, not all records in the database need to be displayed on the screen. The second number tells you the total number of records in the database. Your database can have up to 4,096 records. Since there are no records in the database, it shows 0/0. Next, the word FORM is displayed. This tells you the current database view you are using. The FORM view is opened automatically whenever you create a new database. There are several other views in the database tool, which you will be using later in the labs. The FORM view can be multipage; so the Pg 1 indicator tells you that this is the first page of the form. The next two indicators, X1.30" and Y1.00", tell you the location of the highlight on the screen in inches. The measurement tells you where the entry would appear on the printed page. An entry made at this location would be 1.30 inches from the left edge of the paper and 1 inch from the top of the paper. This information is helpful if you need to design the database structure to match a printed form. The Help reminder is displayed at the right end of the status line. Other information will be displayed in the status line as you use different commands.

The message line tells you how to activate the menu bar and how to create a field. Information in this line will vary as you use the database tool. You will learn how to create a field next.

Planning the Entry Form

Now that you are familiar with the database screen, you will follow Fred as he creates an entry form or **template** to be used to enter the information into the database.

A database file consists of **records** of information. A record is a collection of **fields**, or categories of related information, such as a person's name, address, or phone number. Each field of data is assigned a title or **field name**, such as First Name. The **field contents** consists of the information you enter to complete each field of data. For example, the First Name field contents would consist of the employee's first name.

Fred's first step is to plan how he wants the database organized. Each employee will have a record in the database. Each record will consist of the same pieces of information or fields of data that are currently stored on 5 × 7 index cards. The fields will be:

Social Security Number
First Name
Last Name
Street Address
City
State
Zipcode
Department
Title
Pay
Hours

Once the fields are determined, Fred can create the database entry form. The entry form is used to enter the records into the database. The entry form consists of the field names and blank fields or cells where you will enter the field contents. The database FORM view is used to create the entry form.

Entering a Label

First, Fred wants to enter a label to identify the entry form. The label will be entered at the top of the entry form. The highlight can be moved anywhere within the workspace using the arrow keys.

Mouse Note: You can click with the mouse to move the highlight to where you want to make an entry.

Press: 

The highlight should be positioned on X1.30" and Y1.17". This tells you the label will begin 1.30 inches from the left edge of the paper and 1.17 inches from the top of the paper.

To enter the label in all capital letters,

Press: CAPS LOCK
Type: **EMPLOYEE RECORD**

Your screen should be similar to Figure 9-2.

FIGURE 9-2

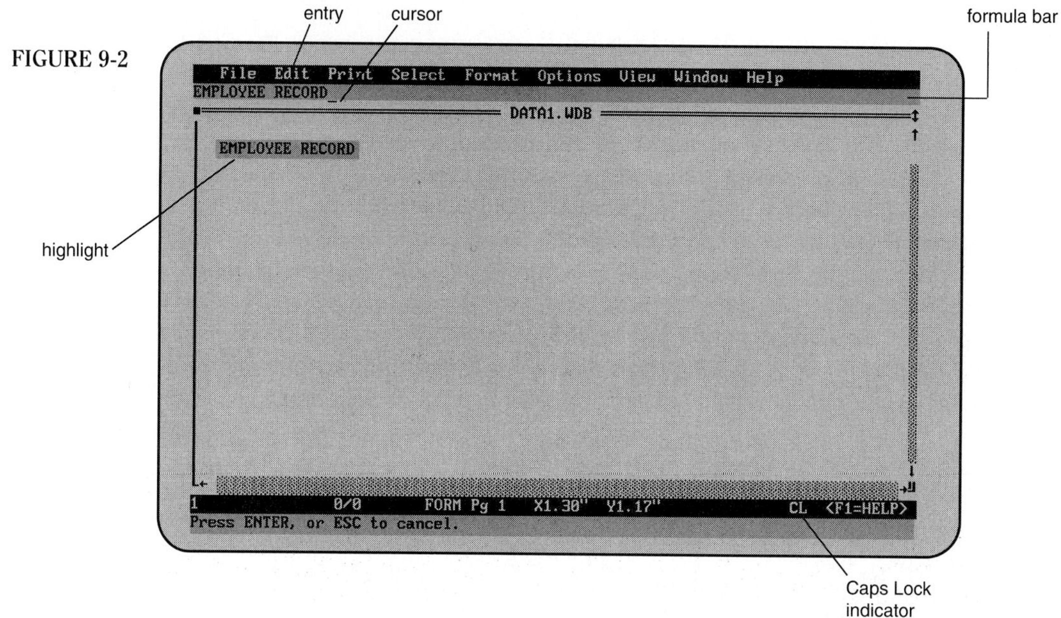

As you type, notice that the highlight extends to accommodate the label. The label is displayed in the formula bar and in the workspace at the highlight location. The cursor shows you where the next character you type will appear in the formula bar. If you see any errors, you can use Bksp to erase them and then type the information correctly.

To complete the label, following the directions in the message line,

Press: ↵

To turn off Caps Lock,

Press: CAPS LOCK

Creating a Field

The first field will be entered two lines below the entry form header. To move to this location,

Press: ↓ (2 times)

Check the status line to verify that the highlight is positioned at X1.30" Y1.50". If it is not, move it there. A field consists of the field name and the field space or cell. The field names can be entered anywhere in the workspace as long as they do not overlap. You will enter the field names as a list down the left side of the workspace.

The first field to be entered is Social Security Number. The field name should be descriptive of the data that will be entered in the field. It can be up to 15 characters long and can contain letters, digits, underscores, and blank spaces. You cannot, however, use a single quotation mark as part of a field name. Each field name in a database must be unique. You can have up to 256 fields in a database file.

Fred has decided to use the field name "SS Number" to represent the Social Security number field contents. The message line in FORM view tells you how to create a field.

Type: SS Number

All field names end with a colon (:). This tells Works the entry is a field name, not a label.

Type: :
Press: ↵

Your screen should be similar to Figure 9-3.

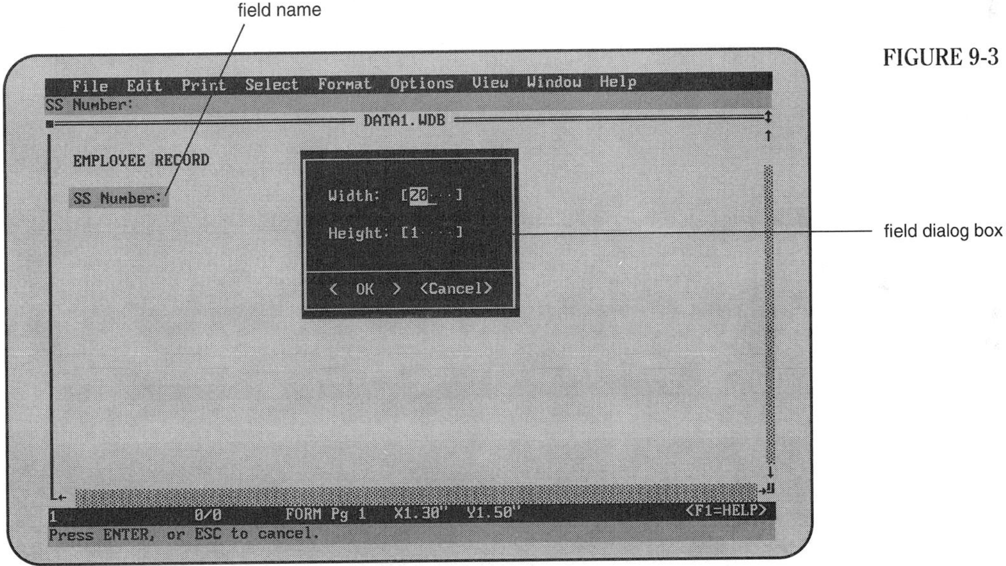

FIGURE 9-3

The Field Width and Height dialog box is automatically displayed whenever you create a field name. Works proposes the field width of 20 spaces and field height of 1 line. The **field width** is the number of spaces needed to hold the largest possible entry in that field. The **field height** is the number of lines needed to display the field contents.

A Social Security number consists of nine numbers and two dashes. So, to display the data, the field width needs to be 11 spaces. The cursor is correctly positioned in the Width text box for you to enter a different width setting. To change the field width to 11 spaces,

Type: 11

The Social Security number will not require more than one line to display the field contents. Therefore the field height setting of 1 is acceptable. To complete the command,

Press: (↵)

The highlight automatically moves to the next line in anticipation that you will create a second field.

The second field is the employee's first name. To enter the second field name,

Type: **First Name:**
Press: (↵)

Note: If you forget to end the field name with a colon, Works will treat the entry as a normal label entry and the Field Width and Height dialog box will not be displayed. To correct this, press (DEL) to delete the label entry and reenter the field name correctly.

Fred estimates that the field width needs to be 10 spaces to accommodate the field contents.

Type: **10**
Press: (↵)

The third field is the employee's last name. It requires a field width of 18 spaces. Complete the specification for the third field as follows:

Type: **Last Name:**
Press: (↵)
Type: 18
Press: (↵)

Your display should be similar to Figure 9-4.

FIGURE 9-4

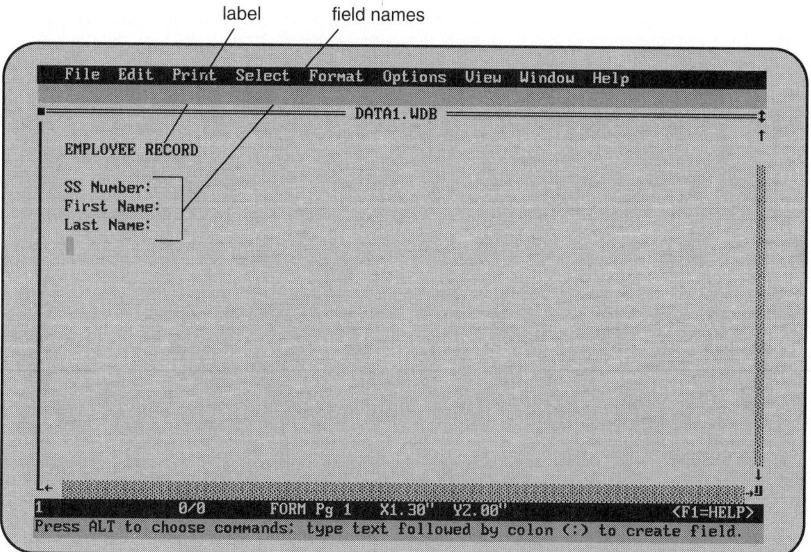

Enter the field name and width for the eight remaining fields shown below. The field height is always 1.

Field:	**Width**
Street:	20
City:	15
State:	2
Zipcode:	5
Department:	11
Title:	10
Pay:	5
Hours:	2

When you have completed the fields, your display should be similar to Figure 9-5.

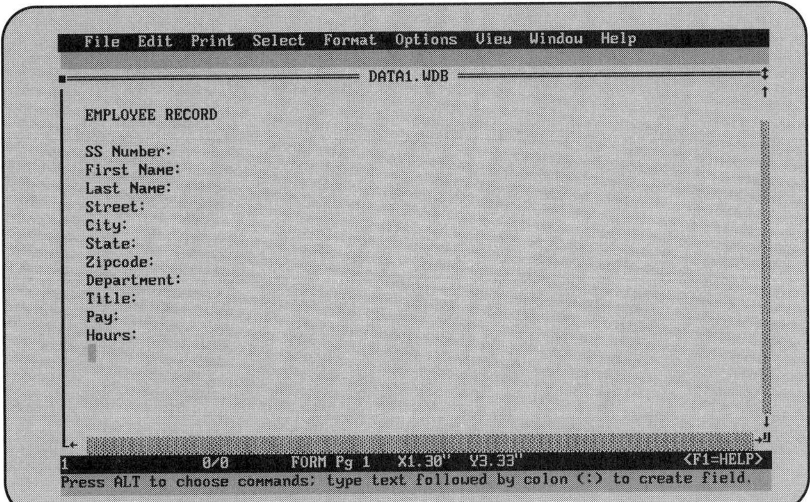

FIGURE 9-5

After looking over the entry form, Fred has decided to change the street field name form "Street" to "Street Address." To do this, you could reenter the complete field definition or use EDIT mode. The Edit (F2) key is used to edit an entry just as you used it in the spreadsheet tool.

Use (↑) to move the highlight to the Street field name.

Press: (F2)

EDIT appears in the status line. To add the word "Address,"

Press: (←)
Press: Space bar
Type: **Address**
Press: (↵)

Your display should be similar to Figure 9-6.

FIGURE 9-6

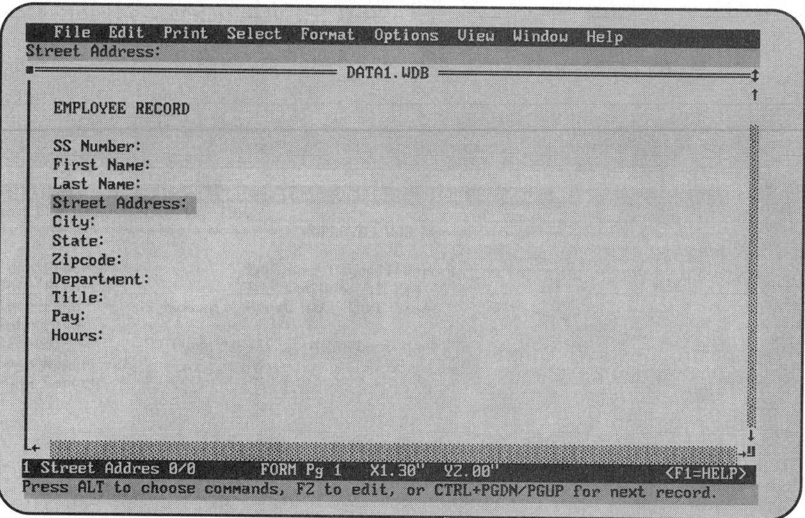

Carefully check your screen to ensure that each field name is the same as those in Figure 9-6. If your screen does not match, correct it now using EDIT.

Once you are satisfied that the entry form fields are correct, the entry form can be saved.

Select: File>Save

Since this is the first time you are saving this file, Works displays the Save As dialog box so you can give the file a new name.

If necessary, change the directory (ALT - I) to the directory where you want works to save the file.

Name this file EMPLOYEE.

The drive light goes on briefly and the entry form is saved on the disk.

Entering and Editing Field Contents

You are now ready to enter a few records into the database.

The data for the first record is:

Field Name	Field Contents
SS Number	527-36-4982
First Name	Edward
Last Name	Becker
Street Address	10326 W. 59th Street
City	Mesa
State	AZ
Zipcode	85205
Department	Restaurant
Title	Counter
Pay	4.35
Hours	40

Although you cannot see it, Works has reserved space for the field contents beginning two spaces to the right of the field name. To move the highlight to the area to enter the Social Security field contents for the first record,

Mouse Note: Click on the area immediately to the right of the field name to move the highlight.

Press: (↑) (3 times)
Press: (→)

The size of the highlight has expanded to correspond to the width of the field or cell. When a field contents cell is highlighted, it is called the **active cell**. The status line displays the field name of the active cell.

You can enter text, numbers, or a formula as a field's contents. The field contents can be up to 256 characters long.

To enter the Social Security number for this record,

Type: **527-36-4982**

The entry is displayed in the active cell and in the formula bar. If you made an error, use (Bksp) to erase the characters and retype the entry correctly. To complete the entry,

Press: (↵)

Your screen should be similar to Figure 9-7.

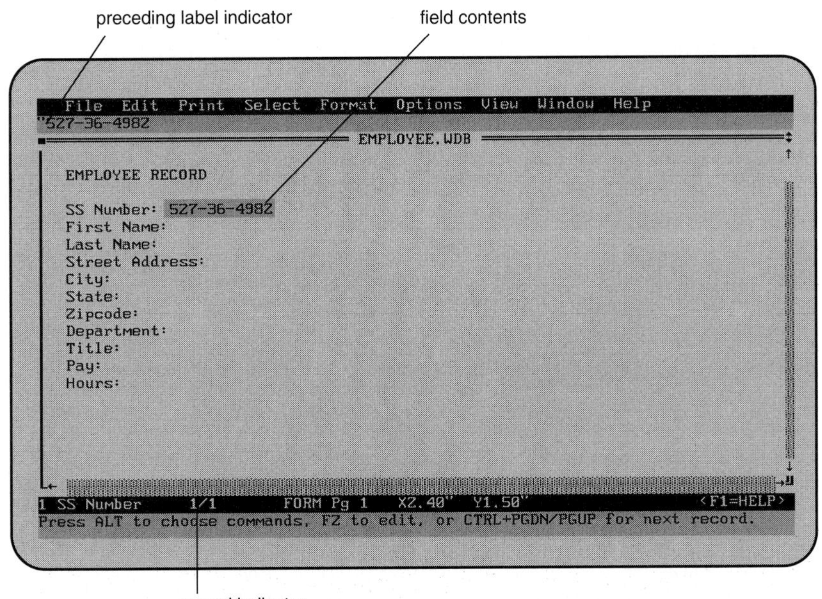

FIGURE 9-7

The field contents are entered into the cell. The formula bar displays the field contents preceded by a label indicator ("). Works treats number and text entries in a database the same as in the spreadsheet tool. The formula bar shows that Works has interpreted this entry as a text entry. This is because hyphens are used within the number. Since this field will not be used in calculations, this interpretation is acceptable.

Once you enter data in a record, the status line changes the number of displayed records over the total number of records indicator. It displays 1/1 because there is one displayed record in the database, which consists of a total of one record.

To move directly to the next field contents cell,

Press: (TAB)

If you press (↓) instead of (TAB), the highlight will move to the field name on the next line, rather than to the field contents cell. You would then need to press (→) to move to the field contents cell. Using (TAB) takes you directly to the next field contents cell.

When entering alphabetic characters in the field contents, enter the information exactly as you want it to appear in the database. It is important to be consistent when entering data into a database. If a field of information is entered in all lowercase letters, it should be entered that way throughout the database. Abbreviations of names or street addresses should also be consistent. In addition, extra spaces before and after entries can cause problems when searching the database for information. Therefore do not include extra spaces at the beginning or end of your field entries.

To enter the field data for the First Name field,

Type: **Edward**
Press: (TAB)

Pressing (TAB) both completes the entry and moves the highlight to the next field contents cell. Now you are ready to enter the information for the Last Name field.

Type: **Becker**
Press: (TAB)

The Street Address field is next.

Type: **1026 West 50th Street**

Your screen should be similar to Figure 9-8.

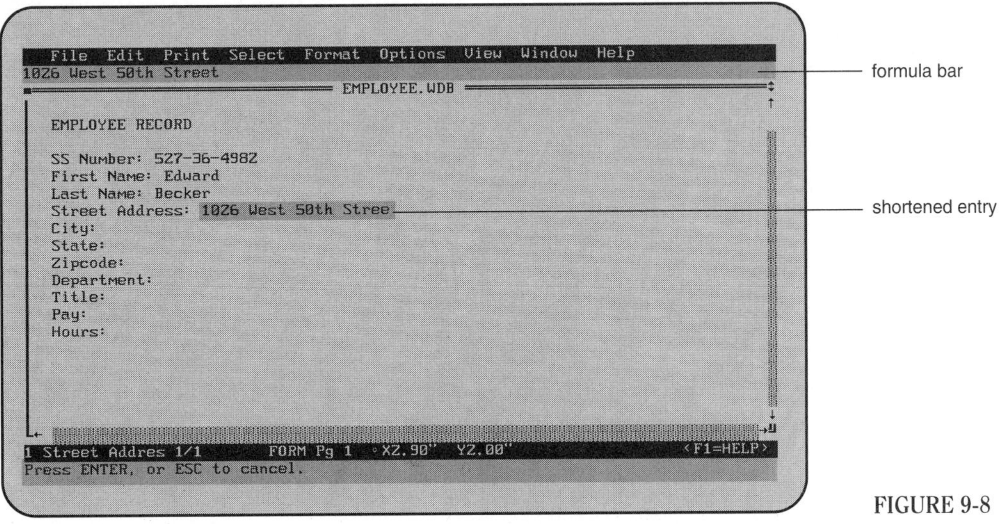

FIGURE 9-8

Notice that the field data is longer than the field width and the entire address cannot be displayed within the highlight. The formula bar displays the entire entry. Shortly, you will learn how to increase the field width so that the entire entry can be displayed.

Press: TAB

Fred notices that he entered the address incorrectly. It should be 10326 West 59th Street.

To move to the previous field contents cell,

Press: SHIFT - TAB

To correct this entry using EDIT,

Press: F2

First, the house number needs to be corrected. To move the cursor to the beginning of the entry,

Press: HOME

To change the number from 1026 to 10326,

Press: → (3 times)
Type: 3

The 3 was inserted into the house number.

When editing in the database tool, you cannot use TAB to move word by word in the formula bar. This is because pressing TAB is the same as pressing ↵; it completes the entry.

Next, to change 50 to 59 by deleting the 0 and replacing it with a 9,

Press: (→) (9 times)

The cursor should be positioned under the the 0 in 50.

Press: (DEL)
Type: 9
Press: (TAB)

Enter the city as follows:

Type: **Scottsdale**
Press: (TAB)

Another error. Fred was looking at the wrong record when entering this field of data. It should be Mesa. To make the City field the active cell,

Press: (SHIFT) - (TAB)

The highlight should be on the City field contents cell. To replace the existing cell contents with the correct data,

Type: **Mesa**
Press: (TAB)

Enter the State field contents as AZ.

The Zipcode field needs to be entered next. With the highlight in this field,

Type: **08525**
Press: (↵)

Your screen should be similar to Figure 9-9.

FIGURE 9-9

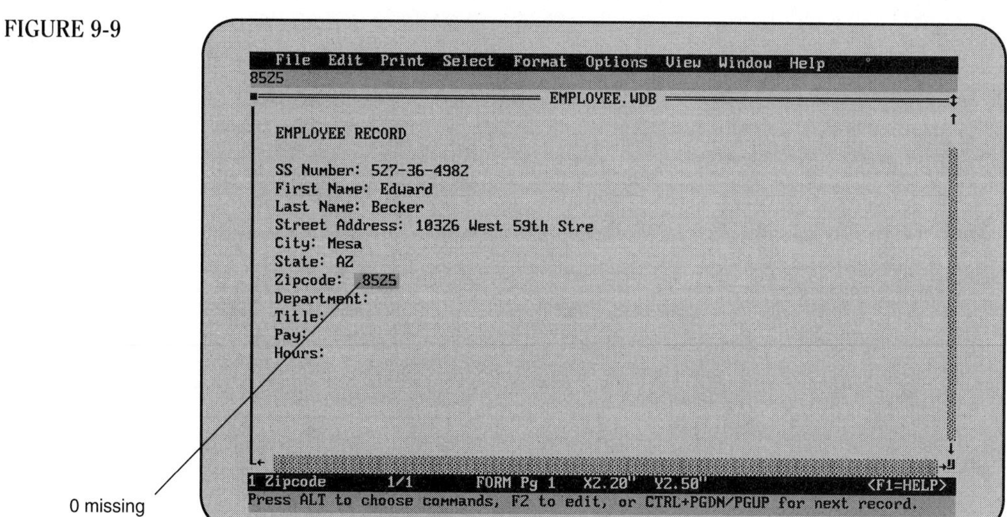

The Zipcode field contents are displayed as 8525. This is because Works has interpreted the entry as a value. When a 0 is the first number in a value entry, Works will eliminate the leading zero. However, the Zipcode field contents needs to be entered as text so that the leading zero will be displayed. Again, since zipcodes are not used in calculations, this is acceptable. To change the zipcode to a text entry, you must begin the entry with a preceding label indicator ("), just as in a spreadsheet. To edit the zipcode,

Press: (F2)
Press: (HOME)
Type: **"0**
Press: (TAB)

The zipcode is now correctly displayed.

Although all zipcodes do not begin with a zero, it is important that all entries in a particular field be either text or numeric. Since you need to make the zipcode a text entry for some zipcodes, you should enter all zipcode entries as text (preceded with a ").

Enter the data for the remaining fields, typing the information exactly as it appears below. If you make typing errors, practice using the editing keys demonstrated above. When entering the field contents for Hours, press (↵) rather than (TAB) to enter the data. If you press (TAB), Works will display a new blank entry form. If this happens, press (CTRL) - (PGUP) to move to the previous record.

Field Name	**Field Contents**
Department	Restaurant
Title	Counter
Pay	4.35
Hours	40

Your screen should be similar to Figure 9-10.

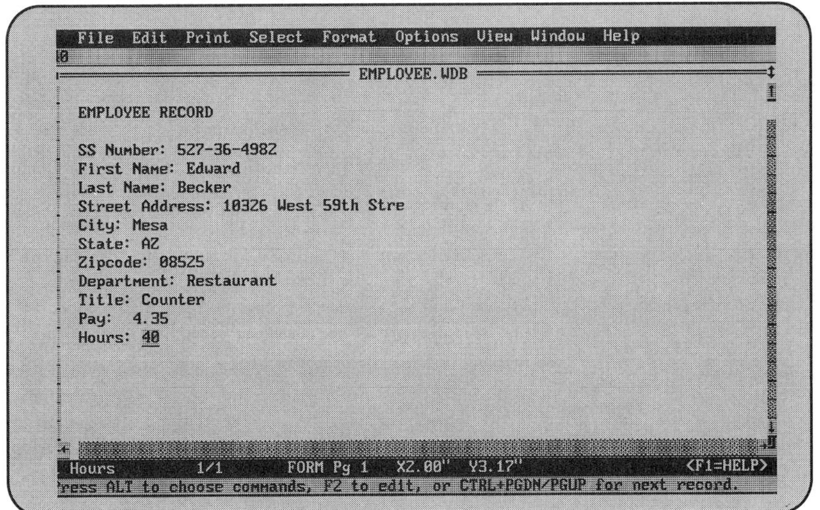

FIGURE 9-10

Notice that the Pay and Hours data do not begin with a preceding label indicator. This is because Works interpreted these entries as values. Also, just as in the spreadsheet tool, Works aligns text entries to the left in the cell space and numeric entries to the right.

The data for the first record is now complete.

To review, the cursor movement and editing keys that you have used so far are shown below.

Key	Result
(TAB)	Moves the highlight to the next field contents cell
(SHIFT) - (TAB)	Moves the highlight to the previous field contents cell
(→)	Moves the highlight right one cell or field; in EDIT moves the cursor one space to the right
(←)	Moves the highlight left one cell or field; in EDIT moves the cursor one space to the left
(↑)	Moves the highlight up one line
(HOME)	In EDIT, moves the cursor to the beginning of the entry
(END)	In EDIT, moves the cursor to the end of the entry
(DEL)	Deletes cell entry; in EDIT, deletes the character at the cursor
(Bksp)	In EDIT, deletes the character left of the cursor
(CTRL) - (PGUP)	Displays the previous record

To enter another record,

Press: (TAB)

When you press (TAB) and you are on the last field in a record, the next record is displayed. Since there is only one record in the database, a second blank entry form is displayed. Notice that the status line displays 2 to show you that the record on the screen is record 2. As records are added to a file, they are assigned a record number in the order they are entered. The number of the **active record** (the record you are viewing) is displayed on the left side of the status line.

Enter the following data as the second record. Complete the last field using (↵) rather than (TAB), so that a blank entry form is not displayed.

Field Name	Field Contents
SS Number	221-55-2321
First Name	Anthony
Last Name	Allbright
Street Address	1766 N. Extension St. #17-24
City	Scottsdale
State	AZ
Zipcode	"85205
Department	Maintenance
Title	Supervisor
Pay	8.25
Hours	45

Your screen should be similar to Figure 9-11.

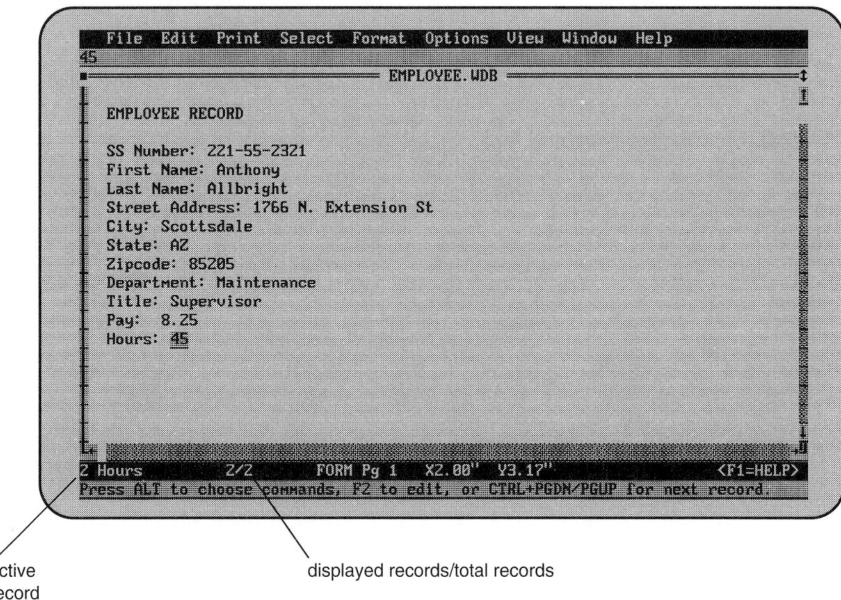

FIGURE 9-11

Once you have completed entering record 2, look at the status bar. It shows 2/2. There are now two displayed records in a database file consisting of two records.

To view the contents of the previous record,

Press: CTRL - PGUP

The first record you entered is displayed on the screen. The record number, 1, is displayed in the status line. Pressing CTRL - PGUP or CTRL - PGDN will move up or down through the records in the file and display the active record, or the record that can be changed or edited. Moving between records is called **scrolling.**

Check both records carefully. Edit if necessary.

Since Fred used abbreviations in the street address for the second record, he wants to use abbreviations in the Street Address field in the first record.

Change the street address in record 1 to 10326 W. 59th St.

To display a blank entry form,

Press: CTRL - END

Pressing CTRL - END quickly takes you to the end of the file and displays a blank entry form. The highlight is in the same field contents cell, Street Address, as it was in the previous record.

Move to the first field contents cell, SS Number.

Enter the next two records. Be careful that you are in the correct field contents cell as you are entering the data for each record.

Field	**Record 3**	**Record 4**
SS Number	492-38-5216	097-12-4879
First Name	Alice	Ellen
Last Name	Patton	Johnson
Street Address	2061 Winchester Rd.	1622 E. Donner Dr.
City	Apache Junction	Tempe
State	AZ	AZ
Zipcode	"85220	"08525
Department	Service	Restaurant
Title	Desk Clerk	Supervisor
Pay	4.55	8.25
Hours	32	40

After you have inserted records 3 and 4, check each of the records by using the (CTRL) - (PGUP) and (CTRL) - (PGDN) keys to scroll to each record. You can move quickly to the first record using (CTRL) - (HOME). As you saw, (CTRL) - (END) takes you to a blank entry form at the end of the database. Therefore, to view the last record in a database, you need to press (CTRL) - (END) and then (CTRL) - (PGUP).

Check that each zipcode begins with a label prefix character. Edit any entries that are incorrect.

Changing the Field Size

The only field width that is too small to display the complete field contents so far is the Street Address field.

Move to: The Street Address field of the second record

The field contents is eight spaces larger than the field width. The procedure for changing the field width in the database tool is just like changing the column width in the spreadsheet tool. The field width is currently set at 20 spaces. To increase the size of the field to 28 spaces to fully display the entry,

Select: Format

Your screen should be similar to Figure 9-12.

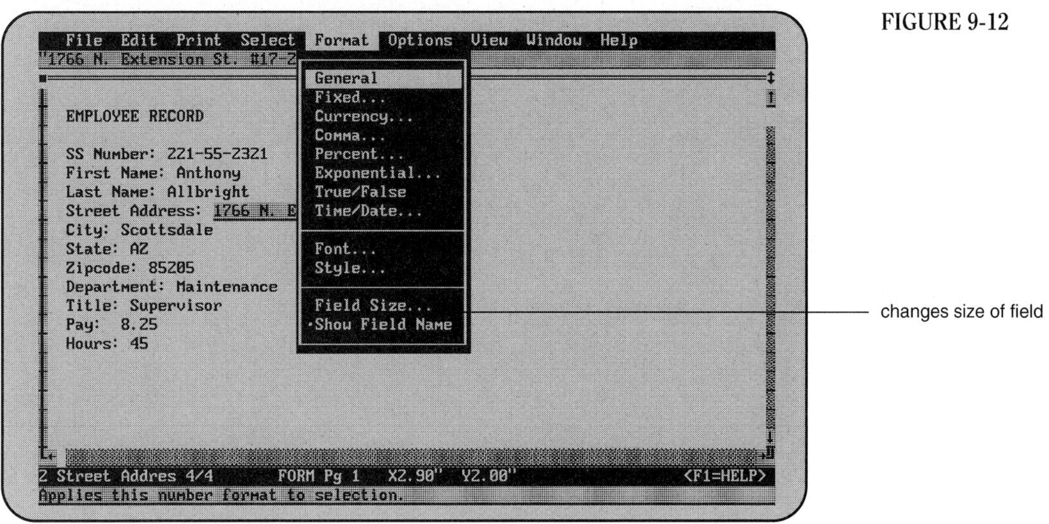

FIGURE 9-12

The Field Size command will change the size of the field in FORM view.

Select: Field Size

To enter the new field size in the dialog box,

Type: 28
Press: ↵

The new field size is now large enough to fully display the street address.

Viewing Multiple Records

There are now four records in the database. In FORM view, you can see one record at a time on the screen. Many times, it is helpful to view many records at once on the screen. Works has a second database view, called LIST view, which lets you do just that.

To move to the first record,

Press: CTRL - HOME

To view all four records on the screen,

Select: View>List

Your screen should be similar to Figure 9-13.

FIGURE 9-13

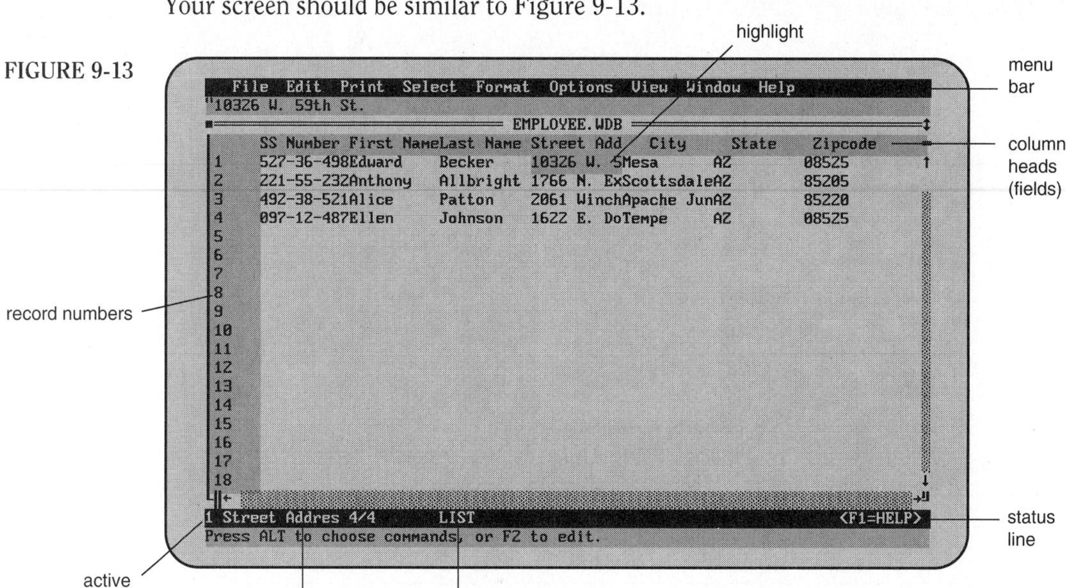

The LIST view screen displays each record as a row and each field as a column. The entry form title is not displayed. Along the left edge of the workspace in LIST view, a row number identifies the **record number** of each record. Eighteen records can be displayed on the screen at a time. This is similar to how data is displayed in a spreadsheet.

The highlight is in the same field and record it was last in when in FORM view. Whichever record you are on in FORM view is the first record displayed in the LIST view screen. Since you were on the first record, record 1 is at the top of the screen.

The menu bar displays the same menu of commands as in FORM view.

The status line displays LIST to remind you that the current database view is LIST. It also displays the record number of the active record (the record containing the highlight) and the field name of the active cell. It does not display the X and Y coordinates and page number, as in FORM view.

Moving Around LIST View

Since the field contents are displayed across a row, only part of each record can be displayed on the screen at a time. To move around LIST view, you use the same keys you used in the spreadsheet tool.

Key	Result
Arrow	Moves one field or record in the direction of the arrow
(PGDN)	Moves down one window
(PGUP)	Moves up one window
(CTRL) - (PGDN)	Moves one window right
(CTRL) - (PGUP)	Moves one window left
(CTRL) - (END)	Moves to the end of the database
(CTRL) - (HOME)	Moves to the beginning of the database
(HOME)	Moves to the leftmost field in the active record
(END)	Moves to the rightmost field in the active record
(CTRL) - arrow	Moves one block of data up, down, right, or left

In Figure 9-13 the active cell is the Street Address field. Notice that the address is not fully displayed in the highlight. This is because LIST view has its own default field width of ten spaces, just like the spreadsheet. This makes reading the information in LIST view very difficult. Look at the other fields of data and you will see that many of them are truncated. The only way to read the field contents in these fields is to move the highlight to the field and look at the entry as it is displayed in the formula bar.

To scroll the fields to the right into view,

Press: (→) (7 times)

Your screen should be similar to Figure 9-14.

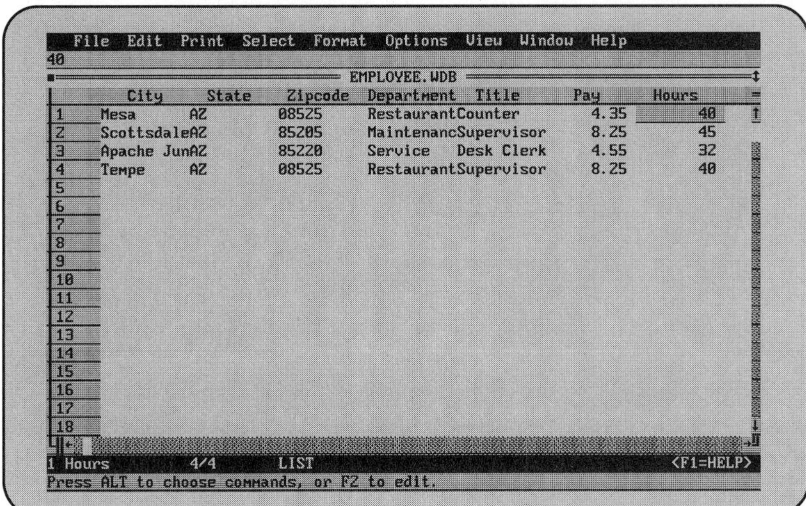

FIGURE 9-14

The Pay and Hours fields have scrolled into view on the right side of the screen, and the Street Address field has scrolled out of view on the left side of the screen. As you can see, many of the fields are too narrow.

To move to the left one window,

Press: (CTRL) - (PGUP)

The first seven fields are displayed again. To move to the last field in a record, you could press (CTRL) - (→) to move a window to the right and then move the highlight to the last field, or you could press (END).

Press: (END)

Pressing (END) positions the highlight on the rightmost field in a row. The Hours field is now the active cell. To move quickly back to the leftmost field in the row,

Press: (HOME)

Changing the Field Width

To make the records in LIST view easier to read, you can change the field width. This is similar to changing the field size in FORM view. When you change the field widths in LIST view, the field sizes in FORM view are not affected. To increase the width of the SS Number field,

Select: Format

Your screen should be similar to Figure 9-15.

FIGURE 9-15

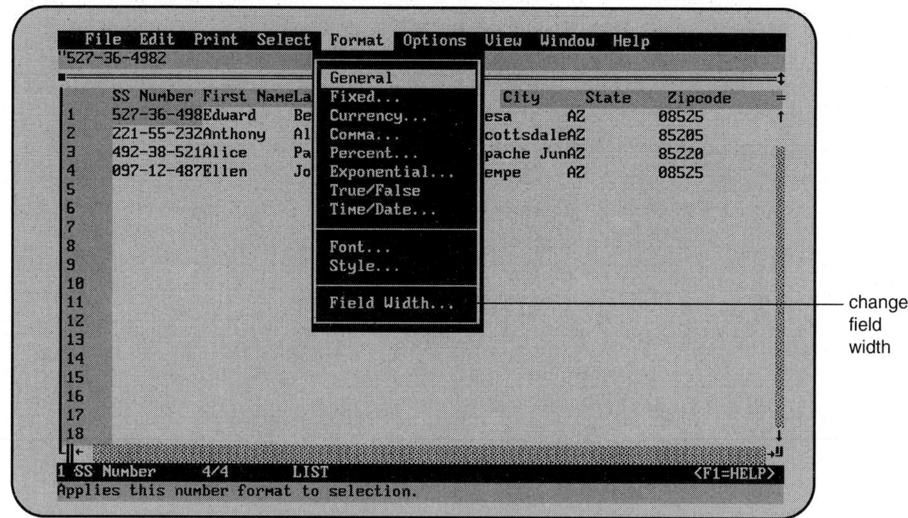

The commands in the LIST view Format menu are slightly different from those in the FORM view Format menu. For example, the command to change the field size is called Field Width rather than Field Size.

Select: Field **W**idth

The default setting, 10, is displayed in the dialog box. The SS Number field contents require 11 spaces. To allow one extra space between columns of data, you will increase the field width to 12.

Type: 12
Press: ↵

Your screen should be similar to Figure 9-16.

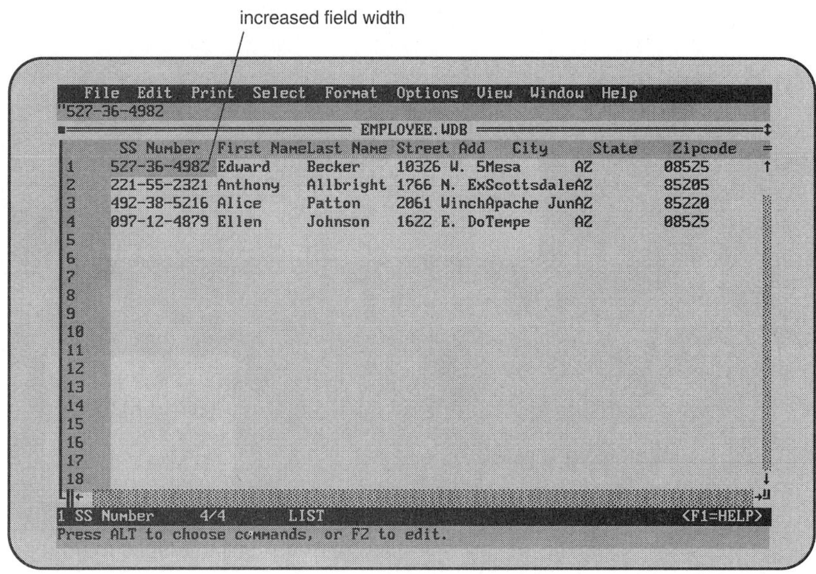

FIGURE 9-16

The entire Social Security number is displayed, and there is one blank space between the SS Number field column of data and the First Name field column of data.

Press: →

The First Name field is wide enough to display the contents; however, there is no space between the "First Name" and "Last Name" field names at the top of the column. To increase the width by one space to add a space between the field names,

Select: Format>Field Width>**11**>↵
Press: →

The Last Name field is correctly displayed and does not need to be changed.

Press: →

Sometimes it is difficult to know how much you need to increase the field width. If you look at the Street Address field, you see that the longest entry is in record 2. It is helpful to move to the longest entry when increasing the width so that you can count the number of characters for the field contents in the formula bar.

Press: ↓

The contents of this field require 28 spaces. However, to allow an extra space between the columns of data, you will increase it to 29.

Increase the field width of the Street Address field to 29.

Next, you will change the width of the City field. To move to the longest entry in this field,

Press: →
Press: ↓

The field contents, Apache Junction, for the third record should be highlighted. The field contents for this record require 15 spaces plus one, to allow a space between columns.

Increase this field width to 16.

Move to the State field.

The State field is larger than it needs to be. Decrease the width to 6 to fully display the field name and leave a blank space between columns.

In a similar way, increase or decrease the field widths of the remaining fields to the settings that follow:

Field Name	**Width**
Zipcode	8
Department	12
Title	11
Pay	5
Hours	6

When you are done, the highlight should be in the Hours field of record 3 and your screen should be similar to Figure 9-17.

FIGURE 9-17

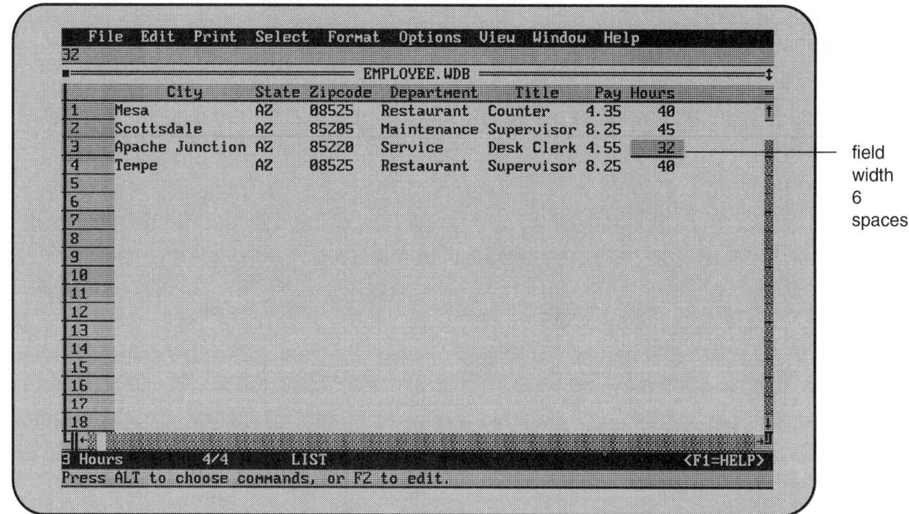

The changes you have made to the field widths in LIST view do not affect the field sizes in FORM view. To verify this, you will switch back to the FORM view. To do this, you can select View>Form from the menu or use the shortcut key (F9).

Select: View>**F**orm

(F9)

Your screen should be similar to Figure 9-18.

FIGURE 9-18

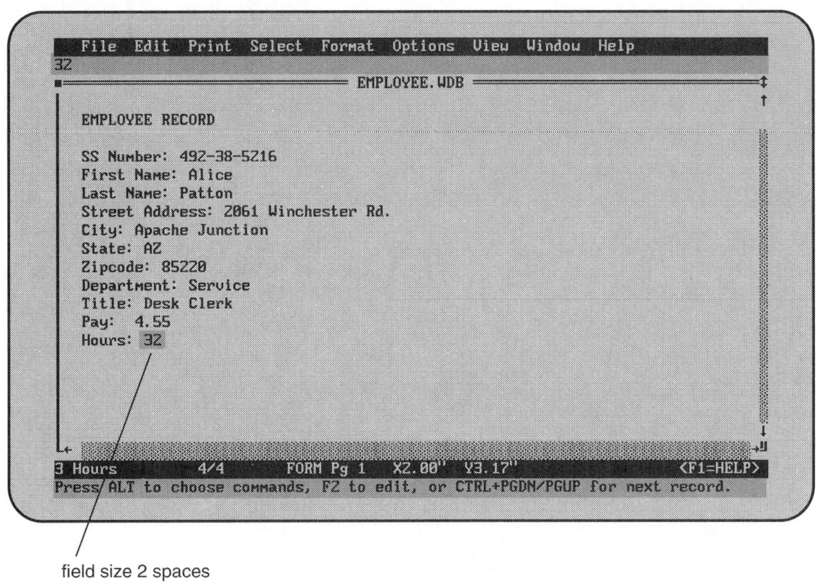

Since the highlight was in the Hours field for record 3 in LIST view, the same record and field are active in FORM view. The Hours cell is only two spaces wide in FORM view; in LIST view it is six spaces wide.

Using (SHIFT) - (TAB), move to each field of this record and verify that the original field sizes you set in FORM view were not altered. When you are done, the SS Number field should be the active cell.

To return to LIST view,

Press: (F9)

Since you were viewing record 3 in FORM view, it is the first record in LIST view. To display the other two records,

Press: (↑) (2 times)

Printing the Database

Fred would like to print a list of the four records in the file. You will decrease the right and left margins so that as many fields of data can be printed across the width of the page as possible. To do this,

Select: **P**rint>Page Setup and **M**argins>**Le**ft Margin>**.5**>**R**ight Margin>**.5**>(↵)

To print the list,

Select: **P**rint>**P**rint>(↵)

Your printed output should be similar to Figure 9-19.

FIGURE 9-19

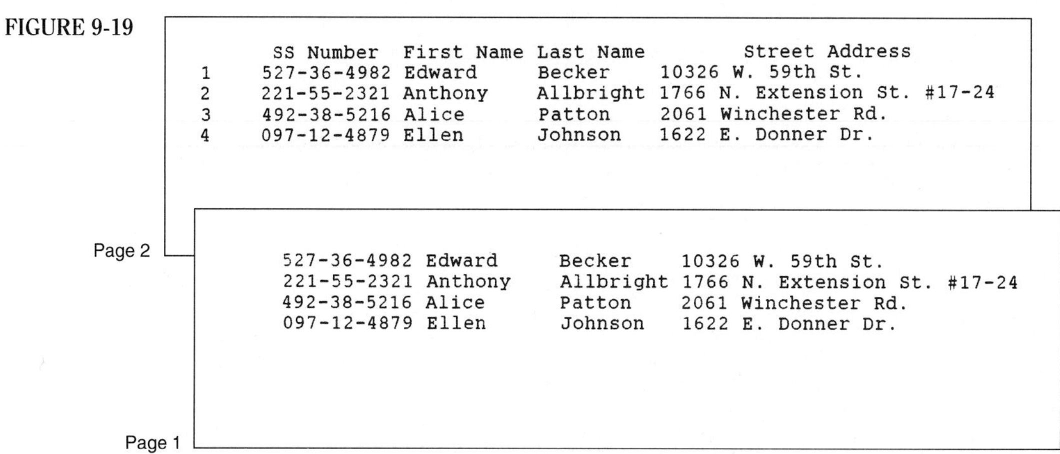

Page 2

	SS Number	First Name	Last Name	Street Address
1	527-36-4982	Edward	Becker	10326 W. 59th St.
2	221-55-2321	Anthony	Allbright	1766 N. Extension St. #17-24
3	492-38-5216	Alice	Patton	2061 Winchester Rd.
4	097-12-4879	Ellen	Johnson	1622 E. Donner Dr.

Page 1

527-36-4982	Edward	Becker	10326 W. 59th St.
221-55-2321	Anthony	Allbright	1766 N. Extension St. #17-24
492-38-5216	Alice	Patton	2061 Winchester Rd.
097-12-4879	Ellen	Johnson	1622 E. Donner Dr.

As many fields as possible are printed across the width of the page. The additional fields are printed on the second page. The record numbers and field names are not printed. To print the record numbers and field names,

Select: Print>**P**rint>Print record and field **l**abels>↵

Your printed output should look similar to Figure 9-20.

FIGURE 9-20

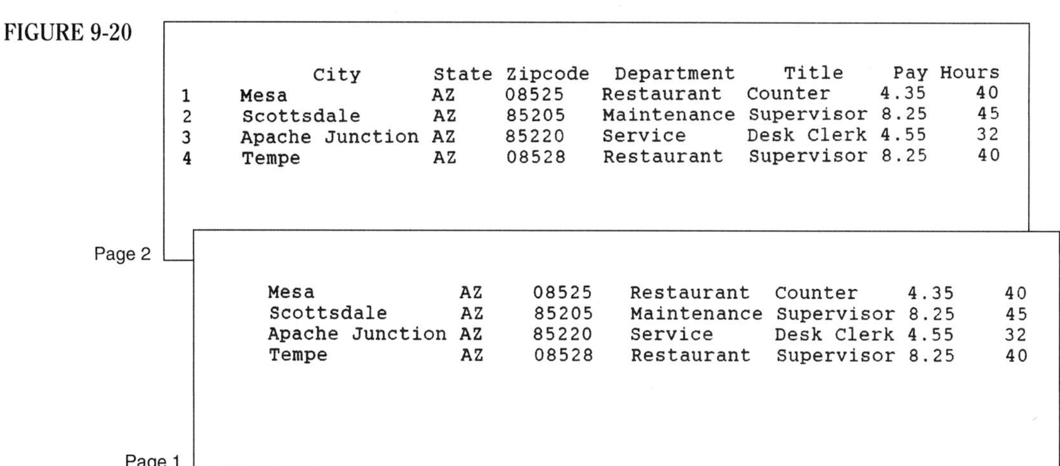

Page 2

	City	State	Zipcode	Department	Title	Pay	Hours
1	Mesa	AZ	08525	Restaurant	Counter	4.35	40
2	Scottsdale	AZ	85205	Maintenance	Supervisor	8.25	45
3	Apache Junction	AZ	85220	Service	Desk Clerk	4.55	32
4	Tempe	AZ	08528	Restaurant	Supervisor	8.25	40

Page 1

Mesa	AZ	08525	Restaurant	Counter	4.35	40
Scottsdale	AZ	85205	Maintenance	Supervisor	8.25	45
Apache Junction	AZ	85220	Service	Desk Clerk	4.55	32
Tempe	AZ	08528	Restaurant	Supervisor	8.25	40

Adding the field labels to the printout makes it easier to understand the output.

You will continue to follow Fred as he builds and uses his database file of employee records in the next lab. To save the current file,

Select: File>Save

Works saves the file using the same filename, EMPLOYEE.

To quit Works,

Select: File>Exit

If you do not want to quit Works, close this file first before continuing. To do this,

Select: File>Close

Key Terms

template
record
field
field name
field contents
field width
field height
active cell
active record
scrolling
record number

Matching

1. 4/4	_____	**a.**	ends a field name entry
2. Forma**t**>Field Si**z**e	_____	**b.**	indicates there are four displayed records in a database of four records
3. (TAB)	_____	**c.**	moves to the last record
4. Forma**t**>Field **W**idth	_____	**d.**	turns on EDIT
5. (F9)	_____	**e.**	moves directly to the next field contents cell in FORM view
6. (CTRL) - (END)	_____	**f.**	indicates the highlight is positioned 1.5 inches from the top of the page
7. Y1.50	_____	**g.**	command to change the size of the field in FORM view
8. :	_____	**h.**	command to change the size of the field in LIST view
9. (F2)	_____	**i.**	moves to FORM view from LIST view
10. (CTRL) - (PGUP)	_____	**j.**	moves to the previous record in FORM view

Practice Exercises

1. Identify the parts of the database FORM screen shown below.

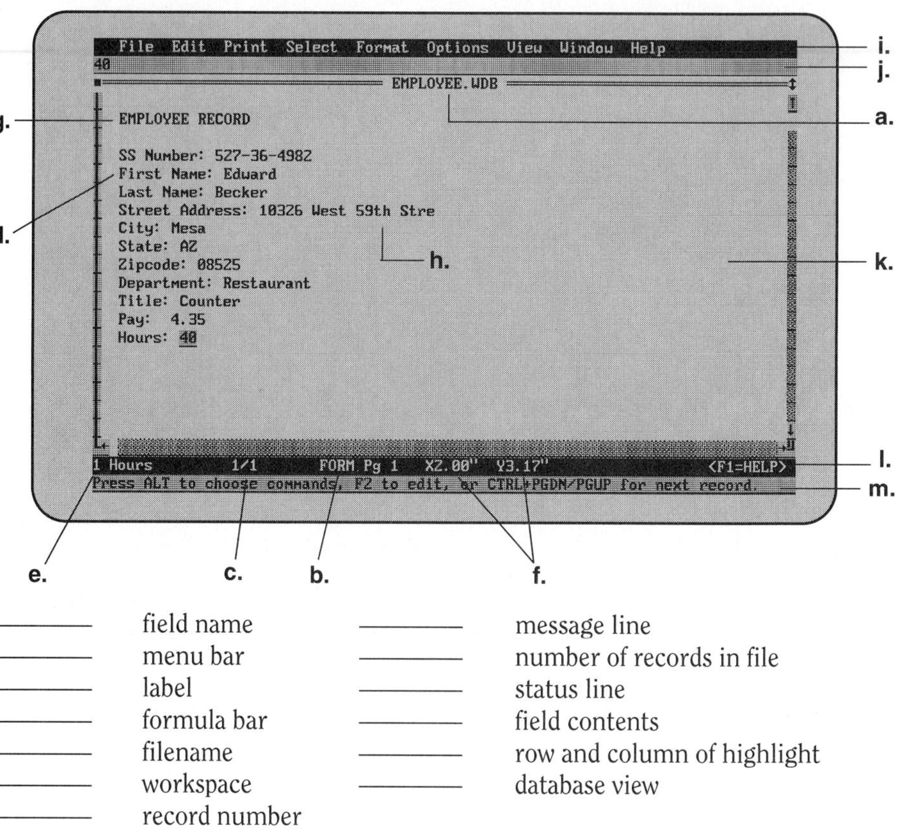

________	field name	________	message line
________	menu bar	________	number of records in file
________	label	________	status line
________	formula bar	________	field contents
________	filename	________	row and column of highlight
________	workspace	________	database view
________	record number		

2. Susannah owns a small business that sells custom-made ceramic tiles. She currently keeps her client orders and payment records in a small accounting ledger. Her business has grown considerably since she first started it a year ago, so she has decided to invest in a computer. She wants to keep track of her client orders and payments using Works. She has defined the fields as follows:

Field Name	Width
LAST NAME	12
FIRST NAME	10
ADDRESS	20
CITY	12
STATE	2
ZIPCODE	5
PHONE	8
UNIT COST	5
QUANTITY	4

- On the second line, enter the entry form title “CLIENT ORDERS” and on the third line “By [Your Name].”

- Beginning on line 5 (Y 1.67"), enter the field names in all uppercase characters and sizes as defined above.
- Save the entry form as TILES.
- Enter the following two records:

Record 1	**Record 2**
Doyle	Miller
Marilyn	Phillip
298 Winding Way	46 South View
Fairview	Albion
PA	PA
“16415	“16401
298-1374	468-9238
4.75	5.85
125	75

- View the records in LIST view.
- Where necessary, increase or decrease the field widths to fully display the field contents and allow one space both between columns of data and between field names. Leave the City and Unit Cost field widths at the default setting.
- In FORM view, enter a third record using your name. The address and phone can be fictitious. You have ordered 356 tiles at a unit cost of $6.75.
- Print a copy of the records in LIST view using “Print command option Print records and field labels.”
- Print the third record in FORM view using the default Print command settings.
- Save the file again as TILES.

3. Joe is a full-time college student. He is in his third full semester of school. He wants to create a database file of all the courses he has taken to date. His fields are:

Field Name	**Width**
COURSE #	6
TITLE	15
SEMESTER	4
GRADE	1

The semester data is entered as F=Fall, Sp= Spring, followed by the year entered as 91 for 1991.

- Create a database file named GRADES using the fields as defined above. Enter two title lines: JOE’S GRADES on the second line of the entry form and “by [Your Name]” on the third line. Leave two blank lines between the title and the field names.

- Enter the following data in numbered order (shown in parentheses):

(1) ENG101
Freshman English
F 91
C

(2) MAT210
Calculus
F 91
D

(3) BUS100
Intro to Business
F 91
B

(4) PSY100
Intro to Psychology
F 91
B

(5) PED101
Physical Education
F 91
A

(6) ENG102
Freshman English
Sp92
B

(7) MAT210
Calculus
Sp92
C

(8) ACC120
Accounting 1
Sp92
B

(9) ART100
World Art
Sp92
B

(10) PED102
Physical Education
Sp92
A

- In FORM view, increase the title field size to fully display the longest course title entry.
- In LIST view, increase or decrease the field widths to fully display the field contents and allow one space between columns of data and between field names.
- Print a copy of the database records in LIST view using the Print command option "Print record and field labels."
- Print the first record in FORM view (use the default FORM view Print command settings).
- Save the file as GRADES.

4. Lynne is the recording secretary for the Future Entrepreneurs Club. She will use Works to help her keep track of the club members.

- Create a database entry form that include each member's full name, complete address, home telephone number, and major.
- Enter your name and appropriate information as the first record.
- Enter 19 additional records using either real or fictitious data.
- Adjust the width of the fields in both FORM and LIST view to fully display the data. In LIST view, where necessary make the width one space wider to allow a space between columns of data.
- Print the database of records in LIST view using the Print command option "Print record and field labels."
- Save the file as ENTRE.

5. Aquanetta owns a gift shop. She has decided to keep track of the store's inventory using Works. The field definitions are as follows:

Field Name	Width
SKU Number	5
Description	20
Quantity	3
Cost	6
Price	6
Vendor	15

- Create a database named STOCK1 using the field definitions above. Begin the field definitions on the fifth line of the form.
- Enter the entry form title "GIFT SHOP INVENTORY" on the first line of the entry form and your name and the date on the second line.
- Enter the following records:

Record 1	Record 2
35001	35005
Large Ceramic Goose	Golden Egg
4	11
14.63	3.12
29.26	6.24
Your Name	Tom Maxwell

- View the records in LIST view.
- Increase or decrease the field widths to fully display the field contents and allow at least one space between columns of data and between field names.
- Print a copy of the records in LIST view using the Print command option "Print record and field labels."
- Print a copy of the first record in FORM view (use the default FORM view print settings).
- Save the file as STOCK1.

Command Summary

Command	Shortcut	Action	Page
Create New File>New **D**atabase		Opens new database file	264
Forma**t**>Field Si**z**e		Changes field size in FORM view	279
Forma**t**>Field **W**idth		Changes field width in LIST view	282
View>**L**ist	F9	Displays LIST view	279
View>**F**orm	F9	Displays FORM view	284
Print>**P**rint>Print record and field **l**abels		Prints records in LIST view with record numbers and field labels	286

LAB

Modifying, Sorting, and Searching a Database

10

OBJECTIVES

In this lab you will learn how to:

1. Edit the database records.
2. Delete records.
3. Insert and move fields.
4. Hide and unhide fields.
5. Copy field contents.
6. Enter field formulas.
7. Search and query the database.
8. Sort the database.
9. Insert records.
10. Format a field.
11. Print selected records.

CASE STUDY

Fred continued to add records to the database file. After a short time, he had 25 records in the file. Before adding more records, he decides to show the club manager a printout of the records in the file. The manager suggests that Fred add two more fields, Sex and Weekly Pay, to the database form. You will follow Fred as he modifies the database structure to include these two new fields of data.

In addition, throughout the day Fred receives several notes asking him for information or telling him about changes that need to be made to the employee records. Updating records and providing information to other departments is a routine part of his job. You will follow Fred as he locates, edits, adds, and deletes records in the database file.

Finally, the accounting department has asked him for a list of employees who are earning $6.00 per hour or more and work in the Restaurant or Service departments. You will create a simple report containing this information.

Opening a Database File

Load DOS. If necessary, respond to the date and time prompts. Load Works. Your data disk should be in the appropriate drive for your computer system.

Select: Open Existing File

Select the appropriate directory for your computer system. Scroll the files in the Files box until the database files are displayed.

The file you created in Lab 9, EMPLOYEE.WDB, as well as several others are listed in the Database section of the Files selection box.

The file EMPLOYE2.WDB is the same as the file EMPLOYEE.WDB you created in Lab 9, except that it now contains 25 records. Open the file EMPLOYE2.WDB.

Your screen should be similar to Figure 10-1.

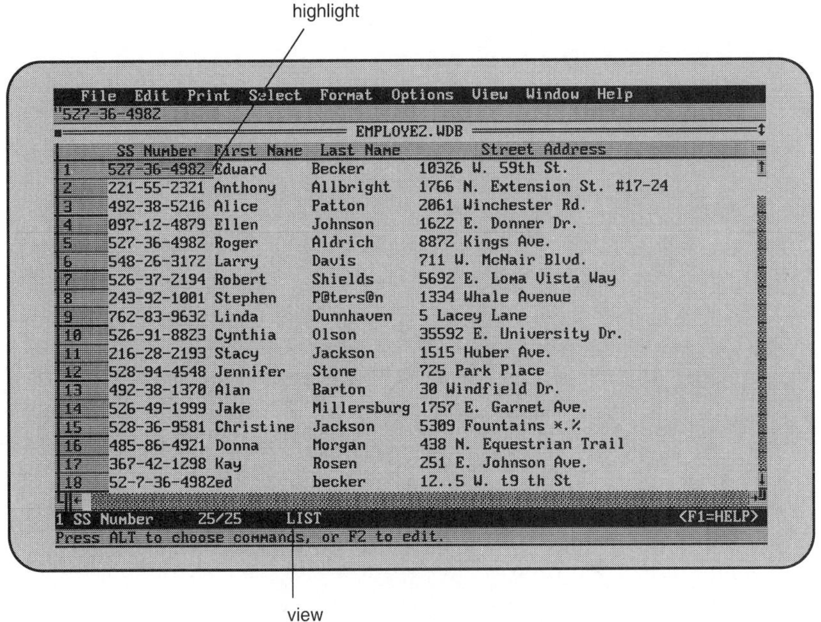

FIGURE 10-1

When the file is opened, the highlight is in the same location it was in when the file was last saved. In this case, the highlight was in the Social Security Number field of the first record. Also, you will notice that the records are displayed in LIST view. This is because the file was saved in LIST view. If it had been saved in FORM view, it would have displayed in FORM view when opened.

Fred notices several errors in the records displayed in the window. For example, the eighth record has several errors in the Last Name field, and record 15 has several errors in the Street Address field. Also, he sees that data for Edward Becker has been entered twice, both as record number 1 and record number 18. Record 18 also contains several errors. Fred figures there are probably several other errors in other fields that are not visible in the window.

To view the fields to the right,

Press: (CTRL) - (PGDN)

Next, Fred notices that several entries in the Pay field have been shortened. For example, record 7 shows the pay value as 4.1 when it should be 4.10. The last error he sees is that the state in record 12 should be AZ, not AX.

To view the rest of the records in the database,

Press: (CTRL) - (END)

The highlight is positioned on the last field of the last record.

Press: (HOME)

He does not see any other errors. To return to the first record,

Press: CTRL - HOME

Editing Records in LIST View

The first record that needs to be corrected is record 8. You could use the arrow keys to move to the record. However, it is often faster to use the Select>GoTo command.

Select: Select>GoTo

Your screen should be similar to Figure 10-2.

FIGURE 10-2

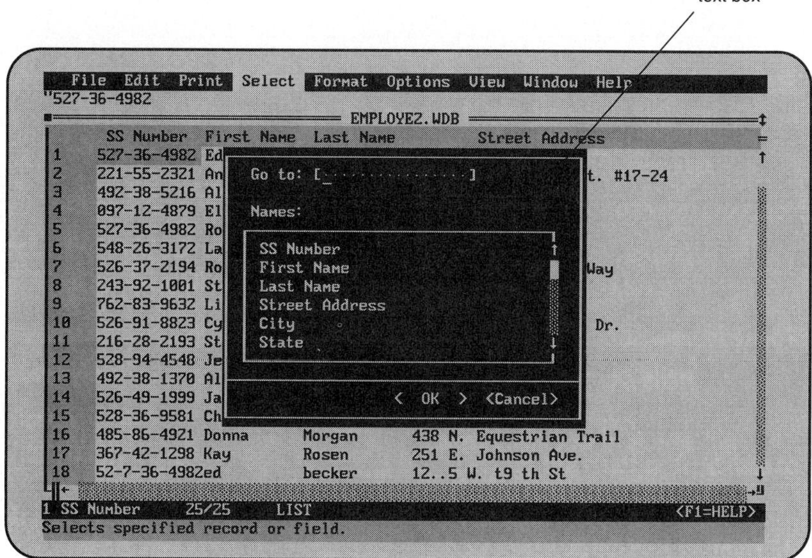

In the Go to: text box you can enter a record number or a field name. To move to record 8,

Type: 8
Press: ↵

The highlight is now positioned on the first field in record 8.

To correct the last name,

Press: → (2 times)
Type: Paterson
Press: →

Fred also notices that the street address in this record is incorrect. To change it to 1334 W. Hale Ave.,

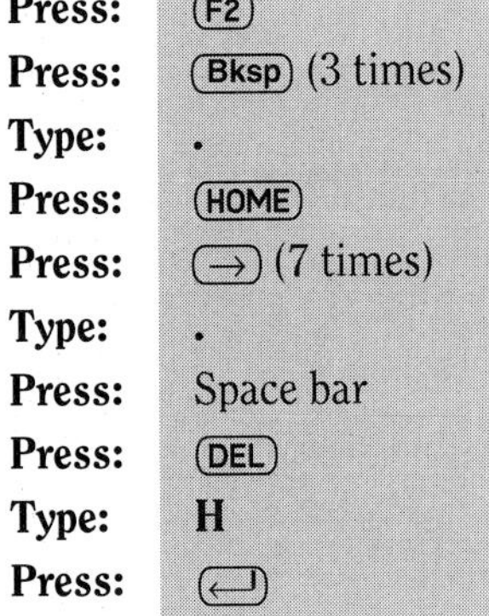

Press: (F2)
Press: (Bksp) (3 times)
Type: .
Press: (HOME)
Press: (→) (7 times)
Type: .
Press: Space bar
Press: (DEL)
Type: H
Press: (↵)

Your screen should be similar to Figure 10-3.

FIGURE 10-3

```
 File  Edit  Print  Select  Format  Options  View  Window  Help
"1334 W. Hale Ave.
                        EMPLOYE2.WDB
    SS Number  First Name  Last Name    Street Address
1   527-36-4982 Edward     Becker      10326 W. 59th St.
2   221-55-2321 Anthony    Allbright   1766 N. Extension St. #17-24
3   492-38-5216 Alice      Patton      2061 Winchester Rd.
4   097-12-4879 Ellen      Johnson     1622 E. Donner Dr.
5   527-36-4982 Roger      Aldrich     8872 Kings Ave.
6   548-26-3172 Larry      Davis       711 W. McNair Blvd.
7   526-37-2194 Robert     Shields     5692 E. Loma Vista Way
8   243-92-1001 Stephen    Paterson    1334 W. Hale Ave.
9   762-83-9632 Linda      Dunnhaven   5 Lacey Lane
10  526-91-8823 Cynthia    Olson       35592 E. University Dr.
11  216-28-2193 Stacy      Jackson     1515 Huber Ave.
12  528-94-4548 Jennifer   Stone       725 Park Place
13  492-38-1370 Alan       Barton      30 Windfield Dr.
14  526-49-1999 Jake       Millersburg 1757 E. Garnet Ave.
15  528-36-9581 Christine  Jackson     5309 Fountains *.%
16  485-86-4921 Donna      Morgan      438 N. Equestrian Trail
17  367-42-1298 Kay        Rosen       251 E. Johnson Ave.
18  52-7-36-4982ed         becker      12..5 W. t9 th St
8 Street Addres 25/25      LIST                          <F1=HELP>
Press ALT to choose commands, or F2 to edit.
```

Editing records in LIST view is the same as editing records in FORM view.

Using EDIT, correct the street address in record 15 to 530 Nine Fountains Dr. and the state in record 12 to AZ.

Deleting a Record

Edward Becker's record is in the database twice, both as record 1 and record 18. Instead of deleting record 1, you will delete record 18 because it contains many errors.

The command to delete a record is in the Edit menu. First, the highlight must be on any field in the record to be deleted.

Move to: Record 18

To delete the record,

Select: Edit

Your screen should be similar to Figure 10-4.

FIGURE 10-4

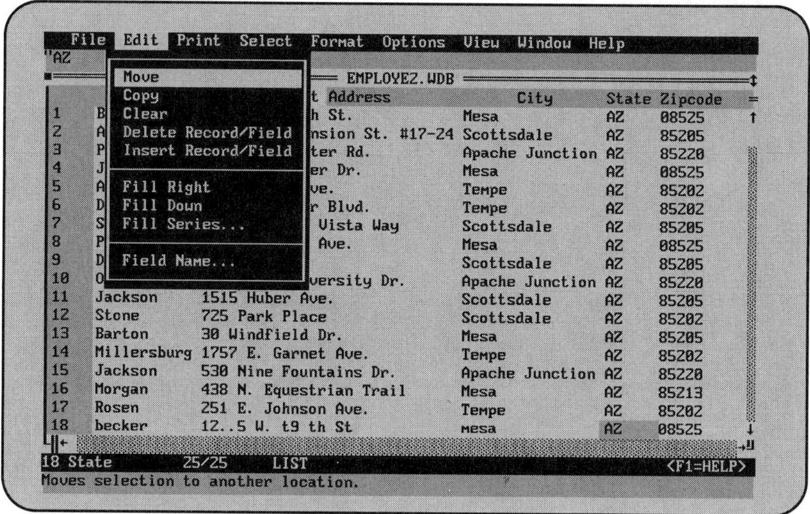

The Delete Record/Field command will remove the record the highlight is on or the entire field the highlight is on. You want to delete the record only. To complete the command,

Select: **D**elete Record/Field>**R**ecord>⏎

The record is permanently removed from the database and the records below have been renumbered. The status line now shows that there are 24 records in the database. To delete a record in FORM view, use the Edit>Delete Record command.

Formatting a Field

Next, the Pay field needs to be changed so that all decimal values are displayed. To correct the display of values, the Format>Fixed command can be used. In the database tool, the Format menu commands affect the entire field. Therefore, it is not necessary to select a range of cells or to position the highlight on a cell containing an incorrect entry. However, you do need to be positioned on any record in the field you want to change. To make this change,

Move to: the Pay field
Select: Forma**t**

Notice that the Format menu commands that control the display of values are the same as the Format menu commands in the spreadsheet tool.

Select: **F**ixed>**2**>⏎

All entries in the field are changed to display two decimal places.

However, Fred thinks this field would look better if it were formatted to be displayed as Currency.

Change the Pay field to Currency with two decimal places.

Your screen should be similar to Figure 10-5.

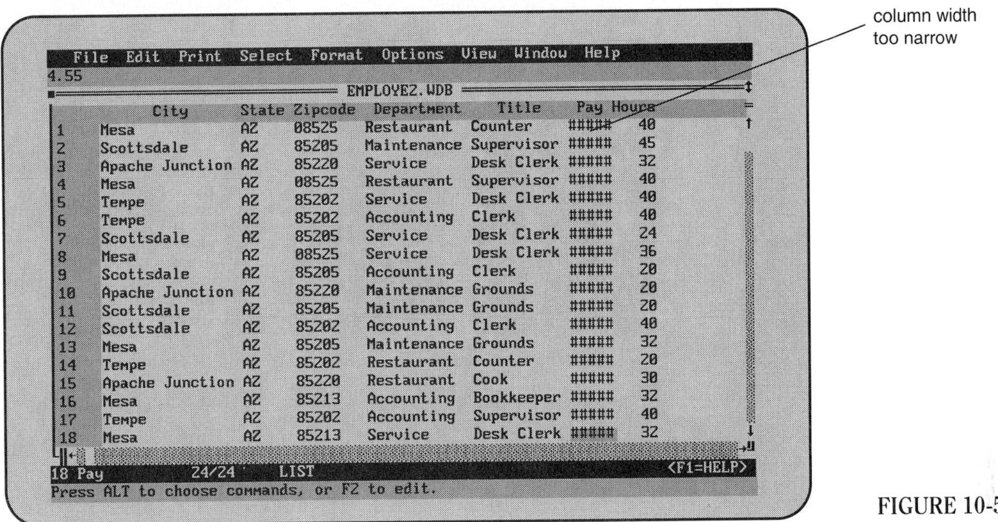

FIGURE 10-5

Just as in the spreadsheet, when the cell is not wide enough to fully display a value, # symbols are displayed. To fix this, increase the field width to six spaces.

The Pay field now displays dollar signs and two places following the decimal.

Inserting a Field in LIST View

Next, Fred wants to add the new field, Sex, to the database entry form. This can be done in either LIST view or FORM view. To add the field in LIST view, you need to create a blank field column and then enter the field name and contents.

Fred wants the new field to appear between the Zipcode field and the Department field. Creating a blank field column is much like entering a blank column in a spreadsheet. First, you position the highlight anywhere within the column where you want the new column inserted. When the field is inserted, the fields to the right of the new field move right to make room.

Move to: the Department field
Select: Edit>**I**nsert Record/Field>**F**ield>↵

Your screen should be similar to Figure 10-6.

FIGURE 10-6

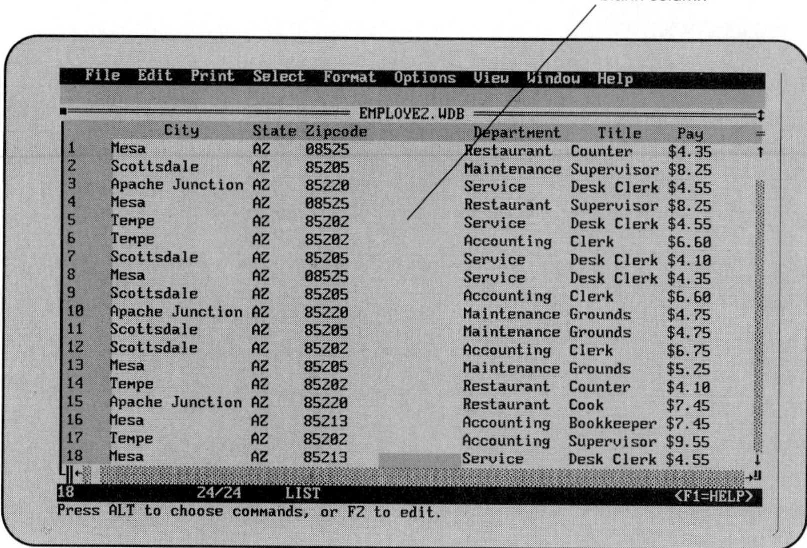

A blank column to be used to enter the field (name) and field (contents) is inserted in the database.

To enter the field name,

Select: Edit>Field Name

Your screen should be similar to Figure 10-7.

FIGURE 10-7

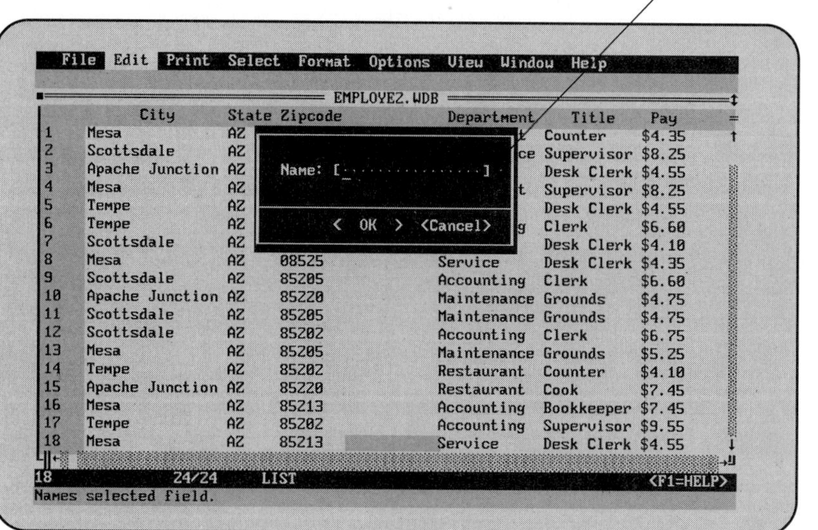

A dialog box appears for you to enter the field name. The name of the field will be "Sex." You do not need to end the field name with a colon as in the FORM view.

Type: Sex
Press: ↵

Your screen should be similar to Figure 10-8.

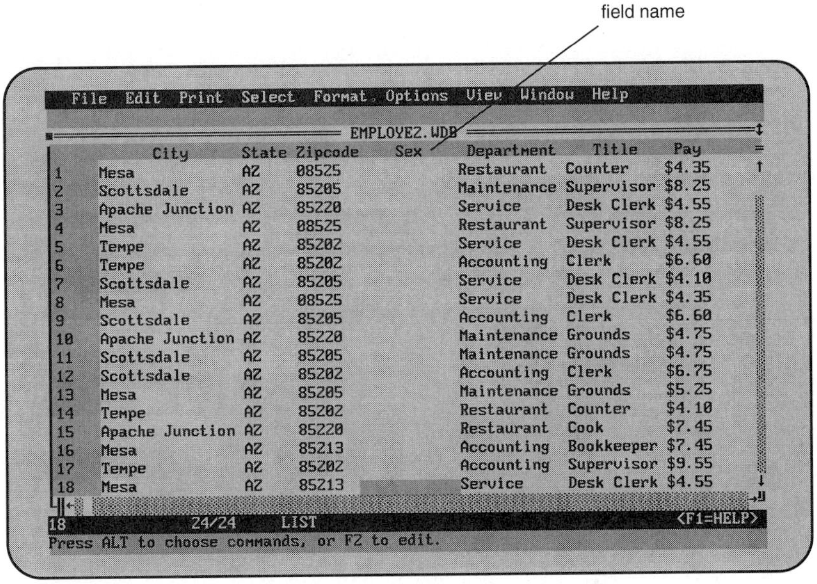

FIGURE 10-8

field name

File Edit Print Select Format Options View Window Help

EMPLOYE2.WDB

	City	State	Zipcode	Sex	Department	Title	Pay
1	Mesa	AZ	08525		Restaurant	Counter	$4.35
2	Scottsdale	AZ	85205		Maintenance	Supervisor	$8.25
3	Apache Junction	AZ	85220		Service	Desk Clerk	$4.55
4	Mesa	AZ	08525		Restaurant	Supervisor	$8.25
5	Tempe	AZ	85202		Service	Desk Clerk	$4.55
6	Tempe	AZ	85202		Accounting	Clerk	$6.60
7	Scottsdale	AZ	85205		Service	Desk Clerk	$4.10
8	Mesa	AZ	08525		Service	Desk Clerk	$4.35
9	Scottsdale	AZ	85205		Accounting	Clerk	$6.60
10	Apache Junction	AZ	85220		Maintenance	Grounds	$4.75
11	Scottsdale	AZ	85205		Maintenance	Grounds	$4.75
12	Scottsdale	AZ	85202		Accounting	Clerk	$6.75
13	Mesa	AZ	85205		Maintenance	Grounds	$5.25
14	Tempe	AZ	85202		Restaurant	Counter	$4.10
15	Apache Junction	AZ	85220		Restaurant	Cook	$7.45
16	Mesa	AZ	85213		Accounting	Bookkeeper	$7.45
17	Tempe	AZ	85202		Accounting	Supervisor	$9.55
18	Mesa	AZ	85213		Service	Desk Clerk	$4.55

18 24/24 LIST <F1=HELP>
Press ALT to choose commands, or F2 to edit.

The field name is displayed at the top of the column.

Hiding Fields

The column of data for the new field, Sex, needs to be completed for each record. You can determine the contents of each record by looking at the member's first name. To begin at the top of the column,

Press: (PGUP)

To see the First Name field for this record,

Press: (←) (6 times)

The Last Name and First Name fields are visible on the screen, but the Sex field is not. Whenever the fields in a record extend beyond a single window, being able to tell what data belongs with which record is difficult. Fortunately, Works lets you hide selected fields so that the fields you want to view can be seen together in a window.

Fred needs to enter the data for the Sex field for every record. To do this, he needs to be able to see the First Name and Last Name field contents while entering the data in the Sex field for each member.

To stop the scrolling of the these two fields off the screen when he moves to the Sex field to enter the data, Fred will hide the Street Address field.

Move to: the Street Address field
Select: Format>Field **W**idth

The current field width of 29 is displayed in the dialog box. To hide a field, you decrease the field width to 0.

Type: 0
Press: ↵

Your screen should be similar to Figure 10-9.

FIGURE 10-9

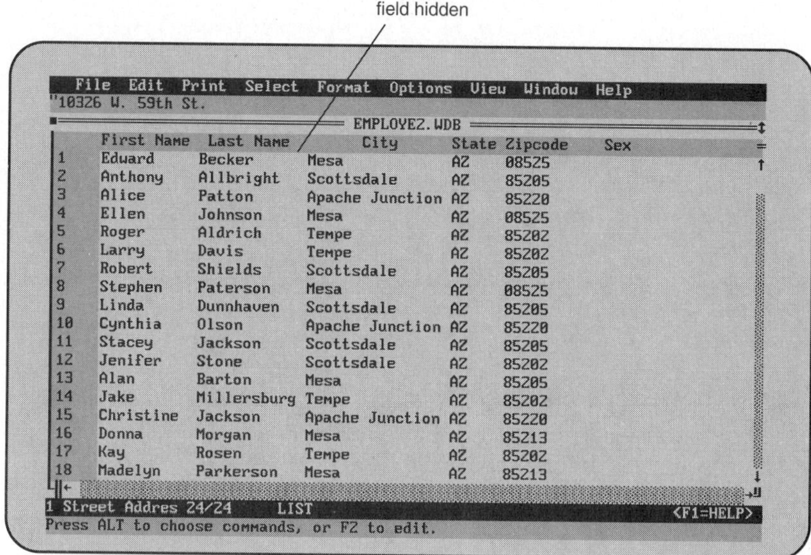

Street Address field hidden
File Edit Print Select Format Options View Window Help
"10326 W. 59th St.
EMPLOYE2.WDB
First Name Last Name City State Zipcode Sex
1 Edward Becker Mesa AZ 08525
2 Anthony Allbright Scottsdale AZ 85205
3 Alice Patton Apache Junction AZ 85220
4 Ellen Johnson Mesa AZ 08525
5 Roger Aldrich Tempe AZ 85202
6 Larry Davis Tempe AZ 85202
7 Robert Shields Scottsdale AZ 85205
8 Stephen Paterson Mesa AZ 08525
9 Linda Dunnhaven Scottsdale AZ 85205
10 Cynthia Olson Apache Junction AZ 85220
11 Stacey Jackson Scottsdale AZ 85205
12 Jenifer Stone Scottsdale AZ 85202
13 Alan Barton Mesa AZ 85205
14 Jake Millersburg Tempe AZ 85202
15 Christine Jackson Apache Junction AZ 85220
16 Donna Morgan Mesa AZ 85213
17 Kay Rosen Tempe AZ 85202
18 Madelyn Parkerson Mesa AZ 85213
1 Street Addres 24/24 LIST <F1=HELP>
Press ALT to choose commands, or F2 to edit.

The field is no longer displayed on the screen. If you switched to FORM view, the information would be displayed. The highlight is not visible because it is in the hidden field.

Fred can now easily look at the First Name field data and complete the data for the Sex field. To redisplay the highlight,

Press: →

The first employee record contains the data for Edward Becker, a male. To enter the sex for the first record,

Move to: the Sex field of record 1
Type: M
Press: ↵

Copying Field Contents

You could enter the field contents for each record individually, or you could copy the same entry down the column and then change only those that are not correct.

To select the column,

Press: 

Extend the highlight down the column through record 24.

To fill the selected column with all Ms for Male,

Select: **E**dit>**F**ill Down

Your screen should be similar to Figure 10-10.

FIGURE 10-10

```
 File  Edit  Print  Select  Format  Options  View  Window  Help
"M
=========================== EMPLOYEZ.WDB ===========================
     First Name  Last Name   City            State Zipcode    Sex
7    Robert      Shields     Scottsdale      AZ    85205      M
8    Stephen     Paterson    Mesa            AZ    08525      M
9    Linda       Dunnhaven   Scottsdale      AZ    85205      M
10   Cynthia     Olson       Apache Junction AZ    85220      M
11   Stacy       Jackson     Scottsdale      AZ    85205      M
12   Jennifer    Stone       Scottsdale      AZ    85202      M
13   Alan        Barton      Mesa            AZ    85205      M
14   Jake        Millersburg Tempe           AZ    85202      M
15   Christine   Jackson     Apache Junction AZ    85220      M
16   Donna       Morgan      Mesa            AZ    85213      M
17   Kay         Rosen       Tempe           AZ    85202      M
18   Madelyn     Parkerson   Mesa            AZ    85213      M
19   Donald      Crane       Mesa            AZ    85213      M
20   Timothy     McHale      Mesa            AZ    08525      M
21   Anita       Robins      Tempe           AZ    85202      M
22   Shelly      Johnson     Tempe           AZ    85202      M
23   Anne        Thomas      Apache Junction AZ    85220      M
24   Leon        Walker      Mesa            AZ    85213      M
1 Sex        24/24      LIST                                <F1=HELP>
Press ALT to choose commands, or F2 to edit.
```

The M in the first cell is copied down the field column.

Now all that needs to be done is to change the records that have female first names to F. The first record with a female first name is record 3.

Press: ↓ (2 times)

To enter the field contents as capital letters,

Press: CAPS LOCK
Type: **F**
Press: ↓

Continue entering the data for this field, looking at the data in the First Name field to determine whether the member is male or female. When you are done, turn off CAPS LOCK.

The default field width is wider than it needs to be. Decrease the Sex field width to four spaces.

Your screen should be similar to Figure 10-11.

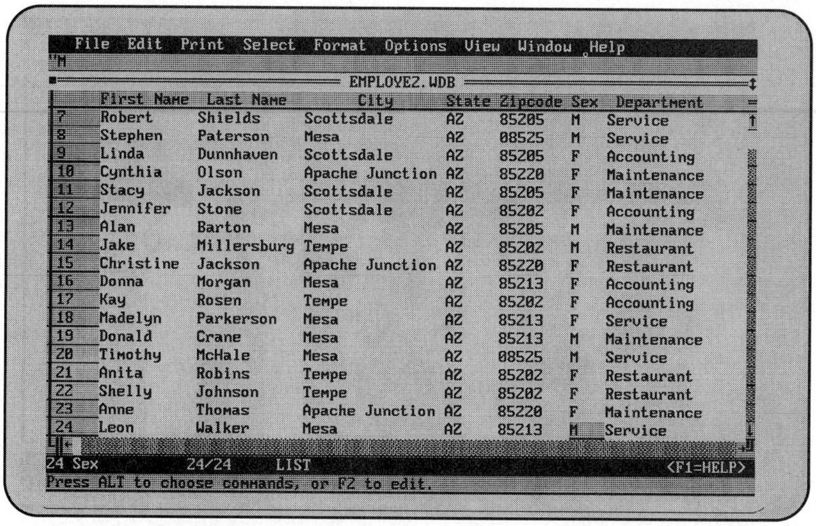

```
 File  Edit  Print  Select  Format  Options  View  Window  Help
"M
                         EMPLOYE2.WDB
    First Name  Last Name    City            State Zipcode Sex  Department
 7  Robert      Shields      Scottsdale       AZ    85205   M   Service
 8  Stephen     Paterson     Mesa             AZ    08525   M   Service
 9  Linda       Dunnhaven    Scottsdale       AZ    85205   F   Accounting
10  Cynthia     Olson        Apache Junction  AZ    85220   F   Maintenance
11  Stacy       Jackson      Scottsdale       AZ    85205   F   Maintenance
12  Jennifer    Stone        Scottsdale       AZ    85202   F   Accounting
13  Alan        Barton       Mesa             AZ    85205   M   Maintenance
14  Jake        Millersburg  Tempe            AZ    85202   M   Restaurant
15  Christine   Jackson      Apache Junction  AZ    85220   F   Restaurant
16  Donna       Morgan       Mesa             AZ    85213   F   Accounting
17  Kay         Rosen        Tempe            AZ    85202   F   Accounting
18  Madelyn     Parkerson    Mesa             AZ    85213   F   Service
19  Donald      Crane        Mesa             AZ    85213   M   Maintenance
20  Timothy     McHale       Mesa             AZ    08525   M   Service
21  Anita       Robins       Tempe            AZ    85202   F   Restaurant
22  Shelly      Johnson      Tempe            AZ    85202   F   Restaurant
23  Anne        Thomas       Apache Junction  AZ    85220   F   Maintenance
24  Leon        Walker       Mesa             AZ    85213   M   Service
24 Sex          24/24        LIST                                 <F1=HELP>
Press ALT to choose commands, or F2 to edit.
```

FIGURE 10-11

Redisplaying Hidden Fields

Now Fred can redisplay the hidden field of data. To unhide the field, you need to increase the field width back to the previous width setting. In order to do this, however, you must be able to move the highlight into the field you want to change. Since the field is hidden, the only way to position the highlight in the field is to use the Select>Go To command.

Select: Select>**G**o To

To tell Works you want to move to a specific field, you can type in the field name exactly as it appears in the entry form, or you can select the field name from the list in the Names: list box. Using the list box ensures that you do not enter the field name incorrectly.

Highlight the Street Address field name.

Your screen should be similar to Figure 10-12.

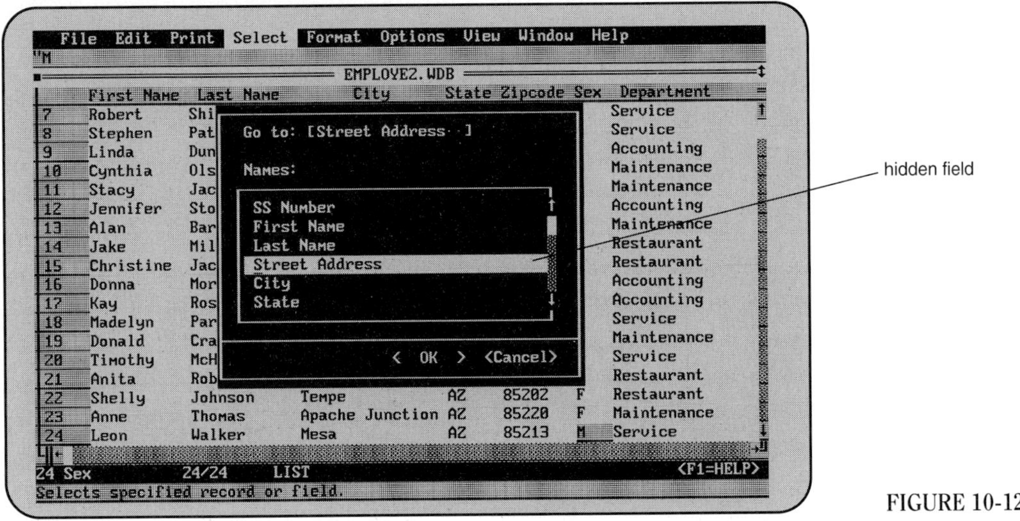

FIGURE 10-12

The field name is displayed in the Go to: text box. To complete the command,

Press: ⏎

The highlight is no longer displayed in the workspace. That is because it is positioned in the hidden field. You can confirm its location by looking at the status line. It tells you the active field is the Street Address field.

To make the field width 29 spaces again,

Select: Forma**t**>Field **W**idth>**29**>⏎

The street address field is displayed again.

Before hiding fields, it is always a good idea to first write down the field widths of the fields you are hiding. This way, when you are redisplaying the field, you will know the correct width to enter. It is easy to forget.

Moving and Inserting Fields in FORM View

To move to the beginning of the file,

Press: CTRL - HOME

The second field that Fred needs to create is the Weekly Pay field. You will enter this field in FORM view.

Press: F9

Your screen should be similar to Figure 10-13.

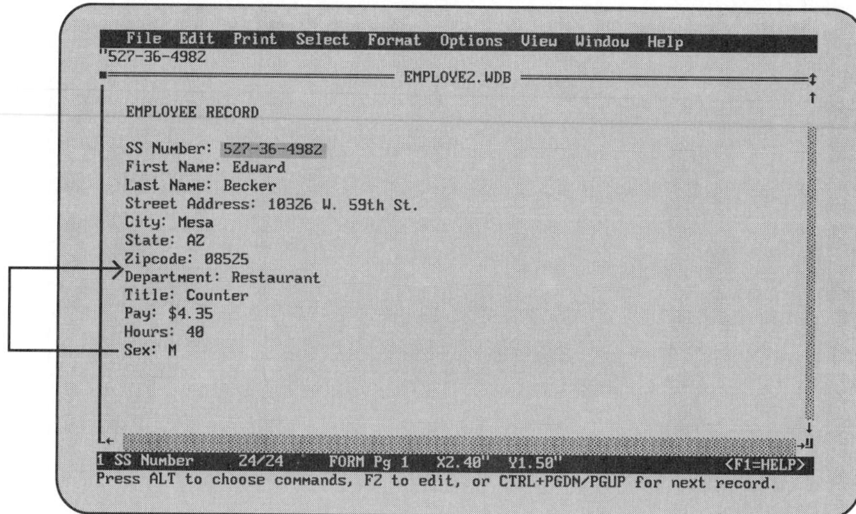

FIGURE 10-13

The first thing you will notice is that the Sex field is not in the same location as you entered it in LIST view. It is at the end of the entry form. The location of a field can be changed for viewing purposes in LIST view without affecting the FORM view. When a field is added in LIST view, it is entered as the last field in FORM view. You must use FORM view to permanently position a field. To move the Sex field after the Zipcode field, first insert a blank line below the Zipcode field. To do this,

Move to: the Department field
Select: **E**dit

Your screen should be similar to Figure 10-14.

FIGURE 10-14

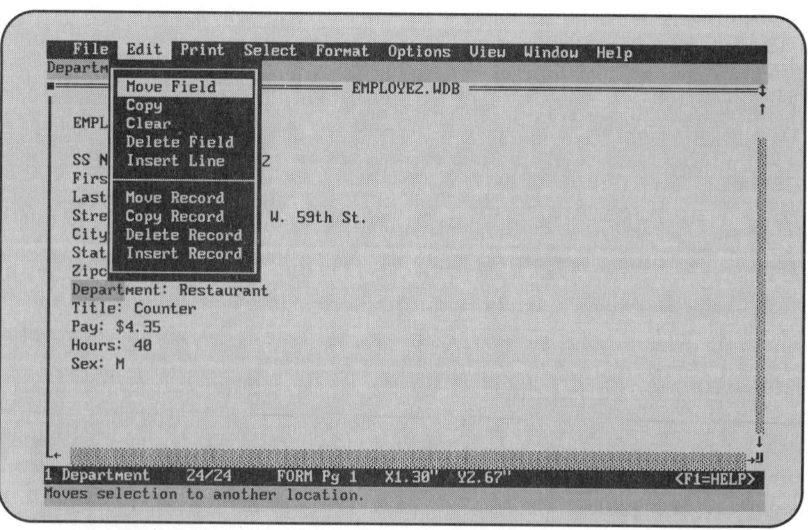

The command that will enter a blank line into the entry form is Insert Line.

Select: Insert Line

A blank line appears below the Zipcode field. Now you can move the Sex field to this location. To do this,

Move to: the Sex field

The highlight can be on the field name or the field contents.

Select: **E**dit>**M**ove Field

The field name and contents are highlighted. Following the directions in the message line,

Move to: the blank line below Zipcode
Press: ↵

The Sex field is now displayed below the Zipcode field.

Highlight the Sex field contents. The field size is set at the default size of 20 spaces. It is much larger than it needs to be. Decrease the field size to 2.

Now you are ready to enter the second new field of data as the last field in the entry form.

Move to: The beginning of the blank line below Hours (X1.30" Y3.50")
Type: **Weekly Pay:**
Press: ↵

To enter a field width of six spaces,

Type: **6**
Press: ↵

Entering a Field Formula

The data for this field is a value that is calculated by multiplying the pay times the hours.

You can use four types of calculations in the database: addition, subtraction, multiplication, and division. Entering a formula in a database is similar to entering a formula in a spreadsheet.

Move to: the Weekly Pay field contents
Type: **=**

The equals sign tells Works you are entering a formula.

In a database, instead of using cell references, you specify the field names of the cells you want Works to use in the calculation. In this case, you want to multiply the hours worked times the hourly pay. The field names must be entered exactly as they appear in the entry form (except for case size). You cannot use pointing to specify the field names.

Type: **pay*hours**

Works displays as much of the entry as possible in the field. The formula bar displays the entire formula.

Press: ⏎

Your screen should be similar to Figure 10-15.

FIGURE 10-15

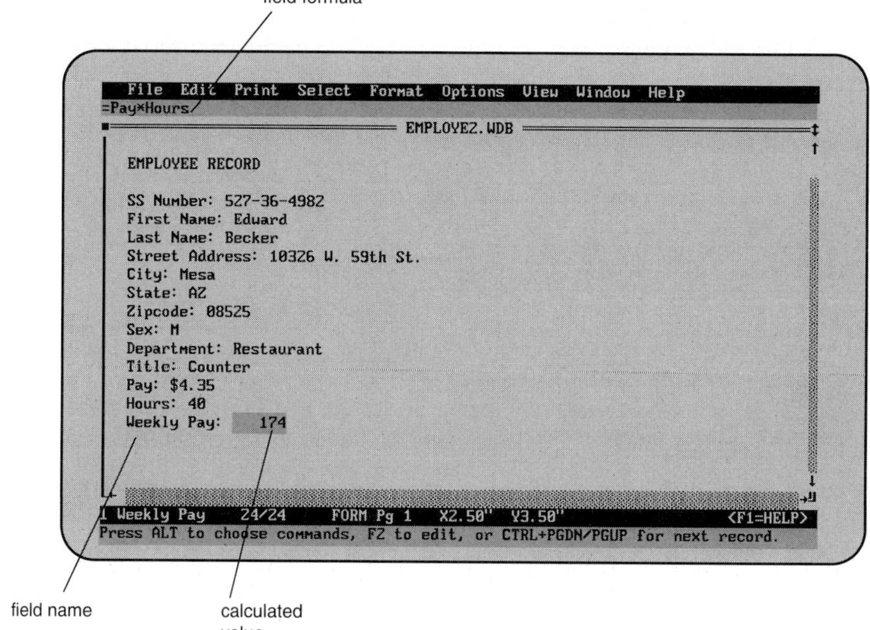

The calculated value is displayed in the field. The formula continues to be displayed in the formula bar.

Format the field to display as Currency with two decimal places and increase the field size to fully display the formatted value.

To see how this change has affected the other records in the database,

Press: F9

Your screen should be similar to Figure 10-16.

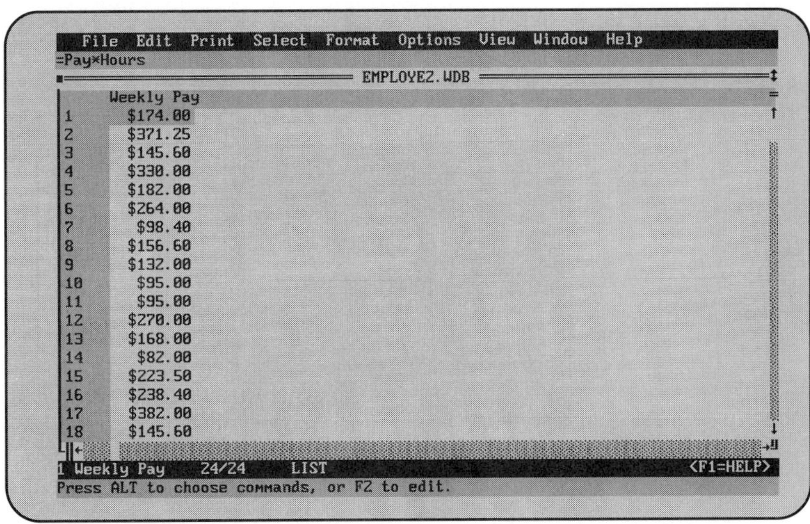

FIGURE 10-16

The Weekly Pay column is displayed. Works calculated the new field for each record in the database. The field width of 10 spaces in LIST view is acceptable, as it fully displays both the value and the field name.

To move to the first field,

Press: HOME

Searching the Database

Next, Fred needs to locate the record for Shelly Johnson and change her last name to Foran. To locate this record, he could look at the First Name and Last Name fields in LIST view; however, that can take a lot of time, especially if the database is large. Instead, Fred will use the Search command to quickly locate a record in the database.

To quickly locate this record,

Select: Select>Search

Your screen should be similar to Figure 10-17.

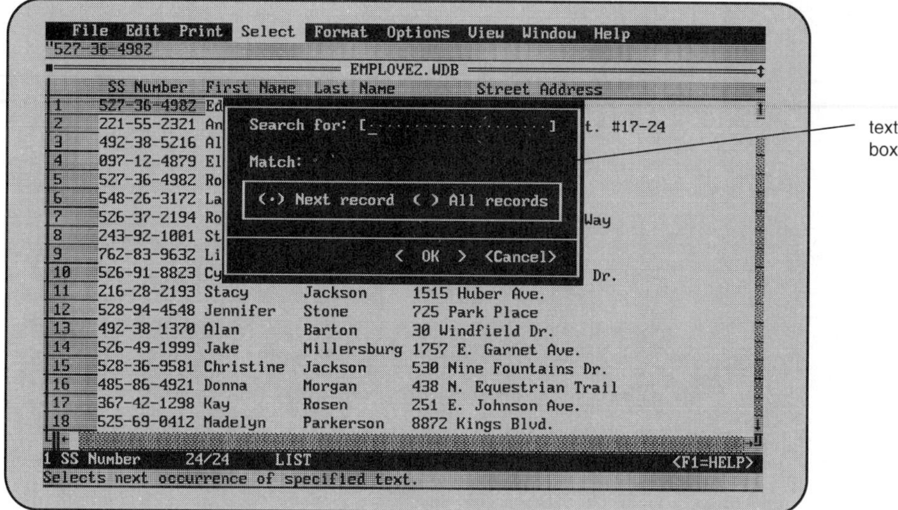

FIGURE 10-17

A dialog box appears in which you type the information you want Works to locate. The Search command will find a record by searching the file for data in a field that matches the text or number you specify. You can enter the text in uppercase or lowercase letters, or a combination of the two. Works is not case-sensitive; it will locate the text regardless of how it is capitalized. Works will also locate the text if it is part of a longer word. In this case, you want to locate the record with a last name of Johnson.

Type: **johnson**

The dialog box's Next record option lets you find the next occurrence of the specified text or number. This is the default setting. To use this setting and tell Works to begin the search,

Press: ↵

Your screen should be similar to Figure 10-18.

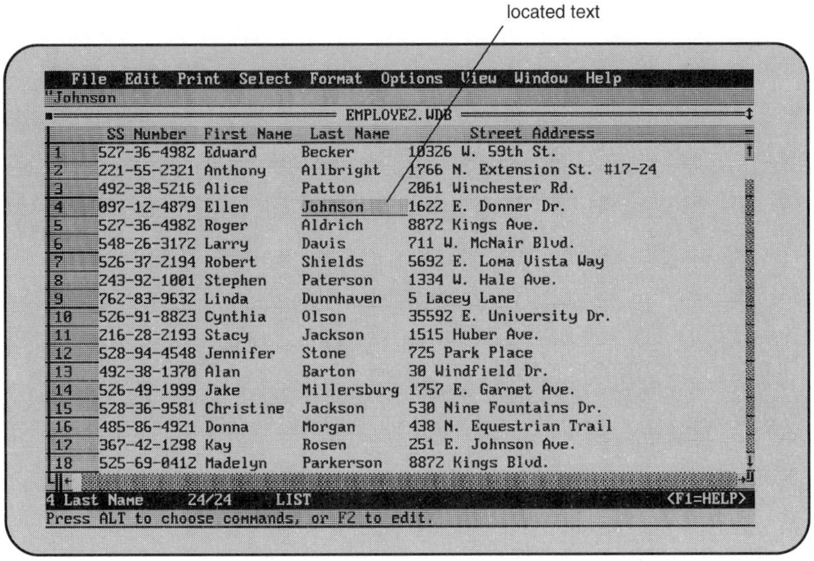

FIGURE 10-18

located text

```
 File  Edit  Print  Select  Format  Options  View  Window  Help
"Johnson
                         EMPLOYE2.WDB
     SS Number   First Name  Last Name      Street Address
1    527-36-4982 Eduard      Becker      10326 W. 59th St.
2    221-55-2321 Anthony     Allbright   1766 N. Extension St. #17-24
3    492-38-5216 Alice       Patton      2061 Winchester Rd.
4    097-12-4879 Ellen       Johnson     1622 E. Donner Dr.
5    527-36-4982 Roger       Aldrich     8872 Kings Ave.
6    548-26-3172 Larry       Davis       711 W. McNair Blvd.
7    526-37-2194 Robert      Shields     5692 E. Loma Vista Way
8    243-92-1001 Stephen     Paterson    1334 W. Hale Ave.
9    762-83-9632 Linda       Dunnhaven   5 Lacey Lane
10   526-91-8823 Cynthia     Olson       35592 E. University Dr.
11   216-28-2193 Stacy       Jackson     1515 Huber Ave.
12   528-94-4548 Jennifer    Stone       725 Park Place
13   492-38-1370 Alan        Barton      30 Windfield Dr.
14   526-49-1999 Jake        Millersburg 1757 E. Garnet Ave.
15   528-36-9581 Christine   Jackson     530 Nine Fountains Dr.
16   485-86-4921 Donna       Morgan      438 N. Equestrian Trail
17   367-42-1298 Kay         Rosen       251 E. Johnson Ave.
18   525-69-0412 Madelyn     Parkerson   8872 Kings Blvd.
4 Last Name     24/24      LIST                              <F1=HELP>
Press ALT to choose commands, or F2 to edit.
```

Note: You can limit the range Works will search in a database by selecting the cells or area of the database before using the command. If no selection is made, Works searches the entire database.

The first record in the file to exactly match the specified search text *johnson* is record number 4. The highlight is positioned on the Last Name field of that record.

Note: If your command did not locate this record, reissue the command and make sure you entered the name *johnson* correctly.

What if there are other records in the database containing the text *johnson?* To continue the search to look for the next record,

Press: F7

The next record containing the word *Johnson* is located. This time, however, the word *johnson* appears in the Street Address field. When the Search command is used, Works does not know that you want to locate only the text in a specific field. Therefore, it searches for the matching text in all fields of the database. To continue the search,

Press: F7

Works has located another record containing the text *Johnson.* This is the record Fred wants to change, since the located text is in the Last Name field and the first name is Shelly.

Press: F7

When Works finds the last record in a database that matches the specified text, it will jump back to the beginning of the database and relocate the first matching record again.

Press: (CTRL) - (HOME)

A quicker way to search the entire database or a selected area of it is to use the All records option in the Search dialog box. To see how this works to locate the same text,

Select: Select>Search

The Search for: text box displays the text you previously entered. All you need to do is to select the All records option.

Select: All Records>(↵)

Your screen should be similar to Figure 10-19.

FIGURE 10-19

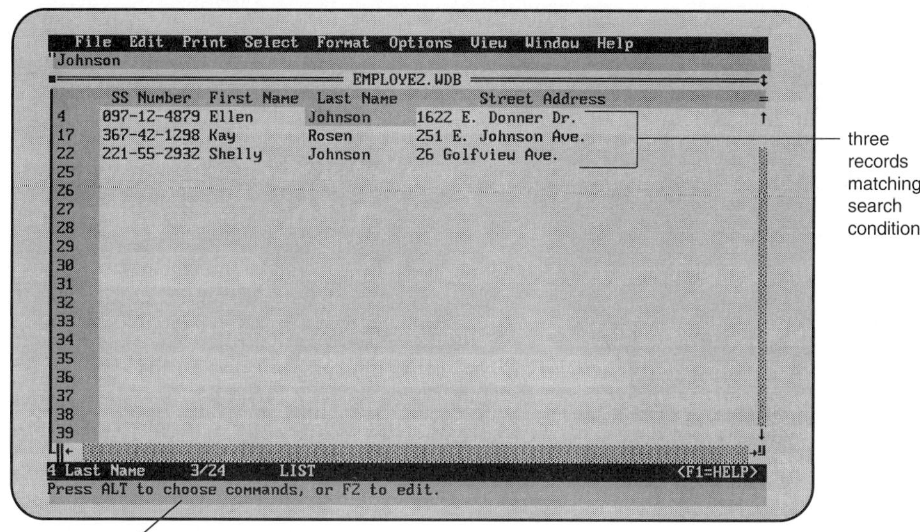

The three records that match the search for text are displayed. All the other records in the database are hidden. The status line shows you that three of the 24 records (3/24) are displayed. In FORM view, the three records would be displayed individually.

To display the hidden records and hide the displayed records,

Select: Select>Switch Hidden Records

All records that do not contain the text *johnson* are displayed. The status line shows that you are displaying 21 of the 24 records in the database.

Finally, to display all the records again,

Select: Select>Show All Records

All 24 records are displayed again.

Querying the Database

An even quicker way to locate a record is to use the Query command. The Search command is useful for locating information in one field; however, it cannot be used to locate information in more than one field. To locate groups of records that fulfill a variety of conditions, a special type of search called a **query** is used.

When you query the database, you are searching for all entries that meet several conditions. The View>Query command lets you specify the conditions.

Select: View>Query

Your screen should be similar to Figure 10-20.

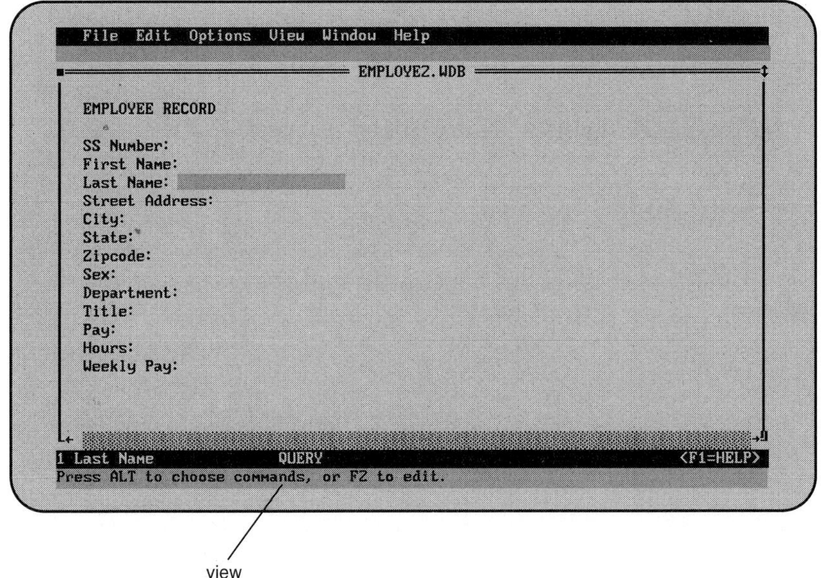

FIGURE 10-20

This is the QUERY view screen. It consists of a blank entry form and a menu of commands. Most of the commands are the same as in the other views. The Edit menu, however, has several commands that are used to edit the query entry form.

The entry form is used to enter the conditions as a formula that you want Works to use to locate the records in the database. If you specify multiple conditions, a record must meet all of them to be displayed.

In this case, Fred wants to locate all records with a last name of Johnson and a first name of Shelly. This query requires that you enter a simple formula in the Last Name and First Name fields. A simple formula looks for an exact match in the field it is entered in.

The highlight should be positioned in the Last Name field. If it is not, move it there.

To locate all records with a last name of Johnson,

Type: **johnson**

Next, to enter the second condition, first name of Shelly,

Press: (SHIFT) - (TAB)

The highlight should be in the First Name field.

Type: **shelly**
Press: (↵)

Both conditions have been entered into the query form. You have asked Works to locate all records with a Last Name field equal to Johnson and a First Name field equal to Shelly. After creating a query, you apply it to the database by returning to the database view you were in when you issued the command. To apply the query,

Select: View>**L**ist

Your screen should be similar to Figure 10-21.

FIGURE 10-21

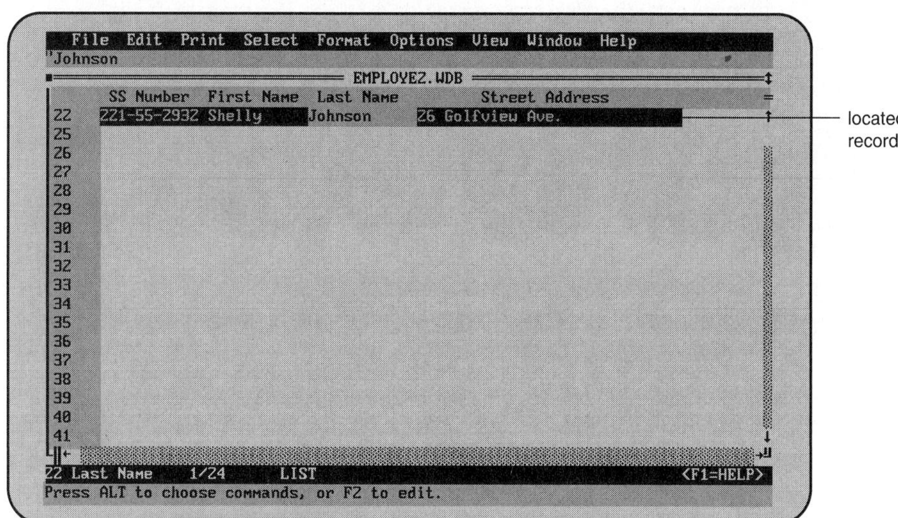

Works has located the record that matches the query conditions and displays it on the screen. As you can see, using Query is quicker and more accurate than using Search to locate information in a database file.

Now, change the last name to Foran.

To display all the records again,

Select: Select>Show **A**ll Records
Press: (CTRL) - (HOME)

Sorting the Database Records

The Accounting Department has asked Fred to provide them with the records for all employees who work in the Restaurant or Service departments and earn $6.00 per hour or more. They would like the list in alphabetical order by last name.

Sorting the Database Records

Works lets you rearrange the order of records in a database into groups of related records based on the contents of a selected field. The field contents on which a database is sorted is called the **sort field**. The Select/Sort Records command is used to rearrange records in the database.

Select: Select>Sort Records

Your screen should be similar to Figure 10-22.

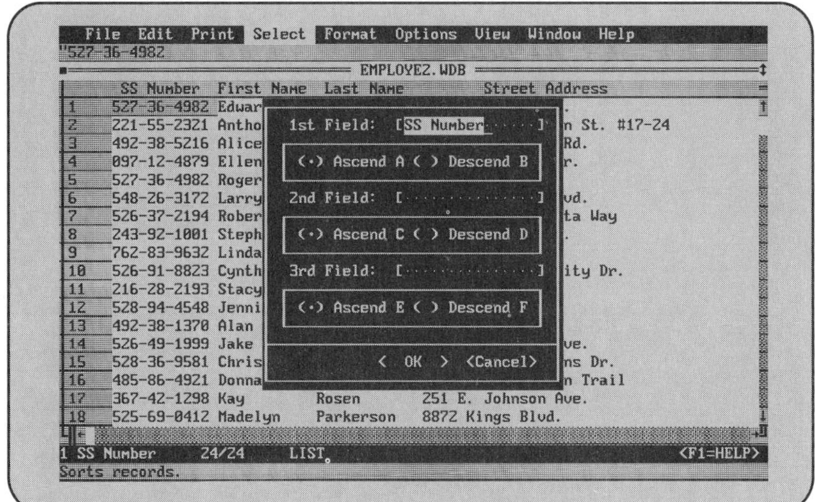

FIGURE 10-22

The Sort dialog box is displayed. To specify a sort field, enter the field name in the Field text box. There are three Field text boxes in the dialog box. This is because Works can sort records using up to three fields at a time.

In the 1st Field: text box, Works has proposed the SS Number field name as the field to sort on. If the database has not been sorted before, Works displays the first field in the database as the proposed field. If the database had been previously sorted, the proposed field would be the field the database is currently sorted by. To tell Works to sort using the Last Name field,

Type: **last name**

Under each Field text box, the options Ascend and Descend are displayed. Works can sort in either ascending (A–Z or 0–9) or descending (Z–A or 9–0) order. Ascending order is the default setting. Since ascending is how Fred wants the records displayed, you do not need to change the setting.

To complete the command,

Press: ↵

Your screen should be similar to Figure 10-23.

FIGURE 10-23

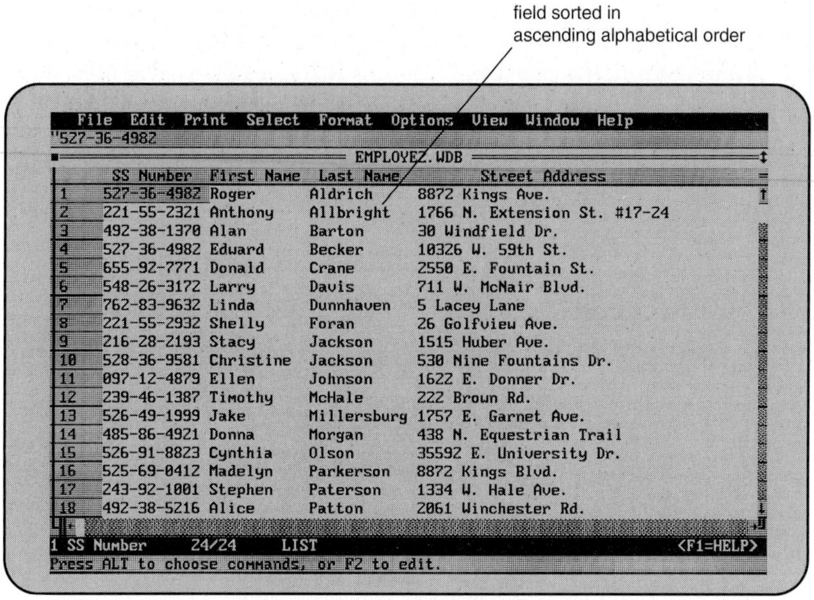

field sorted in ascending alphabetical order

```
 File  Edit  Print  Select  Format  Options  View  Window  Help
"527-36-4982
                         EMPLOYEZ.WDB
    SS Number  First Name  Last Name      Street Address
1   527-36-4982 Roger      Aldrich     8872 Kings Ave.
2   221-55-2321 Anthony    Allbright   1766 N. Extension St. #17-24
3   492-38-1370 Alan       Barton      30 Windfield Dr.
4   527-36-4982 Edward     Becker      10326 W. 59th St.
5   655-92-7771 Donald     Crane       2550 E. Fountain St.
6   548-26-3172 Larry      Davis       711 W. McNair Blvd.
7   762-83-9632 Linda      Dunnhaven   5 Lacey Lane
8   221-55-2932 Shelly     Foran       26 Golfview Ave.
9   216-28-2193 Stacy      Jackson     1515 Huber Ave.
10  528-36-9581 Christine  Jackson     530 Nine Fountains Dr.
11  097-12-4879 Ellen      Johnson     1622 E. Donner Dr.
12  239-46-1387 Timothy    McHale      222 Brown Rd.
13  526-49-1999 Jake       Millersburg 1757 E. Garnet Ave.
14  485-86-4921 Donna      Morgan      438 N. Equestrian Trail
15  526-91-8823 Cynthia    Olson       35592 E. University Dr.
16  525-69-0412 Madelyn    Parkerson   8872 Kings Blvd.
17  243-92-1001 Stephen    Paterson    1334 W. Hale Ave.
18  492-38-5216 Alice      Patton      2061 Winchester Rd.
1 SS Number      24/24      LIST                              <F1=HELP>
Press ALT to choose commands, or F2 to edit.
```

The database now displays the records in ascending alphabetical order by last name. Notice that the records have been renumbered. Once a database is sorted, the original record number order in which the records were entered cannot be restored. If the original order of entry is important to you, be sure to save the database file before you sort it; then save the sorted file using a new filename. Alternatively, you could create a record number field in which you would enter the original record number of each record. The record number in the field would not be altered when the file is sorted. Then you could resort the records by record number if you wanted to restore the original order.

Look at records 9 and 10. Both the employees have the same last name, Jackson. Donna would like the records to be sorted so that the first names are alphabetized within same last names. This would change the order so that Christine Jackson's record would come before Stacy Jackson's. To alphabetize the employees' first names within identical last names, you can specify two sort fields, Last Name and First Name. When a file is sorted on more than one sort field, it is called a **multilevel sort**.

To specify a second sort field,

Select: Select>Sort Records

When you sort on multiple sort fields, enter the most important sort field as the first sort field. Last Name is the field that will be sorted first. Therefore, the first sort field does not need to be changed. To enter a second sort field,

Press: (ALT) - 2
Type: **first name**

Your screen should be similar to Figure 10-24.

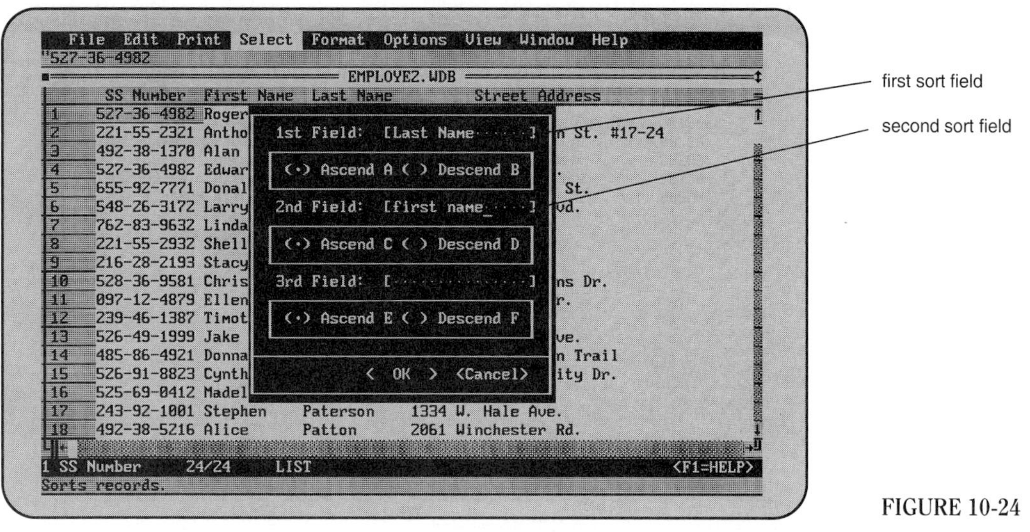

FIGURE 10-24

Again, Fred wants the records sorted in ascending order, so you do not need to change the default selection.

To complete the command,

Press: ↵

Your screen should be similar to Figure 10-25.

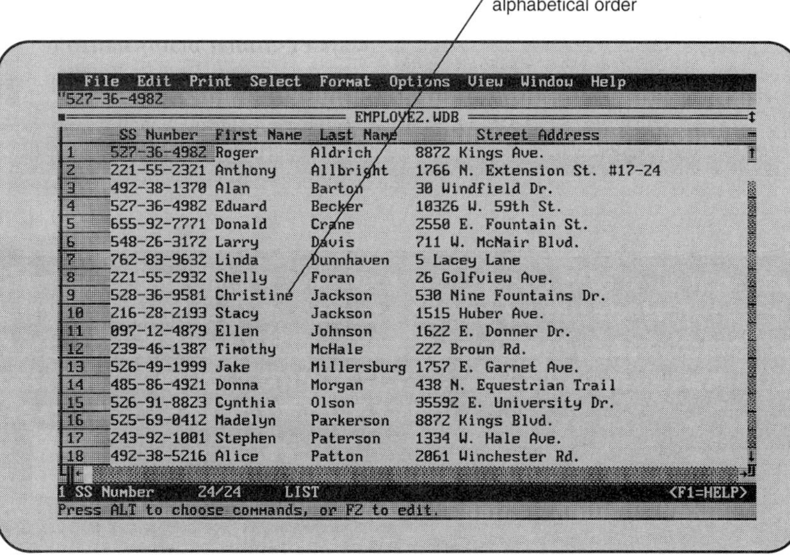

FIGURE 10-25

The employee records are displayed in ascending alphabetical order. Those records with duplicate last names are further sorted by first names within the Last Name field. The employee names are listed with the first name before the last name. Christine Jackson's record (number 9) is now listed before Stacy Jackson's (number 10). Fred is pleased with the results of the multilevel sort.

Inserting Records

Before Fred creates the employee list for the accounting department, he wants to add two more employee records to the database.

A new record can be entered into the database in either FORM or LIST view. Usually, it is easier to use FORM view to insert a record. To return to FORM view,

Press: F9

To insert a record as the last record in the database,

Press: CTRL - END

A blank entry form is displayed.

Enter the following field contents:

Field	Contents
SS Number	**189-25-6730**
First Name	**Sarah**
Last Name	**Fischer**
Street Address	**2562 Winding Way**
City	**Mesa**
State	**AZ**
Zipcode	**"85205**
Sex	**F**
Department	**Maintenance**
Title	**Grounds**
Pay	**4.75**
Hours	**40**

The Weekly Pay field is calculated automatically. To return to LIST view,

Press: F9

To display the beginning of the record,

Press: HOME

Sarah Fischer's record has been added to the file as record 25. Each time a record is added to a sorted file, the file must be resorted in order to maintain the alphabetical order.

As you can see, the Sort command has some drawbacks. Each time a file is sorted, the records are renumbered. This makes locating a record by its original record number unlikely. Also, each time a change is made in the data in the sort field or a record is added to the database, the file needs to be resorted.

You will now need to resort the records because the new record is not in alphabetical order. To resort the database,

Select: Select>Sort Records

The sort settings you entered are displayed. Since you want to sort the database again using the same fields and order, to continue the command by accepting the settings displayed,

Press: (Enter)

Sarah Fischer's record now appears in the correct order, as record 8.

The next record you will enter into the database will contain your first and last name. This time, however, you will insert the record in the correct alphabetic order so that you do not need to resort the file.

To insert a record, position the highlight where you want the record to be entered into the database. For example, if the selected record is record 10 and you insert a new record at that location, the new record becomes record 10 and all the records below are automatically renumbered.

The Edit>Insert Record/Field command is used to insert a record between existing records in LIST view. The Edit>In**s**ert Record command performs the same task in FORM view. The procedure is the same in either view.

To insert your record in LIST view in the correct alphabetic order, first move the highlight to the record that is in the location where you want your record displayed.

Move to: the record location where your name would be in alphabetical order
Select: **E**dit>**I**nsert Record/Field>**R**ecord>(Enter)

A blank line is displayed.

Enter your name in the First and Last Name fields.

The data you enter for all the other fields can be fictitious, except for the following:

Field	Contents
Department	**Service**
Title	**Desk Clerk**
Pay	**6**
Hours	**28**

Because you entered the new record in the correct alphabetic order, the database should not need to be resorted. Generally, if you have a lot of records to add to a database, it is easier to add them in FORM view at the end of the database and then sort the file.

You should now have 26 records in the database.

Press: (CTRL) - (HOME)

Save the database using a new filename, EMPLOYE3.

Entering a Query Formula

The accounting department wants a list of employees who work in the Restaurant or Service departments and earn $6.00 per hour or more. To locate all employees meeting these conditions, you will use the Query command.

Select: View>**Q**uery

The conditions you specified for the previous query are still displayed. To remove them, you could move to each field and press DEL or use the Edit>Clear Field Contents command. However, when you need to delete all the query settings, it is faster to use the Edit>Delete Query command.

Select: **E**dit>Delete Query

The query form is wiped clean and is ready for you to specify all new conditions. The first condition you will enter is the pay rate.

Move to: the Pay field contents

You need to tell Works to locate all records with a pay rate equal to or greater than $6.00. To do this, comparison operators are used to create formulas that find ranges of data. The comparison operators are:

Operator	Meaning
=	Equal to
<>	Not equal to
<	Less than
>	Greater than
>=	Greater than or equal to
<=	Less than or equal to

The comparison operators must be entered exactly as shown above. To enter the formula to locate all records with a pay rate greater than (>) or equal to (=) 6,

Type: **>=6**
Press: ↵

The second condition consists of two parts. You want to locate all employees who work in either the Restaurant or the Service departments.

Move to: the Department field contents

To combine query conditions, you can use the logical operators AND, which is represented by the ampersand symbol (&), OR, which is represented by the pipe symbol (¦), and NOT, which is represented by the tilde symbol (~). The conditions can apply to a single field or multiple fields.

When you use comparison operators or logical operators in a query formula, you must enclose text entries in quotes. Also, when you use a combined query formula, the formula must begin with the = symbol. In this example, to begin the combined formula, you will type an = symbol. Then, to tell Works to locate all records with the Department equal to Restaurant, you need to type ="restaurant". To enter the first part of the formula,

Type: **=="restaurant"**

Note: If you try to enter a query formula that is not entered correctly, the message "Reference not valid or wrong operand type." is displayed. The part of the formula containing the error will be highlighted in the formula bar and you will be placed in EDIT. Correct the formula and press ↵ to continue.

To tell works to combine the first condition with a second, using OR as the logical operator,

Type: **¦**

The ¦ symbol is located above the backslash character (\) on the keyboard. Be careful not to use a colon. Then, to enter the second condition,

Type: **="service"**
Press: ↵

Your screen should be similar to Figure 10-26.

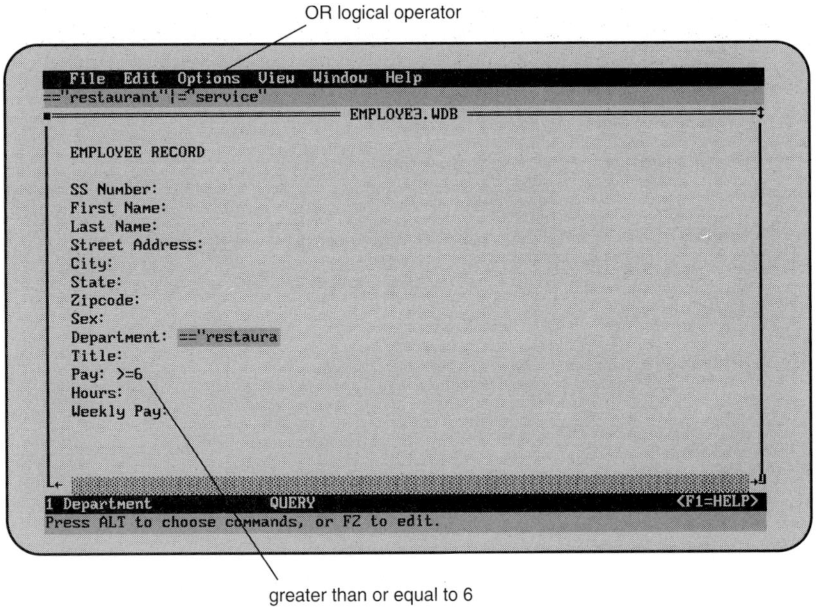

OR logical operator

```
 File  Edit  Options  View  Window  Help
=="restaurant"¦="service"
                    EMPLOYE3.WDB
 EMPLOYEE RECORD

 SS Number:
 First Name:
 Last Name:
 Street Address:
 City:
 State:
 Zipcode:
 Sex:
 Department: =="restaura
 Title:
 Pay: >=6
 Hours:
 Weekly Pay:

1 Department          QUERY                    <F1=HELP>
Press ALT to choose commands, or F2 to edit.
```

greater than or equal to 6

FIGURE 10-2

This formula tells Works to locate all records with a department that is either equal to Restaurant or equal to Service.

To apply the query, you can select View>List, or you can use the shortcut key, F10.

Select: View>List
⋙ F10

Creating a Simple Report

There are four records matching these conditions. The accounting department wants a printout of the names, department, title, and pay rates only. To do this, you will hide the fields you do not want printed (set their field widths to 0).

Hide the SS Number field. Then select the Street Address through Sex fields and hide them. Finally, hide the Hours and Weekly Pay fields.

Press: (HOME)

Your screen should be similar to Figure 10-27, except the record containing your name may be in a different location.

FIGURE 10-27

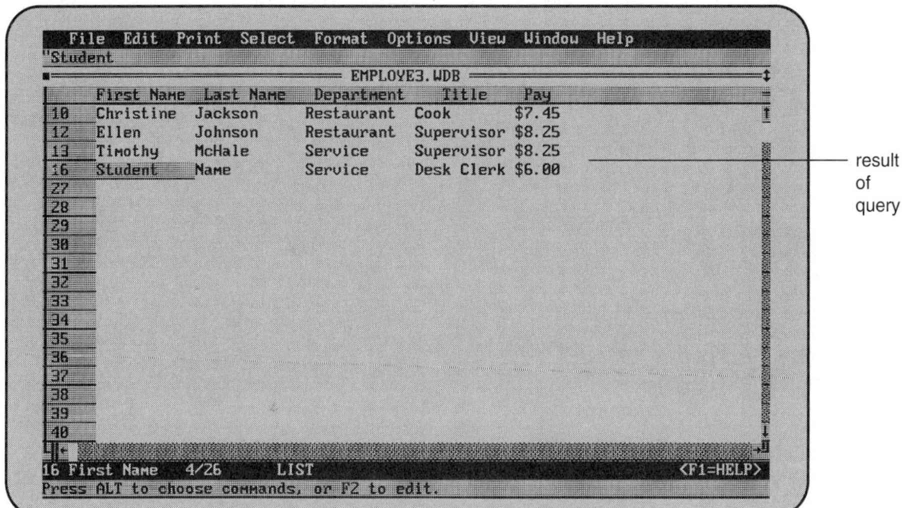

Now you are ready to print a list of the displayed records. Fred would like this report to have a title. He will use the Print>Headers and Footers command to create a header for the page.

Select: Print>**H**eaders & Footers

In the Header: text box,

Type: **Restaurant/Service Employees Earning $6.00 or More**
Select: OK

To print the displayed records and fields only,

Select: Print>**P**rint

Fred wants the printout to display the record numbers and field names. To do this,

Select: Print record and field **l**abels
Press: 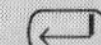

Your printed output should be similar to Figure 10-28.

FIGURE 10-28

```
        Restaurant/Service Employees Earning $6.00 or More

        First Name  Last Name   Department     Title     Pay
   10   Christine   Jackson     Restaurant  Cook        $7.45
   12   Ellen       Johnson     Restaurant  Supervisor  $8.25
   13   Timothy     McHale      Service     Supervisor  $8.25
   16   Student     Name        Service     Desk Clerk  $6.00
```

Although the database of employee records is not complete, the sample list will show the accounting department the type of report that Works is capable of producing.

Rather than unhide the fields, you will close the file without saving it. When you open it again, all the fields and records will be displayed because the file was saved before the fields were hidden. This is a convenient way of saving time when you have hidden fields, since unhiding the fields requires that each field width be respecified individually.

If you want to continue working in Works,

Select: File>Close>No

If you want to close the file and exit Works at the same time,

Select: File>Exit>No

Key Terms

query
sort field
miltilevel sort

Matching

1. query	______	**a.**	field that determines the order of the sort
2. F7	______	**b.**	descending order
3. Search	______	**c.**	logical operator meaning NOT
4. sort field	______	**d.**	less than or equal to
5. < >	______	**e.**	locates all records matching a specified condition
6. F10	______	**f.**	locates all records meeting more than one condition
7. ~	______	**g.**	finds next match in Search

8. Z–A ______ **h.** applies the query

9. LIST ______ **i.** displays each record as a row

10. < = ______ **j.** not equal to

Practice Exercises

1. Open the database file TILES2. This file has the same database structure as the file created in practice exercise 2 in Lab 8 and saved as TILES. Susannah continued to enter her clients' information into her database file. It now contains 19 records.

- In LIST view, increase or decrease the field widths to fully display the entries and to leave a space between columns and/or field names.
- Complete the State field by entering PA for all records. Center the field. (*Note:* Center field is the same as centering in Spreadsheet.)
- Complete the Zipcode field by entering the following zipcodes for the City indicated. (*Hint:* Use Search and Fill Down.)

City	***Zipcode***
Albion	16401
Fairview	16415
Riverton	16410
Springfield	16411

- Insert a new field, Amt. Owed, following the Quantity field. Enter a formula to calculate the value in this field (Quantity * Unit Cost).
- Format the Unit Cost field to Fixed with two decimal places and the Amt. Owed field to Currency with two decimal places.
- In FORM view, decrease the Amt. Owed field to the appropriate field size.
- Edit the following records in FORM view:

5	First Name is Brenda
10	Quantity is 235
12	Unit Cost is 5.65

- Susannah had two cancellations. In FORM view, locate and delete the records for Bonnie Gilson and William Howard.
- Paula Thomas changed her order to a tile with a unit cost of $3.50 and decreased the quantity to 250. In FORM view, search the database for this record and update it.
- Sort the database on Unit Cost as the first field, Last Name as the second field, and First Name as the third field. Use ascending order for all fields. View the database in LIST view.

- Susannah received two new orders. In FORM view, add their records to the end of the database:

Record 1	***Record 2***
Blackmore	Drost
Mary	Beverley
55 Penny Lane	4325 N. Pearl St.
Fairview	Albion
PA	PA
16415	16401
831-9790	963-5353
6.75	4.75
240	632

- Sort the database again using the same fields.
- Save the file as TILES3.
- Print a list of last names, phone numbers, unit cost, quantity, and amount owed for all records with an amount owed value greater than 1000. Use the header "Clients Owing More Than $1000 - [Your Name]." Select the Print option "Print records and field labels."
- Print another list of last names, unit cost, and quantity for all accounts where the unit cost value is less than 4.00 or greater than 5.00. Enter the header: "Unit Cost Less Than $4.00 and More Than $5.00 - [Your Name]." Include the record number and field labels.
- Switch the display to show all records that do not match the query. Print these records using the header "Unit Cost Between $4 and $5 - [Your Name]." Include the record number and field labels.
- Close the file without saving it again.

2. This problem requires that you have completed problem 3 in Lab 9. Open the database file GRADES.

- Joe has decided that he needs to add another field of data to the database file. This field will contain the number of credit hours earned for each class taken. In LIST view, insert this new field after the SEMESTER field. The field name is HOURS.
- Enter the data for the HOURS field for each record in the file. All the classes are three credit hours except MAT210, which is five hours, and PED101 and PED102, which are each one hour. Use the Edit>Fill Down command to fill the field with the number 3, and then edit those records where the credit hours value is other than 3.
- Center the HOURS column of data. Decrease the field width to 6.
- In FORM view, move the HOURS field below the SEMESTER field and decrease the field size to 1.
- Enter three courses you have taken in the past and the grades you earned for each. Enter the semester as F 92.
- Use Search to locate the record for MAT210 taken in Fall 1991. Remove it from the database file.
- Sort the records by GRADE as the first field in ascending order and HOURS as the second field in descending order.

- Save the file as GRADES2.
- Print the TITLE, HOURS, and GRADE fields only. Enter a header for the report: "Courses and Grades - [Your Name]." Print the report using the Print option "Print records and field labels."
- Print a list of all the classes (course number and title only) in which a grade of B was earned. Enter the header "Grade of B - [Your Name]." Do not print the record and field labels.
- Close the file without saving it.

3. Bob is the manager of a small manufacturing company. One of his responsibilities is to keep weekly records for each of the company's 20 employees. Bob has created a database using Works to help him.

- Open the database file STAFF1.
- Insert five blank lines above the first field name.
- Enter the title EMPLOYEE LIST on line 2 and your name on line 3.
- Edit record 1 by entering your first and last name.
- In FORM view, change the field sizes to those shown below:

ID Number	11
Last Name	12
First Name	10
Department	11
Title	20
Pay	4
Hours	2

- In LIST view, increase or decrease the field widths to fully display the entries and to leave a space between columns and/or field names.
- Insert the new field, Sex, between the Pay and Hours fields. Set the field width to 4.
- Complete the Sex field by entering M or F.
- Center the Sex and Hours fields. Format the Pay field to Fixed with two decimal places.
- Edit the following records:

5	First Name is Robert
17	Hours is 35
25	Pay is 5.65

- Bob had three employees terminate their employment with the company. Delete records 3, 7, and 10 (in that order).
- Tom Sanders was promoted from Assembler I to Assembler 2. Search the database for this record and change his job title to Assembler 2 and his pay to $7.25.
- Juanita Williams was also promoted. Locate her record and change her job title from Clerk to Packager and her pay to $5.65.

- Sort the database on Department as the first field, Title as the second field, and Last Name as the third field. Use ascending order for all fields.
- Bob hired two new people. In FORM view, add their records to the end of the database:

Record 1	***Record 2***
539-22-3256	344-09-0804
Fillmore	Jones
Mary	Beverley
Production	Shipping
Assembler 1	Clerk
6.50	4.75
40	32
F	F

- Sort the database again using the same fields.
- Print the records for all female employees earning more than $6.00 per hour. Use the header "Female Employees Earning More Than $6.00/Hr. - [Student Name]." Use the Print option "Print records and field labels."
- Save the file as STAFF2.
- Print a simple report of all employees displaying last name, department, and title. Sort the records by titles as the 1st sort field. Include the record numbers and field labels. Enter the header "Employees by Job Title - [Your Name]."
- Close the file without saving it.

4. In practice problem 5 of the previous lab, you created the file STOCK1 in which you entered two inventory records. Aquanetta, the gift shop owner, continued to enter more inventory records into the database file. To see the database of 26 records, open the file STOCK2.

- Change the vendor in record 1 to your name.
- In LIST view, format the Cost and Price fields to display, as Fixed with two decimal places. Increase the field width if necessary to fully display the values.

  Aquanetta wants to add two new fields. The first field will hold a value that will tell her when she should reorder an item. When the quantity is equal to or less than this value, she will order more. The second new field will calculate the inventory value of the stock on hand.
- In LIST view, insert the first new field after the Quantity field. Enter the field name "Reorder." Set the field width to 7.
- Enter 6 as the reorder point for all records. Change the reorder point for all records whose quantity is equal to or greater than 15 to 12. Center the field.
- In FORM view, move the Reorder field below the Quantity field. Decrease the field size to 2.
- In FORM view, insert the second new field between the Cost and Price fields. Use the field name Inv. Value. Set the field size to 10.

- The Inventory Value is calculated by multiplying Cost times Quantity. Enter this formula. Format the field to display as Fixed with two decimal places.
- In LIST view, query the database to display all items that have a Quantity that is equal to or less than the Reorder value. Print the listing using the "Print record and field labels" option and this header "Reorder Report - [Student Name]."
- Display all records. Sort on Inv. Value as the first field in descending order and Quantity as the second field in ascending order.
- Print all records with the following header "Inventory Valuation Report - [Your Name]". Display the reorder numbers and field labels.
- Sort the database on Price in ascending order.
- Query the database for Price greater than or equal to 20 and less than 30.
- Save the file as STOCK3.
- Print a simple report displaying the Description, Quantity, Price, and Vendor fields only. Use the header "Gifts Between $20 and $30 - [Your Name]." Display the reorder numbers and field labels.
- Exit the file without saving it.

Command Summary

Command	Shortcut	Action	Page
Edit>**M**ove Field		Moves field to new location in FORM	305
Edit>**I**nsert Line		Inserts blank row in FORM	304
Edit>**D**elete Record		Removes record in FORM	296
Edit>In**s**ert Record		Inserts blank record in FORM	317
Edit>**I**nsert Record/Field		Inserts record or field in LIST	297, 317
Edit>Field **N**ame		Enters field name in LIST	297
Edit>**D**elete Record/Field		Removes record or field in LIST	296
Edit>De**l**ete Query		Clears QUERY view screen	318
Print>**H**eader & Footer		Adds headers or footers	320
Select>**G**o to		Moves to field or record	294, 302
Select>**S**earch		Locates record that matches	307
Select>**S**earch>**N**ext record	F7	Locates next record in search	309
Select>Show **A**ll Records		Displays all records	310
Select>S**w**itch Hidden Records		Displays hidden records	310
Select>S**o**rt Records		Rearranges records in order specified	312
Forma**t**>Fi**x**ed		Formats field as Fixed	
Forma**t**>Field **W**idth>**0**		Hides field condition	299
View>**L**ist	F10	Displays LIST view/applies query	312
View>**Q**uery		Locates records meeting query conditions	311

LAB

11 Creating a Report

CASE STUDY

In the previous lab, you created a simple report by searching the database to display selected records and hiding selected fields of data. In this way, the report displayed only the information requested. This procedure is acceptable for creating simple reports; however, it would be a very tedious method to use for producing a more complex report.

In this lab, the accounting department has asked Fred to create a report they will use on a weekly basis. They want the report to list the employees' name, title, hourly pay rate, hours worked, and weekly pay, organized by department. To do this, Fred will use the database REPORT view to create a professional-appearing report.

OBJECTIVES

In this lab you will learn how to:

1. Use REPORT view.
2. Specify a title for a report.
3. Specify report columns.
4. View the report.
5. Modify a report.
6. Define subtotals.
7. Print a report.

Using REPORT View

Load Works and open the file you created at the end of Lab 10, EMPLOYE3.WDB. If the records are not displayed in LIST view, change to that view.

The database should be sorted alphabetically by last name as it was when you saved the file at the end of the previous lab. The record containing your personal data should appear in the database in the appropriate alphabetical order.

You will create the report shown in Figure 11-1 on the next page in this lab.

Employee Payroll Report
by Student Name

First Name	Last Name	Title	Pay	Hours	Weekly Pay
Accounting					
Larry	Davis	Clerk	$6.60	40	$264.00
Linda	Dunnhaven	Clerk	$6.60	20	$132.00
Donna	Morgan	Bookkeeper	$7.45	32	$238.40
Kay	Rosen	Supervisor	$9.55	40	$382.00
Jennifer	Stone	Clerk	$6.75	40	$270.00
	------		------		---------
Total Dept:	5	Average:	$7.39	Total:	$1,286.40
Maintenance					
Anthony	Allbright	Supervisor	$8.25	45	$371.25
Alan	Barton	Grounds	$5.25	32	$168.00
Donald	Crane	Grounds	$5.25	40	$210.00
Sarah	Fischer	Grounds	$4.75	40	$190.00
Stacy	Jackson	Grounds	$4.75	20	$95.00
Cynthia	Olson	Grounds	$4.75	20	$95.00
Anne	Thomas	Cleaning	$4.35	28	$121.80
	------		------		---------
Total Dept:	7	Average:	$5.34	Total:	$1,251.05
Restaurant					
Edward	Becker	Counter	$4.35	40	$174.00
Shelly	Foran	Counter	$4.35	32	$139.20
Christine	Jackson	Cook	$7.45	30	$223.50
Ellen	Johnson	Supervisor	$8.25	40	$330.00
Jake	Millersburg	Counter	$4.10	20	$82.00
Anita	Robins	Counter	$4.10	32	$131.20
	------		------		---------
Total Dept:	6	Average:	$5.43	Total:	$1,079.90
Service					
Roger	Aldrich	Desk Clerk	$4.55	40	$182.00
Timothy	McHale	Supervisor	$8.25	40	$330.00
Student	Name	Desk Clerk	$6.00	28	$168.00
Madelyn	Parkerson	Desk Clerk	$4.55	32	$145.60
Stephen	Paterson	Desk Clerk	$4.35	36	$156.60
Alice	Patton	Desk Clerk	$4.55	32	$145.60
Robert	Shields	Desk Clerk	$4.10	24	$98.40
Leon	Walker	Assistant	$5.25	40	$210.00
	------		------		---------
Total Dept:	8	Average:	$5.20	Total:	$1,436.20
	=======		=======		=========
Total Emp:	26	Average:	$5.71	Total:	$5,053.55

FIGURE 11-1

A **report** consists of introductory text, such as a report title, the sorted groups of data, spacing between the groups, group subtotals, and report totals. Works labels the different parts of a report as follows:

Introductory report rows — These rows contain information that appears on the first page of a report. Typically, a report title is entered in these rows.

Introductory page rows — These rows contain information that appears at the beginning of each page of the report. Typically, the field names are used as column headings in these rows.

Introductory group rows — These rows contain information that describes the contents of the group of data immediately below the row. Generally, an introductory group row is used whenever the report data is grouped in categories of information.

Record rows — These rows contain the field contents of the data in the database file.

Summary group rows	These rows display calculated values about the records displayed in the preceding group.
Summary report rows	These rows display calculated values about all the records displayed in the report.

Works has a preset report definition form that will create a simple report automatically for you. Not all the report rows are used in the preset report. You customize the preset report specifically to meet your needs by adding, deleting, and defining the different report rows.

To use the preset report definition form to create a report,

Select: View>New Report

Your display should be similar to Figure 11-2.

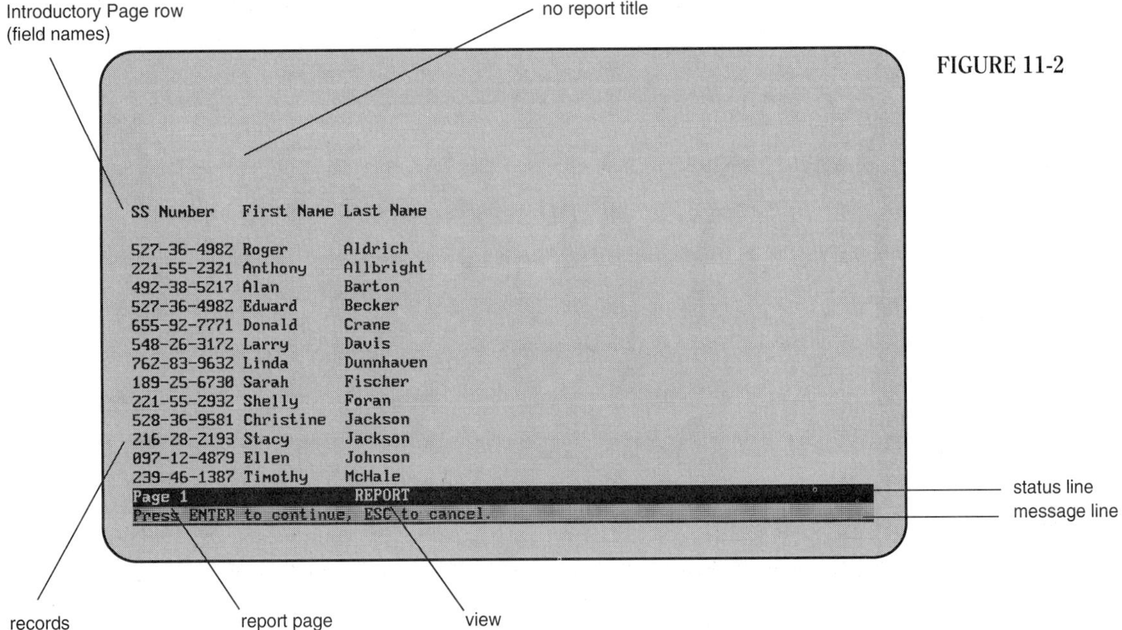

FIGURE 11-2

After a few moments, Works creates the report and displays the first page on the screen. The field names are listed above each column of data in the Introductory Page row. The Record rows contain the fields of information for each record in the database. The records are in alphabetical order because the database is sorted alphabetically. Your record should appear in the appropriate alphabetical order. The width of each column of data is the same as the column widths used in LIST view. The report does not have a report title.

The status line tells you that you are using the REPORT view and the page of the report you are viewing on your screen. You are viewing page 1 of the report. The message line directs you to press ↵ to continue.

Press: ↵

The bottom half of page 1 is displayed. To see the top of page 2,

Press: ↵

The Introductory Page rows are displayed again. To view the rest of the report,

Press: ⏎ (3 times)

The bottom half of page 3 should be displayed. Page 3 is the last page of the report.

Examining the Report Definition Screen

When you reach the end of the report, pressing ⏎ again will display the Report Definition screen.

Press: ⏎

Your screen should be similar to Figure 11-3.

FIGURE 11-3

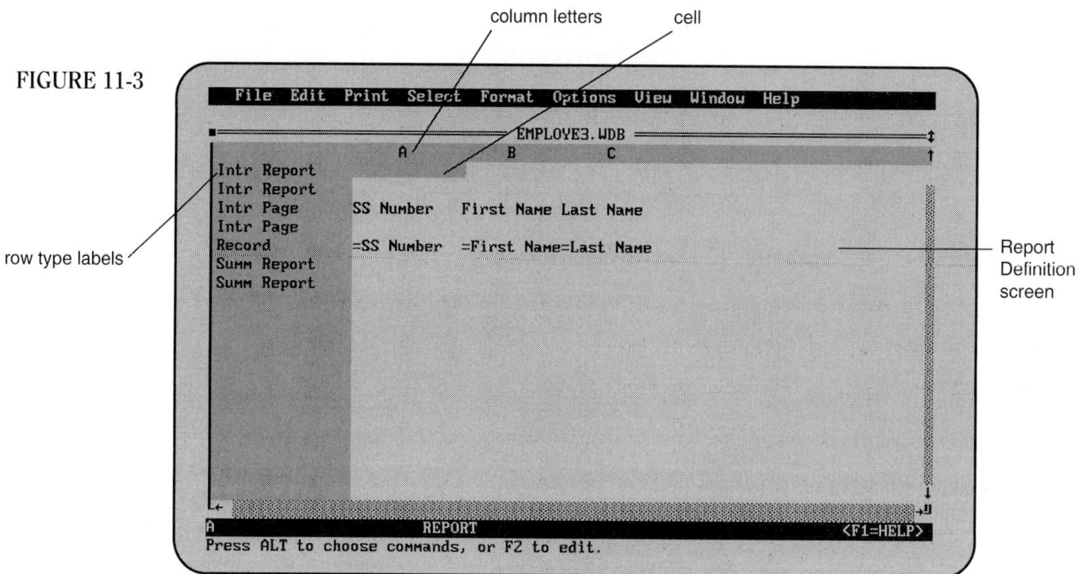

The **Report Definition screen** determines the layout of the report. It is similar to a spreadsheet in that it consists of column letters along the top of the workspace and row labels along the left side. As in a spreadsheet, the intersection of a column and row creates a cell. The cell contents in each row determine what information goes into the report. The information consists of explanatory text, data, or summary statistics.

The row labels identify the **row types**. The row types control the information displayed on each row of the report. They are:

Intr Report — These are the **Introductory Report rows**. They are used to enter report titles that appear on the first page of the report only.

Intr Page — These are the **Introductory Page rows**. Information in these rows appears at the beginning of each page of the report.

Record — **Record rows** print one entry for each record in the report. Works will print the actual data for each record.

Summ Report — These rows are the **Summary Report rows**. They are used to display summary statistics for each column of data.

The row types print in a specific order. However, you can have as many of each row type as you want.

The cells to the right of the row type labels control what information will be displayed in the report. You use the arrow keys to move around the Report Definition screen just as you would use them to move around a spreadsheet screen. The highlight should be positioned in column A of the first Intr Report row. The two Intr Report rows are currently empty.

Press: ↓ (2 times)

Your screen should be similar to Figure 11-4.

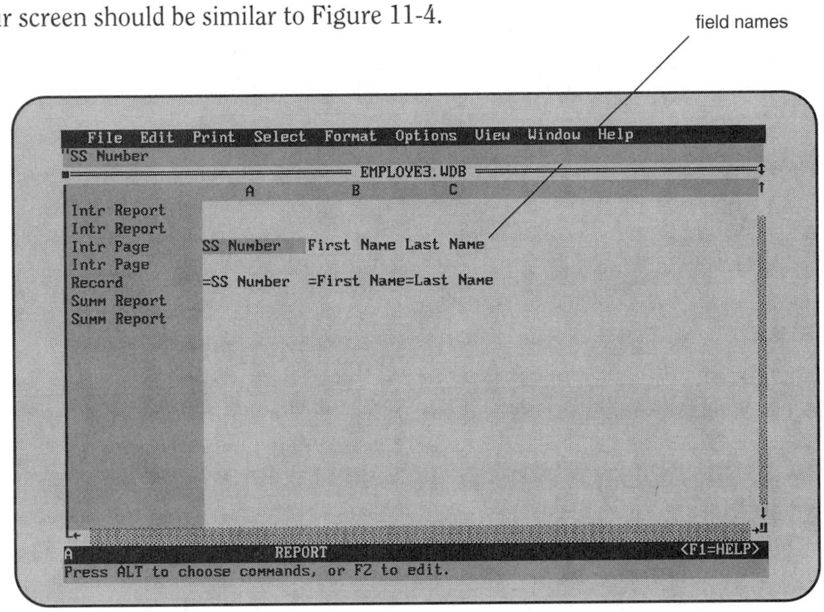

field names

```
 File  Edit  Print  Select  Format  Options  View  Window  Help
"SS Number
                         EMPLOYE3.WDB
                     A            B            C
 Intr Report
 Intr Report
 Intr Page          SS Number    First Name Last Name
 Intr Page
 Record             =SS Number   =First Name=Last Name
 Summ Report
 Summ Report

A                        REPORT                          <F1=HELP>
Press ALT to choose commands, or F2 to edit.
```

FIGURE 11-4

The highlight should be positioned in column A of the first Intr Page row. The cells in this row display the field names as column headings. The first three field names are displayed in columns A through C on your screen. To see the rest of the field names,

Press: → (12 times)

Each cell in the first Intr Page row contains a field name from the database.

Press: HOME

The second Intr Page row is blank.

Press: ↓ (2 times)

Your screen should be similar to Figure 11-5.

FIGURE 11-5

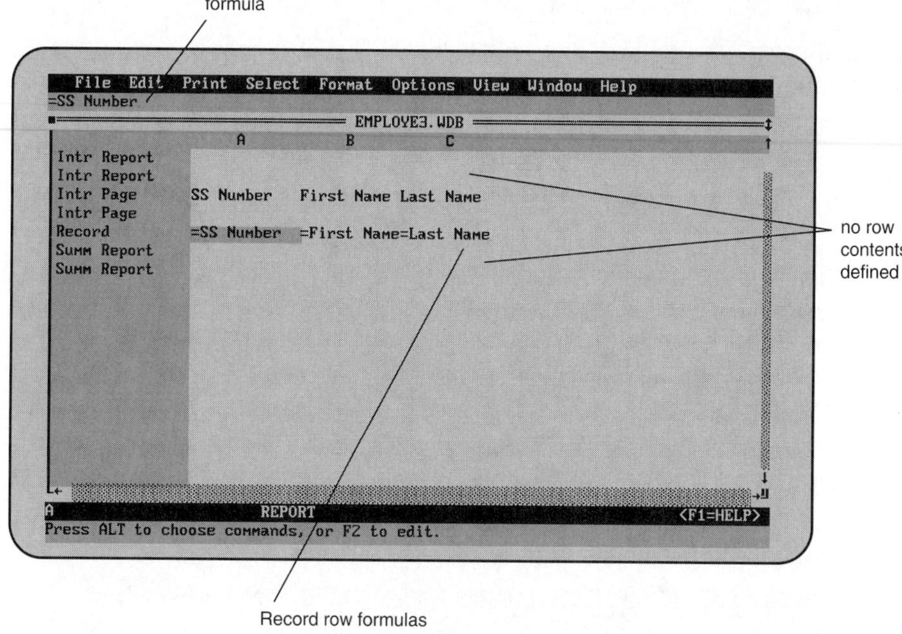

The highlight should be positioned in column A of the Record row. A Record row is printed for each record from the database. Each cell in this row contains a formula. A formula is used because each row contains different data. The formula in column A directs the program to enter the data from the SS Number field in this column for each record.

Press: (→)

The formula in column B of the Record row directs Works to enter the data from the First Name field for each record in the database. To see the rest of the formulas in the Record row,

Press: (→) (11 times)

Each cell in the Record row contains a formula that directs Works to enter data from a specific field for each record in the report column.

Press: (HOME)
Press: (↓)

The highlight should be positioned on the first Summ Report row. Both rows are currently empty.

The report generated by Works provides a basis for you to begin creating a customized report. To customize this report, Fred will begin by adding a title and summary statistics.

Entering a Report Title

The title of this report will be "Employee Payroll Report" as the first title line and "for the Week of May 15, 1992" as the second title line. The first Intr Report row will contain the text for the first title line and the second Intr Report row will contain the text for the second title line.

To enter information into the report definition box, move the highlight to the cell and type the text, numbers, dates, or formulas. This is similar to entering information in a spreadsheet. If the information extends beyond the width of the cell, the entry will be fully displayed as long as the cells to the right are empty.

To enter the first title line in column B,

Move to: column B of the first Intr Report row
Type: **Employee Payroll Report**

If you make a mistake, use (Bksp) to erase the error and retype the entry correctly.

Your screen should be similar to Figure 11-6.

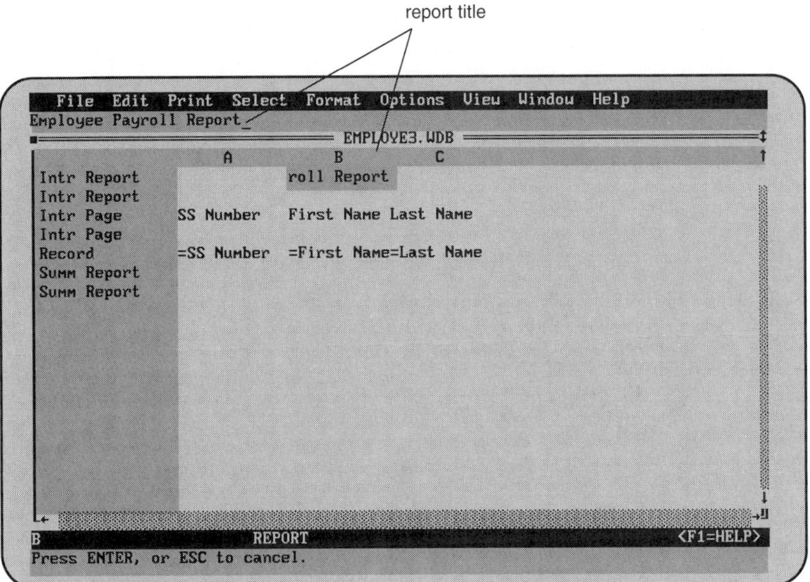

FIGURE 11-6

Just as in the spreadsheet, as you type the information is displayed in the formula bar. If the text is longer than the cell width, it scrolls in the cell space. To complete the entry,

Press: 

The first title line is fully displayed in the cell space because the cells to the right are empty. This is similar to a long label in a spreadsheet cell. If you see an error, do not be concerned; you will learn how to edit the entry shortly.

To enter the second title line,

Press: 

The highlight should be in column B in the second Intr Report row.

Type: **for the Week of May 15, 1992**
Press: ↵

Your display should be similar to Figure 11-7.

FIGURE 11-7

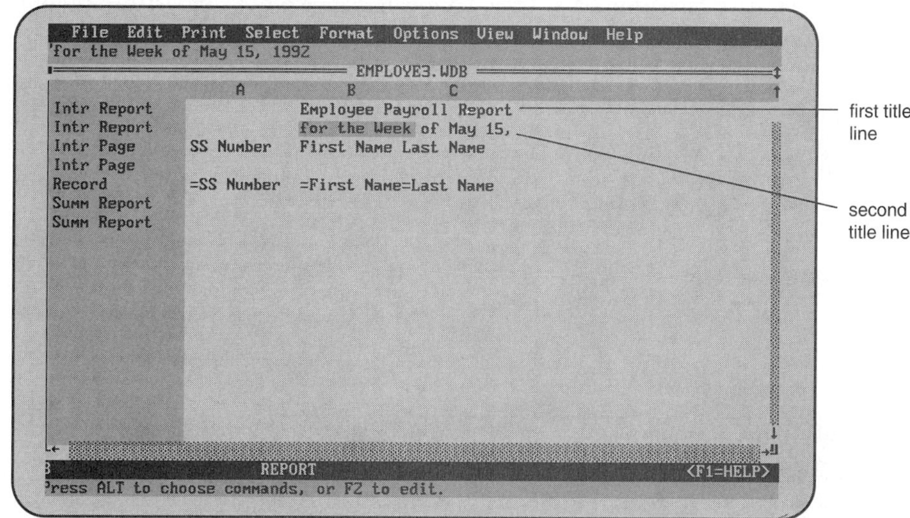

Both title lines are displayed in the Intr Report rows.

Naming and Viewing the Report

To see the title as it appears in the report,

Select: View

Your screen should be similar to Figure 11-8.

FIGURE 11-8

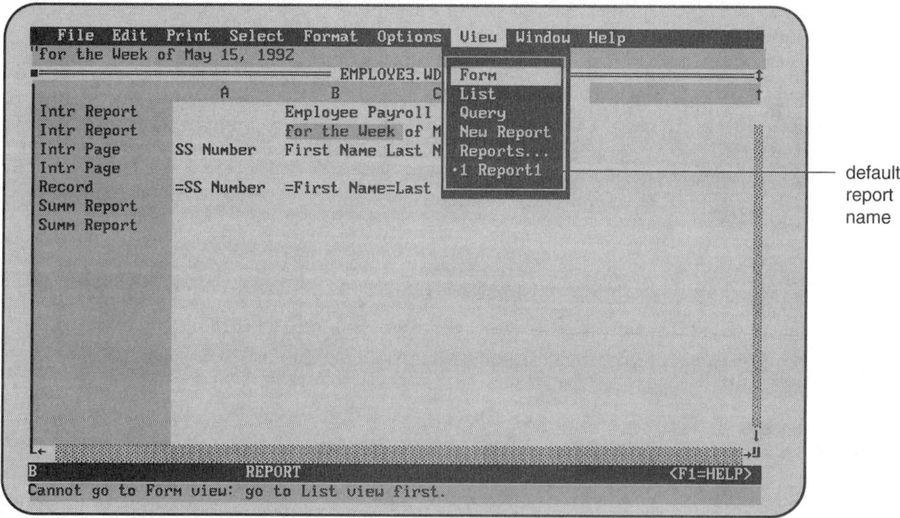

Under the Reports option in the View menu, Report1, the default report name Works assigned to the report, is displayed. This is very similar to how Works automatically assigned a default name to a chart as you created it in the Spreadsheet Chart view. Whenever a new report is created, Works automatically assigns it a name and lists it in the View menu. You can have up to eight reports created using the same database. Since you are using the first report, it is the selected report. However, the name assigned by Works is not very meaningful. To assign it a new name,

Select: Reports

The Reports dialog box is displayed. This is the same as the dialog box used in the Spreadsheet View>Charts command.

Select: Name
Type: **Payroll**

To instruct Works to rename the file by selecting the Rename button,

Press: ↵

Your screen should be similar to Figure 11-9.

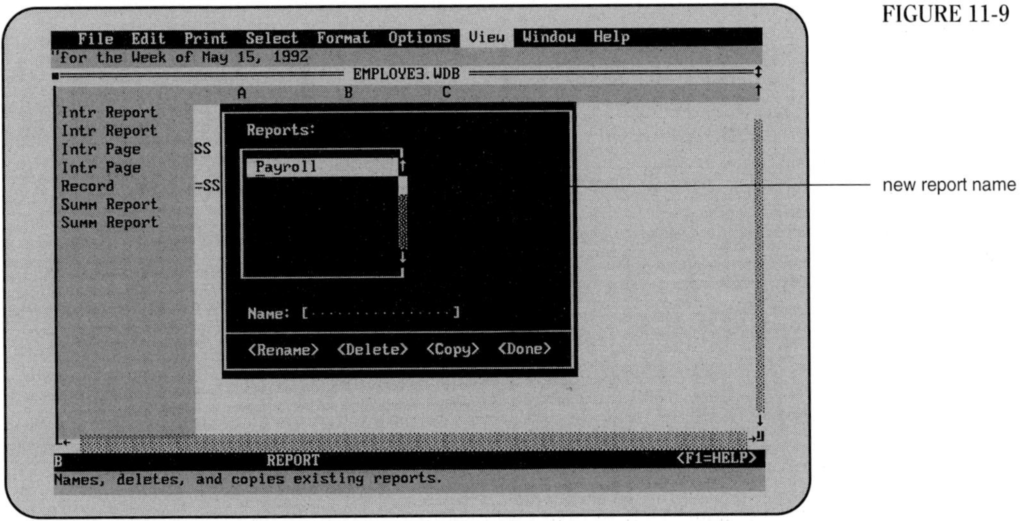

FIGURE 11-9

The new report name has replaced Report1 in the dialog box.

To leave the Reports dialog box,

Press: ESC

You are returned to the Report Definition screen. To view the report to see the title,

Select: View

The new report name is listed as the first report. To select it,

Type: 1

Your display should be similar to Figure 11-10.

FIGURE 11-10

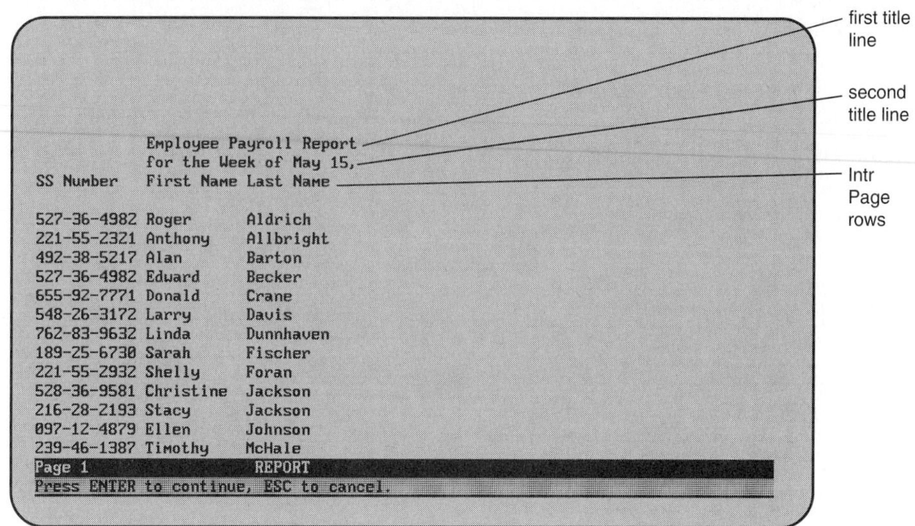

The upper half of the first page of the report is displayed on the screen.

The report title is displayed as the first two lines of the report. The column headings are immediately below the title. Fred does not like how the title looks. He thinks the title would look better if it just read "Employee Payroll Report" on the first line and "Week of May 15, 1992" on the second line.

To return directly to the Report Definition screen without paging through the entire report,

Press: (ESC)

Editing the Report Title

Fred wants to change the second line of the title to "Week of May 15, 1992." To edit this title line,

Move to: column B of the second Intr Report row
Press: (F2)

Most of the same editing keys used in the spreadsheet can be used to edit in REPORT view. However, you cannot use (TAB) and (SHIFT) - (TAB) to move word by word. To delete the words "for the"

Press: (HOME)
Press: (DEL) (9 times)

Do not be concerned that you deleted the preceding label indicator ("), Works will automatically insert it again because it is a text entry.

Press: 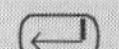

Your screen should be similar to Figure 11-11.

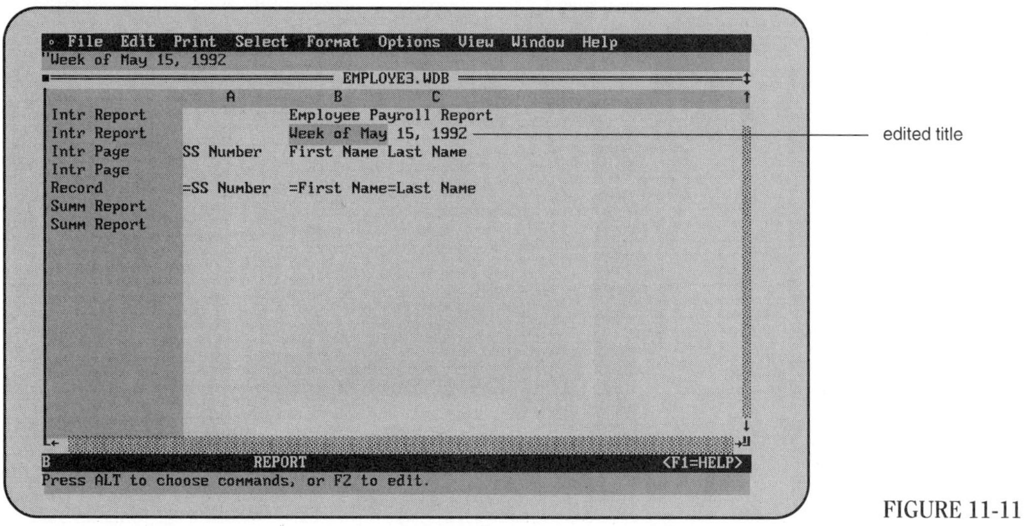

FIGURE 11-11

The two words are deleted from the second line of the title.

Entering Summary Statistics

Next, Fred wants the report to calculate the total number of employees, the average rate of pay, and the total weekly pay.

The Summ Report rows are used to display summary statistics for all records in the report. The first statistic you will enter will calculate the total number of records in the report. Fred wants this formula entered in column C in the second Summ Report row. This way, the calculated value will be displayed below the Last Name column of data. Leaving the first Summ Report row empty will also leave a blank row between the last record in the report and the calculated value.

Move to: column C of the second Summ Report row

The Edit menu contains the command to add summary statistics to a report.

Select: Edit>Insert Field **S**ummary

Your screen should be similar to Figure 11-12.

FIGURE 11-12

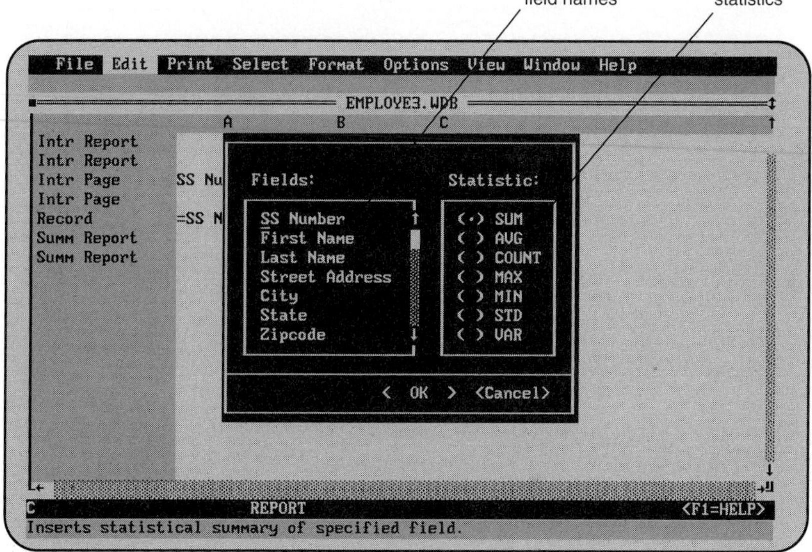

The Insert Field Summary dialog box is displayed. It lists each field in your database in the Fields box and the seven statistical functions you can use in the Statistic box. The statistics perform the following calculations:

Statistic	Calculation
SUM	Total of group
AVG	Average of group
COUNT	Number of items in group
MAX	Largest number in group
MIN	Smallest number in group
STD	Standard deviation of group
VAR	Variance of group

The COUNT function is the formula you want to use to count the records. You need to select the field of data you want the COUNT statistic to use to perform the calculation. To use the Last Name field,

Select: Last Name
Select: COUNT

Your screen should be similar to Figure 11-13.

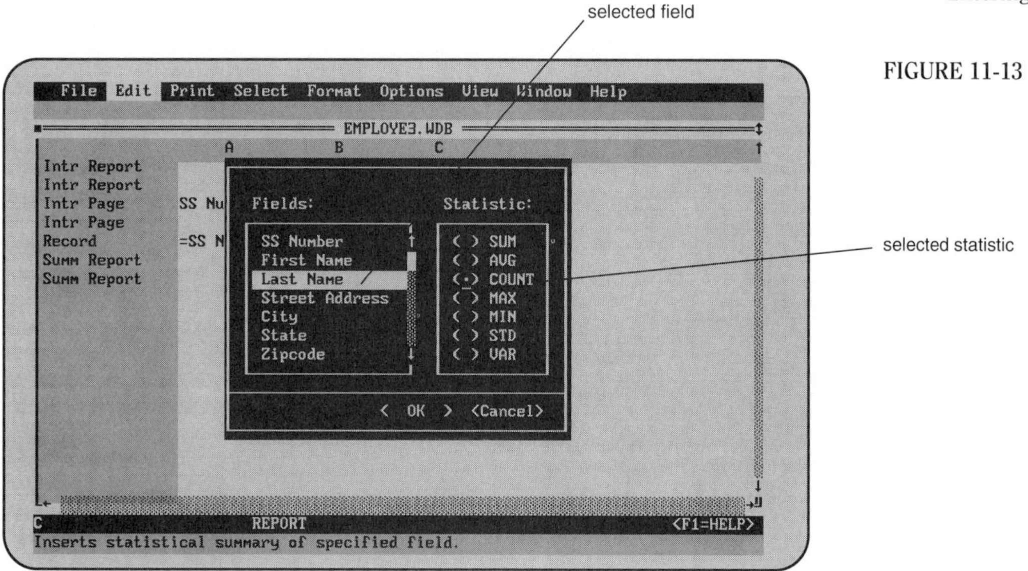

FIGURE 11-13

To complete the command,

Press: ⏎

Your screen should be similar to Figure 11-14.

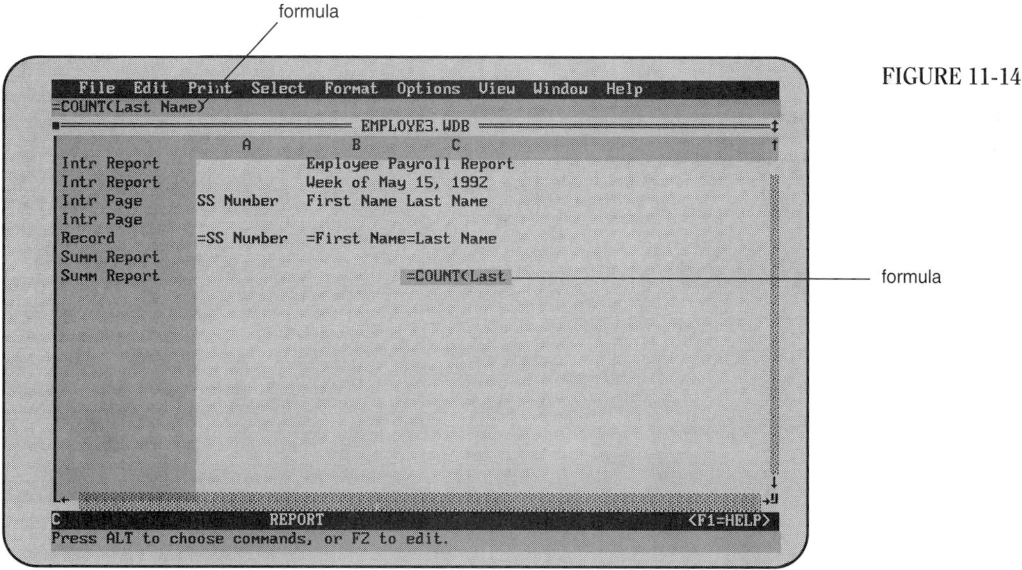

FIGURE 11-14

The formula =COUNT(Last Name) is entered in the cell that the highlight is positioned on. This tells Works to count the number of records in the Last Name field of the report and display the calculated value at the end of the Last Name column of data.

The second statistic you will enter will calculate the average pay. This value will be displayed below the Pay column of data. To move to this location,

Move to: column K of the second Summ Report row
Select: **E**dit>Insert Field **S**ummary>Pay>**A**vg>⏎

The formula =AVG(Pay) is entered in the active cell of the Report Definition screen.

The final summary statistic will calculate the total weekly pay and display it below the Weekly Pay column of data. To move to this column,

Move to: column M of the second Summ Report row
Select: **E**dit>Insert Field **S**ummary>Weekly Pay>**S**um>⏎

The formula =SUM(Weekly Pay) is entered in the active cell.

To see the calculated values in the report,

Select: **V**iew>**1**

The calculated values will appear at the end of the records. To see the bottom of page 1,

Press: ⏎

Your display should be similar to Figure 11-15.

FIGURE 11-15

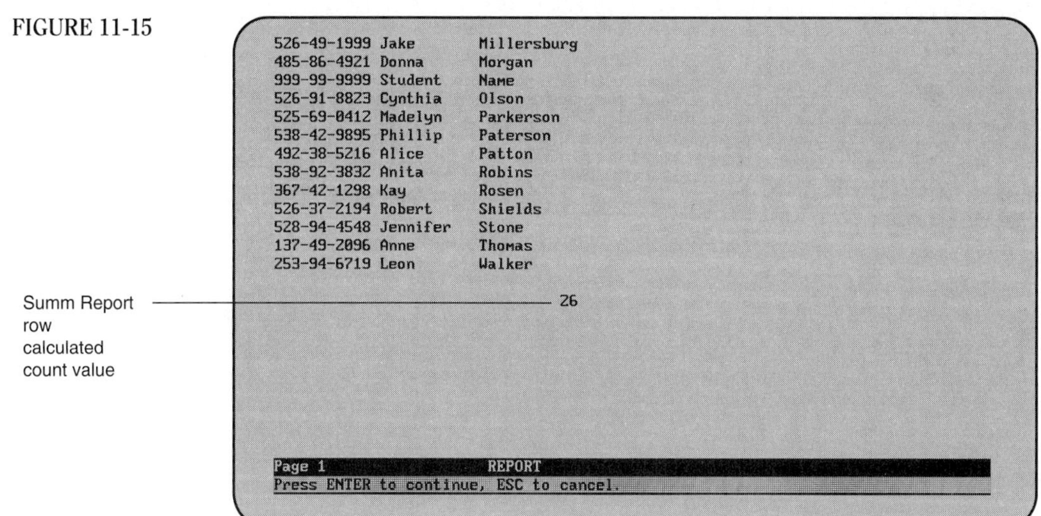

Under the Last Name column, the value 26 is displayed. This is the value calculated by the COUNT function. It tells you there are 26 entries in the Last Name column.

Reminder: The record containing your data will appear in alphabetical order in the report. Therefore your screen will differ slightly from the figures in the text displaying the report.

To see the second page of the report,

Press: 

Notice that the report title is not displayed on this page. A report title is displayed on the first page of the report only. The column headings, however, are displayed on each page of the report.

To see the calculated values for the Pay and Weekly Pay fields on the last page of the report,

Press: (3 times)

Your screen should be similar to Figure 11-16.

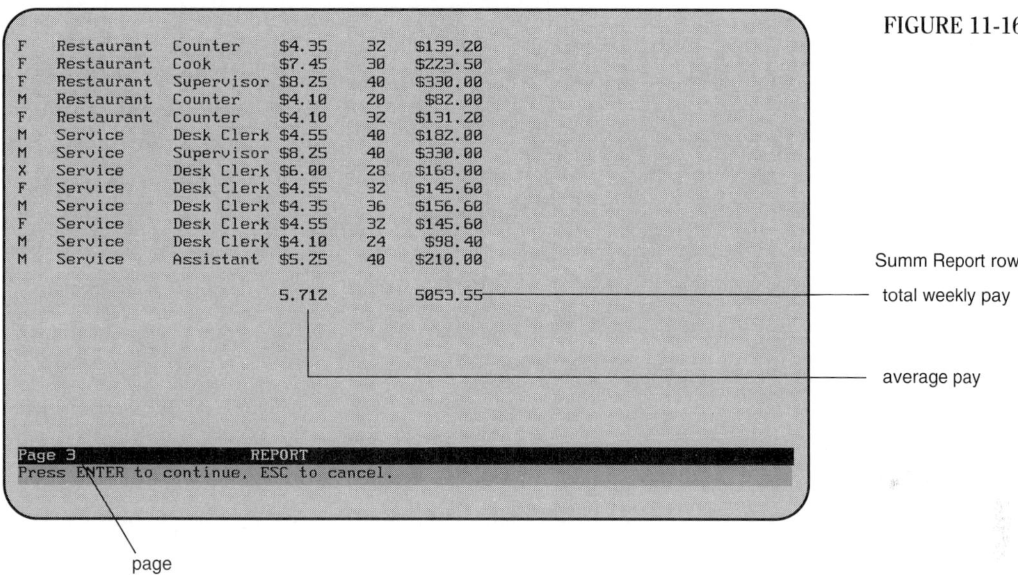

F Restaurant Counter $4.35 32 $139.20
F Restaurant Cook $7.45 30 $223.50
F Restaurant Supervisor $8.25 40 $330.00
M Restaurant Counter $4.10 20 $82.00
F Restaurant Counter $4.10 32 $131.20
M Service Desk Clerk $4.55 40 $182.00
M Service Supervisor $8.25 40 $330.00
X Service Desk Clerk $6.00 28 $168.00
F Service Desk Clerk $4.55 32 $145.60
M Service Desk Clerk $4.35 36 $156.60
F Service Desk Clerk $4.55 32 $145.60
M Service Desk Clerk $4.10 24 $98.40
M Service Assistant $5.25 40 $210.00
5.712 5053.55
Page 3 REPORT
Press ENTER to continue, ESC to cancel.
Summ Report row
total weekly pay
average pay
page

FIGURE 11-16

You should be viewing the bottom half of page 3. The summary statistics for the Hourly Pay and Weekly Pay columns are displayed. The average hourly pay is 5.712, and the total weekly pay is 5053.55.

To return to the Report Definition screen,

Press: 

Grouping the Records

Now Fred is ready to divide the report into groups by department. To do this, the Select>Sort Records command is used.

Select: Select>Sort Records

Your screen should be similar to Figure 11-17.

FIGURE 11-17

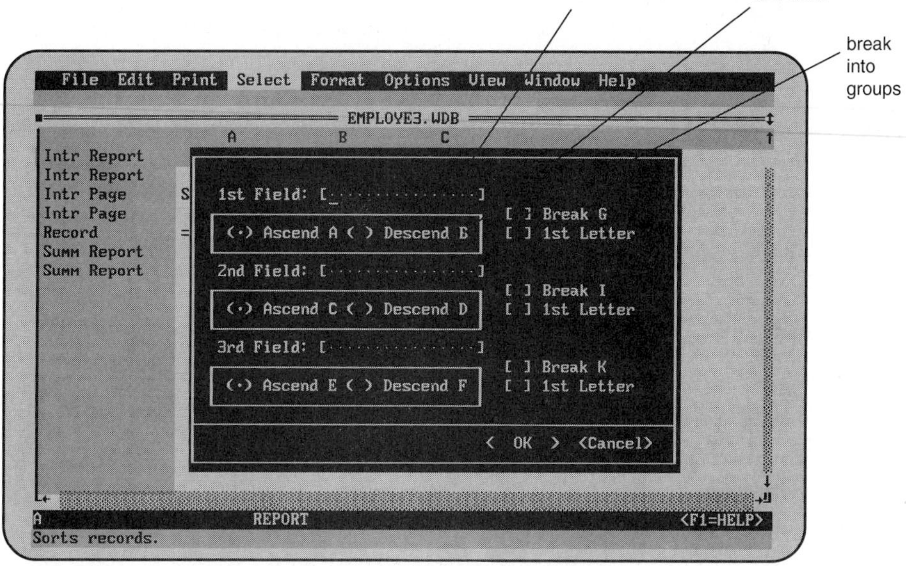

The Sort dialog box is displayed. This is very similar to the VIEW and FORM Sort dialog boxes. Fred wants the records grouped by department. In the "1st Field:" text box,

Type: **department**

Since he wants them organized in ascending alphabetical order, the default setting is acceptable. To the right side of each field text box, there are two additional options, Break and 1st Letter. The Break check box lets you separate a report into groups by inserting a blank Summ Report row in the report each time information in the field changes. If this box is not selected, Works sorts the data on the field specified, but it does not divide the records into groups. Fred wants the report divided into groups. To select the break box for the first field,

Press: (ALT) - G

The 1st Letter check box is used when the sort field contains text and you want the break to occur whenever the first letter of the field changes, rather than breaking after each new word. In this case, since the break will occur for each new word, it is not necessary to select this box. To complete the command,

Press: ↵

After a few moments, the records are sorted and the Report Definition box displays a new row title, Summ Department. Works automatically adds a new row referencing the selected sort field whenever this command is used.

Move to: column A of the Summ Department row

Each cell in this row displays a formula that will calculate the summary statistics for the records in the group. Works automatically enters a formula to count the number of entries if the field contains text and a formula to sum the entries if the field contains values. For example, the first three fields contain text, so the COUNT function is used. To see the summary statistics for the value fields,

Press: END

Your screen should be similar to Figure 11-18.

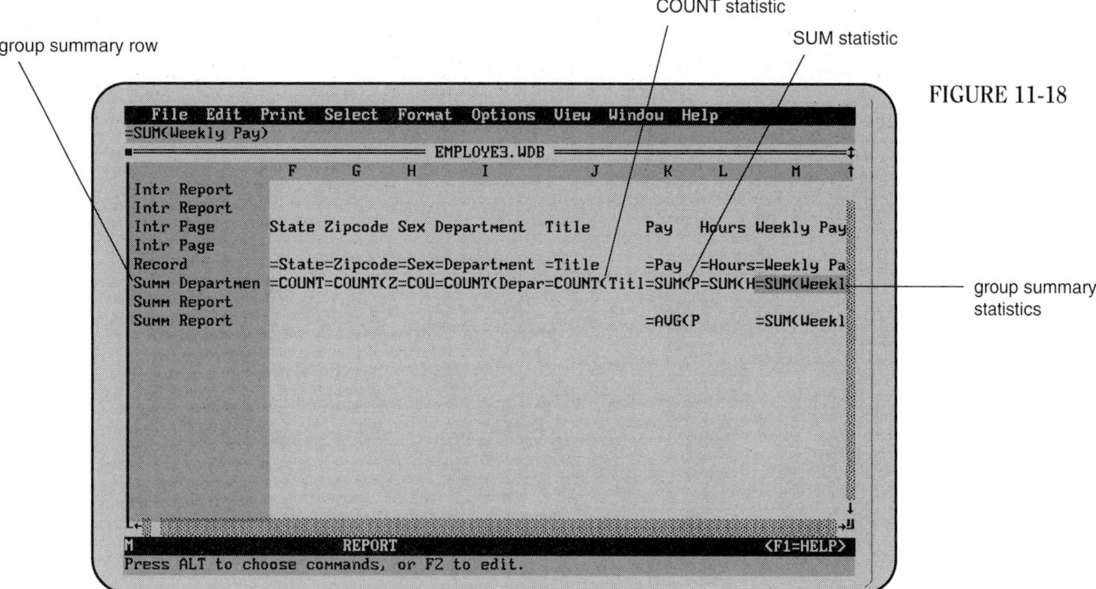

FIGURE 11-18

The three fields Pay, Hours, and Weekly Pay contain a SUM function that will total the values in the field.

Let's view the report to see the calculated value and how this change has affected the report layout.

Select: View>1

Your screen should be similar to Figure 11-19.

FIGURE 11-19

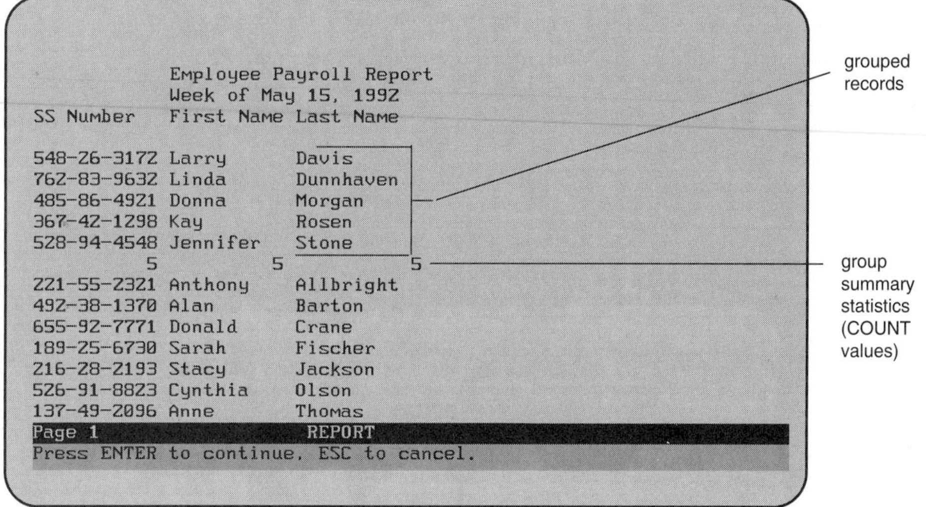

The records have been divided into groups by department. The numbers at the bottom of each column in the first group represent a count of the number of entries in the group. However, it is difficult to know which department each group represents. To clarify the meaning of the values, an introductory group row can to be added to identify the groups.

Press: ⏎ (4 times)

Your screen should be similar to Figure 11-20.

FIGURE 11-20

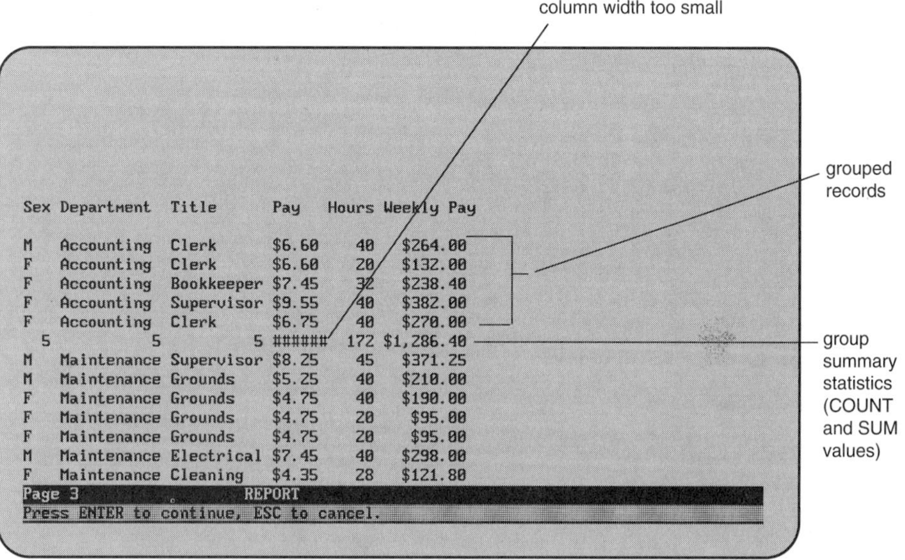

This page of the report displays # symbols in the Pay group summary cell. As in a spreadsheet, this tells you the value is too large to display in the cell width. Since Works summed the Pay data, the total value is larger than the field width. Fred thinks it would be more meaningful if the Pay data were averaged rather than summed. As you will see, it is easy to change the default summary functions to a function that better describes the data.

To return to the Report Definition screen,

Press: ↵ (2 times)

Adding an Introductory Group Row

First, you need to add an introductory group row to the report to identify the groupings of data. The introductory row should identify the departments. To enter the row and specify what type of row you want,

Select: **E**dit>**I**nsert Row/Column>**R**ow>↵

Your display should be similar to Figure 11-21.

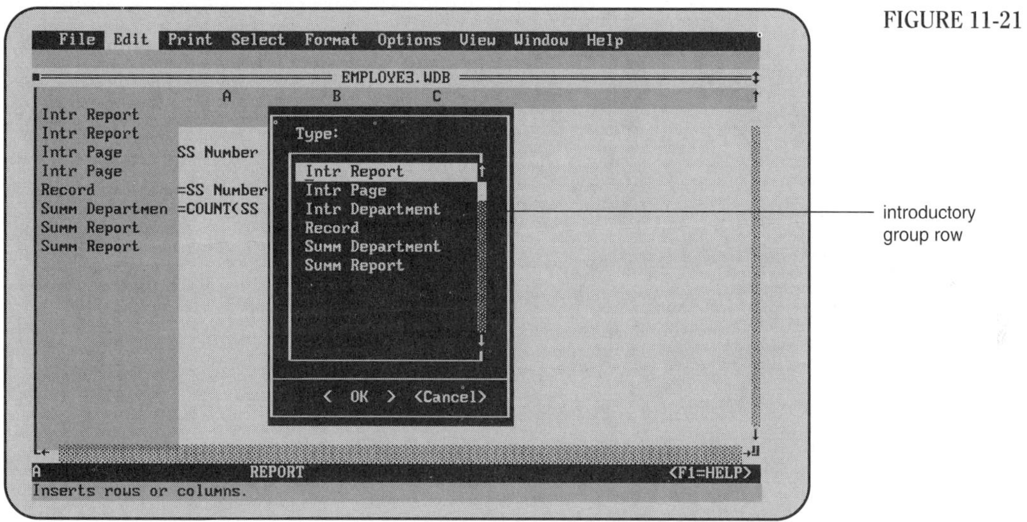

FIGURE 11-21

In the Type dialog box, six row types are listed. You need to select the type of row you want inserted into the report.

Notice that Works displays a row type called Intr Department. Works automatically creates a row type whenever you create a group in a report. The field upon which the report is divided is displayed automatically following the row type label.

Select: Intr Department>↵

The Intr Department row is automatically inserted into the report definition form below the Intr Page rows. The type of row you select will determine where Works will enter the row on the form.

Next, you need to enter a formula that will direct Works to enter the name of the department for each group as the information to be displayed in this line of the report. To display the department name in column B,

Move to: column B of the Intr Department row
Type: **=Department**
Press: ↵

To view the change in the report,

Select: View>**1**

Your screen should be similar to Figure 11-22.

FIGURE 11-22

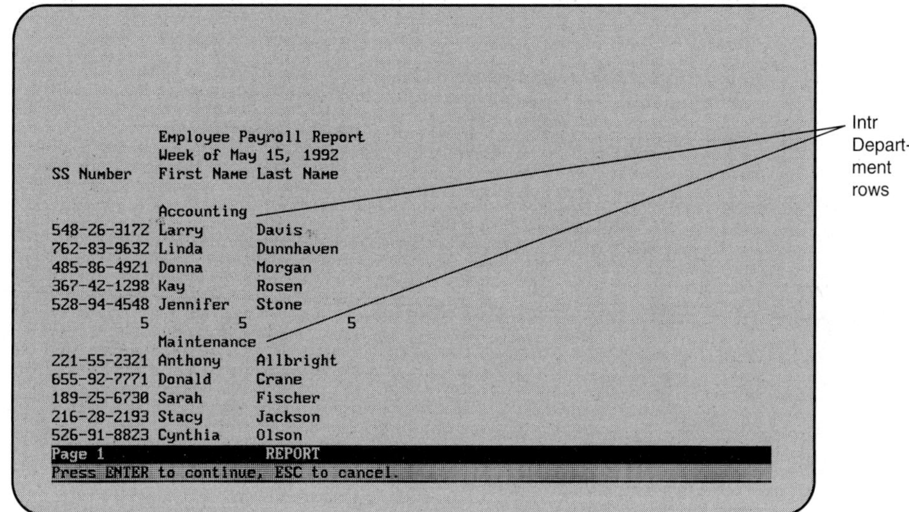

Now you can easily identify the groups by department. Above the First Name column, the department name for the first and second groups of data, Accounting and Maintenance, are displayed on the screen. To see the bottom of page 1,

Press: ↵

The department names for the other two groups are displayed above each group.

To return to the report definition box,

Press: ESC

Editing Cell Formulas

By default, Works sums numeric groups and counts text groups of data. In this case, however, Fred wants the Pay column of data to be an average rather than a sum. To change the formula,

Move to: column K of the Summ Department row
Press: (F2)
Press: (HOME)

To change SUM to AVG,

Press: (→)
Press: (DEL) (3 times)
Type: **avg**
Press: (↵)

View the top of page 3 of the report.

Your screen should be similar to Figure 11-23.

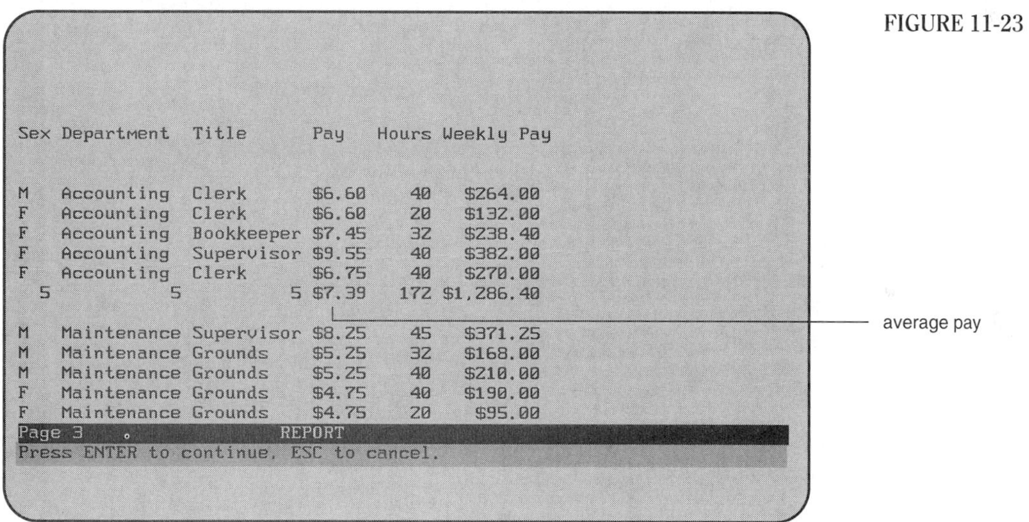

FIGURE 11-23

The Pay field of data is averaged for each group and the calculated value can be fully displayed in the cell space.

To return to the Report Definition screen,

Press: (ESC)

Deleting Report Columns

When Works creates a report, it uses each column of data displayed in the database as a report column. Fred wants the report to display selected fields of data only.

The columns of data Fred wants displayed in the report are First and Last name, Pay, Hours, and Weekly Pay. You will remove the unwanted columns. When you delete a column, the highlight must be positioned anywhere on the column you want to remove.

Your highlight should be in column A. If it is not, move it there.

To remove the SS Number column of data,

Select: **E**dit>**D**elete Row/Column>**C**olumn>(Enter)

Your display should be similar to Figure 11-24.

FIGURE 11-24

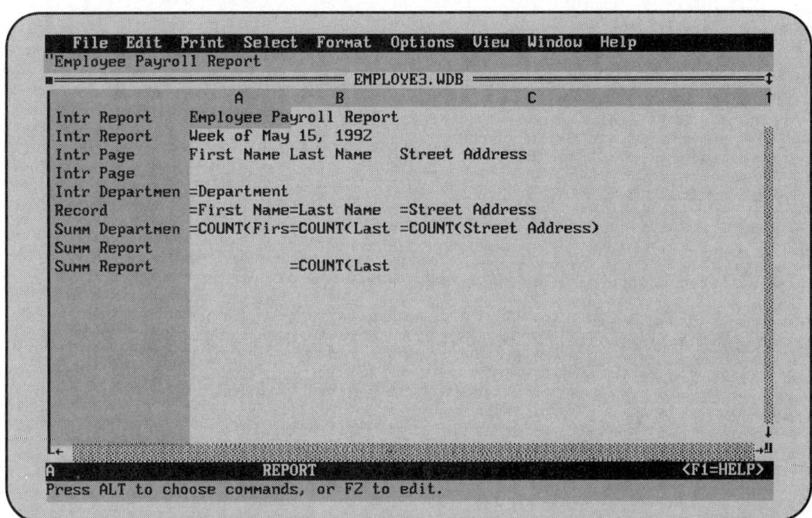

Column A has been deleted and the columns to the right have moved over to take its place. The column has been deleted from the Report Definition screen only. It still exists in LIST and FORM views.

Note: If you accidentally deleted the wrong column, do not be concerned. In the next section you will learn how to insert a column of data and then you can replace the column you deleted.

You could use the same procedure to delete the other columns, however, because they are adjacent to each other, you can save time by selecting them first and then deleting them as a group.

To do this,

Move to: column C

The Street Address field should be highlighted. To extend the highlight,

Press: (F8)

The fields to be deleted are Street Address, City, State, Zipcode, Sex, Department, and Title. To highlight these fields,

Press: (→) (6 times)

The highlight should extend from column C through column I. To remove these columns,

Select: **E**dit>**D**elete Row/Column>**C**olumn>(⏎)
Press: (HOME)

Your screen should be similar to Figure 11-25.

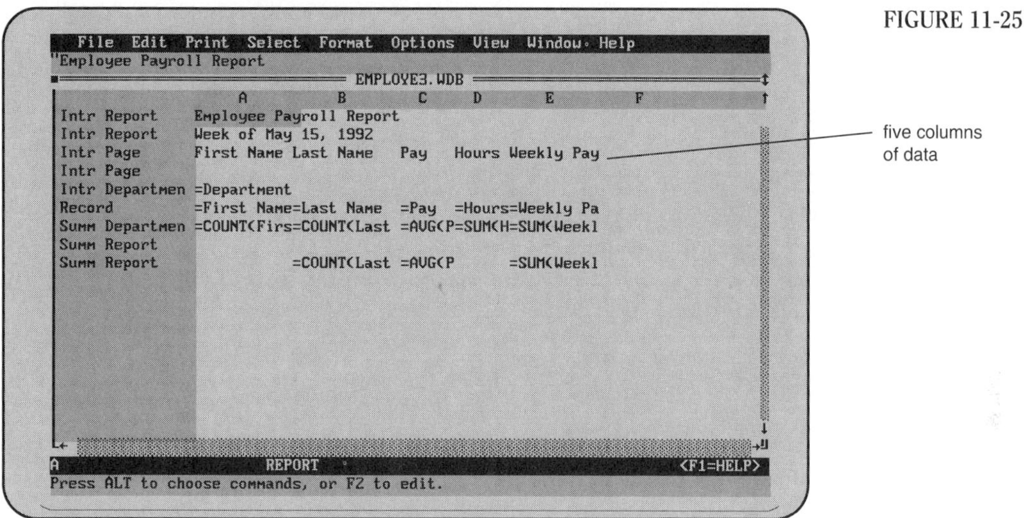

FIGURE 11-25

The Report Definition screen now displays five columns of data, First Name, Last Name, Pay, Hours, and Weekly Pay in columns A through E.

View the report.

Your screen should be similar to Figure 11-26.

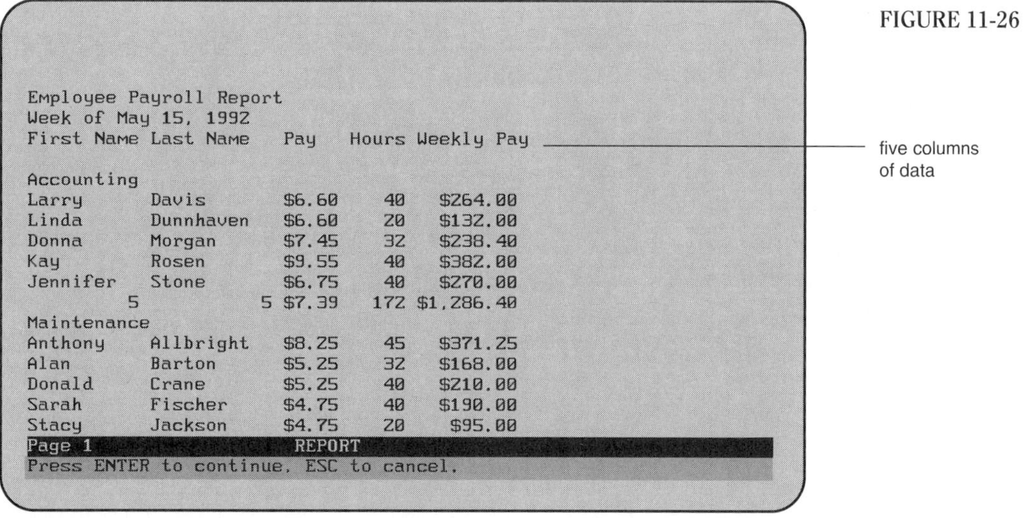

FIGURE 11-26

The report displays the five remaining columns of data.

Press: (ESC)

Inserting a Field of Data

Fred realizes he made a mistake. He deleted the column containing the Title field from the report. To add it back, he needs to create a blank column where it will be displayed and enter the column heading and the record definition for the field.

The Title field will be inserted as column C, between the Last Name and Pay fields.

Move to: column C
Select: **E**dit>**I**nsert Row/Column>**C**olumn>(↵)

A blank column is displayed in the report definition form. To enter the field name as the label for the column of data,

Move to: column C of the first Intr Page row

You could type the field name directly into the cell, or you can use the Edit menu to insert a selected field name. Generally, selecting the field name is easier.

Select: **E**dit>Insert Field **N**ame

A Fields dialog box is displayed. All the field names used in the database are displayed in the box. To select the Title field name,

Select: Title
Press: (↵)

The field name is displayed in the cell.

Next, to define the field contents,

Move to: column C of the Record row
Select: **E**dit>Insert Field C**o**ntents

The Fields dialog box is displayed again. To enter the Title field data for each record in this column,

Select: **T**itle>(↵)

Your screen should be similar to Figure 11-27.

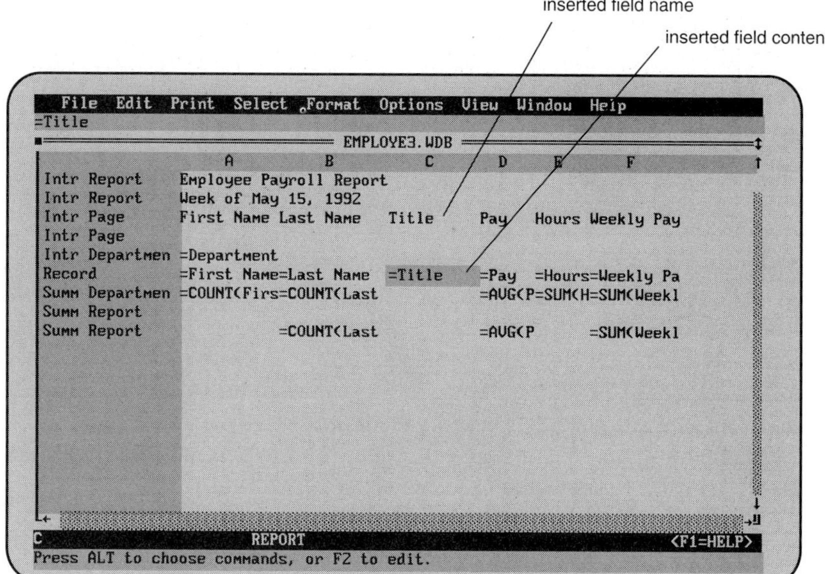

FIGURE 11-27

The Title field name is displayed as a formula (=Title). This formula tells Works to place the contents of the Title field in this column for each record into the report.

View the report.

Your screen should be similar to Figure 11-28.

inserted column of data

```
Employee Payroll Report
Week of May 15, 1992
First Name Last Name   Title       Pay  Hours Weekly Pay

Accounting
Larry      Davis       Clerk      $6.60   40   $264.00
Linda      Dunnhaven   Clerk      $6.60   20   $132.00
Donna      Morgan      Bookkeeper$7.45    32   $238.40
Kay        Rosen       Supervisor$9.55    40   $382.00
Jennifer   Stone       Clerk      $6.75   40   $270.00
         5           5            $7.39  172 $1,286.40
Maintenance
Anthony    Allbright   Supervisor$8.25    45   $371.25
Donald     Crane       Grounds    $5.25   40   $210.00
Sarah      Fischer     Grounds    $4.75   40   $190.00
Stacy      Jackson     Grounds    $4.75   20    $95.00
Cynthia    Olson       Grounds    $4.75   20    $95.00
Page 1                 REPORT
Press ENTER to continue, ESC to cancel.
```

FIGURE 11-28

The Title column of data has been added back into the report. While looking at the report, Fred decides the summary statistics for the First Name and Hours fields do not add any important information to the report. You will delete these statistics next.

Return to the Report Definition screen.

Deleting Field Contents

To delete the group formula that counts the number of entries in the First Name field of data,

Move to: column A of the Summ Department row
Press: DEL
Press: ↵

Delete the formula to calculate the hours (column E) in a similar way. View the report. The First Name and Hours fields no longer display group summary statistics.

Now that the report displays the required information, Fred wants to improve the report's appearance. He plans to add descriptive labels to identify the group and report statistics and format the Summ Report values to display as currency. He also wants to format the department headings so that they are printed in bold.

Finally, he wants to insert several blank lines to separate the information in the report, adjust column widths, and center the report title.

Return to the Report Definition screen.

Adding Descriptive Labels

Because you created the report and specified the formulas, you know what the calculated group and report values mean. However, someone else looking at the report would not know. Adding descriptive labels will help clarify the meaning of these values.

You will enter descriptive labels to the left side of the values. To enter a descriptive label for the group count formula,

Move to: column A of the Summ Department row
Type: **Total Dept:**
Press: ↵

To enter a label to identify the report count values,

Move to: column A of the second Summ Report row
Type: **Total Emp:**
Press: ↵

Your screen should be similar to Figure 11-29.

FIGURE 11-29

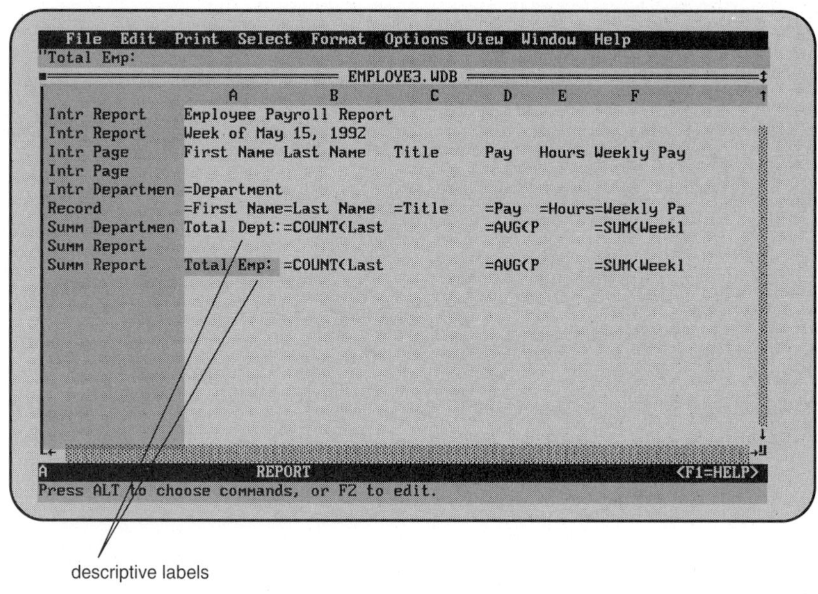

In the same way, enter the label "Average:" in column C for the Summ Dept and Summ Report Pay data and the label "Total:" in column E for the Summ Department and Summ Report Weekly Pay data.

To see how these changes have affected the report layout, view the report.

The descriptive labels for the group summary statistics are displayed. Fred does not like how the count value is so far to the right of the label. He will change this by aligning the value in the center of the cell space.

Press: ↵

The second half of page 1 of the report should be displayed. The report statistics and descriptive labels greatly improve the meaning of the report.

The addition of the labels, however, has made the report look very crowded. When you insert blank lines between categories, this will improve the readability of the report.

Return to the Report Definition screen.

Formatting the Report

First, Fred wants the Summ Report average and total values to be displayed as currency. To change the Pay group,

Move to: column D of the Summ Report row
Select: Forma**t**>C**u**rrency>**2**>↵

Move to column F and change the Weekly Pay summary value to display as Currency with two decimal places.

Fred also wants to change the alignment of the group and report count value to centered.

To change the group count first,

Move to: column B of the Summ Department row
Select: Format>**S**tyle>**C**enter>(↵)

Make the same change for the report count value in column B of the second summary report row.

The last format change Fred wants to make is to have the department group heading printed in bold. To format the heading,

Move to: column A of the Intr Department row
Select: Forma**t**>**S**tyle>**B**old>(↵)

View the report. Your screen should be similar to Figure 11-30.

FIGURE 11-30

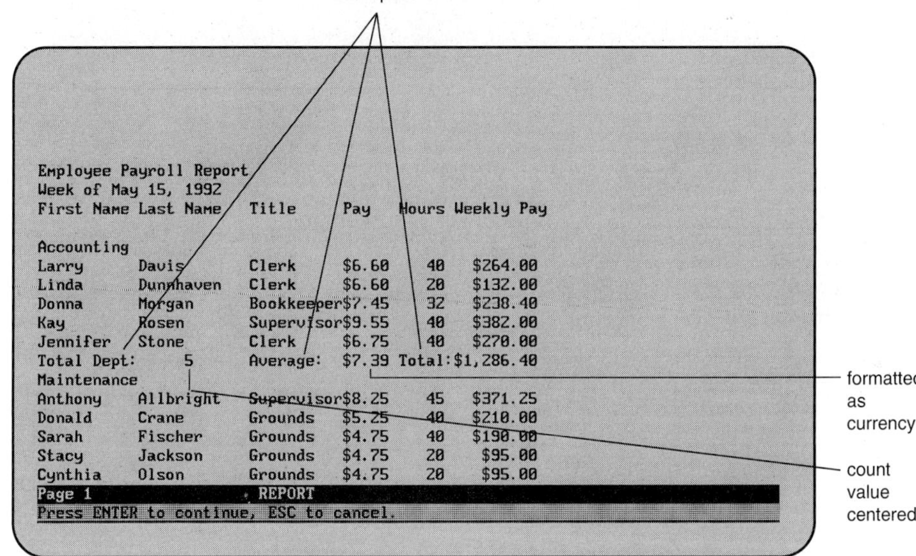

The count value is centered in the cell space and the summary statistics are displayed as currency. When the report is printed, the department headings will be bold.

Press: (↵)

The report looks very crowded and would benefit from the addition of blank space between categories of data.

Return to the Report Definition screen.

Inserting Blank Lines

First, Fred wants to separate the report title from the column heading with a blank line. To insert an additional row below the second title line,

Move to: the first Intr Page row
Select: **E**dit>**I**nsert Row/Column>**R**ow>(↵)

In the Type dialog box, you need to specify the type of row you want to insert. By default, Works highlights the type of row that the highlight is positioned on. However, you want to insert another Introductory Report row at this location.

Highlight: Intr Report
Press: ↵

Your display should be similar to Figure 11-31.

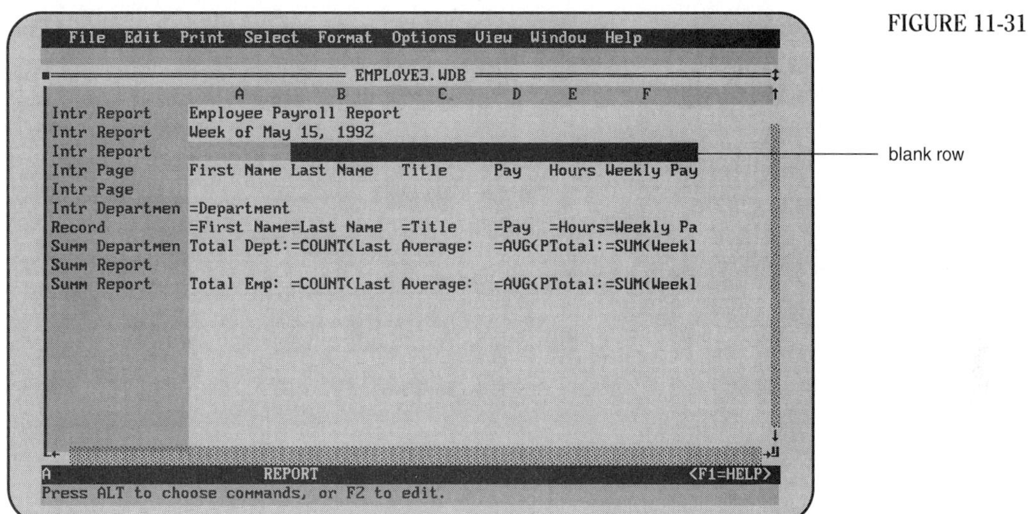

FIGURE 11-31

A blank row has been entered in the Report Definition screen. Leaving the contents of this row blank will insert a blank row between the report title and the column headings.

To add space between the groups of data, you will add several more blank lines in the report. First, to insert a blank introductory department row between the group title and the first record of each group,

Move to: the Record row
Select: **E**dit>**I**nsert Row/Column>**R**ow>Intr Department>↵

Next, to insert a blank row between the last record of each group and the group total,

Move to: the Record row
Select: **E**dit>**I**nsert Row/Column>**R**ow>Summ Department>↵

Then, to add another blank row to separate the group summary statistics from the group heading immediately below it,

Move to: the first Summ Report row
Select: **E**dit>**I**nsert Row/Column>**R**ow>Summ Department>↵

Your screen should be similar to Figure 11-32.

FIGURE 11-32

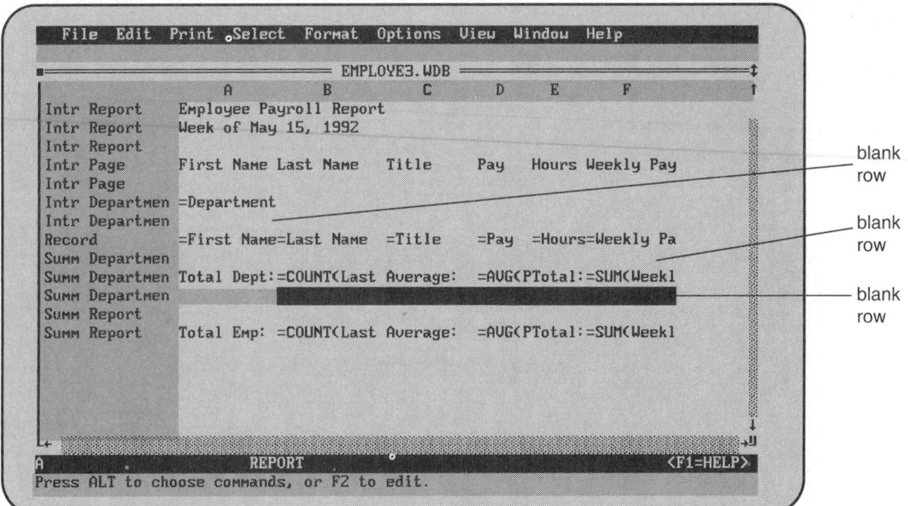

View the report. Your screen should be similar to Figure 11-33.

FIGURE 11-33

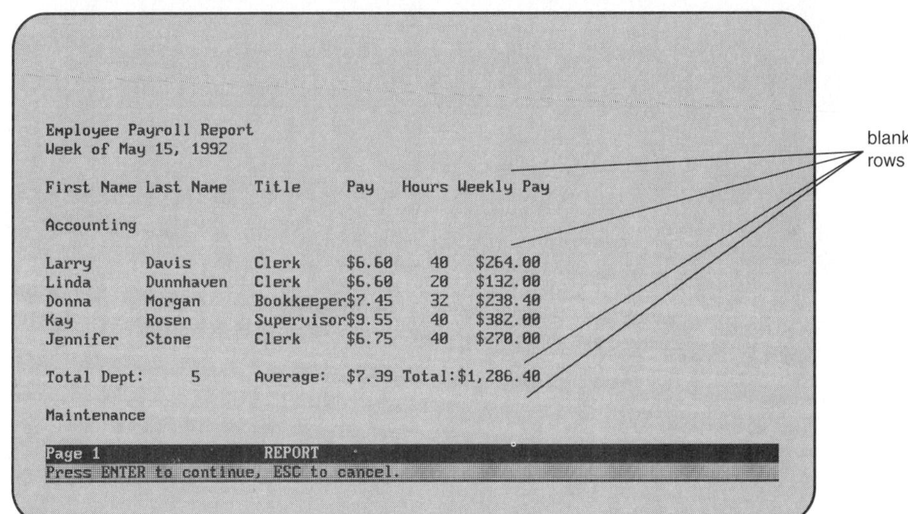

The blank lines separating the different categories make reading the report much easier. Fred notices that the spacing between the Title and Pay columns looks crowded, however. He would like to increase the column widths to improve the report's appearance.

After viewing the entire report, return to the Report Definition screen.

Increasing Column Widths

Next, you will increase the width of the columns of data so that there is more space between the columns and the report is balanced on the page better. The procedure is the same as changing the column width in FORM or LIST view. To increase the width of the First and Last Name fields at the same time to the same size,

Press: F8
Select: columns A and B
Select: Format>Column Width
Type: **12**
Press: ↵

Next, change the column widths of the following fields:

Title	12 spaces
Pay	7 spaces
Hours	7 spaces
Weekly Pay	10 spaces

Changing the column width in REPORT view does not change the widths you set in FORM and LIST view.

View the report. Your screen should be similar to Figure 11-34.

```
Employee Payroll Report
Week of May 15, 1992

First Name  Last Name   Title         Pay    Hours  Weekly Pay

Accounting

Larry       Davis       Clerk         $6.60     40    $264.00
Linda       Dunnhaven   Clerk         $6.60     20    $132.00
Donna       Morgan      Bookkeeper    $7.45     32    $238.40
Kay         Rosen       Supervisor    $9.55     40    $382.00
Jennifer    Stone       Clerk         $6.75     40    $270.00

Total Dept:        5    Average:      $7.39 Total: $1,286.40

Maintenance

Page 1                  REPORT
Press ENTER to continue, ESC to cancel.
```

FIGURE 11-34

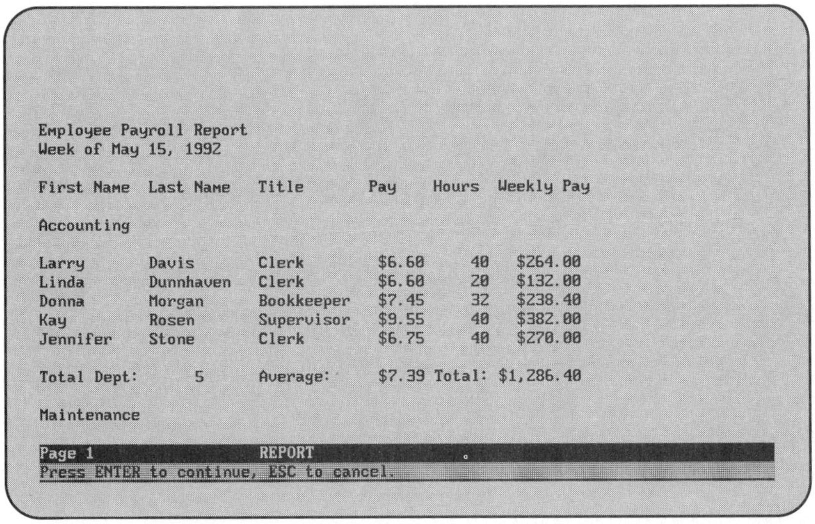

This change makes the report occupy the entire width of the page and increases the readability of the data by adding more white space between the columns of data. The report title, however, should be centered over the columns of data.

Return to the Report Definition screen.

Centering the Report Title

Fred wants the two title lines centered over the five columns of data. To do this, you can move each row individually using Edit>Move, or you can move both lines at the same time by selecting the two lines first. To move the two title lines so that they begin in column B,

Press: (F8)
Select: column A of the first and second Intr Report row
Select: **E**dit>**M**ove

Move to: column B in the first Intr Report row
Press: (↵)

The two titles are displayed in column B. However, this still is not very centered over the report columns. If you moved the title to column C, it would be off-centered to the right. To help center the title, you will add blank spaces preceding the title label in each row of the title. To do this,

Move to: column B of the first Intr Report row
Press: (F2)
Press: (HOME)
Press: (→)

To enter six blank spaces in front of the title,

Press: Space bar (6 times)
Press: (↵)

In the same way, enter eight blank spaces in front of the second title line.

Your screen should be similar to Figure 11-35.

FIGURE 11-35

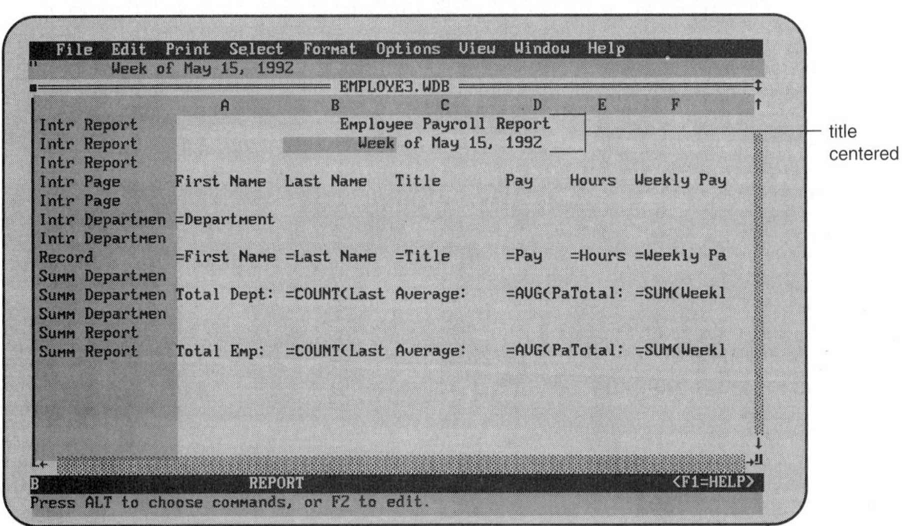

Now the report title is more evenly centered over the report columns.

Finally, Fred wants to add a single dashed line above each group total and average values and a double dashed line above the report total and average values.

To add a single dashed line six characters wide above the Department total formula,

Move to: column B of the first Summ Department row
Type: "------

Note: Do not forget to begin this entry with quotes (") to define it as a label entry.

Press: ↵

In the same row, enter a single dashed line six characters wide above the average pay formula (column D) and a single dashed line nine characters wide above the weekly total formula (column F).

To enter a double dashed line seven characters wide above the total employee formula for the report,

Move to: column B of the first Summ Report row
Type: "=======
Press: ↵

In the same row, enter a double dashed line seven characters wide above the average pay report formula (column D) and a double dashed line nine characters wide above the weekly total report formula (column F).

View the report. Your screen should be similar to Figure 11-36.

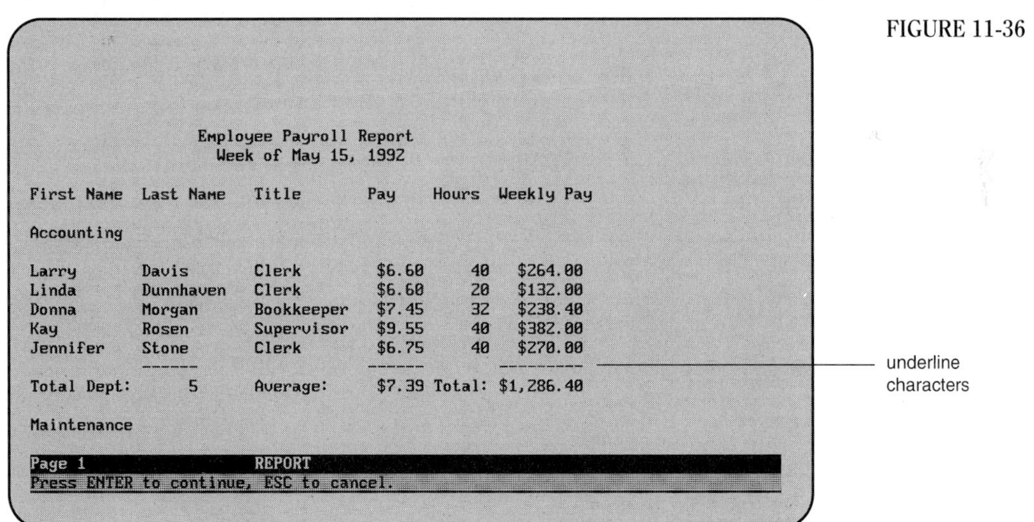

FIGURE 11-36

The first page of the report shows the title centered over the columns of data and the single dashed lines under each column containing group summary statistics.

To view the bottom of the report,

Press: ↵ (2 times)

The double dashed lines are displayed below each column containing report summary statistics. Fred is pleased with how the report looks now and is ready to print a copy of it for the accounting department.

Return to the Report Definition screen.

Before printing the report, change the second title line to "By [Your Name]". Center it below the first title line.

Printing the Report

If you have printer capability, to print a copy of the Weekly Employee Report,

Select: **P**rint>**P**rint>(↵)

Your printed output should be similar to Figure 11-1, at the beginning of the lab.

To return to LIST view from REPORT view, you can select View>List or you can use the shortcut key (F10).

Select: **V**iew>**L**ist

➳ (F10)

Notice that the records are no longer in alphabetical order by last name. This is because when you sorted the report by department, the database was sorted in the same order. To see this,

Move to: the Department field

This is probably not how you want the database records to appear when the file is opened. To restore the original sort order of the database,

Select: **S**elect>S**o**rt Records

The first and second sort fields are the same as they were when you first sorted the database. The report sort settings do not affect the database sort settings. To execute the sort,

Press: (↵)
Press: (CTRL) - (HOME)

The records are resorted back in their original alphabetical order. The report sort order settings are not affected.

Save the file as REPORT.

Exit Works or close the file if you are continuing to use Works.

Key Terms

report
Report Definition screen
row types
Introductory Report rows
Introductory Page rows
Record rows
Summary Report rows

Matching

1. Intr Page	_____	**a.**	the default report column width
2. =AVG(Pay)	_____	**b.**	displays summary statistics for each column of data
3. 10 spaces	_____	**c.**	deletes a row or column
4. (F2)	_____	**d.**	calculates the average of the Pay field
5. (ESC)	_____	**e.**	information that appears at the top of every page of the report
6. Summ Report	_____	**f.**	information that appears at the top of the first page of the report only
7. (F10)	_____	**g.**	EDIT
8. ####	_____	**h.**	returns directly to the Report Definition screen
9. Edit>Delete Row/Column	_____	**i.**	indicates column too narrow to display value
10. Intr Report	_____	**j.**	returns to LIST view

Practice Exercises

1. To complete this problem, you must first have completed problem 1 in Lab 10. Open the database file TILES3. Using the data in this file you will create a report.

Susannah wants to create a report that will display the last names, phone numbers, unit cost, quantity, and amount owed for the clients in her database. She wants the report grouped by the unit cost of the order. The report will have the following basic format:

REPORT TITLE
[Your Name]

LAST NAME	PHONE	UNIT COST	QUANTITY	AMT. OWED
Unit Cost of:	$X.XX			
Data row	_____	_____	_____	$________
Data row	_____	_____	_____	$________
Data row	_____	_____	_____	$________
Number:	X	Total:	XXXX	$X,XXX.XX
Unit Cost of:	$X.XX			
Data row	_____	_____	_____	$________
Data row	_____	_____	_____	$________
Data row	_____	_____	_____	$________
Number:	X	Total:	XXX	$X,XXX.XX
			=====	========
		TOTAL:	XXXX	$XX,XXX.XX

View the present report definition form. Follow the instructions below to modify the report definition form. As you modify the report, view it whenever necessary.

- In column A, enter the title "TILE ORDERS" on the first Intr Report row and your name in the second Intr Report row.
- Rename the report ORDERS.
- In the second Summ Report row, enter formulas to sum the Quantity and Amount Owed columns only.
- Group the report by Unit Cost with a blank line between groups.
- Add an introductory group row that will display the unit cost for each group of data in column B. Format this cell as Currency with two decimal places. In column A, enter the descriptive label "Unit Cost of:" to describe each group. Right align the entry. Bold the entire group heading (columns A and B).
- Delete all columns of data except Last Name, Phone, Unit Cost, Quantity, and Amt. Owed.
- Delete the formulas that sum the Last Name and Unit Cost groups.
- Enter a blank row to separate the report title from the column headings.
- Enter a blank row above and below the group heading.
- Enter the following labels to describe the group summary statistics:

Label	Location	Format
Number:	column A	Right-aligned
Total:	column C	Right-aligned

- Center-align the count value in the group summary row (column B). Center-align the unit cost column of data. Right-align the Amt. Owed column heading.
- Enter the label "TOTAL:" in column C to describe the report summary statistics. Right-align the label. Format the Amt. Owed report summary value as Currency with two decimal places. Center the Quantity report summary value.
- Increase the column widths for Last Name to 15, Unit Cost and Quantity to 12, and Amt. Owed to 14.
- Center the two report title lines over the five columns of data.
- Enter five double-underline characters (=====) above the Quantity summary report value. Center the entry. Enter 10 double-underline characters above the Amt. Owed summary report value. Right-align the entry.
- Print the report.
- Save the file as TILEREPT.

2. To complete this problem you must have completed problem 2 in Lab 10. Using the data in GRADES2, you will create and print a report showing the course title, hours, and semester grouped on the grade earned.

The report will have the following basic format:

```
                    REPORT TITLE
                    [Your Name]

          TITLE         SEMESTER        HOURS

Grade of: X

          __________    .....           .....
          __________    .....           .....
          __________    .....           .....
  Number: X                         Total: XX

Grade of: X

          __________    .....           .....
          __________    .....           .....
          __________    .....           .....
          ===                            ====
  NUMBER: X                         TOTAL: XX
```

View the present report definition form. Follow the instructions below to modify the report definition form. As you modify the report, view it whenever necessary.

- In column B, enter title "Courses and Grades Earned" on the first Intr Report row and your name in the second Intr Report row.
- Rename the report COURSES.
- In the second Summ Report row, enter formulas to count the entries in the Titles fields and sum the data in the Hours field.
- Group the report by grade with a blank line between groups.
- Delete the COURSE # and GRADE columns of data.
- Delete the semester group summary value.
- Insert a blank column at column A and column C (in that order).
- Add an introductory group row that will display the grade for each group of data in column B. In column A, enter the descriptive label "Grade of:" to describe each group. Bold the entire group heading (columns A and B).
- Enter a blank row to separate the report title from the column headings.
- Enter a blank row above and below the group heading.
- Enter the following labels to describe the group summary statistics:

Label	Location	Format
Number:	column A	Right-aligned
Total:	column D	Right-aligned

- Left-align the count value in the group summary row (column B).

- Center the HOURS column of data.
- Enter the following labels to describe the report summary statistics:

Label	Location	Format
NUMBER:	Column A	Right-aligned
TOTAL:	Column D	Right-aligned

- Left-align the count value in the summary report row (column B).
- Center the two report title lines over the columns of data.
- Enter three double-underline characters (===) above the Title count summary report value and four double-underline characters above the Hours total value.
- Print the report.
- Save the file as GRADERPT.

3. To complete this problem, you must first have completed problem 3 in Lab 10. Open the database file STAFF2. Using the data in this file you will create a report.

Bob wants to create a report that will display the employees' last name, title, sex, and pay, grouped by department. The report will have the following basic format:

```
                    REPORT TITLE
                    [Your Name]

Last Name      Title            Sex        Pay


 Department:  XXX

Data row   _____________       ____      $ _____
Data row   _____________       ____      $ _____
Data row   _____________       ____      $ _____

    Number:  X             Average:      $X.XX

 Department:  XXX

_______    _____________       ____      $ _____
_______    _____________       ____      $ _____
_______    _____________       ____      $ _____

    Number:  XX            Average:        $X.XX
             ====                        ======
  NUMBER:    XX            AVERAGE:        $X.XX
```

View the preset report definition form. Follow the instructions below to modify the report definition form. As you modify the report, view it whenever necessary.

- In column B, enter the title "PAY RATE BY DEPARTMENT" on the first Intr Report row and your name in the second Intr Report row.

- Rename the report PAYRATE.
- In the second Summ Report row, enter formulas to average the Pay column and count the Title column only.
- Group the report by Department (ascending with break) as the first sort field, Sex (ascending with break) as the second sort field, and Last Name (ascending, no break) as the third sort field.
- Delete all columns of data except those Bob wants displayed in the report.
- Add an introductory group row that will display the department for each group of data in column B. In column A, enter and right-align the descriptive label "Department:" to describe each group. Bold the entire group heading (columns A and B).
- Delete all formulas in the Summ Sex group row. Delete the group formulas that count the Last Name and Sex groups. Change the Pay statistic for the department group to an average.
- Move the Sex column of data after the Title column.
- Change the column widths for Last Name to 15, Title to 20, and Sex and Pay to 8.
- Enter the following labels to describe the Department group summary statistics:

Label	**Location**	**Format**
Number:	column A	Right-aligned
Average:	column C	Right-aligned

- Enter a blank row to separate the report title from the column headings.
- Enter a blank row above and below the group heading.
- Left-align the Title count value in the Department group summary row and Report summary row (column B).
- Right-align the Pay column heading. Format the Pay column and Average Pay values (both department and report) as Currency with two decimal places.
- Center-align the Sex column of data and column heading.
- Enter the label "NUMBER:" in column A and "AVERAGE:" in column C to describe the report summary statistics. Right-align the labels.
- Center the two report title lines over the four columns of data.
- Enter four double-underline characters (====) above the count summary report value. Left-align the characters. Enter eight double-underline characters above the average Pay summary report value.
- View the report. Bob notices an error in the data for one of the employees. Change the first name of Robert Shields to Roberta and the Sex to F. View the report.
- Add a footer to the report that will print the page number as "Page - #". Use Help for information about this feature. Print the report.
- Save the file as STAFFRPT.

4. To complete this problem, you must first have completed problem 4 in Lab 10. Open the database file STOCK3. Using the data in this file you will create a report.

Aquanetta wants to create a report that will display the Description, Quantity, Price, and Inv. Value for the items in her database. She wants the report grouped by the vendor.

The report will have the following basic format:

```
                              REPORT TITLE
                              [Your Name]

Description       Price          Quantity          Inv. Value

     Vendor:__________

Data row______  ________            __            $________
Data row______  ________            __            $________
Data row______  ________            __            $________
                               Total:   XX         $X,XXX.XX

     Vendor:      XXXXX

______________  ________            __            $________
______________  ________            __            $________
______________  ________            __            $________
                               Total:   XX         $X,XXX.XX
                                      ====         ========

                             TOTAL:  XXX           $X,XXX.XX
```

View the preset report definition form. Follow the instructions below to modify the report definition form. As you modify the report, view it whenever necessary.

- In column B, enter the title "INVENTORY VALUATION REPORT" on the first Intr Report row and your name in the second Intr Report row.
- Rename the report VALUE.
- In the second Summ Report row enter formulas to sum the Quantity and Inv. Value columns only.
- Group the report by Vendor (ascending with break) as the first sort field, and Description (ascending, no break) as the second sort field.
- Delete all unnecessary columns of data. Move the Price column of data after the Description column.
- Delete the group formulas for the Description and Price groups.
- Add an introductory group row that will display the vendor's name for each group of data in column B. In column A, enter the descriptive label "Vendor:" to describe each group. Right-align the label. Bold the entire group heading (columns A and B).
- Enter a blank row to separate the report title from the column headings.
- Enter a blank row above and below the group heading.

- Enter the label "Total:" to describe the group summary statistics in column B. Right-align the label. Enter the label "TOTAL:" in column B to describe the report summary statistics. Right-align the label.
- Change the column widths for Description to 23, Quantity to 13, and Inv. Value to 14.
- Right-align the Price, Quantity, and Inv. Value column headings. Center-align the Quantity column of data and group and report summary values.
- Format the Inv. Value report column and group and summary values as Currency with two decimal places.
- Center the two report title lines over the four columns of data.
- Enter four double-underline characters (====) above the Quantity summary report value. Center the characters. Enter 10 double-underline characters above the Inv. Value summary report value. Right-align the characters.
- Print the report.
- Save the file as STOCKRPT.

Command Summary

Command	Shortcut	Action	Page
Edit>**M**ove		Moves cell contents to new location	358
Edit>**D**elete Row/Column		Removes report rows or columns	348
Edit>**I**nsert Row/Column		Adds new report rows or columns	345
Edit>Insert Field **N**ame		Adds report column head	350
Edit>Insert Field C**o**ntents		Adds report column data	350
Edit>Insert Field **S**ummary		Adds summary report values	337
Select>S**o**rt Records		Creates report categories	341
Forma**t**>C**u**rrency		Displays values as currency	353
Forma**t**>**S**tyle>**B**old		Boldfaces text	354
Forma**t**>**S**tyle>**C**enter		Centers text	354
Forma**t**>Column **W**idth		Adjusts report column widths	357
View>**L**ist	F10	Returns to LIST view	360
View>**N**ew Report		Displays new report	329
View>**R**eports>Name>**name**>**R**ename		Renames report settings	335

LAB

Integrating Works 12

Objectives

In this lab you will learn how to:

1. Insert a spreadsheet and chart into a word processing document.
2. Create a form letter.

CASE STUDY

Fred Morris, the membership coordinator of the Sports Club, continues to prepare for the board of directors meeting on membership growth. Using Works, he has prepared a spreadsheet of the club's growth for the years 1988 through 1992. He has also created several charts of this data. Now he would like to use Works to create a memo to the board about this information. You will follow Fred as he creates a memo using the Works word processing tool and inserts the spreadsheet and chart information from the spreadsheet tool into the memo.

As a second project, Karen Barnes, the membership assistant, submitted the final copy of the welcome letter to the membership coordinator. The membership coordinator is very pleased with the content and form of the welcome letter. However, he would like it to be more personalized. He wants to include the first name of the new member and an inside address. Karen will create a form letter using Works to personalize each welcome letter.

Creating the Word Processor File

First, Fred needs to create a memo to the board of directors. The memo is created using the word processing tool. The spreadsheet and chart are then copied into the word processing document. The completed document will look like Figure 12-1.

```
TO: Board of Directors
FROM: Fred Morris, Membership Coordinator
RE: Sports Club Membership Growth

Over the past five years, the Sports Club has shown steady
growth in all membership categories. The statistics for the
years 1988 through 1992 are shown below.
```

Sports Club Membership
1988 - 1992

	1988	1989	1990	1991	1992
Family	840	930	1274	1380	1442
Individual	615	779	1089	1488	1635
Youth	250	408	535	628	675
Retired	114	168	232	250	398
	=====	=====	=====	=====	=====
Total	1819	2285	3130	3746	4150

```
The growth pattern is even more clearly visible when it is
displayed as a chart. The chart below shows the growth in
the four membership categories for the five years.
```

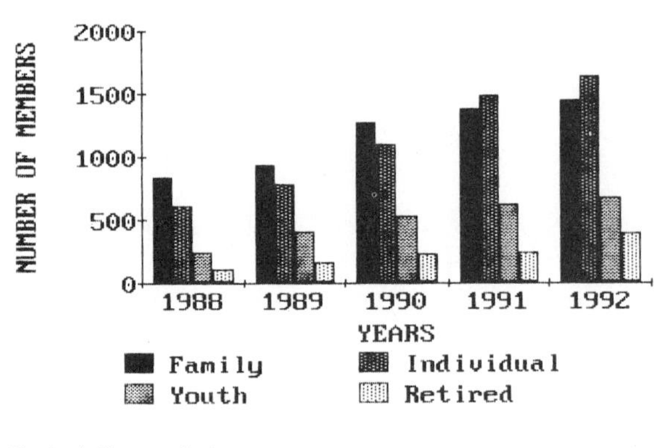

Student Name - Date

FIGURE 12-1

Load Works. Select the commands to create a new word processor file.

A blank word processing screen should be on your display screen. To create the text for the memo,

Type: **TO: Board of Directors**
FROM: Fred Morris, Membership Coordinator
RE: Sports Club Membership Growth

Over the past five years, the Sports Club has shown steady growth in all membership categories. The statistics for the years 1988 through 1992 are shown below.

To create two blank lines,

Press: ↵ (2 times)

Fred will enter the data from the spreadsheet CHARTS.WKS in the memo below this paragraph. The second paragraph of the memo can be entered next. Below this paragraph, Fred will display a chart of the membership growth.

Type: **The growth pattern is even more clearly visible when it is displayed as a chart. The chart below shows the growth in the four membership categories for the five years.**

Press: 

After editing any errors, save the memo as BOARD. Remember to select the appropriate directory first.

Your screen should be similar to Figure 12-2.

FIGURE 12-2

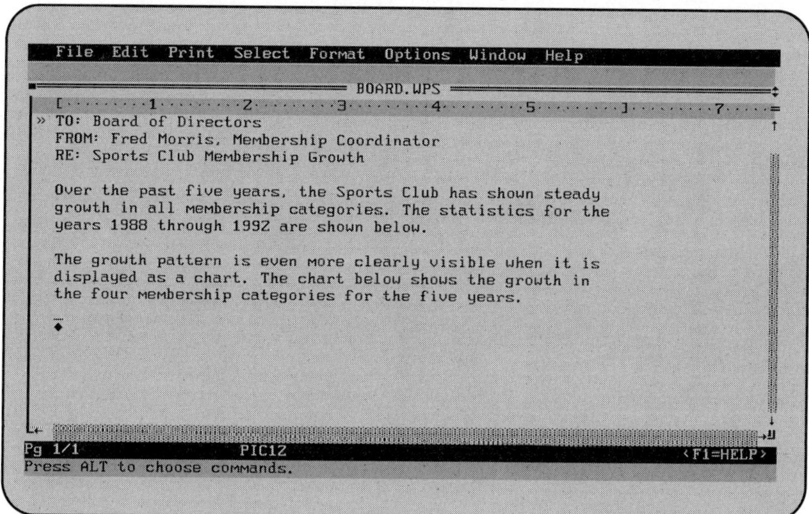

Now you are ready to copy the spreadsheet and chart into the memo. The spreadsheet file you will use is CHARTS. This is the file you created at the end of Lab 8.

Open the spreadsheet file CHARTS.

There are now two open files, BOARD and CHARTS. CHARTS is displayed in the active window. BOARD is open, but not displayed. It is hidden behind the CHARTS window.

The highlight should be in cell A1. If it is not, move it there.

To see both files at the same time,

Select: **W**indow>**A**rrange All

Your screen should be similar to Figure 12-3.

FIGURE 12-3

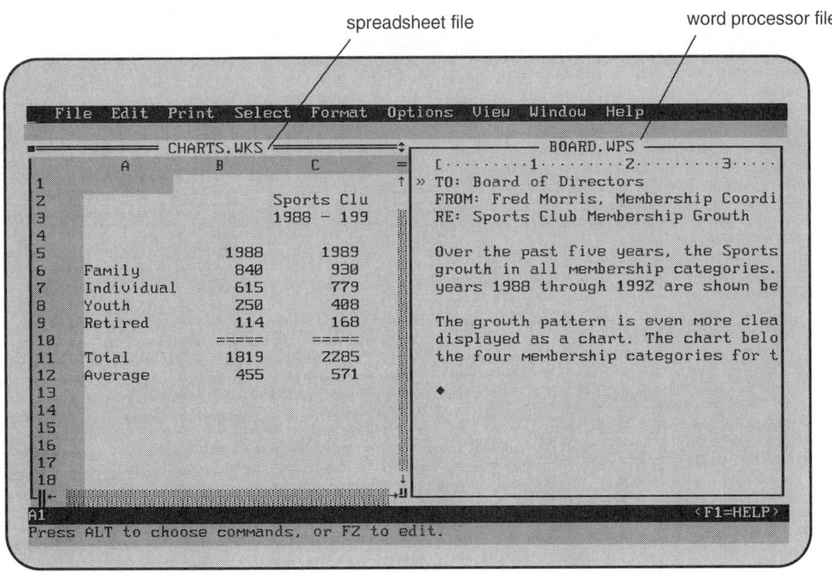

The two files are displayed side by side on the screen. CHARTS is the active window.

Copying a Spreadsheet into a Word Processor File

Fred wants to copy the spreadsheet data into the memo. However, he does not want to include the Average data in row 12. To select the range of cells to copy,

Press: F8

Mouse Note: Remember, you can drag on the cells to select the range.

Highlight cells A1 through F11.

The Edit>Copy command is used to copy data between tools, just as it is used to copy within tools.

Select: Edit>Copy

Now you need to specify the new location where you want the copied information displayed. You want it copied into the word processor file, BOARD. To switch to the BOARD file and make it the active window,

Press: CTRL - F6

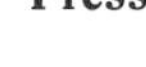

Mouse Note: Remember, you can click on the window to make it active.

Fred wants the spreadsheet data displayed below the first paragraph. Move to the blank line below the first paragraph of the memo.

To complete the command and copy the spreadsheet into the word processor file,

Press: 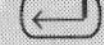

Your screen should be similar to Figure 12-4.

FIGURE 12-4

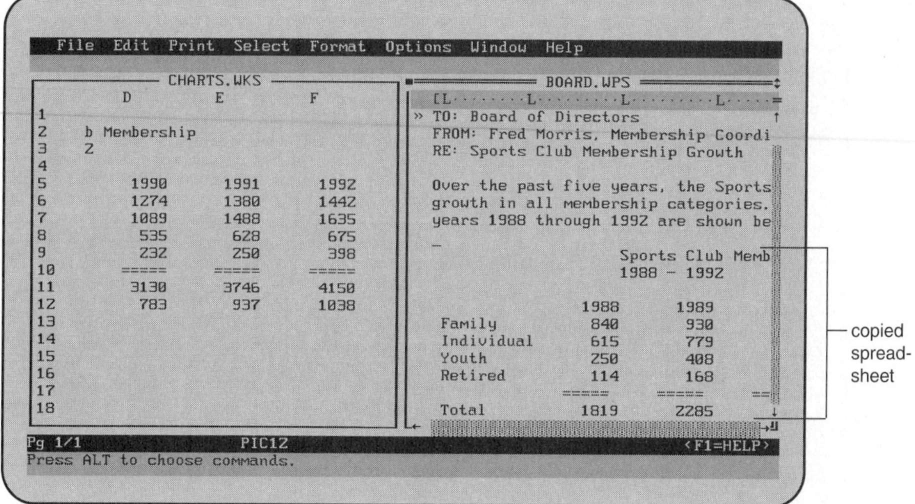

The spreadsheet data has been copied into the word processor file. To enlarge the screen to fully display the memo,

Select: Window>Maximize

Mouse Note: Remember, you can click on the double-headed arrow to enlarge the active window.

Editing the Spreadsheet

Many times, the information you copy into a word processor file from a spreadsheet or database file will not display correctly. This is because data in a spreadsheet or database is stored in rows and columns. When this information is copied into a word processor file, Works inserts a tab marker between each column. This problem has occurred in only one area in the spreadsheet you copied. The double-dashed line above the total values is not aligned correctly in the column.

Move to the left margin of the line containing the double-underline characters.

To see how Works has converted the spreadsheet format to word processor format,

Select: Options>Show All Characters

Your screen should be similar to Figure 12-5.

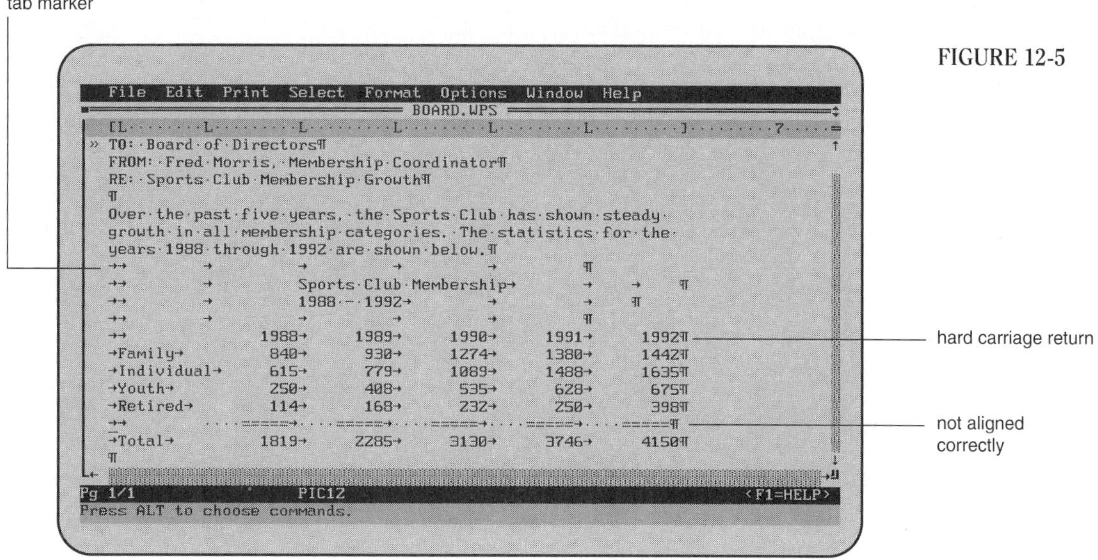

FIGURE 12-5

Each column of data from the spreadsheet is preserved as a column in the word processor file by the insertion of a tab marker (→). Each row of the spreadsheet ends with a hard carriage return symbol (¶) to signify the end of a paragraph.

To correctly align the double underline for the first column of data,

Press: (→) (2 times)
Press: Space bar

Your screen should be similar to Figure 12-6.

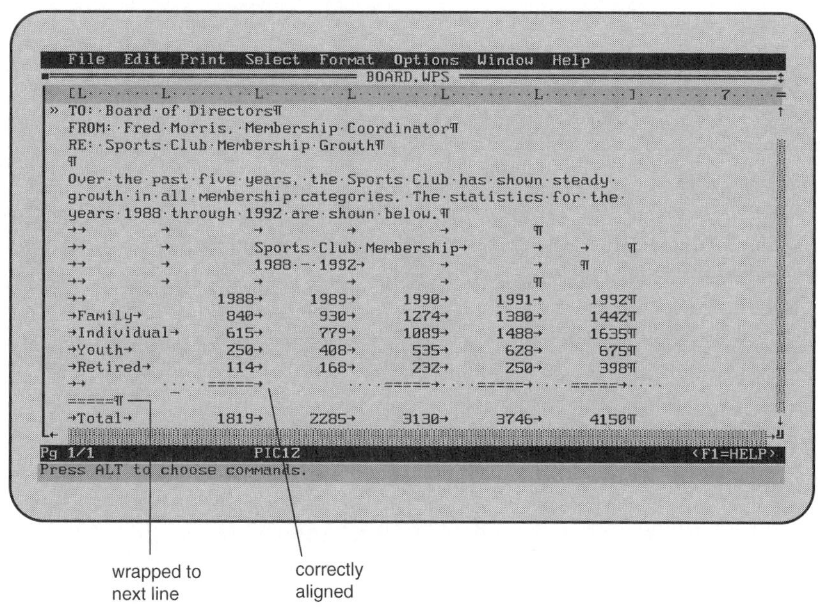

FIGURE 12-6

The double underline is aligned correctly under the first column of data. However, the one extra space you entered forced the other column underlines to the right and word-wrapped the line to the next line.

To correct this, you will need to delete a tab marker and enter a space in its place for each column.

Press: (CTRL)-(→) (2 times)

The cursor should be positioned under the tab marker. To delete it,

Press: (DEL)

To enter a blank space,

Press: Space bar

The double underline in the second column should be aligned correctly.

Repeat this process for the remaining three columns of data. When you are done, your screen should be similar to Figure 12-7.

FIGURE 12-7

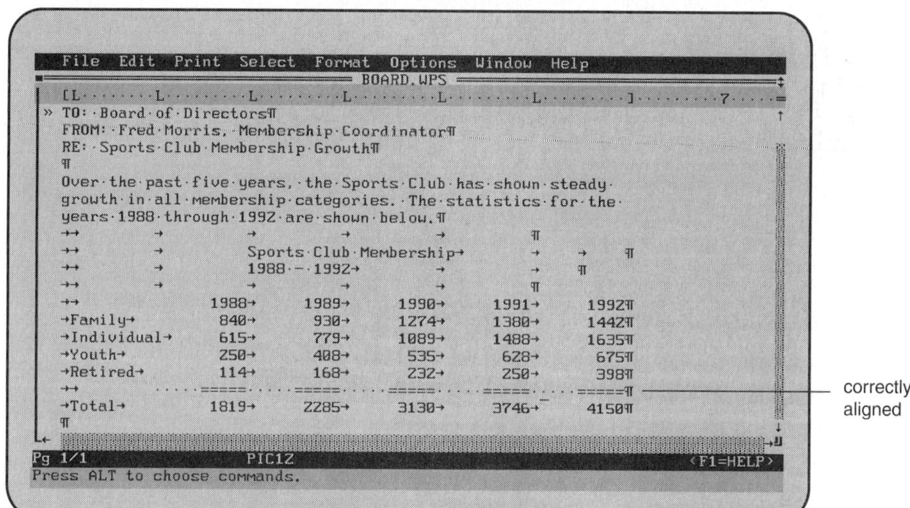

This was a fairly simple problem to fix. However, many times a spreadsheet is too wide to fit the width of the page, and the rows wrap to the next line. You may be able to decrease the margin width to increase the number of characters that can be printed on a page. If the spreadsheet is very wide, however, you may need to transfer the data in multiple segments. It is not always easy to correct the format of a spreadsheet or database file that is copied into a word processor file. A lot of editing may be required. Once a spreadsheet is copied into a word processor file, it can be edited just like normal text.

Turn off the all character display.

To further improve the appearance of the memo, Fred wants to center the heading "1988–1992" in the second spreadsheet title below the first title line and add more blank space between the text of the memo and the spreadsheet.

To center the second spreadsheet title line, move to the 1 in 1988 and enter six spaces.

Next, to add more blank space around the spreadsheet you will enter a second blank line above the spreadsheet title and two blank lines below the Total row of data. Move to the appropriate location in the file and enter another blank line above the spreadsheet title and two extra blank lines below the Total row of data.

Finally, Fred wants to enter a blank line between the column heads containing the years and the first row of data. Move to the appropriate location and enter a blank line.

Your screen should be similar to Figure 12-8.

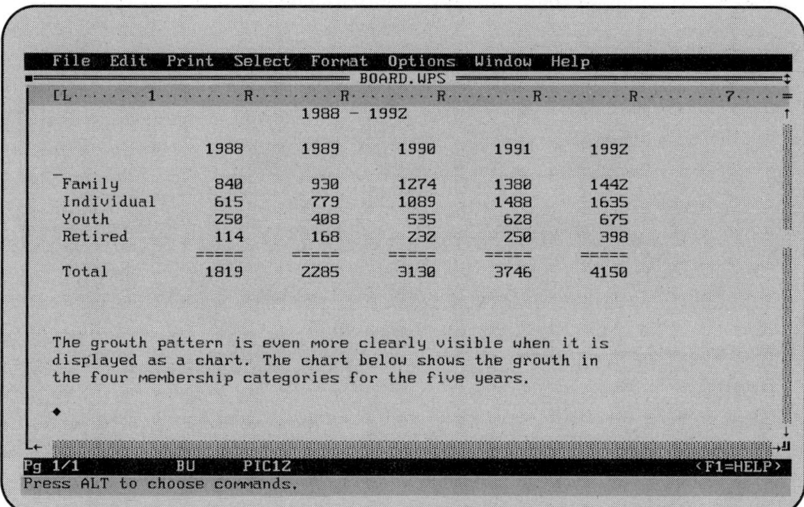

FIGURE 12-8

Inserting a Chart into a Word Processor File

Now Fred is ready to copy the bar chart of the spreadsheet data into the memo. He wants it displayed below the second paragraph. Move to the blank line below the second paragraph.

The procedure for copying the chart into the word processor file is different from copying the spreadsheet data. When copying a chart, Works inserts a **placeholder** for the spreadsheet chart at the location you specify in the word processor file. The chart placeholder consists of the spreadsheet filename followed by the chart name. The placeholder directs Works to access the spreadsheet and copy the chart named in the placeholder into the word processor file.

To insert the placeholder,

Select: **E**dit>**I**nsert Chart

A dialog box is displayed. The Spreadsheets box lists the spreadsheet files you can select. The only spreadsheet file displayed is CHARTS because it is the only open spreadsheet file. The spreadsheet file must be open in order to insert a chart into a word processor file.

To select the spreadsheet file, CHARTS,

Press: ↓

The filename is highlighted and the associated charts are displayed in the Charts box. The chart you want to copy into the memo is BAR. Select the chart named BAR. Your screen should be similar to Figure 12-9.

FIGURE 12-9

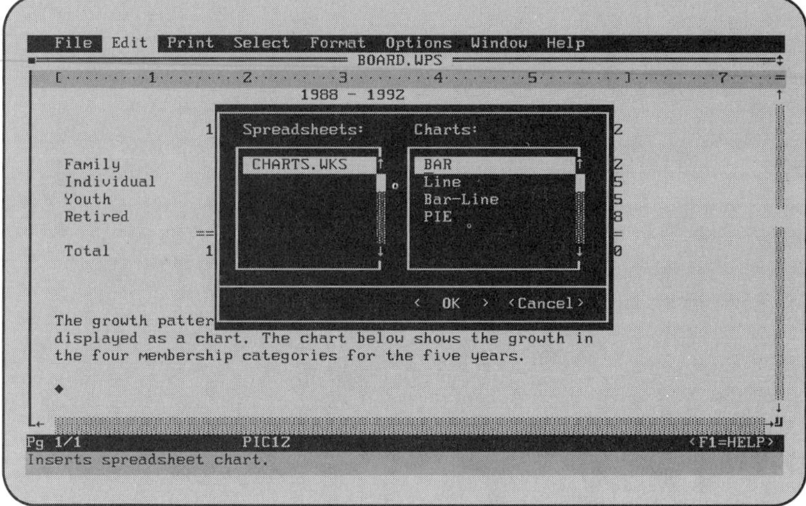

The chart name BAR should be highlighted. To complete the command,

Press: ↵

To view the placeholder,

Press: ↑ (2 times)

Your screen should be similar to Figure 12-10.

FIGURE 12-10

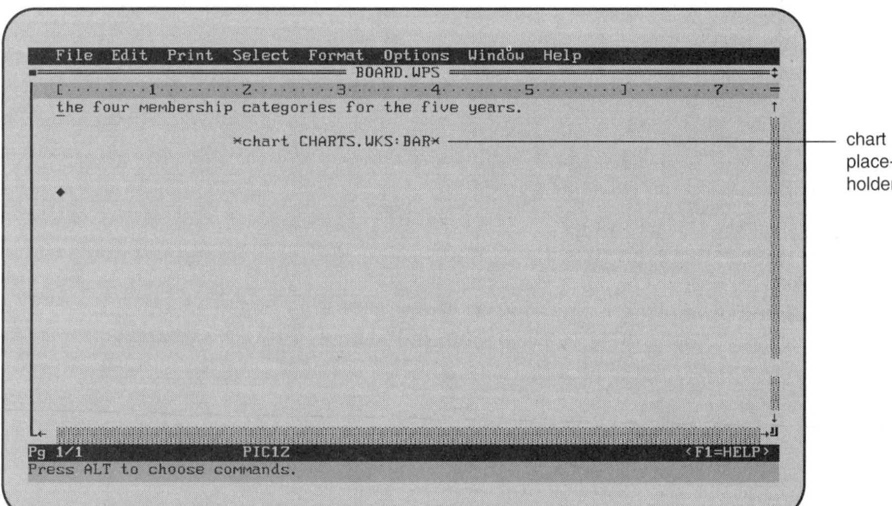

The placeholder "*chart CHARTS.WKS:BAR*" is displayed in the word processor file. When the file is printed, the chart will print in the location specified by the placeholder.

Once a placeholder is entered into a file, you can move or copy it to another location in the file. To do this, first select the placeholder and then use the command to move or copy it to a new location. You can also delete a placeholder by selecting and deleting it.

Since you cannot actually see the chart, it is helpful to preview how it will appear when printed. This lets you see if you want to change the size or layout of the chart before printing it. To preview the memo,

Select: Print>Preview>↵

Your screen should be similar to Figure 12-11.

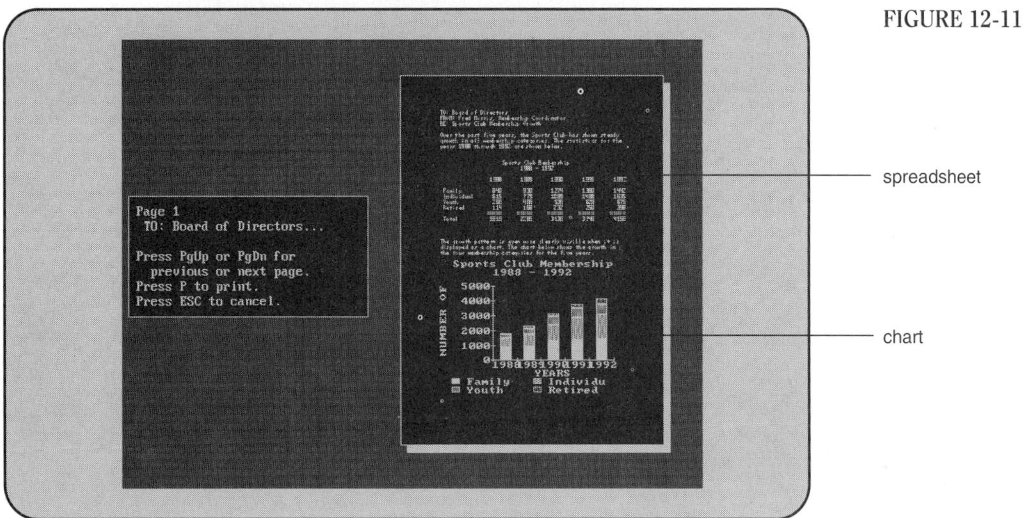

FIGURE 12-11

The memo is displayed, including the chart. Although some of the spreadsheet and chart labels are shortened, they will print correctly when you print the memo.

Works automatically aligns the left and right edges of the chart even with the left and right margins of the word processing document. The program also determines the height of the chart automatically. These settings can be changed, however, if you do not like how they appear.

Sizing a Chart

Fred wants to make two changes. First, he wants to insert an extra blank line above the chart to separate it from the text. Second, he wants to change the chart type from a stacked bar to a bar chart. He feels a bar chart will represent the data more clearly. To clear the preview screen,

Press: ESC

To change the size of the chart in a word processing document, you position the cursor on the chart placeholder you want to modify.

Move to the beginning of the chart placeholder.

Select: Format>Indents & Spacing

Your screen should be similar to Figure 12-12.

FIGURE 12-12

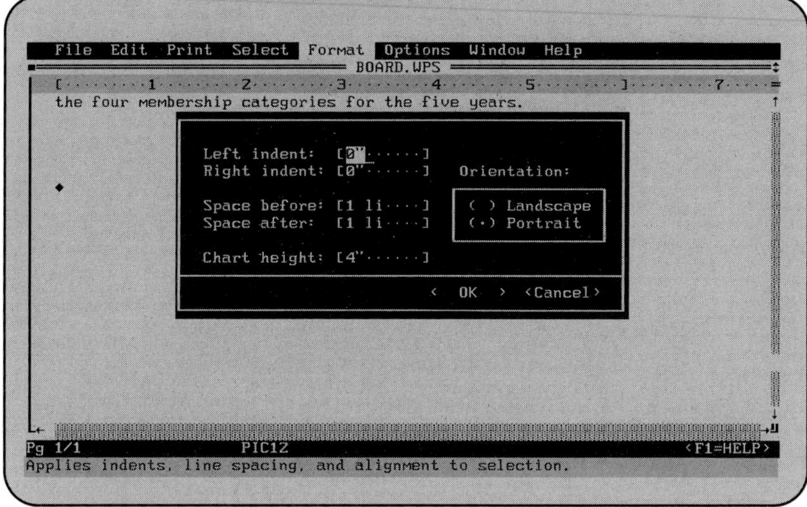

The dialog box displays the default size settings for the chart placeholder the cursor is on. The left and right indents are set at 0". This setting aligns the chart even with the current left and right margins of the word processing document. The Space before: and Space after: options let you specify the number of blank lines above and below the chart. Fred wants to increase the amount of space above the chart title. The default setting is one blank line. To increase this to two blank lines,

Select: Space **b**efore
Type: **2**

The next option, Chart height, specifies the height of the chart. The default setting of 4" is acceptable.

The last two options, Portrait and Landscape, let you change the orientation of the chart on the page. Portrait places the chart on the page vertically, while Landscape places it sideways. Portrait is the preset orientation setting and does not need to be changed.

To complete the command,

Press: ↵

An extra blank line is inserted above the chart placeholder. Now, if you move or copy the placeholder, the blank line will be included also.

Next, Fred wants to change the type of chart to a bar chart. To do this, you need to switch to the spreadsheet file and change the chart type.

Press: CTRL - F6
Select: View>**1**

The stacked bar chart is displayed. To clear the chart,

Press: (ESC)

To change this chart to a bar chart,

Select: Format>**B**ar

To return to the memo and preview the change in the document,

Press: (CTRL) - (F6)
Select: **P**rint>Pre**v**iew>(↵)

Your screen should be similar to Figure 12-13.

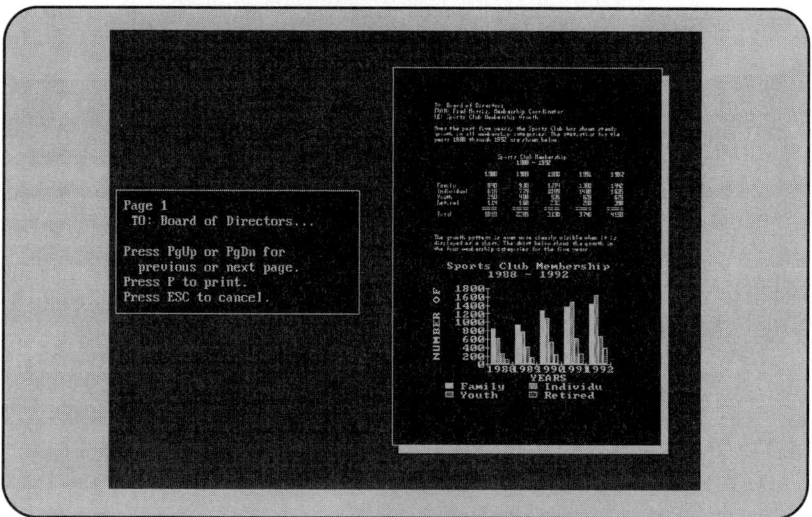

FIGURE 12-13

The bar chart is displayed in the memo. This is because any changes you make in a spreadsheet chart that is specified in the chart placeholder will be automatically reflected in the word processor file. In addition, if you make any changes in the spreadsheet data that affect the chart specified in the chart placeholder, the changes will also be automatically reflected in the chart printed in the memo. Both files must be open when the changes are made.

Press: (ESC)

You are now ready to print the memo. Before doing this, enter your name and the current date on the last line of the memo. Save the memo as BOARD.

Select: **P**rint>**P**rint>(↵)

Note: Do not have the printer set to draft quality. If you do, the chart will not print.

Your printed output should be similar to Figure 12-1 at the beginning of the lab.
Save and close both files.

Creating a Form Letter

In the second project, you will follow Karen as she creates a form letter. A **form letter** is a standard letter sent to many different people.

To create a form letter in Works, you use two files: a word processor file and a database file. The word processor file contains the text that is the same for each letter. It directs the program to take information from the database file and enter it in the form letter. You will modify the welcome letter to be the form letter.

Open the file WELCOME.WPS. The welcome letter you saved at the end of Lab 4 should be displayed on your screen.

Karen needs to change the letter so that each letter sent to a new member includes the new member's first name in the salutation and his or her full name and address as the inside address.

To tell Works where to insert this information, you enter placeholders in the word processing document. Form letter placeholders are similar to chart placeholders. They identify where and what information to print in the document from another file. However, the form letter placeholders identify fields of data from a database file that are to be inserted into the word processing document, whereas the chart placeholder identifies a chart from a spreadsheet file.

The database file MEMBERS.WDB contains the name and address information you will insert into the welcome letter. Open the file MEMBERS.WDB.

Your screen should be similar to Figure 12-14.

FIGURE 12-14

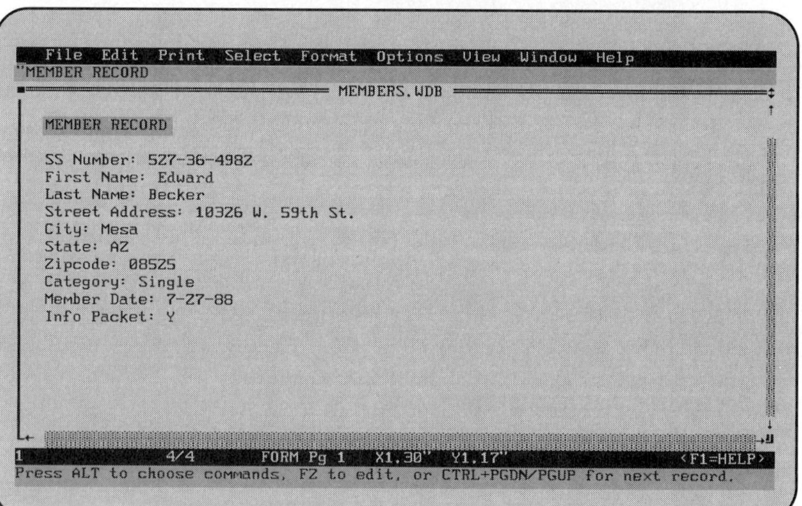

The database file contains the information needed to complete the form letter. The fields of information for each record are:

Field Name	***Field Contents***
==========	=============
SS Number	Social Security Number
First Name	Member's First Name
Last Name	Member's Last Name
Street Address	Street Address
City	City
State	State
Zipcode	Zipcode
Category	Membership Group: Family, Single, Youth, or Retired
Member Date	Membership Date
Info Packet	New Member informational packet mailed: Yes (Y) or No (N)

Enter your name and address as the fifth record in the database file. You do not need to use your real Social Security number or address. Enter a membership category of your choice. Enter the current date for the membership date (such as10-31-92). For the Info Packet field data, enter N for No.

Entering Form Letter Placeholders

Now, Karen will modify the welcome letter to accept information from the database file.

Works takes the field information from the database file and combines it with the form letter file. The form letter placeholders control what fields are used from the database file and where they are entered in the form letter file.

To switch to the letter,

Press: CTRL - F6

The welcome letter should be displayed.

The welcome letter needs to be modified to allow the name and address information for each new member from the database file to be entered into the welcome letter. The inside address will hold the following three lines of information:

First and Last Name
Street Address
City, State, and Zipcode

The first line of the inside address will be entered as the first line of the welcome letter. Karen does not want the date included in the letter.

Delete the line containing the date.

You are now ready to enter a placeholder to identify the First Name field of data. The cursor should be on the first line of the document.

The placeholder will direct the program to accept information from the database file at the location of the placeholder in the form letter file.

Select: Edit>Insert **F**ield

Your display screen should be similar to Figure 12-15.

FIGURE 12-15

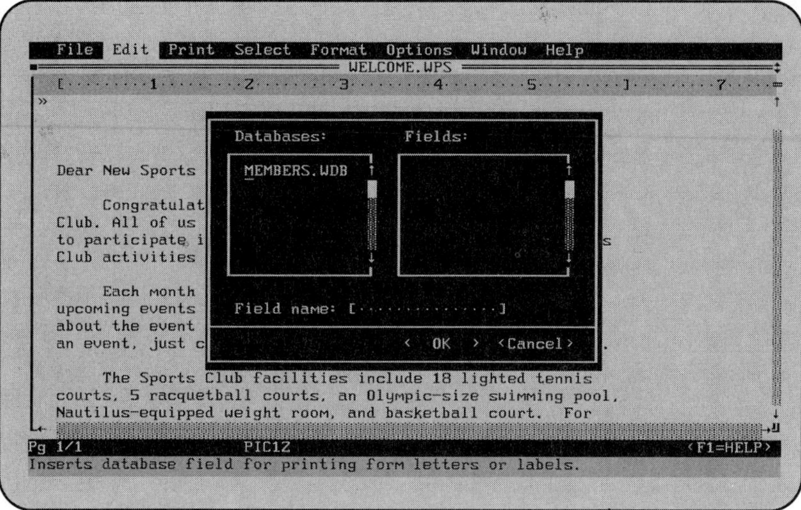

A dialog box is displayed. This dialog box is similar to the one you used to select the spreadsheet chart to enter into the memo. However, it contains a Databases and a Fields box instead of a Spreadsheets and a Charts box. This dialog box operates in exactly the same way and allows you to select the database file and the field names you want to use.

The Databases box displays the name of the open database file, MEMBERS.WDB. To select this file,

Press: 

The filename should be highlighted and the associated field names displayed in the Fields box.

The first field name you want to use is First Name.

Select: First Name

Your screen should be similar to Figure 12-16.

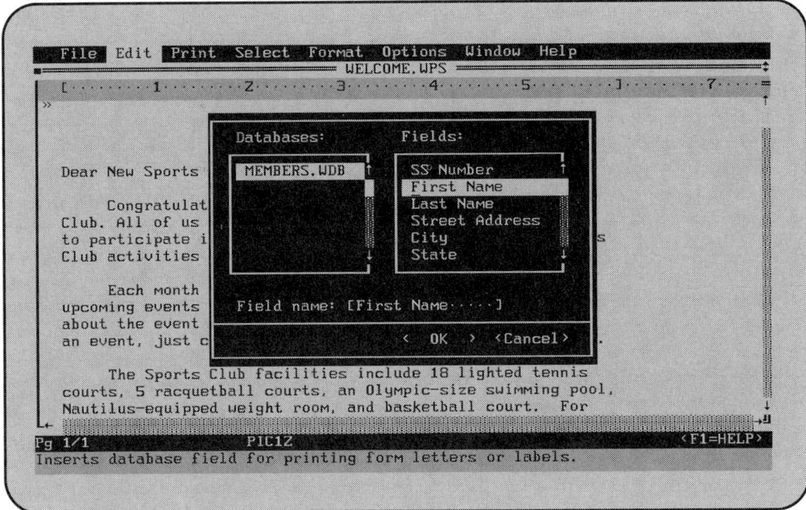

FIGURE 12-16

The First Name field should be highlighted.

Press: ↵

Your screen should be similar to Figure 12-17.

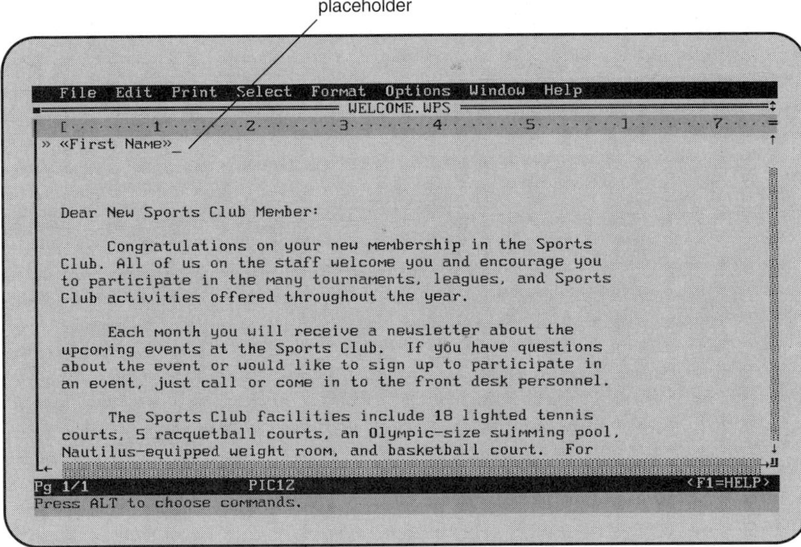

FIGURE 12-17

The placeholder "<<First Name>>" is entered at the cursor location in the welcome letter. When the command to print the form letter is issued, the information for the new member's first name from the database file will be entered at this location in the form letter.

The next piece of information to be entered on the first line of the inside address is the member's last name. To leave a space between the first and last names,

Press: Space bar

To enter the last name placeholder,

Select: **E**dit>Insert **F**ield

The file name is already selected and the field names displayed.

Select: Last Name
Press: ↵

The placeholder for the Last Name field of data is entered on the line.

The next line of the inside address will contain the street address. To move to the next line,

Press: ↓

Enter the placeholder for the street address at this location.

The next line of the inside address will display three fields of data from the database file: City, State, and Zipcode.

Press: ↓

Enter the placeholder for the three fields of data on this line. Separate the City field data from the State with a comma and space, and the State field data from the Zipcode field data with a space.

Your display screen should be similar to Figure 12-18.

FIGURE 12-18

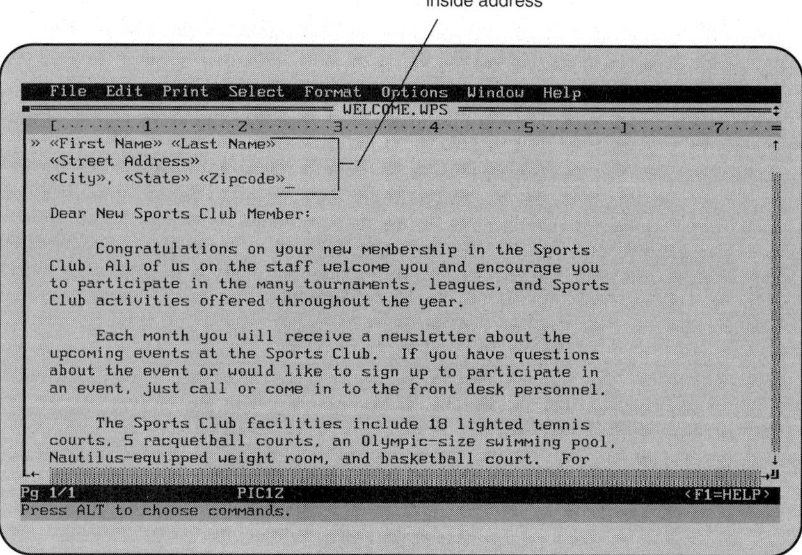

The placeholders needed to enter the inside address data from the database file into the form letter are now complete.

If you see any errors, delete the incorrect placeholder and select the correct placeholder.

The inside address should be separated from the salutation with two blank lines. Make this adjustment if necessary in the form letter.

The last field of information that needs to be entered in the form letter file is the new member's first name in the salutation.

First, delete the words "New Sports Club Member." Do not delete the colon. The cursor should be positioned under the colon. Enter the placeholder for the first name into the salutation.

Your screen should be similar to Figure 12-19.

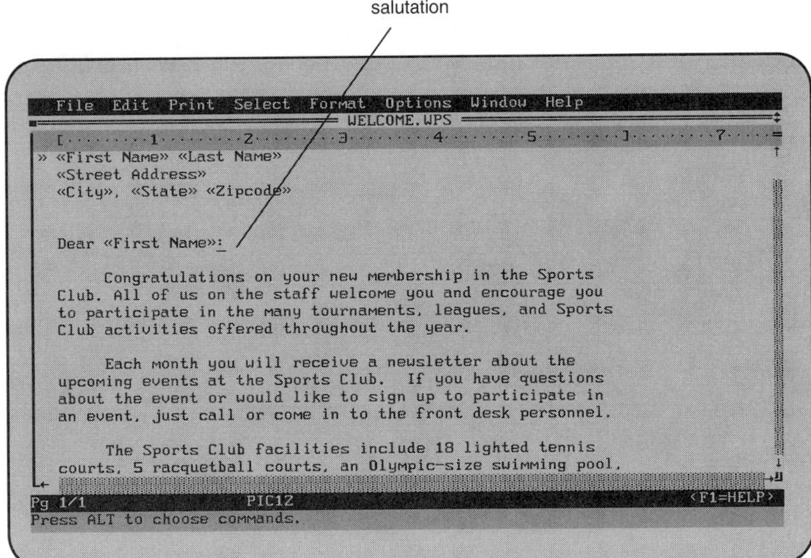

FIGURE 12-19

All the placeholders that are needed for the form letter are complete. Once all the required placeholders are entered in the form letter, the file is saved.

Before saving the file, Fred wants to change the format of the letter to block style. To do this, remove the paragraph indents at the beginning of each paragraph and the seven tabs from the closing lines.

Finally, move to the end of the file. If the end-of-file marker is on the second page of the file, delete as many blank lines below the closing as necessary so that the file is only one page long. (Check the status line for the number of pages in the document. It should be Pg 1/1.)

Save the file as FORM.

Specifying the Records to Print

Now that you have created and saved the form letter, you are ready to print the new personalized welcome letter.

Karen wants the form letter to be printed only for members who have not received the information packet. To locate all records that contain a No in this field, she needs to query the database file.

To switch to the database file,

Press: CTRL - F6

The database file is now the active file. To specify the query,

Select: View>**Q**uery

In the query form, enter N for "No" in the Info Packet field.

To return to the database FORM view,

Select: View>**F**orm

To see the results of the query more easily, switch to LIST view.

There should be two records (4 and 5) matching the query condition of N in the Info Packet field. One of the records should be the record containing your name and information. The other records are hidden. Now, when you print the form letter, only form letters for the displayed records will be printed.

Printing the Form Letter

To switch back to the letter file,

Press: (CTRL) - (F6)

The form letter should be the active window.

If necessary, turn the printer on and adjust the paper.

The Print>Print Form Letters command lets you combine a word processor file and a database file. Both files must be open when you use this command. Works will print one copy of the form letter for each displayed record in the database file.

Select: **P**rint>Print **F**orm Letters

A dialog box is displayed. The filename of the open database file is displayed in the Databases box. To accept the selected filename,

Press: (↵)

The Print dialog box is displayed. Select the options you want to use; then

Select: **P**rint

The status line first displays the number of form letters to be printed, in this case two. Then it displays the number of letters that have been printed.

The printed copy of the form letter for the first displayed record (4) should be similar to Figure 12-20 on the next page.

The second form letter should contain your name and address information.

Now that the form letters have been printed for the two new members, Karen needs to change the Info Packet field data for these records to Y for "Yes."

```
Ellen Johnson
1622 E. Donner Dr.
Tempe, AZ 08528

Dear Ellen:

Congratulations on your new membership in the Sports Club.
All of us on the staff welcome you and encourage you to
participate in the many tournaments, leagues, and Sports
Club activities offered throughout the year.

Each month you will receive a newsletter about the upcoming
events at the Sports Club.  If you have questions about the
event or would like to sign up to participate in an event,
just call or come in to the front desk personnel.

The Sports Club facilities include 18 lighted tennis courts,
5 racquetball courts, an Olympic-size swimming pool,
Nautilus-equipped weight room, and basketball court.  For
your comfort while using the Sports Club, the men's and
ladies' locker rooms each have showers, a sauna, and a steam
room.  A spa for both men and women is located between the
locker rooms. The lounge and cafe are open to serve you
throughout the day and evening.

The regular monthly membership fee is $45.00.  Other
expenses, such as league and lesson fees, pro-shop
purchases, and charges at the Courtside Cafe can also be
billed to your account.  The charges will be itemized on
your monthly statement and added to your regular monthly
fee.

The Sports Club is offering a new program to all its members
that will save you writing a check each month.  Upon your
authorization, the bank will send payment of your monthly
charges directly to the Sports Club.  You will receive a
copy of your monthly statement to confirm the accuracy of
your bill.  If you are interested in the automatic fee
payment program, please contact the accounting department
(931-4285 ext. 33) to make the necessary arrangements.

On behalf of the staff of the Sports Club, I hope your
association with the Sports Club is long and enjoyable.


Sincerely,



Sports Club Manager
```

FIGURE 12-20

To switch to the database file,

Press: CTRL - F6

Change the two displayed records information packet field data to "Y".

Display all records (**S**elect>Show **A**ll Records).

Now each time Karen needs to send a new member welcome letter, all she needs to do is to enter the data for the new member into the database file with the Info Packet field as N. Then she needs to apply the query, open the FORM file, and issue the Print Form Letters command.

Close and save the files.

To review, the steps in creating a customized form letter are:

1. Create the database file. It will contain the fields of data or information needed to complete the form letter.
2. Create the form letter file by entering placeholders in the document to tell Works where and what fields of information to use from the database file. Save the form letter document file.

3. Display only the records in the database file that you want form letters printed for. Use the Print Form Letters command to combine the form letter and database files to create a customized document for each displayed record in the database file.

Exit Works.

Key Terms

placeholder
form letter

Matching

1. →	_____	**a.**	a form letter placeholder
2. Edit>Copy	_____	**b.**	inserts a chart into a word processor file
3. *chart CHARTS.WKS:BAR*	_____	**c.**	tab marker
4. Edit>Insert Chart	_____	**d.**	a chart placeholder
5. Format>Indents & Spacing	_____	**e.**	copies within and between files and tools
6. form letter	_____	**f.**	adjusts sizing of a chart
7. placeholder	_____	**g.**	switches windows
8. Edit>Insert Field	_____	**h.**	specifies the chart or field data to display in a document
9. <<Street>>	_____	**i.**	a standard letter sent to many people
10. CTRL - F6	_____	**j.**	inserts database field data into a document

Practice Exercises

1. In this problem you will create a new word processor file. You will enter the text as directed in the problem and then you will copy a spreadsheet and chart from the file HOME into the document.

- Enter the following text into a word processor document:

  The American dream of owning your own home has become elusive, in part because the prices of homes in most places have risen faster than incomes. The following data shows the average price of a home and the average family income levels from 1976 to 1986.

- Copy the spreadsheet you created named HOME in practice exercise 1 in Lab 8 below this paragraph. Make any editing adjustments necessary. Separate the spreadsheet data from the text with two blank lines.

- Enter the following text below the spreadsheet data:

  The line chart below shows the change in the average cost of a home and family income over the years 1976 to 1986.

- Insert the line chart you created named HOUSING from the spreadsheet HOME below this sentence. Size the chart appropriately. Adjust the spacing of the document so that it completely fills one page.
- Set the left and right margins to one inch. Add a header displaying your name and the current date. (Use Help for information about entering a page number.)
- Save the word processor file as HOME.
- Print the document.

2. In this problem you will create a new word processor file. You will enter the text as directed in the problem and copy a spreadsheet and chart from the file ASSETS into the document.

- Enter the following text into a word processor document:

  Financial planners generally recommend that you allocate your capital into five categories: cash, fixed income producers (bonds), real estate, equities, and precious metals. They also recommend changing how much you allocate to each category as you reach different stages of life.

  On the average, financial planners recommend that the following percentages of your capital be allocated to the five categories according to three age groups as shown below:

- Copy the spreadsheet you created named ASSETS in practice exercise 2 in Lab 8 below this paragraph. Make any editing adjustments necessary. Separate the spreadsheet data from the text with two blank lines.
- Enter the following text below the spreadsheet data:

  The stacked bar chart below shows the percent allocation for each category across the age groups.

- Insert the stacked bar chart you created named STACKED3 from the spreadsheet ASSETS below this sentence. Size the chart appropriately.
- Enter the following text below the stacked bar chart:

  The pie chart below shows the percent allocation for people in their twenties.

- Insert a page break above this text.
- Insert the pie bar chart you created named Pie20s from the spreadsheet ASSETS below this sentence. Size the chart appropriately.
- Set the left and right margins to .5 inch. Add a header displaying your name and the current date. Add a footer as "Page - #." (Use Help for information about entering a page number.)
- Save the word processor file as ASSETS.
- Print the document.

3. In this problem you will create a form letter. You will enter the letter into a new word processor file and use the fields of information in the database file TILES3, which you created in practice exercise 1 of Lab 10.

- Enter the letter below using the placeholders indicated. Center the letter on the page.

Current Date

<<FIRST NAME>> <<LAST NAME>>
<<ADDRESS>>
<<CITY>>, <<STATE>> <<ZIP CODE>>

Dear <<FIRST NAME>> <<LAST NAME>>:

It has come to our attention that your account is now overdue. According to our records you owe <<AMT OWED>>. If you have recently sent a payment for this amount, please disregard this letter. If you have not sent in your payment, please do so within the next seven days.

Thank you very much for your prompt attention to this matter.

Sincerely,

Susannah's Tiles

- Add a record containing your name to the database file. Complete the other field information using data of your choice.
- Print the form letter for your record only.
- Save the form letter as OVERDUE.

4. In this problem you will create a form letter. You will enter the letter into a new word processor file and use the fields of information in the database file STAFF2 that you created in practice exercise 3 of Lab 10.

- Enter the letter (memo) below using the placeholders indicated. Center the memo on the page.

TO: <<First Name>> <<Last Name>>, <<Title>>
FROM: Bob Kind, Manager
DATE: Current date
Re: <<Department>> Meeting

I have decided to hold a brief staff meeting for the employees in the <<Department>> department every Monday at the beginning of your shift. The focus of the meeting will be to set production objectives for

the week. The meeting will also be open for discussion of problems and suggestions.

- Display the record containing your name and field information only.
- Print the memo.
- Save the form letter as MEETING.

Command Summary

Command	*Action*	*Page*
Window>**A**rrange All	Displays all windows	370
Window>Ma**x**imize	Enlarges active window	372
Options>Show **A**ll Characters	Displays hidden symbols	372
Edit>**I**nsert Chart	Specifies chart placeholder	375
Forma**t**>Indents & Sp**a**cing	Sizes a chart	378
Edit>Insert **F**ield	Specifies database placeholders	381
View>**Q**uery	Specifies Query criteria	386
Print>Print **F**orm Letters	Prints form letters	386

INDEX